Responding to Financial Crisis

LESSONS FROM ASIA THEN, THE UNITED STATES AND EUROPE NOW

Changyong Rhee & Adam S. Posen, editors

**A COPUBLICATION OF THE
ASIAN DEVELOPMENT BANK AND
PETERSON INSTITUTE FOR INTERNATIONAL ECONOMICS**

Washington, DC
October 2013

Peterson
Institute for
International
Economics

MIX
Paper from
responsible sources
FSC® C005010

ASIAN DEVELOPMENT BANK
6 ADB Avenue
Mandaluyong City
1550 Metro Manila,
Philippines
Tel +63 2 632 4444   Fax + 63 2 636 2444 www.adb.org

PETERSON INSTITUTE FOR INTERNATIONAL ECONOMICS
1750 Massachusetts Avenue, NW
Washington, DC 20036-1903
(202) 328-9000 FAX: (202) 659-3225 www.piie.com
Adam S. Posen, *President*
Steven R. Weisman, *Editorial and Publications Director*

Cover Design: Peggy Archambault
Printing: Versa Press, Inc.

Printed in the United States of America
15   14   13   5   4   3   2   1

Library of Congress Cataloging-in-Publication Data
Responding to financial crisis : lessons from Asia then, the United States and Europe now /
Changyong Rhee & Adam S. Posen, eds.
    pages cm
    "October 2013."
    Includes bibliographical references.
    ISBN 978-0-88132-674-1
    1. Financial crises—Asia. 2. Financial crises—United States. 3. Financial crises—Europe.
4. Asia—Economic conditions—21st century. 5. United States—Economic conditions—21st cen-
tury. 6. Europe—Economic conditions—21st century. I. Rhee, Changyong, editor of compilation.
II. Posen, Adam Simon, editor of compilation. III. Cline, William R. Sovereign debt and Asia.

HB3808.R47 2013
338.5'42—dc23

                                                                                    2013026764

Contents

Preface

The world still awaits a sustained and sustainable recovery from the global financial crisis of 2008–10, which battered the world economy and disrupted global financial markets to an unprecedented degree. Private credit seized up in the United States and European Union, and global output shrank for the first time in the postwar era. Thanks to initially decisive monetary and fiscal stimulus programs implemented by both advanced and developing countries, a measure of financial stability returned in 2009, only to disappear again in a new bout of turmoil caused by sovereign debt and banking crises in Europe. Despite the actions to date by the European Central Bank, the International Monetary Fund, and European governments, the European crisis awaits a more fundamental resolution.

More broadly, the world is now aware that major financial crises can emerge from even the most advanced economies and more fully appreciates the devastation they can wreak. While this pair of successive crises originated in the world's largest and most financially developed economies, it still affected the rest of the world, including developing Asia, where economic growth suffered especially in those countries dependent on exports. Many of these Asian countries were protected from the worst of the crisis, however, by a combination of improved fundamentals and practices in their own economies and fortuitous circumstance. For example, Asian banks had limited exposure to subprime US assets when the current crisis hit. Many of these practical improvements had been put in place following Asia's own devastating crisis in 1997–98, which indelibly scarred the region's collective psyche.

The learning to date in some Asian economies demonstrates the benefits of revisiting and analyzing past crises. In this volume, we have gathered a team of Asian and American economists with policy experience to draw further relevant lessons from today's crisis for developing Asia as well as for the North Atlantic economies. Of particular relevance is the fact that the lessons learned by Asian countries from their own crisis 15 years ago led directly to some of the improved practices that protected them this time around. Meanwhile, it has become obvious that some policies that US and EU leaders recommended to Asia in the midst of past crises were not adopted in their own practices in recent years. Such inconsistency cost these economies and the world not just in terms of apparent hypocrisy but, more importantly, also in terms of greater damage and lesser resilience once financial crisis did hit the North Atlantic. These and other lessons can help Asian and other policymakers better manage and recover from future financial crises. While prevention of crises would be better, the fact that such crises emerged and persisted in the United States and European Union warns all policymakers everywhere to prepare ahead to respond to and manage crises, for they may be next.

That is why the Asian Development Bank (ADB) and the Peterson Institute for International Economics (PIIE) have teamed up on a major project that examines and compares financial and economic crises then in Asia with now in the North Atlantic. This book is the main output of the study, collecting eight thematic research papers analyzing different dimensions of various past crises, including the global financial crisis of 2008–10, the euro area sovereign debt crisis of 2010 to present, and the Asian financial crisis of 1997–98. One important common element in all the papers is that they draw concrete and specific lessons from past and present crises for today's Asian policymakers and their peers around the globe.

We would like to express our sincere gratitude to ADB and PIIE economists who have contributed their research to this ambitious project. Their backgrounds combine academic excellence with senior-level policymaking experience. As a result, this book combines analytical rigor with practical policy implications. We would also like to give a special thanks to ADB's Donghyun Park and PIIE's Marcus Noland, who jointly managed and coordinated the study, and to ADB's Anna Sherwood and Gemma B. Estrada and PIIE's Madona Devasahayam, Susann Luetjen, and Steven R. Weisman for facilitating the publication of the volume. We believe that this book will be a valuable tool for policymakers in Asia and beyond as a result of their and the contributing authors' efforts.

*****

The Peterson Institute for International Economics is a private, nonprofit institution for rigorous, intellectually open, and honest study and discussion of international economic policy. Its purpose is to identify and analyze important issues to making globalization beneficial and sustainable for the people of the United States and the world and then to develop and communicate practical new approaches for dealing with them. The Institute is completely nonpartisan.

The Institute's work is funded by a highly diverse group of philanthropic foundations, private corporations, and interested individuals, as well as income on its capital fund. About 35 percent of the Institute's resources in our latest fiscal year were provided by contributors from outside the United States. For a list of Institute supporters, see www.piie.com/supporters.cfm. The Institute thanks our collaborators at the Asian Development Bank for their financial as well as substantive support of our work in this area.

The Executive Committee of the Institute's Board of Directors bears overall responsibility for the Institute's direction, gives general guidance and approval to its research program, and evaluates its performance in pursuit of its mission. The Institute's President is responsible for the identification of topics that are likely to become important over the medium term (one to three years) that should be addressed by Institute scholars. This rolling agenda is set in close consultation with the Institute's research staff and Board of Directors, as well as other stakeholders. The President makes the final decision to publish any individual Institute study, following independent internal and external review of the work.

The Institute hopes that its research and other activities will contribute to building a stronger foundation for international economic policy around the world. We invite readers of these publications to let us know how they think we can best accomplish this objective.

The Asian Development Bank's vision is an Asia and Pacific region free of poverty. Its mission is to help its developing member countries reduce poverty and improve the quality of life of their people. Despite the region's many successes, it remains home to two-thirds of the world's poor: 1.7 billion people who live on less than $2 a day, with 828 million struggling on less than $1.25 a day. ADB is committed to reducing poverty through inclusive economic growth, environmentally sustainable growth, and regional integration. Based in Manila, ADB is owned by 67 members, including 48 from the region. Its main instruments for helping its developing member countries are policy dialogue, loans, equity investments, guarantees, grants, and technical assistance.

CHANGYONG RHEE
Chief Economist,
Asian Development Bank

ADAM S. POSEN
President, Peterson Institute
for International Economics

October 2013

1

Introduction

ADAM S. POSEN AND CHANGYONG RHEE

Financial crises are terrible things, and yet they keep happening. During the Asian financial crisis of 1997-98, a substantial amount of policy knowledge was learned through experimentation but at substantial cost. One of the costs was the diminished good will between the then creditor countries of the richer West and the International Monetary Fund (IMF), on the one hand, and the crisis-hit economies of developing Asia, on the other. Policy research and intergovernmental consultation proceeded wholesale from there, with some lessons drawn regarding crisis prevention, mitigation, and resolution. Yet, barely a decade later, the United States and Western Europe suffered a historically significant financial crisis, with large negative spillovers on the whole world economy, particularly on the export-oriented economies of developing Asia. Had we learned nothing? Or were the lessons from Asia's crisis inapplicable to the problems of a global financial crisis (2008-10) that centered on the United States and Europe? Or was there some sort of failure of politics and institutions remaining to be addressed, that somehow extended to the advanced countries of the Organisation for Economic Co-operation and Development (OECD) as well as to emerging Asia?

The studies in this volume address these questions head-on. We came together, Asian and American economists, in order to get past any defensive delusions regarding our own regions' and governments' performance up to and during financial crises, as well as to identify where the commonalities across the Pacific lie. And rewardingly (and perhaps surprisingly), we have been able

Adam S. Posen is the president of the Peterson Institute for International Economics. Changyong Rhee is the chief economist of the Asian Development Bank. They thank Steven Weisman, who contributed greatly to the formulation of this overview and of the volume overall. Wendy Dobson and Morris Goldstein provided helpful comments as well. The views expressed in this chapter are those of the authors and do not necessarily reflect the views and policies of the Asian Development Bank or its Board of Governors or the governments they represent.

to agree broadly on a number of key lessons that do apply to developing Asia as well as to recovering America and Europe. The contrast in Asia's performance during the more recent crisis with its performance during its own crisis 15 years earlier, and the gap between what the US and EU leaders recommended to Asia then and what they practiced on themselves later, is particularly revealing. In short, Asia recovered quickly from the crisis by following the consensus view that emerged after its crisis, while the United States and Europe did themselves harm by not following the advice they gave others and ignoring others' experience. We hope to reaffirm what is good in the developing Asian experience and get it accepted in the North Atlantic economies before the next set of crises emerges.

What kind of lessons are we talking about for the policymakers of such a broad range of economies and polities? General guidelines that are more binding than mere broad bromides, but which will require tailored implementation country by country, emerge very clearly from this volume of essays. In terms of responding to the challenge of financial crises, the arguments of our assembled authors would be:

■ *Prepare as though you cannot prevent.* No economy can ever rule out the possibility that it will suffer a financial crisis. Whether looking at the highly deregulated financial systems of the United Kingdom and United States in the mid-2000s, or at the more limited and concentrated banking systems of Japan and developing Asia of the mid-1990s, or even at the state-controlled financial system of the People's Republic of China today, it seems that everyone is subject to financial fragility. The ability of surveillance and early warning indicators to preempt crises remains more aspirational than practical to date. But governments can meaningfully improve the resilience of their economies ahead of crises and thereby reduce their cost and duration. Having fiscal space, limiting currency mismatch on debt, accumulating sufficient (but not excessive) foreign exchange reserves, and especially preventing excessive domestic credit creation—all are pragmatic policies that should be adopted to promote economic robustness.

■ *Make sure you have room for stabilization policy, and then use it.* Once a financial crisis hits, aggressive monetary easing combined with rapid tough recapitalization or closure of damaged banks can materially improve recovery, in both speed and depth. Japan failed to implement this approach in the 1990s and prolonged its misery; the United States has come closer to following these precepts, and it has had a faster, more sustained, though still suboptimal, recovery as a result. The euro area, on the other hand, has done less on monetary stimulus and far less on bank cleanup than ideal and is suffering stagnation at best as a consequence. Failure to address banking system problems encourages moral hazard and crony capitalism every bit as much in the North Atlantic economies as in East Asia. Lacking macroeconomic room to maneuver because of preexisting debt or vulnerable exchange rate pegs is every bit as costly in Southern Europe today as it was in Southeast Asia in 1998.

- *Address the need for self-insurance globally if we can, regionally if we must.* The biggest gap between the developing Asian and North Atlantic economies arises in the differing needs for self-insurance by accumulation of foreign exchange reserves. This is partly an inevitable matter of need, given respective access to debt markets in home currencies. Still, all countries have the need for some form of liquidity provision in time of financial crisis—hence the very helpful and much used bilateral dollar swap lines that the US Federal Reserve provided to a number of countries in 2008-10, including in Western Europe. All countries recognize that conditional lending, as carried out primarily by the IMF, is a critical component to promoting adjustment in economies, whereas competing conditionality adds to instability. And all countries acknowledge that the current weight of voting in the IMF is out of balance with the actual economic realities of today, which causes both distrust and inequality in the generosity of lending programs. Regional monetary funds, in addition to swaps arrangements, show some promise for diminishing the perceived need to self-insure on hard currency liquidity, but a significant effort at coordination with global institutions is required to make them work.

Our approach in this volume is intentionally based on a comparative case study approach, along specific themes. That is, our authors are neither doing pure cross-sectional regression work with many observations, which while informative miss some critical details, nor focusing solely on the events in one episode in isolation, which loses perspective. Together with our Asian-American set of authors, we believe this framework allows us to deliver practical yet widely applicable lessons about financial crises for developing Asia and beyond. Most of all, by coming together in this approach we hope to get beyond the claims of hypocrisy or the self-serving nature of various policies promoted in the 1990s in Asia versus those pursued by the United States and European Union for their own economies in the last few years. If anything, our message is that the North Atlantic policymakers should have followed the lessons that came out of the Asian financial crisis a decade earlier—where they have "let themselves off easy," with regard to banking cleanup or utilizing fiscal room or trumping IMF conditionality with regional resources, Western countries have done harm to their own economies' recoveries.

In the remaining part of this chapter, we summarize the individual chapters that make up this volume.

The United States and Europe Can Learn from Japan's "Lost Decades"

In chapter 2, Masahiro Kawai and Peter Morgan use the example of Japan's "two lost decades" to draw lessons for other countries. Although other countries have experienced prolonged economic stagnation after the collapse of asset values and resulting banking crises, Japan's period of weak growth, deflation, and mounting debts was exceptionally severe. Japan's plight stemmed from bad policy choices (including inadequate monetary policy) and failure to restructure banks with loans to dead or "zombie" entities. Economic rigidities led to inadequate corporate investment and a slowdown in productivity. Aggravating these factors was the economic and budget cost of Japan's aging society.

The authors use these factors as criteria by which to examine the economic problems in three groups of countries that subsequently experienced economic stagnation resulting from banking crises—the advanced economies of the OECD and the developing or emerging-market countries in Asia and Latin America. Growth in Japan ahead of the crisis was much higher than that in its advanced-country peers and in countries in Latin America but was on a par with the emerging-market countries in Asia. Japan's high growth rate was also related to a higher level of domestic credit than in other countries, and its decline in capital stock was similar to that in developing Asian countries driven by the investment-led growth model. Thus the factors that were unique to Japan were the dramatic decline in stock and real estate prices, price deflation, poor GDP growth, and its aging population. The authors' econometric analysis of long-term growth rates finds that low rates of consumer price index (CPI) inflation (or deflation), low levels of net investment, lack of openness to foreign direct investment, and an aging population explain much of Japan's slowdown.

Turning to policy implications, the authors argue that once bubbles build up and collapse, authorities should undertake accommodative monetary policies, combined with steps to encourage banks to clean up their balance sheets. Japan stands as an example of inadequate policy response and too much forbearance toward the banking sector. Its experience has much in common with the United States and European Union, though it has surface resemblance to the experiences of countries hit by the Asian financial crisis, particularly Indonesia, the Republic of Korea, Malaysia, and Thailand. As for whether the United States and some euro area countries face stagnation comparable to Japan's, the authors' conclusion is mixed. On the one hand, the United States, the United Kingdom, and Italy did not go through as much "excessive" growth in GDP and capital stocks as Japan in the run-up to the crisis. On the other, low consumer price inflation and net investment suggest that these economies are in some danger of "Japanization" of their economies. The slow response to banking sector problems in the euro area is particularly reminiscent of Japan's inadequate responses.

Central Bank Actions in Advanced Economies during the Global Financial Crisis Had Net Positive Impact

In chapter 3, Joseph E. Gagnon and Marc Hinterschweiger assess the responses of central banks in advanced economies (the US Federal Reserve System, Bank of England, Bank of Japan, and European Central Bank) to the global financial crisis. They note that four years after the onset of the crisis, none of the major advanced economies is close to a full recovery. The crisis exposed the fault lines in European monetary policymaking even though central banks generally pushed policy interest rates to historically low levels and undertook nontraditional macroeconomic stimulus to ease financial market strains. Most research indicates that central bank actions have made a positive contribution to economic and fiscal conditions. Central banks sought to renew credit flows by returning liquidity and credit risk spreads to normal levels, reducing some of the "headwinds" impeding economic activity. But the macroeconomic stimulus has been limited.

Gagnon and Hinterschweiger note that preventing the failure of large financial institutions can avert a negative shock but that, by themselves, such actions do not constitute a "positive shock" to the economy. They assess the positive effects from the approach of some central banks, including the US Federal Reserve, especially the policy known as quantitative easing (QE), and the effort to manage expectations about the future path of short-term interest rates. There are potential costs of both "ultra-low" interest rates and QE but so far they are smaller than the benefits. Indeed, more aggressive QE would have been preferred, not less.

The authors acknowledge that "moral hazard" concerns have arisen as a result of steps taken by central banks in cooperation with other authorities to prevent the failure of large financial institutions. The concern arises from the perception of some banks that they will not be allowed to fail and therefore may repeat some of their reckless practices. But such concerns, while legitimate, should be more properly addressed through reforms of the financial system.

Asian Countries Fared Better during the Global Financial Crisis than during the Asian Crisis

In chapter 4, Donghyun Park, Arief Ramayandi, and Kwanho Shin investigate why Asian countries fared better during the global financial crisis than they did during the Asian financial crisis. Asia was hardly immune from the global financial crisis, the authors acknowledge, citing the drop in growth and trade throughout the region. But from the beginning, the global financial crisis had less of an impact on developing countries than on the advanced economies, where the crisis originated, and developing countries "have largely shrugged off the effects" and are recovering. Nevertheless, the crisis heralds a new era of diminished growth expectations in Asia, in part because of the region's reliance on the ailing advanced economies as export markets. But with massive fiscal and monetary stimulus, countries in Asia were able to minimize the downturn and limit the effects of the crisis on financial institutions, eventually using stimulative policies to produce a robust recovery.

The authors caution against "hubris or overconfidence" in Asia, however, recalling that Asian countries suffered the crisis of 1997–98 on their own. Both crises were marked by an abrupt flight of foreign capital from developing Asia. During the Asian crisis, this outflow resulted from a loss of investor confidence in the region, however, whereas in the recent crisis the capital flight resulted from the need of US and European financial institutions to withdraw loans to support their damaged balance sheets at home. As for why the Asian countries fared better in the more recent crisis, the authors say that improved macroeconomic fundamentals helped cushion the blow and provide resources for a response of economic and monetary stimulus.

Among the positive fundamentals shared by the Asian countries was their record of keeping inflation and the growth of domestic credit at a sustainable precrisis rate. These economic fundamentals enabled Asian countries to undertake countercyclical expansionary monetary and fiscal policies to mitigate the crisis. In contrast to the 1990s, the authors call on Asian policymakers to continue to pursue the same sound policies and maintain healthy current account balances (and substantial foreign exchange reserve levels) to be able to counter the effects of shortages of US dollar liquidity of the sort that hurt the region during the Asian crisis. The expansionary response during the recent crisis was far more successful than the contractionary response during the Asian crisis.

The West Failed to Practice What It Preached during the Asian Crisis

Simon Johnson and James Kwak note in chapter 5 that the Western countries, particularly the United States, drew lessons from the Asian crisis of the 1990s but later failed to apply these lessons to themselves. In the 1990s, US policymakers understood the importance of two crucial ingredients in the Asian crisis—tight connections between economic and political elites and dependence on short-term flows of foreign capital. But they wrongly concluded that these problems did not threaten the United States itself. In fact, the events of September–October 2008, when Lehman Brothers collapsed, resembled a "classic emerging-market crisis," and the housing bubble that caused the crisis was an instance of overoptimism and excess debt "worthy of any emerging market."

The policy prescriptions for Asia after the crisis were not applied to the United States. For example, in the recent crisis, the US government rescued major banks overseen by wealthy executives while letting smaller banks fail, thus "bailing out a very specific element of the American elite." By contrast, the United States demanded that emerging-market countries in Asia deal with political and economic factors, such as the grip of elites on the financial sector, even though this insistence was perceived as arrogant in the crisis-stricken countries. The policymakers applied "one set of rules for emerging markets and another for the United States." In Asia, the West forced insolvent financial institutions to undergo resolution or restructuring, wiping out equity, converting debts to equity and replacing management. In the US crisis, authorities instead applied various forms of implicit and government financial support. The result is that the United States has increased moral hazard and enshrined the concept of banks "too big to fail," with negative consequences for global financial stability in the future.

The Role of the International Monetary Fund Is Crucial

In his comparative analysis of the evolution of the Asian and European financial crises, Edwin M. Truman focuses on the role of the IMF in chapter 6. He discusses the experiences of five countries in Asia and ten countries in Europe that went through crises requiring IMF programs in support of economic and financial reforms. In Europe, the IMF's role was supplemented by support from the European Central Bank and the European Stability Mechanism established by euro area countries. While there were many differences among the experiences of these countries, the similarities outweighed the differences.

On the other hand, a major difference was that the European countries received more financial support, despite the fact that their problems derived from deeper issues of solvency and not simply liquidity crises that afflicted Asia. In addition, the programs adopted in the European crisis generally have been less demanding and rigorous than those in the Asian crisis. Partly as a result, the negative global impact of the European crisis has been larger than the crisis in Asia. The main lessons drawn by Truman are that despite promises to the contrary, history does tend to repeat itself and that noncrisis countries should realize they have a stake in preventing and managing crises in other countries. Another lesson is that the IMF and its surveillance mechanisms should focus on monetary unions like the one in Europe and not simply on crises that might afflict individual countries.

Regional Financial Arrangements and Global Institutions Should Increase Coordination

In chapter 7, Changyong Rhee, Lea Sumulong, and Shahin Vallée look at the lessons for the development of regional safety nets and insurance mechanisms that might have prevented the crises of Asia in the 1990s, the global crisis of 2008, and the ongoing European crisis. They conclude that the IMF and other institutions created at Bretton Woods responded "imperfectly" to all of these episodes. The 2008 crisis did lead to an improvement in cooperation to deal with the turmoil, however, and central banks employed currency swap arrangements to provide liquidity when the financial system froze. But these steps did not displace let alone discourage efforts at regional cooperation.

The authors then examine the "alternative insurance mechanisms," which have arisen in recent years, most notably in Europe and Asia. They take the reader through different phases of such cooperation, citing a range of accords and initiatives, starting in the 1970s, that have taken various forms throughout the world. The IMF and the G-20 nations can no longer ignore such regional arrangements; accordingly, much remains to be done to coordinate them with global institutions. IMF governance should better reflect the rising power of emerging-market economies and the ability of these economies to self-insure by building up foreign exchange reserves.

The prospects for such reserve buildups will depend in part on the emergence of the euro and perhaps the renminbi as a reserve currency, making the international monetary system less dependent on the dollar. The authors note that many "innocent bystanders" were hit by the recent crises, a fact calling for more preventive steps to avoid crises in the first place. Regional arrangements could be an important feature of such efforts, but regional and global institutions must coordinate with each other to ensure that "regionalism" does not prevent international cooperation in the future.

Regional Financial Institutions Face the Same Challenges as Global Institutions

In chapter 8, Stephan Haggard also examines the emergence of regional cooperation in global financial crises. While developments in Europe and Asia have focused on regional lenders in these regions, Haggard notes that Latin America also has a subregional experiment that bears scrutiny. Like international institutions, these regional mechanisms face problems of providing assistance without introducing moral hazard concerns. One way to address such concerns in advance of crises is through agreed policy constraints. But such agreements are inherently difficult when membership of regional organizations is heterogeneous. The "turbulent history" of such agreements in Europe offers a case in point, Haggard notes, citing disputes over maintaining the Stability and Growth Pact in Europe. Such commitments have been even weaker in Asia and Latin America.

The chapter explores some of the political, financial, and economic factors affecting these commitments in each region. Once crises hit, it is no less difficult for regional arrangements than it has been for international institutions to enforce preexisting rules on bailouts and lender-of-last-resort rules amid conflicting demands by creditors, borrowers, and political actors. As a result, some regional actors rely on the IMF to help devise rules and negotiations on rescues. Haggard offers a history of such arrangements as they have developed in Europe, Asia, and Latin America. These three diverse regional experiences teach several lessons. Among them is the difficulty of establishing robust surveillance ahead of crises and the design of lender-of-last-resort rules after the crises erupt. While coordination between regional arrangements and the IMF would seem ideal, Haggard explains the difficulties in carrying out such cooperation because of the divergent interests of the regional and international parties. Thus "division of labor" between regional and international players might be a more realistic goal than "coordination."

Most of Emerging Asia Is in a Solid Debt Position, but Japan Faces Challenges

William R. Cline, in chapter 9, looks at three international debt crises—Latin America in the 1980s, East Asia in the late 1990s, and the ongoing European debt crisis—while drawing lessons for the prospects for sovereign creditworthiness in Asia in the future. The countries he examines are the People's Republic of China, India, Indonesia, Japan, the Republic of Korea, Malaysia, the Philippines, Thailand, and Viet Nam. These countries have already learned the lessons of recent sovereign debt crises and have avoided high ratios of external debt to exports and reduced ratios of short-term external debt to reserves. They have also pursued sound management of their fiscal deficits and debts. India faces the challenge of reducing deficits and inflation rates, but its GDP growth has meant that its public debt ratio is not yet at a dangerous level.

Cline concludes that all eight countries "pass the fiscal sustainability test" and are increasingly able to rely on debt denominated in domestic currency instead of foreign currency, another sign of strength. The Republic of Korea and Malaysia have gone the farthest in this direction, he finds. The price paid for relying on domestic market sources has come in terms of higher interest rates, but this premium is relatively small. Perhaps ironically, the inescapable conclusion is that Japan faces the principal sovereign debt challenge in Asia, with high debt ratios and fiscal sustainability challenges. Cline questions whether Japan's pursuit of quantitative easing is addressing the fundamental problem of an aging population and a resulting stagnant labor force. For this reason, monetary expansion might not bring as much growth as many analysts have concluded and could, at the same time, boost interest rates in a way that would compound the debt-to-GDP problems.

2

Banking Crises and "Japanization": Origins and Implications

MASAHIRO KAWAI AND PETER MORGAN

Recent research has found that economic recoveries from banking crises tend to be weaker and more prolonged than those from traditional types of deep recessions (see, for example, IMF 2009, chapter 3). Japan's "two lost decades" perhaps represent an extreme example of this, and the experience has now passed into the lexicon as "Japanese-style stagnation" or "Japanization" for short.[1] A long period of economic stagnation during peacetime is not new, particularly among developing countries—the "lost decade" of Latin America in the 1980s is just one example. But Japanization was a surprising phenomenon observed in a mature market economy where the authorities were supposed to have sufficient policy tools to tackle banking crises and manage the economy. It is characterized by a lack of nominal GDP growth; deflation in prices of goods, services, and assets; weak real economic activity; subdued private demand for credit; and a dramatic rise in government debt. Price deflation and a near-zero short-term interest rate led Japan to be a leader in experimenting with unconventional monetary policies such as quantitative easing.

Several factors may have contributed to Japanization, such as inadequate macroeconomic policy responses, delayed banking sector restructuring, inadequate corporate investment, loss of industrial competitiveness, a slowdown in

Masahiro Kawai is the dean and CEO of the Asian Development Bank Institute. Peter Morgan has been senior consultant for research at the Asian Development Bank Institute since 2008. They are thankful for comments made by two anonymous referees and for competent and dedicated research assistance provided by Asel Kara-muratova. The findings, interpretations, and conclusions expressed in the paper are entirely those of the authors alone and do not necessarily represent the views of the Asian Development Bank, its Institute (ADBI), its executive directors, or the countries they represent.

1. As described in "After Five Years of Crisis, the Euro Area Risks Japanese-style Economic Stagnation," *Economist*, August 4, 2012.

total factor productivity (TFP) growth due to excessive regulation and economic rigidities, and an aging society. Understanding how and why Japanization took place is critical to avoiding similar, prolonged economic stagnation in post-banking crisis periods in other countries, such as the United States and the euro area economies. For this purpose it would be useful to examine how other countries affected by banking crises—such as those in the Organisation for Economic Co-operation and Development (OECD), Asia, and Latin America—recovered from crises through the prism of Japan's postcrisis experience. This will help identify the features of crisis effects and policy lessons and avoid the kind of economic stagnation seen in Japan.

This chapter reviews the features of Japan's long-term economic stagnation by looking at several macroeconomic variables over time. It points out the factors that have likely contributed to the country's prolonged subperformance. It then assesses the experience of banking crises in other developed and emerging-market economies in comparison with Japan's and finds the extent to which Japan's postcrisis economic performance is an outlier from international comparative perspectives. The chapter conducts econometric analysis to examine the determinants of the growth rate of per capita (or per worker) real GDP for an unbalanced panel data of more than 60 countries over the last two decades. The regression analysis focuses on the potential importance of price inflation (or deflation), capital accumulation, bank credit, a banking crisis, and other structural variables such as population aging. The chapter concludes by offering policy recommendations to help avoid long-term stagnation, particularly for the United States and the euro area countries, which may also experience some symptoms of Japanization.

Japan's Stagnation Experience

Carmen Reinhart and Kenneth Rogoff (2009, 2010) compiled an exhaustive list of various types of worldwide financial crises. According to their classification, Japan's banking crisis dated from 1992 to 2001.[2] However, the slow-motion nature of the Japanese financial crisis makes it difficult to describe the process very precisely. Figure 2.1 shows that GDP growth hit a near-term peak in 1988 and fell steadily thereafter, hitting a trough in 1998. Stock and land prices peaked in December 1989 and September 1991, respectively, and then began a long period of decline in subsequent decades.

If one takes 1992 as the year of the onset of the Japanese banking crisis, the data show a clear break in the decades before and after this year. Table 2.1 illustrates that per worker real GDP, which gives a measure of labor productivity, had grown at 2.6 percent in the decade before the crisis, but declined sharply to 0.5 percent growth in the following decade. Moreover, there was no

---

2. We use the data files from Reinhart's website, which are associated with Reinhart and Rogoff (2010), www.carmenreinhart.com/data/browse-by-topic/topics/7 (accessed on July 1, 2013). In many cases, the crisis periods are different from those in Reinhart and Rogoff (2009), including those for Japan.

Figure 2.1　Japanese real GDP and capital investment growth, 1980–2012

percent

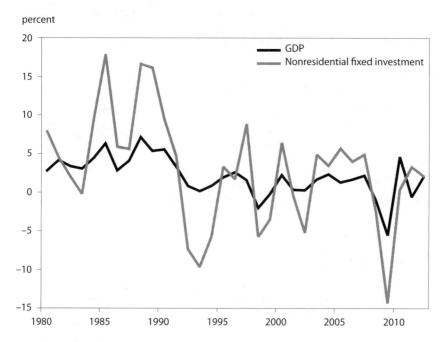

Source: Cabinet Office, Government of Japan.

recovery in the succeeding decade, partly due to the effects of the sharp recession in 2009 following the Lehman Brothers shock. In this sense, the Japanese economy experienced "two lost decades." The growth rate of real GDP per working-age person (aged 15-64) did modestly better, especially in the most recent decade, reflecting a modest worsening in employment. The growth rate of per worker hour real GDP also declined over time from 3.2 percent in 1982–91 to 0.8 percent in 2002–11 though it remained relatively high at 1.5 percent in 1992–2001. For reference, the Conference Board's Total Economy Database shows a rather milder rate of deterioration in Japan, with per worker GDP growth slowing from 2.9 percent in 1982–91 to around 1 percent thereafter. This growth rate is much more in line with the OECD growth average. Moreover, the Conference Board data show substantially higher growth of output per worker hour—closer to 2 percent—than the Japanese government data, also in line with the OECD average.[3]

The main difference between the Conference Board data and the Japanese national accounts data is that the former uses Geary-Khamis (GK) dollars, which are adjusted for both inflation and purchasing power parity (PPP). This

---

3. The Conference Board Total Economy Database is available at www.conference-board.org/data/economydatabase/ (accessed on July 1, 2013).

Table 2.1 Japan's real growth experience, 1972–2011 (average annual growth rate in percent)

Indicator	1972–81	1982–91	1992–2001	2002–11
Japanese government data				
GDP	4.3	4.0	0.6	0.1
Per capita GDP	3.2	3.5	0.3	0.0
Per working age GDP (15 to 64 years)	3.4	3.1	0.6	0.6
Per worker GDP	3.4	2.6	0.5	0.4
Per worker hour GDP	4.1	3.2	1.5	0.8
Conference Board data				
GDP	4.3	4.0	0.8	0.7
Per capita GDP	3.2	3.5	0.6	0.6
Per working age GDP (15 to 64 years)	3.4	3.1	0.9	1.2
Per worker GDP	3.4	2.9	0.9	1.0
Per worker hour GDP	3.8	3.5	1.9	1.7

Note: The Conference Board data for real GDP are measured in 1990 international dollars converted at Geary-Khamis purchasing power parity.

Sources: Cabinet Office, Government of Japan; Organisation for Economic Co-operation and Development statistical database, www.oecd.org/statistics; Conference Board Total Economy Database, www.conference-board.org/data/economydatabase; and authors' estimates.

has the advantage of putting all countries' growth data in comparable units. The use of PPP price measures probably somewhat offsets the effects of the yen's appreciation during the period, and therefore is probably the major reason behind the higher growth estimate. Given that GK dollars are not yet widely used for international comparisons, we focus on the local currency-based or the World Bank's 2005 PPP-based real growth estimates, while bearing in mind that local currency figures may overestimate, and PPP figures underestimate, the extent of Japan's growth slowdown.

The Japanese banking crisis was a classic real-estate-led boom and bust, accompanied by a stock market boom-bust cycle. Figure 2.2 shows that the stock market peaked in December 1989, while land prices on an all-nation basis peaked almost two years later in September 1991.[4] Stock prices and land prices rose by almost 130 and 60 percent to their respective peaks from March 1986. In the subsequent 20 years, however, stock prices came down as a trend to the pre-1985 level, and land prices lost all of their gains between 1980 and 1991 and still have not hit bottom.[5]

---

4. One of the features of Japan's land boom was that the rise in commercial land prices during the bubble was higher than that of residential land prices, and the decline in commercial land prices in the postbubble period was sharper than that of residential land prices.

5. Following the introduction of so-called Abenomics (named after Prime Minister Shinzō Abe), stock prices regained their value to some extent, but land prices have yet to see a solid rise.

Figure 2.2   Stock market and national land prices, 1980–2013

index (March 1986 = 100)

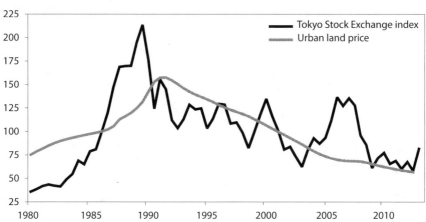

Sources: Japan Real Estate Institute; CEIC Database.

The boom was supported by a steady acceleration of bank loan growth during most of the 1980s, peaking at about 13 percent in 1987 (figure 2.3). Lending growth slumped beginning in 1991, and slid steadily to around zero growth by 1994, where it stabilized until 1998. From 1998 through 2005, bank loans fell sharply due to the beginning of a systemic banking crisis, the Asian financial crisis of 1997–98, the US dot-com bubble collapse in 2000, and aggressive policies to write off bad debts and recapitalize banks. The fall in bank loans was a reflection of substantial deleveraging undertaken by commercial banks. Surprisingly, bank lending continued to contract when economic growth resumed in 2003–05, but it finally made a modest recovery in 2006–08, only to be hit by the Lehman shock in 2008. It began to recover again in 2011, but its level remains well below the peak of 1997.

Features of Japanization

The most remarkable aspect of Japan's postbubble experience has been the lack of growth of nominal GDP in yen terms. Figure 2.4 shows that nominal GDP rose, albeit slowly, throughout most of the 1990s and peaked in 1997, but has declined as a trend since then. As a consequence, nominal GDP in 2012 was 9 percent below its peak level in 1997. However, real GDP rose as a trend because of declines in the GDP deflator. The GDP deflator began to decline in 1994 and the decline has been particularly sharp since 1998. Both the continuous fall of the GDP deflator for more than 15 years and the long-term stagnation of nominal GDP growth for more than 20 years are remarkable phenomena.

The second feature of Japan's postbubble period has been the prolonged deflation of goods and services prices (figure 2.5). The GDP deflator has fallen

Figure 2.3   Growth rates of loans and discounts of domestically licensed banks, 1980–2013

percent

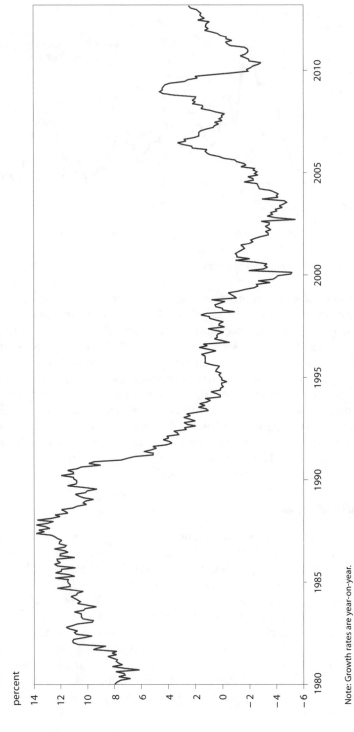

Note: Growth rates are year-on-year.

Source: CEIC Database.

Figure 2.4   Nominal and real GDP and GDP deflator, 1980–2013

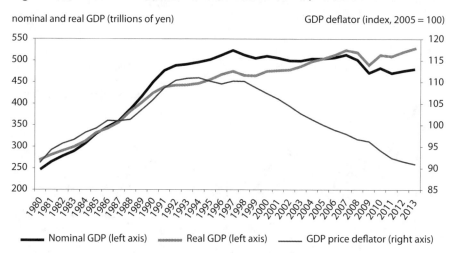

nominal and real GDP (trillions of yen)   GDP deflator (index, 2005 = 100)

━━━ Nominal GDP (left axis)   ▬▬▬ Real GDP (left axis)   ─── GDP price deflator (right axis)

Note: Real GDP is at 2005 constant prices. Data for 2013 are International Monetary Fund (IMF) projections.
Source: IMF, *World Economic Outlook* database, April 2013.

18 percent since its peak in 1993, mostly reflecting large declines in prices of exports and capital investment goods. The only exceptions were a blip in 1997 (due to a hike in the consumption tax rate from 3 to 5 percent) and a slight blip in 2008 (due to the global commodity price rise). The fall in the consumption deflator of the national accounts was also notable, down 12 percent since the end of 1994. In contrast, the decline of the consumer price index (CPI) has been much milder, down only 2 percent since the end of 1994, reflecting differences in methods of computation and the possible upward bias due to using fixed weights for different components. Although both consumer price indicators had shown improvement since 2002, they lost ground again after the Lehman shock in 2008.

The third defining characteristic of Japan's postbubble experience has been the sharp slowdown of private capital investment, especially on a net basis after deducting for depreciation of capital stock. Figure 2.6 shows that the share of gross fixed investment in GDP declined gradually from a peak of 32 percent in 1990 to 20 percent in 2011. However, as depreciation of the capital stock rose steadily, net investment fell sharply as a share of GDP from more than 15 percent at the peak of the bubble to a negative value in the post-Lehman shock period. This slowdown in net investment and, thus, in capital accumulation likely made a significant contribution to the overall slowdown of GDP growth.[6]

---

6. Other developed economies showed milder declines in net investment. The ratios of net investment to GDP for Germany, the United States, and the United Kingdom fell from a range of 6 to 9 percent in 2000 to about 3 percent in 2011. This points to a longer-term decline in growth rates in those countries as well. But Japan's sharp economic decline since the eruption of the global financial crisis—including that in net disinvestment—stands out.

Figure 2.5 Rates of change in GDP deflators and consumer prices, 1980–2012

percent

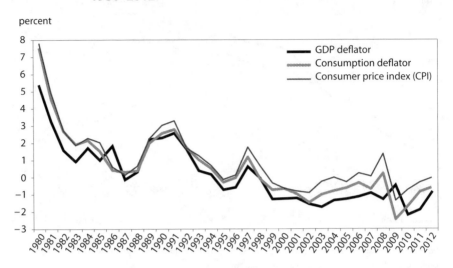

Source: CEIC Database.

Figure 2.6 Gross and net investment and capital depreciation, 1980–2011

percent of GDP

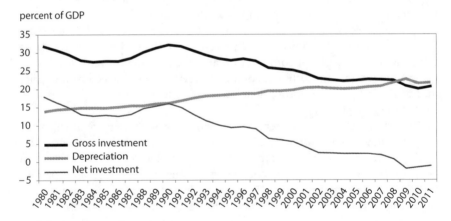

Sources: Cabinet Office, Government of Japan; CEIC Database.

The fourth defining feature of Japan's postbubble stagnation has been the fall of nominal interest rates to extremely low levels, essentially zero in the case of short-term interest rates, reflecting the Bank of Japan's (BOJ) efforts to combat price deflation (figure 2.7). The overnight call rate, the BOJ's normal operating target, has stayed close to zero since 1999, except for two ill-fated

Figure 2.7   Japanese interest rates, 1980–2012

percent

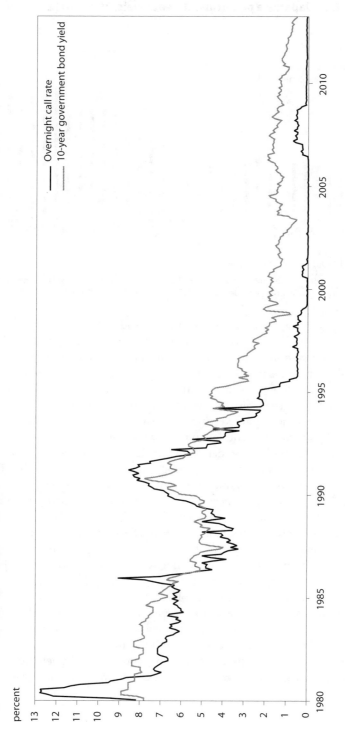

— Overnight call rate
— 10-year government bond yield

Source: CEIC Database.

Figure 2.8   Japanese government debt levels, 1980–2012

percent of GDP

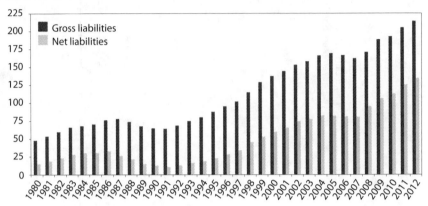

Note: Data for 2012 are OECD projections.

Source: Organisation for Economic Co-operation and Development, *Economic Outlook*, December 2012, http://stats.oecd.org/Index.aspx?DataSetCode=EO92_INTERNET (accessed on July 1, 2013).

and temporary rate hike episodes in 2000 and 2007. The 10-year Japanese government bond (JGB) yield fell steadily from 1990 through 1998, then was somewhat range-bound until 2006, and most recently has been declining gradually, falling below 1 percent in 2012. The phenomenon of very low nominal interest rates has now spread to a number of developed economies, including the United States, the United Kingdom, and the euro area.

The final major characteristic of Japan's stagnation has been the ballooning of government debt. Japan now has the dubious honor of having the highest levels of both gross debt and net debt as a percent of GDP among the OECD countries (figure 2.8), although it has not suffered obviously for it. This sharp rise has been due to continuously large fiscal deficits as a result of declining tax revenues reflecting weak economic growth and of numerous large fiscal stimulus packages, as well as a steady rise in old-age-related social security spending (for pensions and health) reflecting the rapidly aging society.

To summarize, the key aspects of Japanization appear to be a combination of a lack of growth in nominal GDP (due to prolonged weak real growth and outright deflation), sustained deleveraging of the private sector in the aftermath of the bursting of the bubble, a large increase in government debt, and a fall in nominal interest rates to near-zero levels. Although the United States and a number of European countries have also experienced low real GDP growth, rising government debt, and low interest rates in the aftermath of the global financial crisis, none has experienced outright deflation or a lack of nominal GDP growth to any significant extent. In this sense, Japan's experience has been unique.

Possible Factors behind Japanization

Japan's poor economic performance in the postbubble period can have several explanations, including

- inadequate monetary policy responses, leading to persistent price deflation and yen appreciation;

- prolonged pace of deleveraging, leading to persistent asset price stagnation;

- slow reaction to banking sector problems in the form of regulatory forbearance and "zombie" financing;

- lack of structural reform resulting in excessive regulation, economic rigidities, limited openness, and inefficiency; and

- aging of the population.

The first factor is basically one of monetary policy, that is, the BOJ reacted too slowly and reluctantly to ease policy in the face of the collapse of the asset price bubble and the developing banking crisis in the early to mid-1990s. Alan Ahearne et al. (2002) find that Japanese monetary policy was not excessively tight at that time but that the authorities did not take out sufficient "insurance" against downside risks to the outlook. They show some evidence of a liquidity trap, especially after 1997, but still believe that monetary policy could have been more aggressive. Kazuo Ueda (2012) notes that the BOJ did not recognize the negative interaction between real economic and financial factors in its official report until late 1993. It was not until 1995 that the overnight call rate was lowered below 2 percent (figure 2.7). Fabio Canova and Tobias Menz (2012), using an augmented neo-Keynesian model, find that the money stock—rather than technology shocks—was responsible for the slowdown of Japanese economic growth and that restrictive monetary policy during 1998–2003 contributed to weak growth.

Inadequate monetary policy is clearly the primary reason behind outright deflation and a lack of nominal GDP growth throughout the 1990s and 2000s. Deflation likely stifled incentives for household consumption (as holding cash was more attractive) and for corporate investment (due to deflationary prospects). Nominal wages remained depressed, further discouraging household consumption. Deflation was also a driver of the persistently strong yen, particularly during 1990–95 and 1998–2000, having likely harmed the manufacturing sector.[7] However, it is difficult to make a strong case for this in more recent post-

---

7. Koichi Hamada and Yasushi Okada (2009) argue that the yen's estimated 78 percent overvaluation in real terms against the US dollar by 1995 exerted a large long-term depressing effect on the Japanese economy, which was only masked at times by favorable movements in the terms of trade, chiefly due to declines in energy prices. Robert Dekle and Kyoji Fukao (2011) find that TFP growth in Japanese industries was generally higher than in the United States in 1980–90, but slowed well below US rates in 1990–2004, and that this was correlated with the long period of yen overvaluation during 1985–2000.

Lehman shock years, as the real effective yen rate was not especially strong.[8] In addition, deflation did not help in halting the deleveraging process or the continuous declines in land prices. Essentially, deflation either was one of the primary factors behind stagnant economic activity or at least failed to provide a favorable economic environment for consumption and business investment.

The second factor is the process of deleveraging by commercial banks and indebted corporations. According to this view, commercial banks extended "excess" bank loans to the corporate sector with real estate as collateral during the asset-price-bubble period of the late 1980s. The collapse of the asset market exposed the large claims of banks on the corporate sector and the high debt of the corporate sector to banks, forcing both banks and corporations to accelerate deleveraging. This reinforced the declines in financial and real estate prices, further weakening economic activity. Thus, Jenny Corbett and Takatoshi Ito (2010) argue that the main reason for weak growth in the 1990s was the collapse of the financial and real estate bubble.

The third factor relates to the slow response to banking sector nonperforming loans (NPLs) and the emerging banking crisis. It is widely recognized that the Japanese authorities' initial policy was one of "forbearance," i.e., allowing Japanese banks to carry NPLs on their balance sheets in the hopes that client companies would eventually recover. Thus, banks financed overdue loan payments, rather than lending to viable companies willing to invest. This likely led to the development of inefficient "zombie" companies that contributed to excess capacity and price deflation while stifling investment by more productive companies.[9] This phenomenon is analyzed by Takeo Hoshi and Anil Kashyap (1999) and others. Takeo Hoshi, Satoshi Koibuchi, and Ulrike Schaede (2011) find that corporate restructuring efforts during the 1990s and 2000s were less aggressive than in the 1980s. Many studies, including by Toshitaka Sekine (1999) and Hiroyuki Kasahara, Yasuyuki Sawada, and Michio Suzuki (2011), have also identified a link between banks' weak balance sheets and declines in investment spending during this period.[10]

Several underlying factors likely contributed to the slow response on the part of the financial authorities (Kawai 2005). One is the lack of an acute crisis—such as a currency crisis that would have prompted the authorities to respond quickly and decisively—due to the presence of large domestic savings and foreign exchange reserves, which provided substantial breathing room for

---

8. Nonetheless, there is some evidence that the automobile sector—a large exporter in Japan—faced much more significant real effective yen appreciation in the late 2000s and the early 2010s.

9. Hoshi and Kashyap (2011) cite research showing that the estimated share of assets of listed companies made up of "zombie" firms rose from about 3 percent in 1991 to 16 percent in 1996.

10. It is also recognized that the shift to a stricter regulatory regime following the recapitalization of Japanese banks in 1997 and 1998 had a short-run impact of weakening economic activity. Ueda (2012) notes that once banks had sufficient capital to write off their NPLs, their deleveraginq became more aggressive, worsening the credit crunch. However, the bank recapitalization helped Japanese banks in bottoming out their loans in the 2000s and had paved the way toward recovery until 2008.

policymakers but also caused a delay in action. Another is the sustained use of emergency fiscal policy packages, which maintained a minimum degree of aggregate demand and may have delayed decisive policy action. The financial authorities reacted decisively only after Japan faced a systemic banking crisis in 1997–98.

The fourth factor, structural rigidities, is not directly linked to the crisis, but can be another reason for slow growth, since they tend to inhibit the reallocation of resources to sectors with potentially higher productivity (see box 2.1). These negative effects may have been exacerbated in periods of slow growth that likely started due to other factors. High regulation and barriers to entry are important examples of rigidity. Hoshi and Kashyap (2011) cite a number of studies finding a negative relationship between the degree of regulation and productivity growth. Many observers have noted that Japan's very low ratios of imports and the stock of inward foreign direct investment (FDI) to GDP could be a manifestation of the closed nature of the Japanese economy, which constrains growth.[11]

The government of Prime Minister Shinzō Abe has taken up structural reform as the "third arrow" of its "Abenomics" program to restore Japanese economic growth and end deflation. A detailed program has yet to be formulated, but the government is focusing on industrial revitalization, strategic market creation (health, agriculture), and international partnerships. Most notably, the government has joined or begun negotiations on the Trans-Pacific Partnership, the Japan-European Union Economic Partnership Agreement, and the Regional Comprehensive Economic Partnership. The Japanese agricultural sector is notoriously inefficient, so trade concessions in that sector could open the way for significant improvements in economic efficiency. However, it is too early to judge the results of this program.

A fifth possible factor, also structural, is the aging of society. This should not directly affect our measure of labor productivity, which is output per working-age (15–64 years old) person or per worker hour, except to the extent that older workers remain in the labor markets. However, aging could have a number of other possible impact channels, including lower savings, higher old-age-related expenditures, a loss of economic "dynamism" (a lack of development of new high-growth industries), and lower TFP growth. Declining savings could also raise the cost of capital, thereby reducing capital investment, although this has not been apparent yet.

Growth Accounting

A useful step for analyzing the factors for economic slowdown is to decompose GDP growth into the major contributing factors. Using the standard growth accounting framework, GDP growth is a function of the weighted shares of

---

11. In 2011, Japan's import-to-GDP ratio and stock-of-inward-FDI-to-GDP ratio were 14.5 and 3.9 percent, respectively. Those ratios ranked 167th out of 172 countries and 194th out of 198 countries, respectively.

Box 2.1 Structural reforms in Japan

Attempts to promote structural reform in Japan have a long history. Contrary to popular belief, some notable progress has been made, although much remains to be done. These attempts initially came from abroad, reflecting perceptions that structural features of Japan's economy tended to discourage imports and push up Japan's current account and trade surplus.

At the macroeconomic level, numerous factors were perceived to contribute to a high level of savings relative to investment, including preferential taxation of savings and inadequate infrastructure investment.

At the microeconomic level, excessive government regulation, burdensome import procedures, collusive market practices, closed *keiretsu* business networks, and high land prices were seen as contributing to low levels of imports and inward foreign direct investment (FDI). Although foreign reform pressures—called *gaiatsu*—were aimed primarily at trying to correct the trade balance, it was also argued that many such reforms would benefit Japanese consumers by lowering costs and increasing competition. After the Japanese financial crisis of the 1990s and the sharp slowdown in trend growth, calls for structural reforms to boost potential growth were taken up domestically as well.

Structural reform efforts had started before the collapse of the bubble. The Mayekawa Report (Mayekawa et al. 1986) was perhaps the first Japanese call for extensive structural reforms since the economic reforms immediately after World War II. The report identified six major areas for policy changes to reduce current account balances: (1) expansion of domestic demand, including both consumption and infrastructure investment; (2) transformation of the industrial structure, including promotion of inward FDI; (3) promotion of manufactured imports and further improvements in market access; (4) international financial liberalization and stabilization of international currency values; (5) increased contribution to the global economy and international cooperation; and (6) fiscal and monetary policy support. However, there was no concerted move to act on these proposals, presumably because there was little domestic support or perceived need for reforms at the time.

In 1989, the US and Japanese governments started the Structural Impediments Initiative, a series of discussions with Japan to address Japanese economic policies and business practices that the United States claimed impeded US exports and investments. These included Japan's high savings–low investment imbalance; the Japanese retail distribution system, particularly its Large-Retail Store Law that restricted entry by large-scale retailers; land use policies that inhibited market entry of new firms and kept land prices high; the *keiretsu* business conglomerates that restricted market entry; exclusionary business practices, such as the formation of cartels to limit competition; and discriminatory pricing practices.

The bilateral negotiations produced a number of tangible results, including a much expanded program of public works spending on infrastructure, a reduction in working hours of government employees, changes in the taxation of savings, and, most notably, substantial revisions of the Large-Retail Store Law,

(continues on next page)

Box 2.1 Structural reforms in Japan *(continued)*

including shortening the approval process to 12 months, restraining local authorities from enacting their own restrictive regulations, and exempting from the approval process new or expanded floor expansion up to 1,000 square meters for import sales (Cooper 1993).

The Big Bang reform of the financial sector beginning in 1996 under Prime Minister Ryutaro Hashinoto had an important effect of opening up the financial sector to greater competition. Measures included introducing new investment trusts and over-the-counter sales of investment trusts by banks and other financial institutions; fully liberalizing dealings in securities derivatives; promoting entry of banks, securities companies, and insurance companies into each other's business; switching from the licensing system to a registration system for securities companies; liberalizing cross-border capital transactions and foreign exchange business; fully liberalizing brokerage commissions; abolishing the requirements to trade stocks only through stock exchanges; introducing stock exchanges for startup companies; and improving disclosure systems and setting up fair trading rules (Lincoln and Litan 1998).

Facing long-term economic stagnation, Prime Minister Junichiro Koizumi focused on deregulation and structural reform comprising three parts: reforming the administrative system such as the postal saving system and various special semigovernmental corporations; decentralizing or transferring administrative power to local governments by reducing subsidies, reallocating local government block grants, and transferring taxation power to local government; and deregulating the employment, medical care, education, transportation, and communication sectors (Teranishi 2009). In addition, Prime Minister Koizumi urged the Financial Services Agency to put greater pressure on Japanese banks to write off their nonperforming loans, and their improved capital position allowed them to do so with surprising rapidity. Takeo Hoshi and Anil Kashyap (2011) judge that only Koizumi's financial sector reforms were notably successful.

---

the growth of capital and labor inputs, plus TFP—the "residual" that cannot be explained by capital and labor inputs. Labor inputs in turn can be decomposed into the number of workers employed, labor quality, and changes in working hours per employee. Here we follow the notation of Fumio Hayashi and Edward Prescott (2001) with slight modification for the specification of the aggregate production function:

$$Y = AK^{\theta} (hqE)^{1-\theta},$$

where Y is aggregate output, A is TFP, K is aggregate capital, E is aggregate employment, h is working hours per employee, and q is an index of labor quality. The parameter θ is the share of capital in national income, and the production function is assumed to have constant returns to scale, so the share of labor income is $1 - \theta$.

Following their notation further, let P be the total population and N be the working-age population (15–64) and define

$$y = Y/P, \, n = N/P, \, e = E/N, \, x = K/Y,$$

where n is the working-age population share and e is the employment ratio—the ratio of employed labor force to total working-age population—which comprises the labor force participation rate and the employment rate in the total workforce. Using these definitions and by simple algebra, we obtain:

$$y = A^{1/1-\theta} \, hqnex^{\theta/1-\theta}.$$

Table 2.2 shows the contributions to Japanese real per capita GDP growth. The data through 1991 in the table are from Hayashi and Prescott (2001). The table shows a sharp slowdown in productivity growth since 1992, which was the time of the onset of the Japanese banking crisis according to Reinhart and Rogoff (2009). In the period 1992–2001, productivity rose at an average rate of only 0.3 percent. By far the biggest factor behind this slowdown was the actual drop of TFP during the period, with smaller contributions from a larger decline in the workweek compared with previously, a decline in the employment rate, and a decline in the share of the working-age population. Somewhat surprisingly, the contribution from capital deepening rose sharply from the previous decade. However, this mainly seems to reflect the relatively slow response of capital spending during the early stages of the crisis, which led the capital stock to grow faster than output.

Per capita real GDP growth slowed significantly in the 1992–2011 period, mainly reflecting a large decline in the working-age population share, a decline in working hours, and a TFP growth slowdown relative to the previous periods. The contribution from capital intensity was large during the 1992–2001 period but came down sharply during 2002–11, reflecting the sharp drop in net investment discussed above. This growth was well below the OECD average, and this, together with the very low contribution from capital accumulation, points to a longer-lasting impact on growth from the crisis.

International Comparative Perspectives of Banking Crisis Experiences

Financial crises are typically divided into systemic banking crises, sovereign debt crises, and currency crises, and two or more of these may occur in combination. In the 1990s (or in any postwar period), Japan did not suffer sovereign debt crises or currency crises, so we focus our attention in this chapter on banking crises. Two of the most recent large international databases on systemic banking crises are provided in studies by Luc Laeven and Fabian Valencia (2008) and Reinhart and Rogoff (2009).

Table 2.2 Accounting for Japan's per capita real GDP growth, 1962–2011 (percent)

Period	Per capita growth rate (percent)	Contributing factors (average percent contribution)					
		Total factor productivity	Capital intensity	Workweek length	Employment ratio	Labor quality	Working-age population share
1962–71	8.1	5.5	2.3	–0.2	–0.5	0.4	0.6
1972–81	3.2	1.3	2.1	–0.3	0.0	0.4	–0.2
1982–91	3.5	2.9	0.2	–0.5	0.2	0.4	0.4
1992–2001	0.3	–0.7	1.6	–0.9	–0.1	0.7	–0.3
2002–11	0.0	0.6	0.1	–0.6	0.2	0.4	–0.6

Notes: The growth rate is that of per capita real GDP. Working-age population is population aged 15 to 64.

Sources: Based on Hayashi and Prescott (2001) for the first three periods; Cabinet Office, Government of Japan; Conference Board Total Economy Database, www.conference-board.org/data/economydatabase, for total factor productivity and labor quality; Japan Statistics Bureau; authors' estimates for the last two periods.

Banking crises tend not to be as clear-cut as currency or sovereign debt crises. Laeven and Valencia (2008, 5) define a systemic banking crisis in the following way:

> a country's corporate and financial sectors experience a large number of defaults and financial institutions and corporations face great difficulties repaying contracts on time. As a result, non-performing loans increase sharply and all or most of the aggregate banking system capital is exhausted.

Reinhart and Rogoff (2009, 10) define a banking crisis as

> two types of events: (1) bank runs that lead to the closure, merging, or takeover by the public sector of one or more financial institutions (as in Venezuela in 1993 or Argentina in 2001); and (2) if there are no runs, the closure, merging, takeover, or large-scale government assistance of an important financial institution (or group of institutions) that marks the start of a string of similar outcomes for other financial institutions (as in Thailand 1996–97).

Laeven and Valencia (2008) identify only the year associated with the onset of a banking crisis, while Reinhart and Rogoff (2009) identify the entire period of a crisis. Laeven and Valencia's database identifies 124 systemic banking crises over the period from 1970 to 2007. They also provide detailed information on crisis management strategies for 42 systemic banking crises from 37 countries, e.g., whether or not there was forbearance. The Reinhart and Rogoff (2009, 2010) database goes all the way back to 1800. For the most part, the beginnings of crisis periods in the two databases correspond, but there are exceptions, some quite notable. For example, Laeven and Valencia date Japan's crisis as starting in 1997, when major bankruptcies and bailouts took place, while Reinhart and Rogoff (2009) date it from 1992, when the bubble began to burst. This suggests caution in putting too much emphasis on the exact date of a crisis.

Banking Crisis and Growth

Many studies have analyzed the effect of banking crises on economic growth, but most of these have focused on measuring cumulative output losses or the pace of the subsequent economic recovery. Relatively few have analyzed the impact of banking crises on long-term economic growth. Stephen Cecchetti, Marion Kohler, and Christian Upper (2009) examined whether the timing of financial crises coincided with downward breaks in trend growth rates. This comes close to the objective of our study. Their regression equation attempts to find out whether the growth rate of real GDP shows a break in the level and/or the long-term trend at the time of the crisis by including dummies for the timing of the crisis and the interaction between time and the dummy variable. They identify crisis periods based on Laeven and Valencia (2008).

Using a sample of 40 crises for both developed and emerging/developing economies from all regions, they found a drop in the level of GDP after the crisis in over half of the cases, although only significant for one-fifth of the sample. Postcrisis trend growth rates actually rose in most cases, but this did not necessarily compensate for the initial loss of output. In eight cases they found lower trend growth rates, including in Indonesia, Japan, Malaysia, and Thailand, and most of these were associated with downward-level breaks as well. It is interesting to note the concentration of Asian countries in this group.

Davide Furceri and Annabelle Mourougane (2009) analyzed financial crises in 30 OECD economies from 1960 to 2007, estimating a univariate autoregressive growth equation and deriving the relative impulse response functions where the left-hand side variable was potential growth and explanatory variables were crisis period dummy variables. They found that financial crises lowered trend growth rates on average by two percentage points. As potential growth rates are hard to estimate, they used two approaches as a cross-check—the OECD estimates based on a production function approach, and simpler smoothing techniques using a Hodrick-Prescott filter—and found relatively similar results.

However, these studies attempted only to measure the effects of banking crises on growth, with no attempt to analyze what other variables may have contributed to the deterioration of growth performance after crises. Also, they used the overall growth rate of GDP as the dependent variable, rather than the growth rate of per capita or per worker GDP, so did not fully take account of changes in demographic patterns.

Robert Barro (2001) analyzed the impact of various factors on longer-term growth rates of per capita real GDP and the ratio of investment to GDP for a panel of 67 countries. He regressed five-year average growth rates against a number of explanatory variables—such as the initial level of per capita GDP, quality of human capital, measures of government policy and institutions, trade openness, inflation, the fixed-investment-to-GDP ratio, and crisis period dummies. He found that the five Asian crisis-affected countries (Indonesia, the Republic of Korea, Malaysia, the Philippines, and Thailand) grew during 1995–2000 at about 4 percent per year below the rate that would otherwise have been predicted by the set of explanatory variables—a highly significant shortfall. For the overall sample of countries, he found that crises did not affect output growth five years later, but his result excluded the effects of the output losses during the crisis period.

Barro's approach is very useful, as it develops predicted values for growth rates based on various factors, and identifies cases when countries' growth rates were higher than predicted before a crisis as well as when they were lower than predicted after a crisis. This provides much more information than just comparing precrisis and postcrisis growth rates.

International Experiences of Banking Crises

This section compares Japan's experience with those of other countries. Specifically, we compare Japan with three groups of countries that also experienced banking crises in the 1990s—OECD, Asian, and Latin American countries. Figures 2A.1 to 2A.3 in appendix 2A show the performance of per capita real GDP in these countries. Japan did not experience a sharp decline in per capita real GDP—unlike Finland (1991–93), Sweden (1991–93), Indonesia (1998–99), or Thailand (1996–97)—but saw a significant slowdown in the growth of per capita real GDP during the 1990s and 2000s. Japan's per capita real GDP reached a peak in 1997 and then contracted for two years, taking six years to recover the previous peak in 2003. Six years is much longer than the recovery period among the developed economies that contracted due to banking crises in the 1990s, except for Finland, which took seven years to recover to the previous peak. (Australia took three years; France, two years; Italy, two years; Sweden, five years; the United Kingdom, three years; and the United States, two years.) Interestingly, most emerging Asian countries that were affected by banking crises had to spend as many years as Japan before recovering their previous peaks, except the Republic of Korea, which recovered in only two years. (Indonesia took eight years; Malaysia, six years; the Philippines, five years; and Thailand, six years). Per capita real GDP in Latin America was much more volatile than in Japan.

OECD Countries

Table 2.3 compares Japan's experience with those of seven other OECD countries that also had banking crises during the 1990s, based on the Reinhart-Rogoff data. Choosing countries on this basis allows us to analyze the growth experience in the decade before the crisis, the decade during the crisis, and the decade after the crisis. However, the comparison is not perfect, as some countries experienced crises in either the 1980s or the 2000s as well as in the 1990s. For example, Australia and the United States had banking crises in the 1980s that continued until the 1990s. The United Kingdom had banking crises in the 1980s and the 2000s in addition to the 1990s. France and the United States also had banking crises in the 2000s. The table shows averages for each decade for the level of per capital real GDP, the growth rate of per capita real GDP, the contribution to GDP growth from the capital stock, the ratio of domestic credit to GDP, and the change in housing prices. Barro (2001) examined the ratio of investment to GDP, but we believe that the contribution to growth from the capital stock is a better measure, as it likely captures net investment rather than gross investment, as described earlier in this chapter.

Table 2.3 shows that all of these countries had relatively similar levels of per capita GDP, and Japan's level was quite close to the average, so this can be considered a peer group. However, Japan's experience stands out in several ways. First, it had by far the highest growth rate of per capita real GDP during the 1980s, nearly twice the average rate, while it had the lowest growth rate in the 1990s. By the 2000s, its growth rate was only slightly below the average for these countries, perhaps because of the severe negative impact of the global and euro area financial crises on the United States, Italy, and France. Second, its capital stock contribution was the highest in the 1990s, but at the low end in

Table 2.3 OECD countries' experience with banking crises in the 1990s

Period	Australia (1989–92)	Finland (1991–94)	France (1994–95, 2008–10)	Italy (1990–95)	Japan (1992–2001)	Sweden (1991–94)	United Kingdom (1984, 1991, 1995, 2007–09)	United States (1984–91, 2007–10)	Average
	Per capita real GDP (2005 international dollars)								
1980–1990	21,172	19,922	21,500	20,470	20,946	22,083	20,137	28,059	21,786
1990–2000	25,409	22,675	25,303	25,061	27,885	24,927	24,929	34,115	26,288
2000–2010	32,055	30,237	29,240	28,164	30,017	31,913	32,090	41,493	31,901
	Growth rate of per capita real GDP (annual average percent)								
1980–1990	1.9	2.6	1.8	2.3	4.0	1.9	2.5	2.3	2.4
1990–2000	2.1	1.7	1.5	1.6	0.9	1.7	2.2	2.2	1.7
2000–2010	1.6	1.4	0.4	-0.2	0.7	1.6	1.2	0.6	0.9
	Capital stock contribution to GDP growth (average percentage points)								
1990–2000	0.8	0.6	1.1	0.7	1.6	0.6	1.2	0.9	0.9
2000–2010	1.7	0.6	1.2	0.8	0.6	1.0	1.0	0.9	1.0
	CPI inflation rate (annual average percent)								
1980–1990	8.4	7.3	7.4	11.2	2.5	7.9	7.0	5.6	7.2
1990–2000	2.5	2.1	1.9	4.1	1.2	3.3	3.3	3.0	2.7
2000–2010	3.2	1.8	1.7	2.3	-0.3	1.5	1.8	2.6	1.8

(continues on next page)

Table 2.3 OECD countries' experience with banking crises in the 1990s (continued)

Period	Australia (1989–92)	Finland (1991–94)	France (1994–95, 2008–10)	Italy (1990–95)	Japan (1992–2001)	Sweden (1991–94)	United Kingdom (1984, 1991, 1995, 2007–09)	United States (1984–91, 2007–10)	Average
			Domestic credit/GDP (percent)						
1980–1990	36.8	61.2	91.9	51.1	152.7	85.9	60.4	106.3	80.8
1990–2000	69.2	69.7	88.3	58.3	205.3	107.1	113.0	139.0	106.2
2000–2010	107.2	71.4	95.5	90.0	186.6	104.6	163.7	190.3	126.2
			Rate of change in housing price (period average percent)						
1980–1990	10.3	12.2	6.9	13.0	n.a.	7.4	4.6	n.a.	9.1
1990–2000	4.1	0.8	1.9	2.4	n.a.	2.9	3.8	n.a.	2.7
2000–2010	9.2	6.1	7.5	5.0	n.a.	7.2	3.0	n.a.	6.3

n.a. = not available

CPI = consumer price index; OECD = Organisation for Economic Co-operation and Development

Note: Crisis years (in parentheses) cover all the periods and are based on Reinhart and Rogoff (2009, 2010).

Sources: World Bank, *World Development Indicators* database, for per capita real GDP (in constant 2005 international dollars) and domestic credit/GDP; IMF, *International Financial Statistics*, for CPI inflation rates; Conference Board, Total Economy Database, www.conference-board.org/data/economydatabase, for capital stock contribution to GDP growth; Bank for International Settlements for housing prices.

the 2000s.[12] Third, all countries saw substantial declines in CPI inflation rates over the last three decades, but only Japan experienced outright deflation in the 2000s. Fourth, Japan's ratio of domestic credit to GDP was by far the highest, almost twice the group average in the 1980s and 1990s. Moreover, it saw the largest decline in the credit-to-GDP ratio in the 2000s, while Sweden was the only other country in the group to experience a decline. However, in the 2000s, the domestic credit ratio of the United States exceeded that of Japan, and the United Kingdom was not far behind. Finally, though housing price data are not available in the Bank for International Settlements database, the persistent land price decline suggests that Japan was the only country to experience housing price declines throughout the 1990s and 2000s, which presumably were closely related to the substantial deleveraging observed during that period.

Thus, in comparison with its OECD peers, Japan's growth experience was relatively extreme in terms of the initial growth rate of per capita real GDP, growth of the capital-output ratio, and degree of leverage. It seems reasonable to conclude that these extreme levels—together with inadequate monetary policy—contributed to the severity of the subsequent slowdown of trend growth, the degree of deleveraging, and the extent of deflation. This seems to be a byproduct of rapid investment-driven growth financed by banking sector loans with real estate as collateral in the precrisis period. Among other OECD peers, the high government debt levels seen in the United States and the United Kingdom make them the most likely candidates for Japanization. However, the more stable performance of per capita real GDP growth and the capital stock growth contribution in those countries suggests that their reactions are likely to be less severe than was the case for Japan.

Asian Financial Crisis Countries

Table 2.4 shows similar data for seven emerging Asian countries plus Japan (as a reference). The data are the same as in table 2.3, except that housing price data are not available for most countries, so they are replaced with the ratio of external debt to national income. Most emerging Asian countries were affected by the Asian financial crisis of 1997–98, but the People's Republic of China (PRC) and India also experienced banking crises that started in the early 1990s. It is interesting to see that the Republic of Korea, Malaysia, the Philippines, and Thailand experienced banking crises in the 1980s in addition to the 1990s and that no country had a banking crisis in the 2000s, except that the crises in the 1990s did not end until the early 2000s for most countries.

In the emerging Asian economies, the average level of per capita real GDP in the 1980s was only about 15 percent of that of Japan, and rose to about 25 percent by the 2000s. Nonetheless, Japan's growth rate in the 1980s was only slightly below the average for the emerging Asian economies during that period, which suggests that it was overachieving. Interestingly, the countries

---

12. Data are not available in all countries for capital stock contribution to GDP growth in the 1980s.

Table 2.4 Emerging Asia's experience with banking crises in the 1990s

Period	People's Republic of China (1992–99)	India (1993–98)	Indonesia (1992, 1994, 1997–2002)	Republic of Korea (1983, 1985–88, 1997–2002)	Malaysia (1985–88, 1997–2001)	Philippines (1981–87, 1997–98)	Thailand (1980–87, 1996–2001)	Average	Japan (1992–2001)
Per capita real GDP (2005 international dollars)									
1980–1990	779	1,005	1,559	7,673	5,702	2,592	2,704	3,145	20,946
1990–2000	1,766	1,391	2,500	14,813	8,917	2,543	5,073	5,286	27,885
2000–2010	4,164	2,191	3,092	22,391	11,843	3,023	6,481	7,598	30,017
Growth rate of per capita real GDP (annual average percent)									
1980–1990	7.7	3.2	4.3	7.5	3.1	-1.0	5.9	4.4	4.0
1990–2000	9.3	3.6	2.7	5.1	4.4	0.6	3.4	4.2	0.9
2000–2010	9.8	6.0	4.0	3.6	2.6	2.8	3.4	4.6	0.7
Capital stock contribution to GDP growth (average percentage points)									
1990–2000	4.0	2.4	3.6	3.2	3.8	1.8	4.4	3.3	1.6
2000–2010	5.0	3.1	2.4	1.7	1.3	1.6	1.5	2.4	0.6
CPI inflation rate (annual average percent)									
1980–1990	14.8	8.8	9.6	8.4	3.7	14.9	5.8	8.5	2.5
1990–2000	7.8	9.5	14.5	5.7	3.7	9.0	5.0	7.6	1.2
2000–2010	1.8	5.6	8.4	3.1	2.2	4.6	2.4	4.2	-0.3

	Domestic credit/GDP (percent)								
1980–1990	66.1	23.5	19.7	46.2	76.8	24.4	54.8	44.5	152.7
1990–2000	93.9	23.5	48.5	58.4	119.9	33.8	125.1	71.9	205.3
2000–2010	115.2	37.8	24.2	92.0	113.7	31.9	104.9	74.2	186.6
	External debt/GNI (percent)								
1980–1990	7.7	16.9	45.6	n.a.	56.3	76.9	36.2	39.9	n.a.
1990–2000	16.2	27.1	80.1	n.a.	44.3	63.1	57.6	48.1	n.a.
2000–2010	11.7	18.5	57.1	n.a.	42.2	59.6	35.7	37.5	n.a.

n.a. = not available

CPI = consumer price index; GNI = gross national income

Note: Crisis years (in parentheses) cover all the periods and are based on Reinhart and Rogoff (2009, 2010).

Sources: World Bank, World Development Indicators database, for per capita real GDP (in constant 2005 international dollars) and domestic credit/GDP; IMF, International Financial Statistics, for CPI inflation rates and external debt/GNI; Conference Board, Total Economy Database, www.conference-board.org/data/economydatabase, for capital stock contribution to GDP growth.

hit hardest by the Asian financial crisis—Indonesia, the Republic of Korea, Malaysia, and Thailand—saw sharp declines in the contribution to growth from capital stock in the 2000s, and Malaysia's drop was bigger than that of Japan. In contrast, both the PRC and India showed greater contributions from the capital stock in the 2000s than in the 1990s, reflecting their higher investment ratios. CPI inflation rates generally fell over the period in emerging Asian economies, particularly in the 2000s, but only Japan experienced outright deflation. The ratio of domestic credit to GDP in Japan was much higher than those of emerging Asian economies throughout the period, even though those of the PRC, Malaysia, and Thailand had become relatively high by the 2000s. Domestic credit fell significantly in some Asian-crisis-affected countries (Indonesia, Malaysia, and Thailand) during the 2000s, but they were still able to maintain much higher growth rates than Japan was.

Latin American Countries

Table 2.5 summarizes comparable data for seven Latin American countries that experienced banking crises during the 1990s. Five of them (Argentina, Bolivia, Costa Rica, Mexico, and Brazil) also experienced banking crises during the 1980s, and the other two (the Dominican Republic and Guatemala) had banking crises in the 2000s before the outbreak of the global financial crisis, which makes their situation less comparable with that of Japan. Although the earlier crises were much shorter than those in the 1990s according to the Reinhart-Rogoff data, all Latin American economies exhibited stagnant growth in the 1980s.[13]

Again, average per capita real GDP was far below that of Japan, ranging from 24 to 29 percent, and highest in relative terms during the 1980s. Remarkably, almost all the Latin American countries in the table saw declines in per capita real GDP in the 1980s—often called the "lost decade"—but recovered to moderate but steady growth in the following two decades. The Latin American countries were able to maintain steady growth of their capital stocks in the 1990s and 2000s, unlike Japan, but again, the pace was fairly moderate. Argentina and Brazil experienced periods of hyperinflation in the 1980s and 1990s and Bolivia in the 1980s, but all countries, except Costa Rica and the Dominican Republic, achieved single-digit inflation in the 2000s. The ratios of domestic credit to GDP in Latin America were far lower than that of Japan and fell in the 2000s in Argentina, Bolivia, Brazil, and Mexico. External debt ratios also fell in Bolivia, Costa Rica, the Dominican Republic, and Mexico in the 2000s.

---

13. Colombia, Peru, and Uruguay also experienced major banking crises in the 1980s, but sufficient data are not available for that period.

Table 2.5 Latin America's experience with banking crises in the 1990s

Period	Argentina (1980–82, 1989–90, 1995–96, 2001–03)	Bolivia (1986–87, 1994–97, 1999)	Brazil (1985, 1990, 1994–97)	Costa Rica (1987, 1994–96)	Dominican Republic (1996, 2003)	Guatemala (1990, 2001, 2006)	Mexico (1981–92, 1994–2000)	Average	Japan (1992–2001)
Per capita real GDP (2005 international dollars)									
1980–1990	8,822	3,237	7,239	5,842	3,887	3,416	10,035	6,084	20,946
1990–2000	9,618	3,329	7,496	7,081	4,552	3,611	10,471	6,642	27,885
2000–2010	10,051	3,804	8,566	9,100	6,589	4,118	12,136	8,102	30,017
Growth rate of per capita real GDP (annual average percent)									
1980–1990	–3.0	–2.0	–0.5	–0.2	0.2	–1.5	–0.2	–0.5	4.0
1990–2000	3.3	1.5	1.0	2.7	4.2	1.7	1.7	2.3	0.9
2000–2010	2.1	2.0	2.5	2.5	3.8	0.8	0.5	2.0	0.7
Capital stock contribution to GDP growth (average percentage points)									
1990–2000	1.0	1.0	1.0	2.5	3.3	1.6	2.0	2.1	1.6
2000–2010	1.1	0.9	1.1	1.8	3.5	1.3	2.4	2.0	0.6
CPI inflation rate (annual average percent)									
1980–1990	565.7	1383.2	354.2	27.1	20.9	12.1	69.0	96.7	2.5
1990–2000	252.9	10.4	843.5	16.9	15.3	14.8	20.4	182.2	1.2
2000–2010	8.9	5.1	6.9	10.9	13.1	7.0	5.2	8.6	–0.3

(continues on next page)

Table 2.5   Latin America's experience with banking crises in the 1990s *(continued)*

Period	Argentina (1980–82, 1989–90, 1995–96, 2001–03)	Bolivia (1986–87, 1994–97, 1999)	Brazil (1985, 1990, 1994–97)	Costa Rica (1987, 1994–96)	Dominican Republic (1996, 2003)	Guatemala (1990, 2001, 2006)	Mexico (1981–92, 1994–2000)	Average	Japan (1992–2001)
Domestic credit/GDP (percent)									
1980–1990	26.2	17.7	61.3	17.3	31.5	17.2	14.7	28.4	152.7
1990–2000	19.3	47.2	56.2	14.1	21.2	16.8	25.5	26.8	205.3
2000–2010	14.8	44.5	37.6	36.3	25.7	24.8	18.5	28.6	186.6
External debt/GNI (percent)									
1980–1990	55.9	94.6	40.2	102.3	52.4	28.1	56.1	55.8	n.a.
1990–2000	39.7	78.3	29.2	39.1	35.0	25.3	40.0	33.7	n.a.
2000–2010	76.8	59.3	30.0	32.1	26.0	31.2	22.7	28.4	n.a.

n.a. = not available

CPI = consumer price index; GNI = gross national income

Note: Crisis years (in parentheses) cover all the periods and are based on Reinhart and Rogoff (2009, 2010).

Sources: World Bank, *World Development Indicators* database, for per capita real GDP (in constant 2005 international dollars) and domestic credit/GDP; IMF, *International Financial Statistics*, for CPI inflation rates and external debt/GNI; Conference Board, Total Economy Database, www.conference-board.org/data/economydatabase, for capital stock contribution to GDP growth.

Summing Up

Several findings emerge from these international comparisons. First, Japan's growth rate of per capita real GDP in the 1980s was much higher than the rates of its peers in the OECD country group, as well as in Latin American countries, and was nearly on a par with those of emerging Asian economies that had far lower per capita GDP. But Japan's growth rate together with the CPI inflation rate came down in the 1990s and 2000s. Second, Japan's high growth rate in the 1980s was closely related to its high level of domestic credit at the time, far higher than any other country examined here. Third, the sharp decline in the contribution from the capital stock in Japan in the 2000s, which we identify with lower net investment, was found neither among the OECD peer group nor the Latin American countries, but was observed in the four Asian countries hit hardest by the Asian crisis. Thus, this phenomenon seems to be associated with the investment-led "Asian" growth model.

Econometric Analysis of Banking Crises and Growth

In this section, we attempt to identify the determinants of long-term growth rates econometrically, using a variety of explanatory variables, including dummies related to banking crises. Our estimation model is similar to that of Barro (2001) except that we focus on a different set of variables that may explain a structural slowdown in growth. Also, we take advantage of the fact that another decade of data is available, which provides a sufficient time lag after banking crises in the 1990s to provide more evidence of their long-term effects.

We use an unbalanced panel of 64 countries, including both developed and emerging/developing economies, over the 1990-2009 period, which is split into four five-year subperiods. The left-hand variables are the five-year average growth rate of per capita or per worker real GDP in constant 1990 dollar PPP terms from the World Bank database. As explanatory variables, first we include standard determinants of per capita real GDP growth: the initial level of log per capita real GDP (expected to be a negative factor due to the convergence hypothesis), and two alternative measures of capital accumulation: the ratio of net investment to GDP and the contribution to growth from the capital stock (positive factor). Second, we include a financial factor—the change in the ratio of domestic credit to GDP from the previous period—which may affect growth positively. Third, we include the CPI inflation rate to see if low inflation (or deflation) can cause a decline in per capita or per worker real GDP growth. Fourth, we include the real effective exchange rate (REER), the appreciation of which may retard per capita or per worker real GDP growth. Two measures of the REER—the log difference from the average of the previous five-year period and the five-year average of the deviation from the 10-year moving average—are tried. Fifth, to capture the effect of banking crises, a crisis dummy variable is included with a value of unity if a crisis is identified in the Reinhart-Rogoff database and zero otherwise. A separate dummy is also included for the 2007-09 period to capture the effect of the global financial crisis.

Structural variables that may affect growth include the ratio of the stock of inward FDI to GDP (*Inward FDI stock/GDP*) as a measure of economic openness, the share of the population with a secondary education in the total population (*Education*), and demographic factors (*Aged/Pop*), i.e., the share of the population aged 65 or higher in the total population.[14]

The first equation (1) to estimate per capita real GDP growth is:

$$(\text{Growth rate of GDP/Pop})_{jt} = \alpha * \text{Constant} + \beta * \ln(\text{GDP/Pop})_{jt0}$$
$$+ \gamma * (\text{Net investment/GDP})_{jt} + \delta_1 * (\text{CPI inflation})_{jt} + \delta_2 * [(\text{CPI inflation})_{jt}]^2$$
$$+ \varepsilon_1 * (\text{REER deviation})_{jt} + \varepsilon_2 * \Delta(\text{Domestic credit/GDP})_{jt}$$
$$+ \varepsilon_3 * (\text{Banking crisis dummy})_{jt} + \varepsilon_4 * (\text{GFC dummy})_{jt}$$
$$+ \varepsilon_5 * (\text{Inward FDI stock/GDP})_{jt} + \varepsilon_6 * \text{Education}_{jt} + \zeta_1 * (\text{Aged/Pop})_{jt}$$
$$+ \zeta_2 * [(\text{Aged/Pop})_{jt}]^2 + u_{tj}, \tag{1}$$

where j refers to country, t is the sample period, and t_0 is the initial year of period t. The next equation (2) is the same as equation (1), except that the net investment term (*Net investment/GDP*) is replaced by the contribution to GDP growth from the capital stock (*Capital contribution*). Equations (3) and (4) are the corresponding specifications to estimate the growth rate of per worker (employed) real GDP using the initial level of log per worker (employed) real GDP as an explanatory variable. Table 2A.1 in appendix 2A summarizes variable definitions and data sources.

The estimation procedure is three-stage least squares, which takes into account the possible endogeneity of the CPI inflation rate, the ratio of domestic credit to GDP, the REER deviation, and the alternative measures of net investment. Table 2.6 shows the regression results for growth rates of per capita real GDP using the two alternative measures of net investment—net investment ratio (equation 1) and capital stock contribution (equation 2)—and for the same alternatives for per worker real GDP (equations 3 and 4). Constant terms are not reported.

The estimation results are broadly similar for the per capita and the per worker real GDP growth rate.

In equations (1) and (2), the initial year's per capita real GDP level coefficients have the expected positive signs, implying income convergence, but are not significant. The corresponding coefficients for per worker real GDP growth in equations (3) and (4) have the expected signs but only that in equation (3) is statistically significant.

The coefficients on the ratio of net investment to GDP in equations (1) and (3) are positive, but only the latter is statistically significant. The coefficient in equation (3) implies that a one percentage point rise in the net investment ratio raises per capita real GDP growth by 0.1 percentage point. In equations

---

14. A number of steps were taken to reduce outliers in the data, including deleting observations with inward FDI stock/GDP over 100 percent, CPI inflation over 30 percent, and changes in the ratio of private domestic credit to GDP over 40 percent (in absolute terms). Also, observations with per capita GDP levels less than $1,000 were dropped.

Table 2.6 Regression results for growth rates of per capita/worker real GDP

Explanatory variable	Growth rate of GDP/Population (1)	Growth rate of GDP/Population (2)	Growth rate of GDP/Worker (3)	Growth rate of GDP/Worker (4)
ln(GDP/Pop)$_0$ * 100	−0.593 (0.626)	−0.315 (0.314)	—	—
ln(GDP/Worker)$_0$ * 100	—	—	−1.257** −0.568	−0.443 −0.397
Net investment/ GDP * 100	0.012 (0.026)	—	0.111*** (0.014)	—
Capital contribution * 100	—	1.340*** (0.094)	—	1.581*** (0.126)
CPI inflation * 100	−0.412 (0.287)	0.513*** (0.181)	0.869*** (0.180)	0.606*** (0.235)
[CPI inflation]^2 * 100	0.009 (0.010)	−0.021*** (0.007)	−0.036*** (0.006)	−0.024*** (0.009)
REER deviation * 100	−20.259*** (6.578)	9.277* (4.401)	16.033*** (5.846)	7.488 (5.883)
Δ(Domestic credit/ GDP) * 100	−0.077*** (0.027)	−0.039* (0.024)	−0.007 (0.026)	−0.087*** (0.026)
Banking crisis dummy * 100	−1.827*** (0.704)	−0.392 (0.622)	−0.605 (0.631)	0.151 (0.750)
GFC dummy * 100	−0.777 (0.515)	−0.541* (0.308)	0.241 (0.460)	−0.58 (0.390)
Inward FDI stock/ GDP * 100	−0.003 (0.011)	0.019*** (0.007)	0.022** (0.009)	0.021** (0.010)
Education * 100	0.003 (0.014)	−0.008 (0.012)	0.002 (0.012)	−0.006 (0.014)
Aged/Pop * 100	0.002 (0.432)	0.982*** (0.232)	0.734** (0.342)	0.923*** (0.307)
[Aged/Pop]^2 * 100	−0.009 (0.016)	−0.037*** (0.009)	−0.022* (0.013)	−0.030*** (0.012)
Number of observations	104	140	98	139
R^2/Chi^2	−0.24 / 39.05	0.26 / 299.83	−0.34 / 91.4	−0.17 / 224.64

GFC = global financial crisis

Notes: The results are for three-stage least squares where the consumer price index (CPI) inflation rate, the change in the domestic credit ratio, the real effective exchange rate (REER) deviation, and net investment (or capital contribution) measures are treated as endogenous variables. The equations for these four endogenous variables are not shown here. Numbers in parentheses are standard deviations, and statistical significance is measured * at the 10 percent level, ** at the 5 percent level, and *** at the 1 percent level.

Source: Authors' calculations.

(2) and (4), where the alternative measure of the contribution from the capital stock is used, the coefficients are also positive and statistically highly significant. The coefficients imply that a one percentage point contribution from capital stock growth raises the per capita and per worker GDP growth rate by 1.3 and 1.6 percentage points, respectively.

The coefficients on CPI inflation rates—the average of each five-year period—in equations (2), (3), and (4) reveal the expected signs, with the linear term positive and the quadratic term negative, and are statistically significant in these equations. The coefficients imply that the growth rate of per capita real GDP is low in countries with low inflation, increases with the rise of inflation up to 24 to 26 percent, and then declines with the rise of inflation thereafter. The coefficients for equation (1) have the wrong signs and are not statistically significant. The results for equations (2) to (4) support the view that Japan's growth was negatively affected by its persistent price deflation.

The coefficients for a banking crisis are negative as expected in equations (1) to (3) but statistically significant only in equation (1). The coefficient in equation (1) implies that a banking crisis lowers the five-year average growth rate of per capita GDP by 1.8 percentage points. We tried to identify longer-term effects using the lagged value of the banking crisis dummy, but this did not work well, probably because of multicollinearity. The global financial crisis dummy had the expected negative sign in equations (1), (2), and (4) but was significant only in equation (2). The coefficient in equation (2) implies that the global financial crisis likely reduced per capita GDP growth by 0.5 percentage point.

The coefficients for the ratio of the inward FDI stock to GDP are positive as expected, and statistically significant in equations (2) to (4). The coefficient estimates imply that a one percentage point increase in the inward FDI stock ratio raises per capita and per worker growth by 0.2 percentage point. This suggests a positive structural effect from economic openness.

The coefficients on the ratio of the aged population to the total population have the expected signs of a positive coefficient for the linear term and a negative coefficient for the quadratic term and were significant in equations (2), (3), and (4). The positive sign of the linear term probably reflects the positive growth experience of many developing and emerging economies, while the negative sign for the quadratic term reflects the expected negative impact of highly aged societies, which tend to be in developed countries. The coefficient estimates in equations (2), (3), and (4) imply that the per capita and per worker real GDP growth rate rises until the aged population ratio reaches 27 to 33 percent, begins to decline after such a threshold ratio, and actually turns negative once the ratio reaches 56 to 66 percent, a relatively high level.[15] The results in equations (3) and (4) are powerful, as they correct for changes in the share of the labor force in the total population due to aging and thus imply that there is a direct effect of aging on labor productivity.

---

15. Japan's aging population share averaged 21 percent in the period 2005–09, so this factor may have contributed to the country's low growth.

Figure 2.9 Model estimates of Japanese per capita/worker real GDP growth

annual average rate of growth in percent

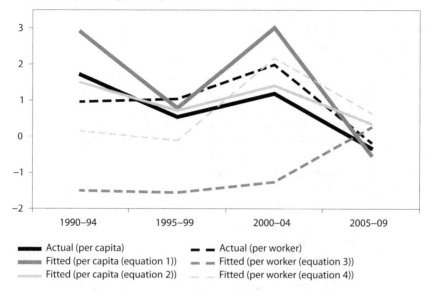

Actual (per capita)
Fitted (per capita (equation 1))
Fitted (per capita (equation 2))

Actual (per worker)
Fitted (per worker (equation 3))
Fitted (per worker (equation 4))

Notes: The data plotted are actual and fitted values of the annual average growth rates of per capita and per worker real GDP. The fitted vales are based on the results reported in table 2.6.

Source: Authors' estimates.

The coefficient on the REER deviation—the log difference from the previous five-year period average which turns out to yield better results than the alternative measure—is negative as expected and significant in equation (1), but positive in the other equations and significant in equations (2) and (3). The results do not provide strong support for the view that growth rates were negatively affected by currency appreciation. The coefficients on the change in the ratio of domestic credit to GDP are negative and statistically significant in all equations except (3), a surprising result contrary to our prior expectations. The coefficients for the education variable are not consistent in terms of signs and are not significant, a surprising result, as other estimates indicated that it was positive and significant. These results suggest that further investigation may be needed.

Interpretations of Results

Figure 2.9 shows the actual and predicted values for Japanese per capita and per worker real GDP growth rates based on the estimation results reported in table 2.6. The fitted values for per capita real GDP growth, particularly based on equation (2), capture the trend well, while equation (1) shows somewhat higher growth than actual growth in 2000-04. The fitted values for per worker real GDP growth do not have as good a fit as those for per capita real GDP growth, though equation (4) performs better than equation (3). Overall, use of the capital stock contribution, rather than the net investment ratio, provides a better fit. In general, the biggest negative contributions to growth come from the slowdown in the pace of capital accumulation, the decline in the CPI inflation rate, the lack of openness of the economy, and the rise in the aging population share, though the contributions vary by equation. The contributions from the domestic credit ratio and the REER deviation are significant in some cases, but usually with the wrong sign. Other potentially important variables—such as the banking crisis dummy—make only modest contributions to growth.

The model predicts a slowdown in growth of other advanced economies as well, including the United States, Germany, Italy, and the United Kingdom, which were hit by the global financial crisis. Aside from the crisis dummy, this mainly reflects declines in the net investment ratio or the capital stock contribution. In the case of the United States, this effect is moderate during the estimation period, but recent slowdowns in the pace of capital accumulation suggest this will likely be more important in future. The aging effects are generally much smaller in these economies—such as the United Kingdom and United States—compared with Japan, although Germany and Italy both show significant effects of aging.

Aside from banking crises and aging, the main factor behind lower growth is lower inflation (or deflation) and lower capital accumulation. This is particularly a problem in the near term for developed economies, since the rate of inflation is expected to remain low and the depreciation of the capital stock is high. The latter suggests that until a new equilibrium between new gross investment and depreciation of the capital stock is reached, net investment levels in developed economies are likely to remain depressed. These observations point to a need for continued monetary policy easing to avoid deflation and for structural measures to increase the attractiveness of investment—including deregulation, an improved investment climate, and open policies toward FDI—and measures to stimulate the labor supply.

Conclusion and Policy Implications

In this chapter, we have attempted to identify the major factors associated with Japanization, a broad-based and long-lasting stagnation in economic performance following the collapse of asset price bubbles that led to a large-scale banking crisis. This stagnation in performance includes a significant slowdown in trend growth of per capita real GDP, a substantial period of deleveraging, slow or no growth in the capital-stock-to-GDP ratio, a decline in short- and long-term interest rates, and a substantial increase in the ratio of government debt to GDP. Other phenomena that may be unique to Japan include a prolonged, substantial decline in stock and real estate prices, moderate but persistent price deflation, and a lack of nominal GDP growth. Japanization may have been aggravated by the rapid aging of the population.

The first best solution to avoid long-term stagnation following a collapse of asset price bubbles is to prevent the bubbles themselves by containing economic overheating, excessive credit growth, overinvestment in fixed assets, and asset market speculation. From this perspective a combination of macroeconomic and macroprudential policy measures is essential to prevent asset price bubbles. However, once the bubbles build up and then collapse, the second best policy is to quickly minimize the negative impact of such a collapse on the banking sector and overall economic activity through accommodative monetary policy and rapid financial policy responses to encourage banks to clean up their balance sheets. One of the reasons for Japan's poor economic performance in the 1990s was an inadequate policy response on the part of the central bank and financial authorities—the latter of which adopted forbearance toward the banking sector until 1997, when a systemic banking crisis erupted. Lack of policy urgency—facilitated by large domestic savings and foreign exchange reserves as well as by sustained fiscal stimuli—was a serious mistake.

We have compared Japan's experience with those of a number of other countries that also had banking crises in the 1990s. Against these comparators, Japan's performance stands out in several ways. First, the growth rate of per capita real GDP it achieved during the 1980s—4 percent per year—was quite high compared with its peer group of OECD countries, and more in line with the experience of Asia's emerging economies with much lower per capita income levels. Second, its pace of capital accumulation was high among the OECD countries (but low in comparison to emerging economies) in the 1990s, but declined to the low end even among the OECD countries in the 2000s. Third, its ratio of domestic credit to GDP was significantly higher than the ratios in other OECD countries, and much higher than the norm for emerging economies, but fell unusually sharply in the 2000s. Fourth, housing prices declined on average throughout the decades of the 1990s and 2000s. In some ways, Japan's experience most resembles those of the countries hit directly by the Asian financial crisis—Indonesia, the Republic of Korea, Malaysia, and Thailand. This suggests that the origin of "Japanization" may lie partly in the adoption of the investment-led growth model financed by the banking sector.

Our econometric analysis—which accounts for a possible simultaneity bias of the key endogenous variables—shows that capital accumulation, the CPI inflation rate, economic openness measured by the stock of inward FDI as a ratio of GDP, and the share of the aged population (age 65 and over) in the total population are mostly significant determinants of long-term growth of per capita (or per worker) real GDP. In particular, very low rates of CPI inflation (or deflation) and subdued capital accumulation, coupled with the closed nature of the economy and an aging population, explain much of Japan's slowdown. Although the very large yen appreciation in the mid-1990s may have had a negative impact on growth, the regression analysis has not found the overall negative impact of the REER.

A decomposition of growth of Japan's real GDP per working-age person shows that, during the 1990s—the period of Japan's banking crisis—TFP declined and the average work week also shortened significantly, although the contribution to growth from the capital stock remained relatively strong. During the 2000s, the contribution from the capital stock slowed considerably, while TFP growth recovered somewhat. The overall slowdown of TFP growth in the postbubble period could be due to the lack of structural reform and the aging of society. Our analysis suggests that structural policies to restore growth—directed toward promoting capital accumulation and further opening of the economy—would be critical particularly in postcrisis periods. Measures to stimulate corporate investment should include deregulation, liberalization of trade and FDI, increased labor market flexibility, and lower taxation of investment. Although little can be done to affect the share of the aged population, policies can encourage greater labor force participation, higher fertility rates, and labor immigration.

The question is whether the United States and a number of major euro area economies that experienced recent large-scale financial (particularly banking) crises would face a similar risk of long-term stagnation or Japanization. There are some positive and negative factors regarding this. On the positive side, the experience of the United States, United Kingdom, and Italy shows that the average per capita GDP growth rates prior to the global financial crisis period were much lower than in Japan, ranging from 1.2 percent for Italy to 2.5 percent for the United Kingdom. Therefore, the initial extent of "excess" growth was much less. The contribution to growth from the capital stock was also lower in these countries than in Japan, again indicating less excess investment. On the negative side, low CPI inflation and a decline in net investment as a share of GDP after the global financial crisis—though not to the same extent as Japan—suggest some risk of Japanization. The very high levels of domestic credit relative to GDP in the precrisis period add to this risk. The slow response to banking sector problems in the euro area economies also points to a risk of long-term stagnation. Aging can be a significant negative factor for growth in major developed economies, such as Germany and Italy, but much less so in the United Kingdom and the United States.

References

Ahearne, Alan, Joseph Gagnon, Jane Haltmaier, and Steve Kamin. 2002. Preventing Deflation: Lessons from Japan's Experience in the 1990s. *International Finance Discussion Papers* no. 729. Washington, DC: Board of Governors of the Federal Reserve System.

Barro, Robert. 2001. *Economic Growth in East Asia Before and After the Financial Crisis.* NBER Working Paper 8330. Cambridge, MA: National Bureau of Economic Research.

Canova, Fabio, and Tobias Menz. 2012. Japan's Lost Decade: Does Money Have a Role? *Journal of the Japanese and International Economies* 24: 178–95.

Cecchetti, Stephen, Marion Kohler, and Christian Upper. 2009. Financial Crises and Economic Activity. Paper prepared for a symposium on "Financial Stability and Macroeconomic Policy" organized by the US Federal Reserve Bank of Kansas City, Jackson Hole, Wyoming, August 20–22.

Cooper, W. 1993. *Japan–U.S. Trade: The Structural Impediments Initiative.* Congressional Research Service (March 15). Library of Congress, Washington, DC. Available at http://digital.library.unt.edu/ark:/67531/metacrs77/m1/1/high_res_d/93-341e_1993Mar15.txt (accessed on July 1, 2013).

Corbett, Jenny, and Takatoshi Ito. 2010. What Should the US and [the People's Republic of] China Learn from the Past US-Japan Conflict? In *The US-Sino Currency Dispute: New Insights from Politics, Economics and Law*, ed. S. Evenett. London: Centre for Economic Policy Research. Available at www.voxeu.org/sites/default/files/currency_dispute.pdf (accessed on July 1, 2013).

Dekle, Robert, and Kyoji Fukao. 2011. The Japan-US Exchange Rate, Productivity, and the Competitiveness of Japanese Industries. In *Japan's Bubble, Deflation and Long-term Stagnation*, ed. Koichi Hamada, Anil Kashyap, and David Weinstein Cambridge, MA: MIT Press.

Furceri, Davide, and Annabelle Mourougane. 2009. *The Effect of Financial Crises on Potential Output: New Empirical Evidence from OECD Countries.* OECD Economics Department Working Paper 699. Paris: OECD Publishing. Available at http://dx.doi.org/10.1787/224126122024 (accessed on July 1, 2013).

Hamada, Koichi, and Yasushi Okada. 2009. Monetary and International Factors behind Japan's Lost Decade. *Journal of the Japanese and International Economies* 23, no. 2: 200–19.

Hayashi, Fumio, and Edward C. Prescott. 2001. The 1990s in Japan: A Lost Decade. *Review of Economic Dynamics* 5, no. 1: 206–35.

Hoshi, Takeo, and Anil Kashyap. 1999. *The Japanese Banking Crisis: Where Did It Come From and How Will It End?* NBER Working Paper 7250. Cambridge, MA: National Bureau of Economic Research.

Hoshi, Takeo, and Anil Kashyap. 2011. *Why Did Japan Stop Growing?* NIRA Research Report. Tokyo: National Institute for Research Advancement. Available at www.nira.or.jp/pdf/1002english_report.pdf (accessed on July 1, 2013).

Hoshi, Takeo, Satoshi Koibuchi, and Ulrike Schaede. 2011. Corporate Restructuring in Japan during the Lost Decade. In *Japan's Bubble, Deflation and Long-Term Stagnation*, ed. Koichi Hamada, Anil Kashyap, and David Weinstein. Cambridge, MA: MIT Press.

IMF (International Monetary Fund). 2009. *World Economic Outlook* (April). Washington, DC.

Kasahara, Hiroyuki, Yasuyuki Sawada, and Michio Suzuki. 2011. Investment and Borrowing Constraints: Evidence from Japanese Firms. Paper presented at the Japan Project Meeting of the National Bureau of Economic Research, Tokyo, June 24–25.

Kawai, Masahiro. 2005. Reform of the Japanese Banking System. *International Economics and Economic Policy* 2, no. 4 (December): 307–35.

Laeven, Luc, and Fabian Valencia. 2008. *Systemic Banking Crises: A New Database.* IMF Working Paper 8/224. Washington, DC: International Monetary Fund.

Lincoln, Edward J., and Robert E. Litan. 1998. *The "Big Bang"? An Ambivalent Japan Deregulates Its Financial Markets.* Washington, DC: Brookings Institution. Available at www.brookings.edu/research/articles/1998/12/winter-globaleconomics-lincoln (accessed on July 1, 2013).

Mayekawa, Haruo, et al. 1986. Report of the Committee on Economic Structural Adjustment for International Cooperation (in Japanese). Tokyo. Available at www.ioc.u-tokyo.ac.jp/~worldjpn/documents/texts/JPUS/19860407.O1J.html (accessed on July 1, 2013).

Reinhart, Carmen, and Kenneth Rogoff. 2009. *This Time Is Different: Eight Centuries of Financial Folly.* Princeton, NJ and Oxford, UK: Princeton University Press.

Reinhart, Carmen, and Kenneth Rogoff. 2010. *From Financial Crash to Debt Crisis.* NBER Working Paper 15795. Cambridge, MA: National Bureau of Economic Research.

Sekine, T. 1999. *Firm Investment and Balance-Sheet Problems in Japan.* IMF Working Paper 99/111. Washington, DC: International Monetary Fund.

Teranishi, Juro. 2009. *Neo-liberalism and Market-Disciplining Policy in Koizumi Reform: Were We Really Development-Oriented?* (October 6). Nihon University. Available at www.ier.hit-u.ac.jp/~nisizawa/teranishi.pdf (accessed on July 1, 2013).

Ueda, Kazuo. 2012. Deleveraging and Monetary Policy: Japan since the 1990s and the United States since 2007. *Journal of Economic Perspectives* 26, no. 3: 177–202.

Appendix 2A

Figure 2A.1 Per capita real GDP of OECD countries that experienced banking crises in the 1990s (in local currency)

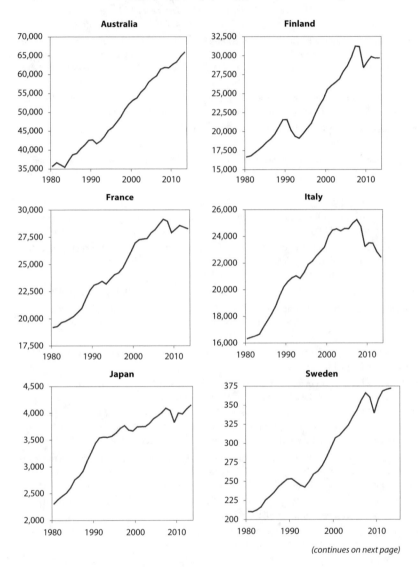

(continues on next page)

Figure 2A.1   Per capita real GDP of OECD countries that experienced banking crises in the 1990s (in local currency) *(continued)*

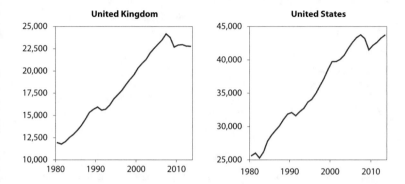

Notes: Figures are in local currency in real terms with varying base years. Units are 1,000 yen for Japan and 1,000 kronor for Sweden.

Source: IMF, *World Economic Outlook* database, April 2013, www.imf.org/external/pubs/ft/weo/2013/01/weodata/index.aspx (accessed on July 1, 2013).

Figure 2A.2 Per capita real GDP of Asian countries that experienced banking crises in the 1990s (in local currency)

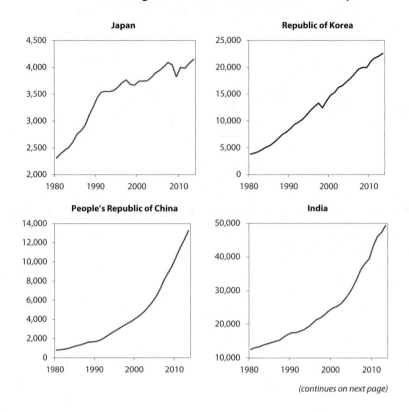

Japan

Republic of Korea

People's Republic of China

India

(continues on next page)

Figure 2A.2   Per capita real GDP of Asian countries that experienced banking crises in the 1990s (in local currency) *(continued)*

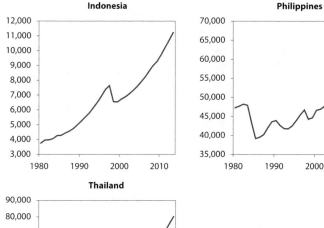

Indonesia

Philippines

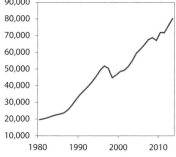

Thailand

Notes: Figures are in local currency in real terms with varying base years. Units are 1,000 yen for Japan, 1,000 won for the Republic of Korea, and 1,000 rupiah for Indonesia.

Source: IMF, *World Economic Outlook* database, April 2013, www.imf.org/external/pubs/ft/weo/2013/01/weodata/index.aspx (accessed on July 1, 2013).

Figure 2A.3   Real per capita GDP of Japan and Latin American countries that experienced banking crises in the 1990s (in local currency)

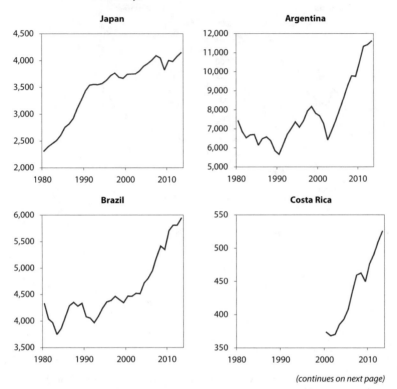

(continues on next page)

Figure 2A.3   Real per capita GDP of Japan and Latin American countries that experienced banking crises in the 1990s (in local currency) *(continued)*

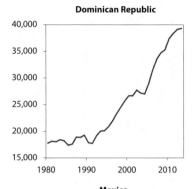

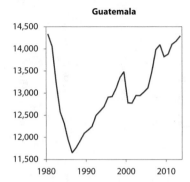

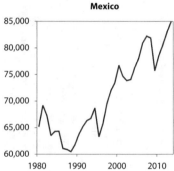

Note: Figures are in local currency in real terms with varying base years. Units are 1,000 yen for Japan.

Source: IMF, *World Economic Outlook* database, April 2013, www.imf.org/external/pubs/ft/weo/2013/01/weo-data/index.aspx (accessed on July 1, 2013).

Table 2A.1 Definitions of variables used in regression analysis

Variable	Definition	Description and comments	Source
GDP/Pop	Per capita real GDP in constant 2005 international dollars; the growth rate is five-year average	GDP converted to constant 2005 international dollars using purchasing power parity (PPP) rates, divided by the total population	World Bank, *World Development Indicators*
GDP/Worker	Per person employed real GDP in constant 1990 international dollars; the growth rate is five-year average	GDP converted to constant 1990 international dollars using PPP rates, divided by total employment in the economy	World Bank, *World Development Indicators*
Net investment/GDP	Ratio of net fixed capital formation to GDP, five-year average	The net value calculated as gross fixed capital formation minus consumption of fixed capital	CEIC; IMF, *International Financial Statistics*
Capital contribution	Contribution of capital services growth to GDP growth, five-year average	Sum of contribution of information and communications technology (ICT) and non-ICT capital services to GDP growth	Conference Board, Total Economy Database
CPI inflation	Consumer price index (CPI) inflation rate, five-year average	Consumer price indices, nationally defined	World Bank, *World Development Indicators*; IMF, *World Economic Outlook* database
REER deviation	Deviation of the real effective exchange rate index (2005 = 100) from the previous five-year period average	Real effective exchange rate is the geometric weighted average of bilateral exchange rates adjusted by relative consumer prices (2005)	World Bank, *World Development Indicators*; Bank for International Settlements; CEIC
Δ(Domestic credit/GDP)	Change in the ratio of domestic credit to private sector to GDP from the previous five-year period average	Domestic credit to private sector includes loans, purchases of nonequity securities, trade credits, and other accounts receivable that establish a claim for repayment. For some countries these claims include credit to public enterprises	World Bank, *World Development Indicators*

Banking crisis dummy	An event of a banking crisis, taking on value 1 if crisis occurs during five-year period and 0 otherwise	Two types of banking crises are included: (1) systemic/severe and (2) financial distress/milder	Reinhart and Rogoff (2009)
GFC dummy	The global financial crisis (GFC) event, taking on value 1 during the 2005-09 period and 0 otherwise		
Inward FDI stock/GDP	Ratio of inward foreign direct investment (FDI) stock to GDP, five-year average	The stock of inward foreign direct investment as a ratio of GDP	UN Conference on Trade and Development (UNCTAD)
Education	Ratio of secondary school enrollment to the total secondary-school-age population, five-year average	The total gross enrollment in secondary education, regardless of age, as a ratio of the total population of official secondary education age. The ratio can exceed 100 percent because of the inclusion of overaged and underaged students due to early or late school entrance and grade repetition	World Bank, *World Development Indicators*
Aged/Pop	Ratio of the aged population to the total population, five-year average	The aged population (age 65 and above) as a ratio of the total population	World Bank, *World Development Indicators*

Source: Authors' definitions.

3

Responses of Central Banks in Advanced Economies to the Global Financial Crisis

JOSEPH E. GAGNON AND MARC HINTERSCHWEIGER

The first tremors of the global financial crisis and recession began in 2007. Financial strains peaked in the fall of 2008 after the bankruptcy of Lehman Brothers. Economic activity continued to decline until the middle of 2009, but, four years later, none of the major advanced economies is close to a full recovery. The crisis exposed fault lines in the design of monetary union in Europe that have caused years of declining output in large countries such as Italy and Spain with important spillovers to the rest of the world. Over this period, central banks have pushed policy interest rates to historically low levels and have engaged in a variety of measures, both traditional and nontraditional, to ease financial market strains and provide additional macroeconomic stimulus.[1]

With few exceptions, most researchers agree that these central bank actions have made positive contributions to economic and financial conditions. Many of the policies were aimed at returning liquidity and credit risk spreads on financial assets to normal levels, thereby encouraging a renewed flow of credit through the economy. To the extent that these policies have succeeded, they have reduced the "headwinds" that restrain economic activity, but they have not provided additional macroeconomic stimulus beyond that implied by the level of the short-term policy interest rate. Similarly, policies aimed at preventing the disruptive failure of systemically important financial institutions can help

Joseph E. Gagnon has been senior fellow at the Peterson Institute for International Economics since September 2009. Marc Hinterschweiger has been a research analyst at the Peterson Institute for International Economics since 2008. They thank William Cline, Simon Johnson, Marcus Noland, Edwin Truman, and two anonymous referees for helpful comments and advice.

1. This chapter focuses solely on central bank actions and thus does not explore issues surrounding reform of financial regulation, fiscal policy, emergency programs for countries in the euro area, or reforms to improve economic integration in Europe.

to prevent a negative shock to economic activity, but they do not constitute an independent positive shock. Most observers agree that the US Federal Reserve should have prevented the disruptive bankruptcy of Lehman Brothers if it had the authority to do so, but Chairman Ben Bernanke has said the Fed lacked such authority.[2] The Treasury, in cooperation with the Federal Reserve, was granted new powers and resources soon after the Lehman bankruptcy, and no other systemically important institution has failed. The European Central Bank faced unique difficulties among the central banks studied here owing to the cross-border nature of the euro area and the enormous strains that developed with the sovereign debt crisis there.

With short-term policy rates constrained by the zero lower bound, central banks in some of these economies have sought to ease monetary conditions through large-scale purchases of long-term assets, also known as quantitative easing (QE). Many studies suggest that such purchases can stimulate economic activity by lowering long-term interest rates. Another tactic pursued by some central banks for lowering longer-term interest rates is to provide guidance aimed at lowering expectations about the future path of short-term interest rates. There is some evidence that such guidance does have an effect, although there are limits to how far guidance can be extended credibly.

We believe that the extraordinary liquidity measures and emergency loans should be judged a success to the extent that they were implemented. They do raise concerns about moral hazard, but those concerns ultimately must be addressed through reforms of the financial system to prevent such a crisis from occurring again. There are potential costs of ultra-low interest rates and QE, but to date the costs are far smaller than the benefits. This suggests that more QE would be preferable to less.

How Have Central Banks Responded to the Crisis?

This chapter focuses on the responses of the four main advanced-economy central banks: the US Federal Reserve System (Fed), the European Central Bank (ECB), the Bank of Japan (BOJ), and the Bank of England (BOE). This section reviews the actions taken by these central banks during and after the crisis. The following section reviews economic research on the effectiveness of the actions taken and the potential costs of these actions.

Timeline of Crisis Responses

In early 2007, market participants began to be concerned about potential losses on financial assets that might result from the incipient downturn in housing

---

2. Ben Bernanke, "Federal Reserve's Response to the Financial Crisis," lecture at George Washington University, Washington, DC, March 27, 2012, www.federalreserve.gov/newsevents/lectures/about. htm (accessed on July 13, 2013).

prices around the world.[3] These concerns were most intense with respect to structured credit products based on US subprime mortgage loans, which the rating agencies were beginning to downgrade on a widespread basis. Prices of such assets dropped sharply and a number of US mortgage companies specializing in subprime products failed. At the end of July, IKB, a mid-sized German bank with substantial exposure to US subprime assets, came under severe pressure and was recapitalized by its state-owned largest shareholder.

These concerns spilled over into broader financial markets on August 9, 2007, when BNP Paribas, a large French bank, suspended withdrawals from three investment funds it sponsored, citing an inability to value some of the mortgage-related assets. Funding pressures quickly emerged across a wide range of European and US financial institutions because banks decided to hoard cash to meet potential calls on their credit lines to off-balance-sheet conduits, and because of concerns about potential losses in the portfolios of counterparty financial institutions. In particular, the spreads of bank term funding rates over comparable-maturity overnight index swap (OIS) rates soared and liquidity in the interbank and other credit markets vanished. Figure 3.1 displays the Libor-OIS spreads in each of the four currencies (dollar, yen, euro, and pound) since January 2007.[4] Figure 3.2 displays indices of the implied volatilities of equities in each of these economies. These volatility measures capture both underlying uncertainty and reduced willingness of investors to hold risky assets during the crisis.

The ECB and the Fed quickly responded to these pressures by injecting overnight funds into the banking system. By the end of August 2007, both the ECB and the Fed had increased their supplies of longer-term funds to the banks and the Fed had narrowed the spread between the target federal funds rate and the rate on discount window borrowing. The BOE and BOJ did not noticeably alter their operating procedures in August 2007. All four central banks held their main policy rates constant that month. See table 3A.1 at the end of the chapter for a timeline of central bank responses to the financial crisis.

Over the remainder of 2007, the Fed, ECB, BOE, and other central banks adopted further measures to increase liquidity in the banking system, including frontloading reserves into the banking system during each maintenance period (ECB and BOE), widening the penalty-free range for banks' reserve holdings

---

3. This subsection is based on the public record as documented in newspapers and on the websites of these four central banks and various issues of the *OECD Economic Outlook*. The first several paragraphs are based on Gagnon (2011). Good overviews may be found in Fawley and Neely (2013), IMF (2013a), and on the "Credit and Liquidity Programs and the Balance Sheet" tab on the website of the Board of Governors of the Federal Reserve System, www.federalreserve.gov/monetarypolicy/bst.htm (accessed on July 1, 2013).

4. Libor stands for London inter-bank offered rate. The Barclays scandal in 2012 called into question the accuracy of Libor as a measure of the true average cost of funding for large international banks. Nevertheless, movements in Libor over time are well correlated with market perceptions of underlying funding difficulties for major banks.

Figure 3.1   Three-month Libor-OIS spreads, 2007–13

percentage points

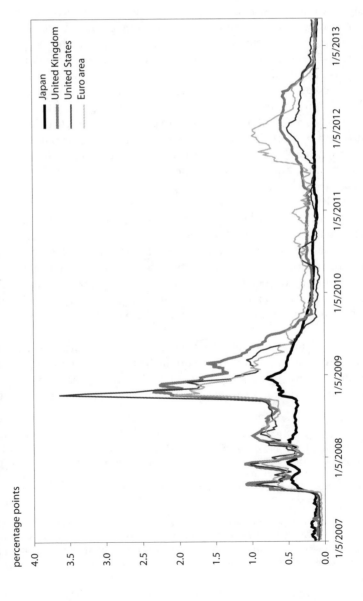

Libor = London interbank offered rate; OIS = overnight index swap

Source: Bloomberg.

Figure 3.2 Implied stock market volatilities, 2007–13

standard deviation of 30-day changes, annualized percentage points

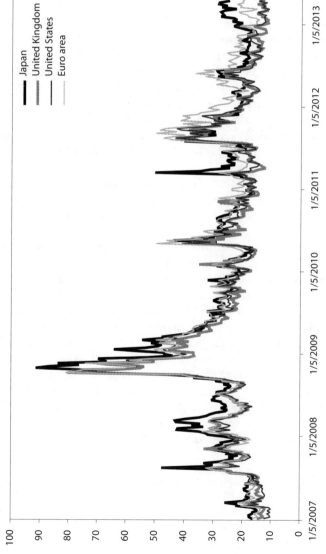

Note: Indices refer to S&P 500 (United States), Nikkei 225 (Japan), Euro Stoxx 50 (euro area), and FTSE 100 (United Kingdom).
Source: Bloomberg.

(BOE), undertaking more frequent auctions of longer-term credit to banks (Fed, ECB, and BOE), and providing term dollar funding to banks outside the United States through swap lines between the Fed and the ECB and Swiss National Bank (SNB). In conjunction with the UK Treasury, the BOE set up a special liquidity support facility for Northern Rock. Japanese markets were relatively unaffected by these strains, reflecting a much lower exposure to the housing bubble and lower dollar funding needs, so the BOJ did not adopt measures to increase liquidity. The Fed lowered its policy rate 100 basis points over the last four months of 2007 and the BOE lowered its policy rate 25 basis points late in the year, while the ECB and BOJ held their policy rates steady.

In the first few months of 2008, financial conditions deteriorated sharply, culminating in the nationalization of Northern Rock and the assisted takeover of Bear Stearns by JPMorgan. By April 2008, the Fed had lowered its policy rate another 225 basis points and the BOE had lowered its policy rate another 50 basis points. The ECB and BOJ continued to hold their policy rates steady. Over this period the Fed increased the size of its term credit auctions for banks and its swap lines with the ECB and SNB, established a term securities lending facility, and established a direct credit facility for nonbank primary bond dealers similar to the discount window for banks. The Fed also made an emergency loan secured by assets of Bear Stearns to facilitate the acquisition of Bear Stearns by JPMorgan. The BOE established a term securities lending facility for banks.

Over the summer of 2008, financial conditions improved somewhat and inflation became a more prominent concern for central banks as commodity prices soared. The ECB raised its policy rate 25 basis points in July 2008 and the Fed, BOE, and BOJ held their rates constant.

Financial turbulence returned even more strongly in September 2008 with the entry into conservatorship of the housing agencies Fannie Mae and Freddie Mac, the failure of Lehman Brothers, and the rescue of AIG. The crisis peaked in October 2008 as market participants lost confidence in financial institutions around the world. On October 8, the Fed, ECB, BOE, and other central banks (but not the BOJ) announced an unprecedented coordinated cut in policy rates of 50 basis points. Later in October the Fed cut its policy rate another 50 basis points and the BOJ cut its policy rate 20 basis points. In November and December 2008, all four central banks made further policy rate cuts, totaling 85, 75, 200, and 20 basis points for the Fed, ECB, BOE, and BOJ, respectively.[5] The Fed also tried to push down expectations of the future path of the policy rate by stating that "economic conditions are likely to warrant exceptionally low levels of the federal funds rate for some time."[6]

---

5. The Fed cut its policy rate target in December 2008 to a range of 0 to 25 basis points from a previous level of 100 basis points. The federal funds rate has fluctuated around 15 basis points since year-end 2008.

6. Federal Open Market Committee (FOMC) statement, December 16, 2008, www.federalreserve. gov/newsevents/press/monetary/20081216b.htm (accessed on July 11, 2013).

Central banks aggressively expanded nontraditional measures during the last few months of 2008. All four central banks broadened the collateral they accept in lending operations. The Fed established swap lines with the BOE, BOJ, and other central banks, and the limits on Fed swap lines with the ECB, SNB, BOE, and BOJ were eliminated. All four central banks increased their supply of longer-term funding to the banking system. The Fed and the BOJ took measures to support the commercial paper market. The Fed announced plans to support the asset-backed securities market and to undertake large-scale purchases of longer-term debt issued or guaranteed by the federal housing agencies. In coordination with the US Treasury, the Fed provided emergency support to AIG, Bank of America, and Citigroup secured by assets of those institutions. Governments in the euro area and the United Kingdom provided emergency support to several large financial institutions. The ECB narrowed the corridor between its standing deposit and lending facilities from 200 to 100 basis points and coordinated with the SNB to provide term Swiss franc liquidity to European banks. The BOE converted its temporary securities lending scheme to a permanent discount window facility that lends liquid government bonds against a wide range of collateral. The BOJ announced increased purchases of Japanese government bonds and lowered the fee on its securities lending operations. In addition to these nontraditional central bank measures, governments in the euro area, United States, and United Kingdom increased their guarantees of certain classes of bank liabilities, including deposits and senior debt. The US Treasury also issued a temporary guarantee of money market mutual fund accounts.

Although the worst of the financial strains had passed by the end of 2008, the outlook for global economic activity continued to plunge in the first few months of 2009. The worsening economic outlook, including notably in Eastern Europe, compounded the problems faced by financial institutions. The Fed and the BOJ had already lowered their policy rates to their implicit lower bounds of 0 to 25 and 10 basis points, respectively, but the Fed strengthened its guidance concerning future policy rates by replacing the phrase "some time" with "extended period."[7] The BOE lowered its policy rate 150 basis points to an implicit lower bound of 50 basis points by March 2009 and liberalized the payment of interest on reserves by suspending reserve targets for banks. The BOE's *Inflation Reports* subsequently hinted that the policy rate was likely to remain at this level for the next two years, since such a policy path was projected to lead to an inflation outcome closer to the 2 percent target than the higher policy path implied by market interest rates. The ECB lowered its main policy rate 150 basis points to a level of 100 basis points by May 2009. The ECB widened the corridor between its standing facilities back to 200 basis points in January 2009 and then narrowed it to 150 basis points in May. With the substantially increased provision of longer-term liquidity to banks in the

---

7. FOMC statement, March 18, 2009, www.federalreserve.gov/monetarypolicy/fomccalendars.htm (accessed on July 11, 2013).

euro area, the overnight interbank rate dropped below the main refinancing rate, though not below the 25 basis point rate paid on the standing deposit facility. In this sense, the ECB appears to have eased policy somewhat more than would be implied by holding the main refinancing rate at 1 percent, and the true lower bound for the overnight interbank rate may have been the 25 basis points paid by the ECB's deposit facility, which is equivalent to the 25 basis points paid by the Fed on excess reserves.

In the first half of 2009, the Fed expanded its purchases of long-term agency securities and began to buy longer-term Treasury securities. These purchases, now referred to as QE1, reached $1.7 trillion by early 2010. The Fed also expanded the range of securities eligible for financing under its Term Asset-Backed Securities Loan Facility (TALF). The BOE announced a program to buy long-term gilts, commercial paper, and corporate bonds. The initial target was £75 billion, but it was raised to £200 billion by the end of the year. The ECB announced a program to buy covered bonds, albeit to a smaller extent (€60 billion) than the Fed and BOE programs. The BOJ began outright purchases of commercial paper and corporate bonds with residual maturities of up to one year, although the amounts undertaken were small.

Figures 3.3 through 3.5 show that 2009 was the year of maximum economic contraction, with output falling sharply relative to potential and unemployment rising in all four economies. The rate of increase in domestic (GDP) prices fell sharply in 2009 in three of these economies; in Japan inflation fell sharply in 2010.

After aggressive actions in the first half of 2009, central banks were relatively quiet in the second half of 2009 and the first few months of 2010. However, in late 2009, the BOE expanded the target for its total long-term asset purchases moderately in order to prevent undershooting its inflation target. In December 2009, the BOJ announced further small increases in its operations to supply liquidity to financial institutions. Total assets of these central banks were broadly stable over this period, but for the Fed and the BOE, this stability at the aggregate level masked sharp changes in the composition away from lending to financial institutions (reverse repo in the United Kingdom) toward purchases of long-term bonds (figures 3.6a to 3.6d.) During this period, the Fed gradually reversed and wound down the extraordinary liquidity measures enacted during the financial meltdown.

By the spring of 2010, the situation started to deteriorate again in the euro area as the economic slowdown and assistance to the financial sector gave rise to large fiscal deficits and dramatic increases in government debt. In peripheral countries such as Greece, Ireland, and Portugal, market participants began to be concerned about a possible default on sovereign debt, and interest rates spiked. In May 2010, a variety of policy measures were implemented by several European institutions to counter the intensifying European debt crisis. The ECB announced that it would commence purchases of private and government debt securities from the secondary markets in the affected countries. It also reactivated measures to supply unlimited three- and six-month liquidity

Figure 3.3   Output gaps, 2000–2013f

percent of potential GDP

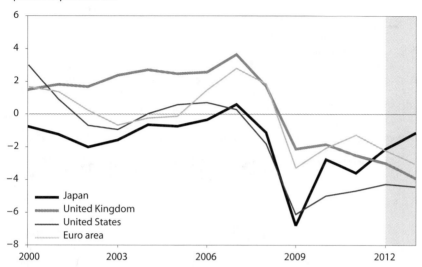

f = forecast

Note: 2013 data are IMF forecasts.

Source: IMF, World Economic Outlook database, April 2013.

to banks (longer-term refinancing operations [LTROs]). Additionally, bilateral currency swap arrangements with the Fed were resumed in order to ensure dollar liquidity for European financial institutions. The ECB also eased collateral eligibility requirements with respect to Greek government and government-guaranteed bonds.

Also in May 2010, the BOJ published a framework to strengthen the basis for economic growth by providing one-year loans of up to ¥3 trillion to financial institutions. As shown in figure 3.5, Japanese deflation intensified during 2010, leading the BOJ in October to reduce its policy rate to a range of 0 to 0.10 percent, clarify the conditions for exiting its zero-interest-rate policy, and establish a program to purchase longer-term assets, including corporate and government bonds, equities, and real estate investment trusts.

The European and Japanese slowdowns spread to the United States by mid-2010. In addition, some measures of US inflation declined further in early 2010, raising fears of outright deflation. In August, the Fed decided to keep the size of its portfolio constant by reinvesting maturing assets. In November 2010, it announced its intention to purchase a further $600 billion of longer-term Treasury securities. The objectives of this so-called QE2 program were to reduce long-term real interest rates, speed up the economic recovery, and ensure that inflation would stay in line with the Fed's mandate.

A short period of relative calm in financial markets in the first half of 2011, along with slightly higher inflation expectations, led the ECB to increase its

Figure 3.4 Unemployment rates, 2000–2013f

percent of total labor force

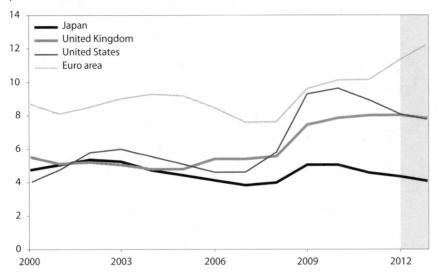

f = forecast
Note: 2013 data are IMF forecasts.
Source: IMF, *World Economic Outlook* database, April 2013.

policy rate by a total of 50 basis points. The Fed decided not to extend QE2 and stopped buying long-term assets in June 2011. The BOE kept its asset purchases on hold through the first half of 2011. Japan, however, was hit by a severe earthquake and tsunami in March 2011 that massively damaged its economy. The BOJ provided liquidity to the markets and increased its purchases of long-term assets.

In the second half of 2011, the sovereign debt crisis flared up again in the euro area. In response, the ECB announced a series of new and reactivated measures. In August, it said that it would continue to provide liquidity to banks through fixed-rate tender procedures with full allotment until at least early 2012 and introduce an LTRO with a maturity of about six months. In September, the ECB announced that it would resume purchases of government bonds in affected countries, and it extended the dollar swap agreements with the Fed. In October, it announced two additional LTROs for October and December as well as a second round of covered bond purchases. In November and December, it reduced its policy rate by 0.50 percent and eased collateral requirements and reduced the required reserve ratio for banks. Most notably, it announced two LTROs with unlimited size and a three-year maturity that eventually injected more than €1 trillion of long-term funding into the European banking system.

In the United Kingdom, the BOE undertook several measures to ease credit conditions and stimulate the economy. It broadened the eligible collat-

Figure 3.5   Inflation rates, 2000–2013f

GDP deflator, percent change

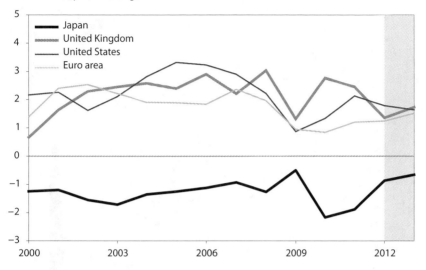

f = forecast

Note: 2013 data are IMF forecasts.

Source: IMF, *World Economic Outlook* database, April 2013; authors' calculations.

eral requirements in its operations as of July 2011. In September 2011, it announced plans to provide dollar funding to UK banks through a reactivated swap line with the Fed. And in December, the BOE announced the creation of a contingency liquidity facility to mitigate risks to financial stability arising from a perceived shortage of short-term sterling liquidity. This facility offers sterling credit for 30 days against a preapproved list of collateral.

Once again, the tensions in Europe contributed to a slowdown in US economic growth prospects in the second half of 2011, probably intensified by uncertainty about US fiscal policy after the debt ceiling debacle of mid-2011. In September, the Fed introduced the Maturity Extension Program (MEP), which eventually led to the sale of all Fed assets with maturities of less than three years in exchange for new assets with maturities in excess of six years. The Fed also changed its forward rate guidance, noting that economic conditions were likely to warrant exceptionally low levels for the policy rate at least through mid-2013. And it decided to reinvest principal payments from its holdings of agency debt and agency mortgage-backed securities (MBS) in agency MBS instead of Treasury securities.

In January 2012, the Fed extended its guidance for exceptionally low rates to at least until late 2014. It also started to publish the longer-run inflation objective and provide information about individual committee members' expectations of the future policy rate, conditional on their projected economic outlook. In June 2012, the Fed extended the MEP to the end of the year. During the first

Figure 3.6a US Federal Reserve assets, 2007–13

trillions of dollars, weekly

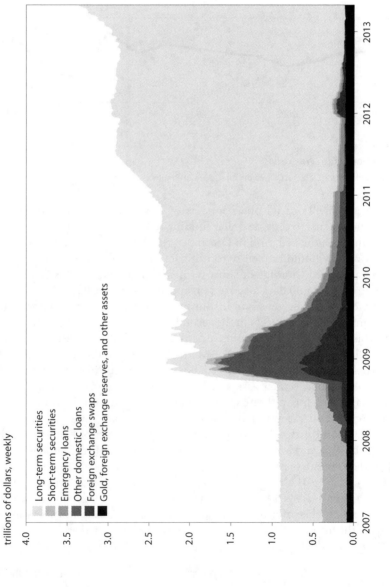

Legend:
- Long-term securities
- Short-term securities
- Emergency loans
- Other domestic loans
- Foreign exchange swaps
- Gold, foreign exchange reserves, and other assets

Source: US Federal Reserve.

Figure 3.6b   European Central Bank assets, 2007–13

trillions of euros, weekly

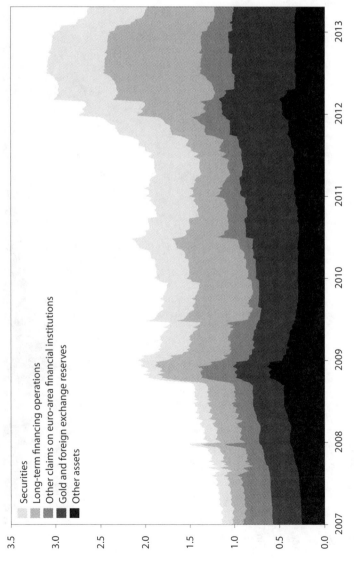

Securities
Long-term financing operations
Other claims on euro-area financial institutions
Gold and foreign exchange reserves
Other assets

Source: European Central Bank.

Figure 3.6c Bank of Japan assets, 2007–13

trillions of yen, monthly

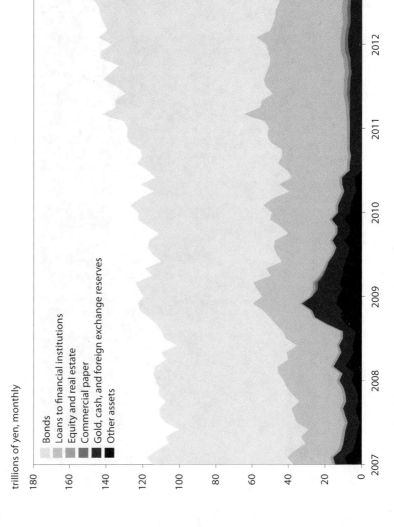

Source: Bank of Japan.

Figure 3.6d   Bank of England assets, 2007–13

billions of pounds, weekly

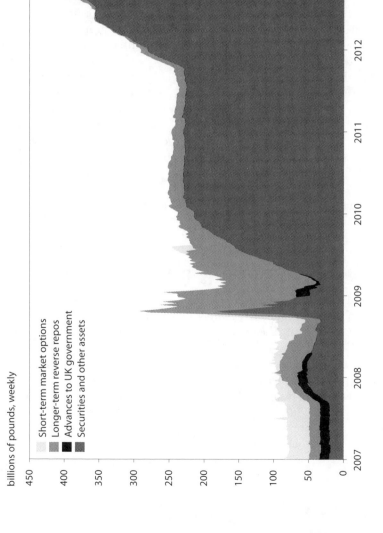

Short-term market options
Longer-term reverse repos
Advances to UK government
Securities and other assets

Source: Bank of England.

half of 2012, the ECB expanded collateral eligibility for banks, the BOE increased purchases of long-term assets, and the BOJ established an explicit price stability goal of inflation at 1 percent, expanded its long-term asset purchases, and extended the maximum maturity of bonds purchased from two to three years.

In July 2012, the BOE expanded its target holdings of long-term bonds to £375 billion. It also launched a new lending scheme to provide incentives for banks and other financial intermediaries to boost lending to UK households and companies. This scheme was at least partly intended to offset funding costs for banks, which had risen in 2012 due to adverse developments in the euro area. In September 2012, the Fed launched a third program of net asset purchases (QE3) focused on MBS. When the MEP ended in December (because there were no more short-term assets to sell), the Fed expanded QE3 with additional purchases of long-term Treasuries at the same pace as under the MEP, for a total of $85 billion per month in purchases of long-term bonds. Additionally, the Fed changed its forward guidance on the policy rate, moving from calendar-based guidance to guidance based on the economic outlook. It said that it expected exceptionally low rates to be appropriate as long as the unemployment rate was above 6.5 percent and inflation two years ahead was forecast to be below 2.5 percent.

Around the same time, the ECB specified the elements of its Outright Monetary Transactions (OMT) program that had been preannounced by ECB President Mario Draghi in July. OMTs are sterilized interventions conducted in secondary markets that allow the ECB to buy unlimited amounts of short-term debt (up to three years' maturity) of those governments that have accepted funds from the European Stability Mechanism (ESM) and that comply with the ESM's terms and conditions. As of this writing, no country has applied to benefit from the OMT program.

In October 2012, the BOJ introduced a facility to provide funds of up to 100 percent of depository institutions' net increase in lending to the nonfinancial sector.

Similarities and Differences in Responses across the Regions

The similarities in responses across these regions are manifold. Central banks moved to supply liquidity to dysfunctional markets by increasing their lending operations, extending their loan maturities, broadening the range of collateral accepted, and making outright purchases of assets. They also responded to macroeconomic weakness by lowering policy rates and purchasing long-term assets to reduce long-term interest rates.

Differences in responses by central banks, on the other hand, reflect differences in the exposure of local financial institutions, financial industry structures, macroeconomic shocks, and, perhaps most importantly, perceptions of the appropriate role of monetary policy.

The BOJ responded far less aggressively in most areas—despite suffering a comparable initial shock to output and inflation—mainly because of the much lower exposure of Japanese financial institutions to troubled assets and because of the perceived limited room for additional monetary stimulus. However, at the very end of our review period, Shinzō Abe was elected prime minister on a campaign to change the management of the BOJ and raise its inflation objective.[8]

With respect to financial strains, all four central banks moved quickly to deal with problems in individual markets as they arose, with the temporary exception of the BOE in the opening weeks of the crisis. Although it is difficult to prove statistically, market participants widely credit these programs as having prevented a much worse outcome. The Fed appeared to face the greatest obstacles arising from the greater role of nonbank financial institutions in the United States and the limitations on Fed lending to those institutions. Fed loans to nonbanks are allowed only under "unusual and exigent circumstances," must be fully collateralized, and must be approved by a super-majority of the Board of Governors. That the Fed was able to support the commercial paper and asset-backed securities markets is a testament to the resolve of its governors and the ingenuity of its lawyers. The obvious exception to this pattern of extraordinary support is the failure of Lehman Brothers. Fed Chairman Bernanke has stated that he lacked the authority to save Lehman because Lehman did not have sufficient collateral to back a loan of the size that was needed.[9] Fed and Treasury officials tried to find a buyer for Lehman, but the two main candidates—Barclays and the Korea Development Bank—backed out. Shortly after the Lehman failure, the US Congress passed legislation to enable the Treasury to support critical nonbank financial institutions.

With respect to monetary policy, all four central banks lowered their traditional target rates to historically low levels and took some quantitative measures. The Fed acted the fastest, at least in part because the United States was the initial focal point of the financial crisis but also because it was more institutionally disposed to play an active role in supporting the economy. The BOJ and the ECB were more reluctant to ease policy, with the ECB actually raising rates in mid-2008 and again in early 2011. The Fed and the BOE have been the most aggressive in outright purchases of longer-term assets that go beyond measures to stabilize specific markets, but they will soon be joined by the BOJ. The ECB has been the most aggressive in lending at short and medium terms to financial institutions. It has characterized these loans not

---

8. In April 2013 (outside the scope of this study), the new governor of the BOJ, Haruhiko Kuroda, announced an aggressive program of purchases of long-term assets designed to raise Japan's inflation rate to 2 percent within two years.

9. Bernanke, "Federal Reserve's Response to the Financial Crisis." At the times of their loans, Bear Stearns and AIG were judged to have supplied collateral in excess of the loan amounts, and both loans eventually were repaid in full with interest. Lehman Brothers is expected to distribute about 21 cents for each $1 of its debt, suggesting that it was grossly insolvent. See Jonathan Stempel, "Lehman Plans to Distribute $14.2 Billion to Creditors," Reuters, March 27, 2013, www.reuters. com/article/2013/03/27/us-lehman-bankruptcy-idUSBRE92Q0HV20130327 (accessed on July 1, 2103).

Table 3.1 Central bank balance sheet expansion, July 2007 to December 2012

Central bank	July 2007	December 2012	Change (percent)	Change (percent of GDP)
US Federal Reserve[a]	$850 billion	$2,966 billion	249	13
European Central Bank	€1,213 billion	€3,018 billion	148	18
Bank of Japan[a]	¥108 trillion	¥158 trillion	46	12
Bank of England	£80 billion	£410 billion	413	21

a. The US Federal Reserve and the Bank of Japan are engaged in open-ended purchases that will expand their balance sheets by an undetermined amount in 2013 and beyond.

Sources: Bank of England; Bank of Japan; Board of Governors of the Federal Reserve System; European Central Bank; IMF, *World Economic Outlook* database; authors' calculations.

as a channel for monetary easing but as a means of ensuring financial stability and the smooth functioning of financial markets. However, the ECB's loans to financial institutions probably have helped to combat an unwanted tightening of credit standards by banks that has been a headwind for the euro area economy. The strains associated with the sovereign debt crisis in the euro area are unique among the economies studied in this chapter and they have greatly complicated the decisions of the ECB. In contrast, there are no concerns about the breakup of Japan, the United Kingdom, or the United States as monetary or political unions.[10]

Table 3.1 presents changes in the size of central bank balance sheets, which are a crude measure of the overall extent of central bank responses to the financial crisis. This measure does not capture changes in operating procedures or in the composition of central bank assets and liabilities. For example, these central banks initially financed the increase in longer-term loans to the banking system by reducing short-term loans or selling off short-term government bonds (figures 3.6a to 3.6d). Nevertheless, efforts to increase monetary stimulus beyond that implied by the level of short-term interest rates generally require an increase in the overall balance sheet. By these measures, the BOE has been most aggressive, whereas the ranking of the others depends on whether one focuses on the change in percentage terms or as a percent of GDP. However, almost all of the increases in the balance sheets of the BOJ and ECB reflect short-maturity assets (under three years), which have less effect on long-term interest rates than the BOE's and Fed's purchases of longer-term assets. The Fed, in particular, has gone the furthest in extending the maturity of its balance sheet. As of late 2012 it held no assets with maturities less than three years and it has not purchased any asset with a maturity of less than four years since then.

---

10. There is an independence party in Scotland, but there is no perceived risk to the pound as a currency or to the solvency of the UK government.

How Effective Were the Responses?

First we consider effectiveness in terms of influencing measurable market variables in the desired direction. Policies are divided into three categories: (1) the traditional short-term interest rate instrument, (2) purchases of long-term assets designed to push down longer-term interest rates, and (3) liquidity facilities and emergency loans designed to ease financial stress and improve the functioning of financial markets. We then consider the effects of all of these actions on the macroeconomy. Finally, we discuss potential costs and risks of these central bank actions.

Policy Rates and Policy Guidance

All the central banks covered here lowered their traditional short-term policy rates in response to the financial crisis (figure 3.7). In this case, effectiveness in influencing market variables in the desired direction is tautological.

The Fed, BOE, and BOJ have gone somewhat further and attempted to lower longer-term interest rates by indicating that policy rates are likely to remain close to their current levels for an extended period.[11] Jeffrey Campbell et al. (2012) present evidence that Fed policy communications prior to the crisis had significant effects on expectations of the future policy rate as measured by the term structure of market interest rates. They argue that forward guidance is a potentially important policy tool at the zero lower bound on short-term interest rates. However, two discussants of their paper (Charles Calomiris and Michael Woodford) say that the evidence on movements in policy expectations most likely reflects the fact that Fed communications provide information concerning the Fed's view of the economy and not any change in how the Fed is expected to react to a given state of the economy. This distinction is important because markets may have interpreted the Fed's promises to hold rates low for a long time as bad news about the economic outlook, which would dampen spending, as opposed to good news about lower borrowing costs, which would support more spending.

During the second half of 2009, the term structure of interest rates continued to slope upward in both the United Kingdom and the United States over a two-year horizon to a greater extent than implied by historical estimates of the term premium,[12] suggesting that policy communications of their central banks

---

11. For the BOE, this guidance is implicit in the inflation forecasts, which show outcomes closer to the target under paths that assume near-zero policy rates than under higher levels for the policy rate. For the BOJ, this guidance is related to raising inflation toward its desired level, which is not projected to happen in the near term.

12. Don Kim and Athanasios Orphanides (2007) show that the term premium over a two-year horizon has been close to zero in recent years and the average over a longer period is much lower than 100 basis points, which was roughly the average yield on two-year Treasury securities in the second half of 2009. It is plausible that the term premium could have increased in response to the financial crisis. However, two-year interest rates did not exhibit substantial and sustained declines

Figure 3.7   Short-term policy rates, 2007–12

percent, monthly

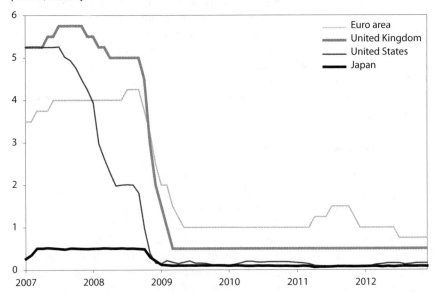

Sources: IMF, *International Financial Statistics;* Bloomberg.

had only limited success in persuading markets that ultra-low policy rates would last more than a few months. However, as policy rates remained near zero in the following years, the term structures eventually flattened. In all four of these monetary regions, two-year government bond yields in December 2012 were roughly equal to the yields on one-month government bonds.[13] Because this decline in term slope occurred equally for central banks that communicated an intention to hold rates low for a long time (BOE, BOJ, and the Fed) as well as for a central bank that did not make such a communication (ECB), this simple look at the data does not provide useful information concerning the effectiveness of communication.

Daniel Thornton (2012a) examines two dates on which the Fed provided new guidance about the period of time over which the policy rate was likely to remain near zero without announcing any new asset purchases: August 9, 2011, and January 25, 2012.[14] On the former date, the period of low rates was said to

---

immediately after Fed and BOE announcements in early 2009 aimed at guiding near-term policy expectations lower.

13. German yields are used for the euro area.

14. Other dates on which the Fed provided new information about future policy rates also involved increases in planned purchases of long-term bonds. Thus, movements in yields on those dates conflate the effects of forward guidance and asset purchases.

continue at least until mid-2013, whereas on the latter date the period of low rates was said to continue at least until late 2014. On both dates, however, this guidance was made conditional on the future state of the economy. Thornton notes that OIS yields dropped on both dates, consistent with some effect of the guidance, but he points out that the two-year OIS yield remained around 0.5 percent on both dates, which suggests that markets did not fully believe that the policy rate would remain in its range of 0 to 0.25 over the announced horizon. Thornton also argues that the decline in OIS rates across the term structure seems inconsistent with an effect of policy guidance that is focused on the next two or three years.

Table 3.2 replicates Thornton's analysis using one-year forward rates derived from Treasury securities.[15] The first two columns display forward yields that span the period covered by the Fed's announcement on August 9, 2011. Note that these rates are considerably lower than the OIS rates reported by Thornton (2012a), suggesting that Thornton's analysis may be polluted by counterparty risk in the swaps market. The one-year yield one year forward dropped by 15 basis points that day, a two-standard-deviation movement that brought the level of the forward yield into the range of the policy rate of 0 to 25 basis points. The Fed's announcement on January 25, 2012, covered a period of between two and three years ahead. Forward yields over the next two years dropped into the range of 0 to 25 basis points, but the forward yield beginning in two years remained noticeably above this range. This is consistent with the fact that the guidance extended only until late 2014, which allows for a possible rate increase within the third year and also may reflect a risk premium. Note that the Fed's policy guidance was conditional on its economic outlook. On both dates, forward yields declined over the term structure, with the largest declines at the four-year horizon. There is no reason to believe that policy guidance focused on the next two or three years would not affect expectations of the policy rate somewhat beyond that horizon. Note that the effect dies off with more distant horizons.

Purchases of Long-Term Assets

A number of recent studies have focused on the effects of large-scale purchases of long-term assets by the BOE and the Fed since 2008. Almost all agree that such purchases do significantly reduce long-term interest rates. Figure 3.8 displays long-term bond yields in these economies; the yield for the euro area is a GDP-weighted average of government bonds in member countries.[16]

---

15. These rates are based on the work of Gürkaynak, Sack, and Wright (2007), and they are regularly updated on the Fed website at www.federalreserve.gov/Pubs/feds/2006 (accessed on July 1, 2013).

16. The weighted average yield is appropriate for an assessment of the macroeconomic effects of ECB policy on the entire euro area. Using a German yield is not appropriate because flights to safety within the euro area push up peripheral yields at the same time that they push down the German yield.

Table 3.2   Forward one-year Treasury yields (basis points)

	Year 0	Year 1	Year 2	Year 3	Year 4	Year 5	Year 6	Year 7	Year 8	Year 9
					August 9, 2011					
Level	13	21	73	142	215	283	342	390	428	456
Change	–4	–15	–24	–29	–31	–30	–28	–26	–22	–19
					January 25, 2012					
Level	14	25	69	128	190	249	302	345	380	406
Change	–0	–7	–12	–14	–14	–12	–10	–7	–4	–1
	Standard deviation of daily changes, August 2007–December 2012									
Standard deviation	5	8	9	9	9	9	9	9	9	9

Sources: US Federal Reserve Board; authors' calculations.

Figure 3.8   Long-term government bond yields, 2007–12

percent, monthly

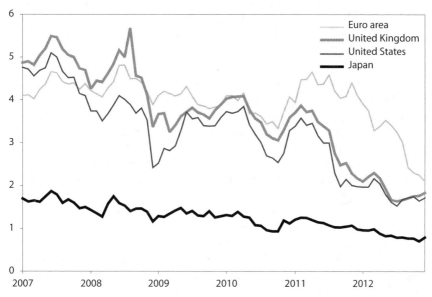

Source: IMF, *International Financial Statistics*.

Event Studies

Many studies focus on the movements of bond yields on the day (or within the hour) of an announcement by a central bank that it plans to purchase a large quantity of long-term bonds. The first study was released by one of us and colleagues (Gagnon et al. 2011) and shows that yields on a wide range of longer-term assets declined significantly on days when the Fed first announced that it would (or might) purchase MBS or long-term Treasury bonds, or that it would increase its purchases.[17] By adding up the cumulative yield changes on all days in which the Fed released information about future bond purchases, Gagnon et al. estimate that the initial Fed program of $1.7 trillion of purchases of MBS and longer-term Treasury bonds (QE1) lowered the 10-year Treasury yield by between 50 and 100 basis points, and that most of this decline reflected a reduction in the term premium as opposed to a reduction in expected future short-term interest rates. Other long-term interest rates, including those on corporate bonds and swap agreements, also declined by comparable amounts. MBS yields declined by even more, probably because the MBS market was unusually strained prior to QE1.

---

17. The initial version of Gagnon et al. (2011) circulated as a working paper in March 2010.

Michael Joyce et al. (2011) find that BOE announcements about bond purchases also had significant effects on UK bond yields, and that the first £200 billion of announced purchases "may have depressed gilt yields by about 100 basis points." Martin Daines, Michael Joyce, and Matthew Tong (2011) provide further support and relate yield movements across the term structure to amounts purchased across the term structure.

Arvind Krishnamurthy and Annette Vissing-Jorgensen (2011) extend Gagnon et al. (2011) to cover the second Fed purchase program (QE2). They find that the $600 billion QE2 program lowered the yields on highly rated 10-year bonds about 20 basis points, an effect that is consistent with Gagnon et al. after adjusting for the difference in the sizes of QE1 and QE2.[18] Carlo Rosa (2012) extends the event study analysis to include other financial variables, such as equity prices and exchange rates, and a set of event dates based on analysis of articles in the *Financial Times*. He finds that bond yields declined significantly when the Fed announced bond purchases and that the comovements of financial prices on event days are similar to those associated with conventional monetary policy.

Eric Swanson (2011) shows that an event-study approach applied to the Treasury purchase program of the early 1960s (Operation Twist) finds an effect on yields that is similar in magnitude to the estimates of Gagnon et al. (2011) after scaling for the size of the program relative to GDP. Jonathan Wright (2012) uses the extra variance of bond yields on event dates associated with Fed bond purchases to identify their effects. He does not link bond purchase amounts to specific yield movements, but he instead finds that monetary policy during the period of near-zero short-term interest rates was able to significantly affect long-term Treasury and corporate bond yields, though the effects appear to die out within a few months.

Two papers (Bauer and Rudebusch 2011, Christensen and Rudebusch 2012) find that bond yields declined sharply on event dates in both the United Kingdom and the United States. They argue that most of the declines in the United Kingdom reflect a declining term premium, whereas much or most of the declines in the United States reflect declining expectations of the future short-term interest rate, a difference that the second paper acknowledges as puzzling. Gagnon and Matthew Raskin (2013) show that movements in the term premium are an important part of the effects of asset purchases in the United States and that a survey-based measure of the term premium declined significantly in late 2011 and 2012, beyond the periods examined by Bauer and Rudebusch (2011) and Christensen and Rudebusch (2012).

Several studies examine the international financial effects of asset purchases by the BOE and the Fed (Neely 2010, Bauer and Neely 2012, Glick

---

18. They argue that agency MBS are not in this "safe" class of assets and that MBS yields were not much affected by QE2 because it did not include purchases of MBS. However, MBS yields fell almost exactly as much as yields on 10-year Treasuries during the period leading up to QE2 from early August to early November 2010.

and Leduc 2012). The effects on bond yields are quite large, even for the BOE purchases. This result is consistent with previous research that finds a high correlation of bond yields across countries. The effects on exchange rates are modest but generally in the expected direction.

Other Studies

Even before the launch of large-scale asset purchases, a number of empirical researchers had found that changes in the supply of long-term Treasury bonds affect the slope of the Treasury yield curve (Friedman 1981; Frankel 1985; Agell, Persson, and Friedman 1992; Kuttner 2006; Greenwood and Vayanos 2008). All of these studies focused on the United States. Their results suggest that central bank purchases of long-term bonds, which reduce the supply of those bonds available for private investors, should push down long-term interest rates.

In addition to their event study, Gagnon et al. (2011) estimated a long-term relationship between the net supply of long-term bonds by the public sector and the term premium on 10-year Treasury bonds. Based on this relationship, they estimated that QE1 reduced the term premium on 10-year bonds by about 50 basis points.

Two other studies examine the effect of bond supply factors on the term structure in the United States in the years before the launch of large-scale asset purchases. James Hamilton and Cynthia Wu (2012) find that the average maturity of Treasury debt held by the public (excluding Fed holdings) has an important influence on the term premium, and that the size of this effect is somewhat smaller but of a similar magnitude to that found by Gagnon et al. (2011). Iryna Kaminska, Dimitri Vayanos, and Gabriele Zinna (2011) find that purchases of long-term Treasury bonds by foreign central banks have an important effect on the term premium, again of a magnitude that is comparable to that found by Gagnon et al. (2011).

Jack Meaning and Feng Zhu (2011, 2012) regress the term premium on the average maturity of outstanding Treasury securities, the average maturity of Fed holdings of Treasury securities, and total Fed holdings of Treasury securities as a share of the total outstanding. They estimate that QE1 and QE2 together may have reduced the 10-year Treasury yield by 180 basis points, somewhat more than would be implied by the estimates by Gagnon et al. (2011) after scaling up to include QE2. Jane Ihrig et al. (2012) estimate a term structure model that includes both Treasury and MBS supply effects as well as projections of the future holdings of these assets by the Fed. They estimate that the combined effect of all Fed asset purchases as of June 2012 is to reduce the 10-year Treasury yield by 65 basis points. Francis Breedon, Jagjit Chadha, and Alex Waters (2012) estimate a term structure model for the United Kingdom and find that the BOE purchase programs as of early 2010 had lowered the 10-year bond yield between 50 and 100 basis points. All of the results of these studies imply permanent effects of QE on bond yields in the sense that the yield remains lower as long as the central bank holds the extra long-term bonds.

Sharon Kozicki, Eric Santor, and Lena Suchanek (2011) regress long-term bond yields on central bank assets relative to GDP as well as other control variables such as inflation expectations and fiscal variables. For the United States, their results imply that QE1 may have reduced the 10-year Treasury yield by 108 basis points, somewhat more than implied by Gagnon et al. (2011). In a panel framework with other advanced economies, however, they obtain noticeably smaller, though still significant, effects.

Andreas Fuster and Paul Willen (2010) and Diana Hancock and Wayne Passmore (2011) find that Fed MBS purchases had large effects on MBS yields and on primary mortgage rates. Neither study is able to disentangle the permanent effect on mortgage rates from the temporary effect associated with the extreme financial stress that existed at the start of the purchase program in late 2008.

Stefania D'Amico and Thomas King (2013) take a novel approach. They estimate a model of supply effects on the yield curve that includes every Treasury security outstanding. Differences in the quantities of Fed purchases across specific securities can be used to model differences in the movements of yields across the same securities between the beginning and end of the first purchase program (QE1). These estimated effects include own-price and cross-price supply elasticities. The model is then used to show that the $300 billion of purchases of Treasuries in QE1 lowered the 10-year yield by about 50 basis points. This estimate is at the low end of the results in Gagnon et al. (2011), but it is important to note that this estimate is based only on the Treasury portion of QE1. D'Amico and King are silent on the effects of the much larger MBS purchases. If these also reduce Treasury yields, as most other researchers believe, then the results of D'Amico and King are consistent with a much larger effect of QE1 on Treasury yields than found by Gagnon et al. Stefania D'Amico et al. (2012) extend and refine the D'Amico and King results. They find that QE1 lowered the 10-year Treasury yield by 44 basis points and QE2 lowered it by 55 basis points. Again, they do not include the effects of MBS purchases.

IMF (2013b) takes an indirect approach. A monetary policy shock is defined as the change in the one-year-forward three-month Libor rate on days in which the central bank made a policy announcement. The study then examines the correlations of other interest rates and asset prices to these monetary policy shocks pre-QE and post-QE. In the United Kingdom and the United States, monetary policy has a greater effect on long-term yields of all types post-QE than pre-QE. The opposite result holds for Japan, but this should not be too surprising because the BOJ never bought long-term bonds during the post-QE sample. For all countries, there is little effect of monetary policy on exchange rates or equity prices in either period.

Two studies challenge these numerous positive findings. Using weekly data from 2007 through 2009, Johannes Stroebel and John Taylor (2012) find that increases in Fed holdings of agency MBS do not have a significant effect on the MBS yield spread. Based on this result, the authors question the efficacy of the Fed's MBS program. However, this study has a serious shortcoming because its sample is too short to include the long-term swings that are needed to identify the relationship found in Gagnon et al. (2011), Hamilton and Wu (2012), and other papers cited above. Moreover, Stroebel and Taylor find that the announcement of the Fed purchase program did cause a large and significant reduction in the MBS yield spread, a result they downplay. Daniel Thornton (2012b) finds that the long-term relationship estimated by Gagnon et al. is sensitive to the inclusion of a fixed time trend in the regression. He does not provide any reason to believe that a fixed time trend is an appropriate variable for this regression, nor does he provide any evidence against the other time series or event-study results discussed above.

Overall, the cumulated evidence supports the view that large-scale alterations in the relative supply of short- and long-term bonds in private hands can affect the term structure of interest rates. In order to have a substantial impact on rates, large quantities must be purchased. For example, in the United States, it takes $1 trillion in purchases of long-term bonds to lower the 10-year bond yield by 25 to 50 basis points, according to most studies. Importantly, the effect seems to spill over to at least some degree across all long-term bonds, including classes that are not included in the purchase programs, such as corporate debt in the United States and swaps in the United Kingdom and the United States.

Liquidity Facilities and Emergency Loans

Another common policy response was to combat elevated spreads and reduced liquidity in the interbank funding market. Policies include increasing the amount and term of collateralized lending to financial institutions, front-loading the provision of bank reserves, broadening the range of collateral accepted, and narrowing the spreads between deposit and credit facilities. Central banks surely lowered spreads in this market below where they would otherwise have been, particularly during the periods of greatest financial strain. These programs probably do not have much effect on interbank spreads during noncrisis periods, when spreads are already low.

Measuring the effectiveness of these programs is extremely difficult. A simple correlation of the size of these central bank programs with the size of the spreads is not informative because causality runs in both directions: Higher spreads induced central banks to expand their programs and larger programs helped to hold down spreads. The former effect clearly dominated between mid-2007 and late 2008. Jens Christensen, Jose Lopez, and Glenn Rudebusch (2009) attempt to disentangle these effects by comparing the behavior of interest rates in markets with and without a Fed lending program. They conclude that the Fed's Term Auction Facility (TAF) lowered three-month dollar interbank rates roughly 300 basis points as of late 2008. As shown in figure 3.1, spreads in the interbank funding market have declined considerably since their peaks in late 2008, but they remain slightly higher than before the onset of the financial crisis.

James McAndrews, Asani Sarkar, and Zhenyu Wang (2008) analyze the three-month Libor-OIS spread and find that it narrows on both TAF announcement and operation dates. The cumulative effect of the program as of April 2008 was 57 basis points. John Taylor and John Williams (2008) do not find such a statistically significant effect, but they do not take announcement effects into consideration. Using a similar methodology on Libor-OIS spreads, Tao Wu (2011) identifies a permanent effect of 50 to 55 basis points and a similar effect on other money market spreads. Christensen, Lopez, and Rudebusch (2009) compare the effects of TAF on different markets and find that three-month Libor rates were 70 basis points lower than expected from December 2007 to the middle of 2008. Thornton (2011) finds that TAF reduced Libor spreads by about 35 basis points and that this effect dies out over time. However, one would expect the benefits of TAF to be greatest during the period of greatest financial stress and that they should decline as markets return to normal.

Several studies analyze the central bank swap agreements that were intended to ease strains in dollar funding markets around the world. Michael Fleming and Nicholas Klagge (2010), Linda Goldberg, Craig Kennedy, and Jason Miu (2011), and Naohiko Baba and Frank Packer (2009) find that the swaps had the intended effects. Joshua Aizenman and Gurnain Kaur Pasricha (2010) and Andrew Rose and Mark Spiegel (2012) analyze the effects of the swap agreements on credit default swap spreads in a cross-section of countries and find that countries receiving swap lines see their spreads fall by more, though the effect is not always significant. It varies with the exposure of the respective countries to trade with the United States or holdings of dollar assets.

Hancock and Passmore (2011) find that spreads on agency securities over comparable-maturity Treasury securities, which had been elevated before the announced Fed purchase program, declined sharply with the announcement of the agency purchase program and have drifted down further since then.

Michael Fleming, Warren Hrung, and Frank Keane (2009) show that the Term Securities Lending Facility (TSLF) program reduced the repo spreads between less liquid and more liquid collateral. In a study published a year later, the same three authors find that the amounts outstanding under the program and changes in the repo spreads are negatively correlated (Fleming, Hrung, and Keane 2010).

In a review article on the liquidity provisions of the Federal Reserve, Michael Fleming (2012) finds that most studies establish a positive effect of the liquidity programs, such as the TAF or the TSLF, on financial markets. However, he notes that there is a lack of studies on certain programs such as single-tranche, open-market operations and the Primary Dealer Credit Facility. Additionally, he points to a lack of research based on institution-level as opposed to financial market data, though the release of transaction-level data for the new liquidity programs starting in 2011 will likely improve the situation.

Several studies focus on other liquidity programs such as the Asset-Backed Commercial Paper Money Market Mutual Fund Liquidity Facility (Duygan-Bump et al. 2013), the Commercial Paper Funding Facility (Adrian,

Kimbrough, and Marchioni 2011), and the TALF (Ashcraft, Garleanu, and Pedersen 2011; Campbell et al. 2011). All these papers usually find the expected calming effects of the programs on financial markets.

Stéphanie Stolz and Michael Wedow (2010) compare public measures to support financial markets in the United States and the European Union. They find that as of 2010, the crisis responses had been relatively similar in size and scope. They conclude that the measures averted a further escalation of the crisis and reduced banks' default risk. They assess capital injections to be more successful than debt guarantees or asset purchases in doing so. Also, central bank programs had eased but not fully resolved tensions in the money market as of early 2010.

Fabian Eser et al. (2012) conclude that the ECB's monetary policy instruments have proven effective and versatile. They especially highlight the positive role of the LTROs in reducing liquidity risk and bringing down term spreads and credit default swap premia with respect to euro area banks. The LTROs are not a panacea, however, and they did not prevent renewed widening of sovereign spreads later in 2012. Andrew Rose and Tomasz Wieladek (2012) find that the interventions by the BOE and the UK Treasury were successful in improving funding conditions of UK banks.

John Beirne et al. (2011) assess the effects of the ECB's Covered Bond Purchase Program (CBPP) on primary and secondary markets. Using cointegration techniques, they show that the CBPP did support the primary market for covered bank bonds, though at the expense of uncovered bonds. As for the secondary market, the authors combine an event-study approach of price reactions to ECB announcements, a comparison with benchmark bonds, and a regression analysis to conclude that the CBPP led to a reduction in average covered bond spreads by 12 basis points. However, they note that the effect differs across euro area countries, with Germany and Spain benefiting the most, while the decline has been offset by rising yields in crisis countries. Additionally, they find the effect only for announcement dates, but not for actual purchase dates.

José Manuel González-Páramo (2013) analyzes the ECB's response to the crisis from a lender-of-last-resort perspective. He finds that the ECB's interventions in the money market, covered bond, and sovereign debt markets have helped to maintain market functioning and reduce uncertainty. The ECB's role may more accurately be described as a market maker of last resort that acted as an intermediary and ensured a meaningful price of assets in dysfunctional markets. González-Páramo also points out that emergency liquidity assistance targeting individual banks played an important role in preventing a further escalation of the crisis.

Samuel Cheun, Isabel von Köppen-Mertes, and Benedict Weller (2009) compare the crisis response of the Fed, ECB, and BOE in terms of the collateral accepted by the respective central bank. They conclude that a broader collateral framework in terms of the range of securities accepted and the number of counterparties allows a central bank to more effectively use it as a crisis mitigation tool. In this regard, the ECB's standard liquidity-injecting operations were better suited to address the liquidity issues arising during the financial market meltdown, since they accepted a wider range of collateral from more institutions than the conventional monetary operations of the Fed and the BOE. However, the latter two central banks quickly reacted to the problems in financial markets with the creation of ad hoc measures that reached more banks with a wider range of collateral. The Fed, in particular, has long accepted a much wider range of collateral (including bank loans) at its discount window than the other two central banks. The problem for the Fed was not in liberalizing collateral rules, as the ECB and BOE eventually had to do, but in eliminating the stigma banks traditionally attached to borrowing at the discount window. The Fed achieved this through the TAF. The open auction format and the large quantities of credit on offer in the TAF were attractive to banks, which did not mind being seen to bid on a good deal. This TAF setup was very different from traditional discount window borrowing, in which banks approach the Fed individually to negotiate a loan that may be seen by other banks as a signal of distress. Overall, the three central banks' collateral frameworks turned out to be adequate in addressing liquidity issues, even if they started from different institutional and legal backgrounds. However, Cheun, von Köppen-Mertes, and Weller (2009) point out the associated risk of a broader collateral framework, such as moral hazard and distortions in the proper functioning of markets.

Nathaniel Frank and Heiko Hesse (2009) are more downbeat about the effectiveness of central bank intervention. They examine the Fed's TAF and the ECB's LTROs using a range of statistical and econometric techniques, such as Markov switching models as well as bivariate vector autoregression and generalized autoregressive conditional heteroskedasticity models. They find that the announcement of TAF reduced the Libor-OIS spread in the United States by 35 basis points in the long run, while LTROs compressed the spread in the euro area by 15 basis points. They also show small effects of these programs on each other's markets. Additionally, these measures helped to reduce the volatility of the Libor-OIS spreads both on announcements and implementation dates. Frank and Hesse interpret these results to suggest that the measures undertaken have helped to ease liquidity concerns, but they insist that the economic magnitudes are not very large, and that the programs did not bring the liquidity crisis to a halt. As with most studies, there is a difficult identification problem because the liquidity programs respond to financial strains as well as help to ameliorate them.

Focusing on the Fed, ECB, BOE, and SNB, Petra Gerlach-Kristen and Peter Kugler (2010) pay special attention to the identification problem, namely that changes in money market spreads may influence central banks' decisions very nearly at the same time that the measures they take have effects on these spreads. First, they provide evidence that central banks' tools did indeed respond to liquidity pressures. Interestingly, the tools at their disposal were used as substitutes; in other words, the use of one particular liquidity provision tends to make it less likely that an alternative provision will be used. Second, the authors show that liquidity provisions through repo auctions in the United States, euro area, and United Kingdom had the largest effect in reducing Libor-OIS spreads, while foreign-currency repos and swaps seem to have had no effect. They reveal that the pricing rather than the quantity of liquidity mattered more for the reduction of money market spreads.

Using an event study of policy announcements, Yacine Aït-Sahalia et al. (2012) find that liquidity support measures in the four major advanced economies caused decreases in interbank risk premia: in a pooled sample, the US dollar Libor-OIS spread fell by about six basis points on average in the wake of announcements related to domestic currency liquidity support. There were 10 announcements in the sample, suggesting a total reduction in the spread of about 60 basis points. The authors highlight a similarly favorable effect of bank recapitalizations, but a large negative effect of ad hoc bank bailouts. However, on a disaggregated level, liquidity programs seem to have been more effective in the United Kingdom and the euro area, while the swap agreements benefited mostly the United States and the United Kingdom.

Uwe Vollmer and Ralf Bebenroth (2012) analyze the case of Japan in great detail. They note that, initially, Japan was less immediately exposed to the subprime crisis than were Europe and the United States because Japanese banks did not directly invest in subprime mortgages, nor was their business model reliant on structured financial products. Rather, the authors describe how falling Japanese equity prices reduced banks' Tier 1 capital because Japanese banks hold a significant amount of corporate equity. Declining capital ratios at banks reduced loan volumes and drove up interest rate spreads on commercial paper and bonds. The authors maintain that the measures undertaken by the BOJ to address this credit crunch were effective in reducing commercial paper issuance rates, directly targeting the commercial paper market.

Macroeconomic Effects

It is widely accepted that lower short-term interest rates provide macroeconomic stimulus. It is an open question whether financial strains and uncertainty about future financial regulations reduce the magnitude of stimulus for a given policy rate reduction. Many of the extraordinary liquidity measures may be viewed as attempts to unblock the transmission channels for traditional policy. What about the other actions taken by these central banks? How effective were they at preventing deflation, stimulating activity and employment, and preventing financial collapse?[19]

Figure 3.3 shows that the gap of output below potential has roughly stabilized in the euro area and the United Kingdom, while it is closing in Japan and the United States. Figure 3.4 shows that unemployment is still worsening in

---

19. A related question, not covered in this chapter, is whether fiscal policies were set appropriately both before and after the crisis. We take the conventional view that monetary policymakers should take the stance of fiscal policy as given.

the euro area but has stabilized in the United Kingdom and is declining in Japan and the United States. Figure 3.5 shows that inflation has recovered at least partially from its initial plunge in all four economies.

Governors of these central banks have unanimously stated that their programs were successful in preventing even worse macroeconomic outcomes.[20] The most common defense of these programs starts with the evidence cited above regarding the effect of central bank actions at lowering longer-term interest rates and reducing risk spreads in private markets. These financial prices can be used in existing macroeconomic models to generate implied effects on employment, output, inflation, and other objectives. Hess Chung et al. (2011) use the estimates of Gagnon et al. (2011) to calibrate the effect of QE1 and QE2 on the US economy. They project that the US unemployment rate in mid-2012 was 1.5 percentage points lower than it would have been without these programs and that the asset purchases "probably prevented the US economy from falling into deflation" (p. 4). Janet Yellen suggests that "$500 billion in longer-term asset purchases would serve to lower the unemployment rate by close to 0.25 percentage point within three years."[21] Extrapolating Yellen's statement based on Fed holdings of $3 trillion in long-term assets as of December 2012 suggests that QE reduced the prospective US unemployment rate by about 1.5 percentage points. Han Chen, Vasco Cúrdia, and Andrea Ferrero (2012) find a somewhat smaller effect: $600 billion of purchases raise US GDP by about 0.35 percent, with little effect on inflation. Using a typical rule of thumb that each percentage point increase in GDP reduces the unemployment rate by half a percentage point, these results suggest that QE2 lowered the unemployment rate about 0.2 percentage points. However, their general equilibrium framework imposes restrictions on the ways in which QE may affect the economy.

George Kapetanios et al. (2012) use three statistical models to assess the effects of the decline in long-term interest rates caused by the BOE's asset purchases. They estimate that these purchases may have increased UK real GDP by 1.5 percent and inflation by 1.25 percentage points, although there is considerable uncertainty surrounding these estimates. Christiane Baumeister and Luca Benati (2010) estimate a model with a time-varying effect of the slope of the yield curve on economic activity. They introduce estimates of the effect of

20. Bernanke, "Federal Reserve's Response to the Financial Crisis"; Mario Draghi, "The Role of Monetary Policy in Addressing the Crisis in the Euro Area," speech at the Faculty of Economics and Business, Amsterdam, April 15, 2013, www.ecb.europa.eu/press/key/date/2013/html/sp130415. en.html (accessed on July 1, 2013); Mervyn King, speech at the University of Exeter, January 19, 2010, www.bankofengland.co.uk/publications/Documents/speeches/2010/speech419.pdf (accessed on July 1, 2013); Masaaki Shirakawa, "Recent Economic and Financial Developments and the Conduct of Monetary Policy," speech at the Kisaragi-kai Meeting, Tokyo, November 4, 2009, www.bis.org/review/r091110b.pdf (accessed on July 1, 2013); Jean-Claude Trichet, "Lessons from the Crisis," speech at the European American Press Club, December 3, 2010, www.ecb.int/press/key/date/2010/html/sp101203.en.html (accessed on July 1, 2013).

21. Janet Yellen, "Challenges Confronting Monetary Policy," speech at the Economic Policy Conference of the National Association for Business Economics Policy, March 4, 2013, www.federalreserve.gov/newsevents/speech/yellen20130302a.htm (accessed on July 1, 2013).

Fed and BOE asset purchases on the yield curve into their model and find that in both the United States and the United Kingdom these purchases "averted significant risks both of deflation and of output collapses comparable to those that took place during the Great Depression" (Baumeister and Benati 2010, 5).[22] Jonathan Bridges and Ryland Thomas (2012) use a monetarist framework and suggest that the increase in broad money associated with BOE policy may have raised UK GDP by 2 percent as of early 2011 with an increase of 1 percentage point on inflation as of early 2012. Domenico Giannone, Michele Lenza, and Lucrezia Reichlin (2012) find that the ECB's policies reduced the unemployment rate in the euro area by 0.6 percentage points as of January 2011.

Leonardo Gambacorta, Boris Hofmann, and Gert Peersman (2012) estimate a statistical model only over the crisis period, starting in 2007. They find that central bank balance sheets responded strongly to financial market volatility, but that increases in balance sheets that were exogenous to this and other factors have effects on output and prices similar to monetary policy shocks in normal times. They focus on short-term effects only, but their results are shared broadly across a range of advanced economies.

IMF (2011) looks at correlations of financial flows, trade flows, asset prices, and GDP. The focus is on the spillovers of policies across systemically important countries as well as the emerging-market countries. The report finds that QE1 and QE2 in the United States had positive effects on growth in all regions of the world, including of course on US GDP. The bond market and links between bond markets are the most important channel, but there are positive effects through stock markets in all regions. Despite vocal complaints by policymakers in some emerging-market countries, the effects via the foreign exchange markets were very small: positive in the United States and negative in other countries (but not enough to offset the positive effects mentioned above).

Few studies look at the macroeconomic effects of the liquidity programs (as opposed to QE). One study that does so is by Seth Carpenter, Selva Demiralp, and Jens Eisenschmidt (2012), who argue that it is important to consider both supply and demand effects. They find that without the US liquidity programs of both the Fed and the Treasury, commercial and industrial loans would have been 23 percent lower. The comparable figure for programs in the euro area is a reduction of nonfinancial corporate loans of 4 percent.

Costs and Risks

Overall, the evidence that central bank programs had macroeconomic benefits is extremely strong. However, these benefits may entail offsetting costs or risks. A key risk is that the extraordinary liquidity programs and emergency loans

---

22. This finding may seem surprisingly large, but it is important to note that the output collapse during the Great Depression reflected the interaction of a financial shock with a bad policy response. Bernanke has said that the shocks that caused the Great Depression and the more recent global financial crisis were of a comparable magnitude (Bernanke, "Federal Reserve's Response to the Financial Crisis").

create moral hazard on the part of financial institutions, which may come to rely on such government help too much. There has been an explosion of work on the need for major reforms of financial supervision and regulation to prevent future financial crises (Johnson and Kwak 2010, Claessens et al. 2011, Admati and Hellwig 2013). Assessing the reform agenda is beyond the scope of this chapter. We take the view that the liquidity programs were necessary and desirable under the circumstances and that major reforms are needed to minimize the harm from moral hazard going forward. These reforms may take the form of higher capital standards for banks and other important financial institutions, greater protection of consumers with respect to financial products (including limitations on loan-to-value and debt-income ratios), and plans for the orderly resolution of complex and systemically important institutions that are insolvent.

With respect to QE, Bernanke has identified four potential costs: (1) large purchases of specific assets that could impair the functioning of markets in those assets; (2) a large balance sheet that could reduce public confidence in the central bank's ability to exit smoothly from QE; (3) ultra-low long-term yields that could encourage risky investor behavior, including perhaps generating asset price bubbles; and (4) a large maturity mismatch in the central bank's balance sheet that makes future remittances of profits to the Treasury more risky.[23]

As one of us has stated, none of these potential costs is significant or likely to become significant in the foreseeable future.[24] Indeed, some of these costs may at present be negative (i.e., benefits). For example, if the first cost (illiquid markets) were to become significant, the Fed could address it by adopting adjustable daily target ranges for yields on the bonds in question, which would give traders confidence about the prices at which they could buy or sell, which is the main benefit of a liquid market. Fed communication and resolute action against inflation are the keys to minimizing the second cost.

The third cost is undoubtedly the most worrisome. Central banks everywhere are beefing up their analysis of macroprudential risks and developing tools to deal with these risks, such as countercyclical capital charges and loan-to-value ratios. If such tools prove unworkable or ineffective, central banks may have to factor in financial stability concerns in the setting of monetary policy. However, for the immediate future at least, these risks appear very low (Posen 2011).[25] Indeed, further retarding recovery and risking a double-dip recession

---

23. Bernanke, "Monetary Policy since the Onset of the Crisis," speech at Federal Reserve Bank of Kansas City Economic Symposium in Jackson Hole, August 31, 2012, www.federalreserve.gov/newsevents/speech/bernanke20120831a.htm (accessed on July 1, 2013).

24. Joseph Gagnon, "America Needs More Expansionary Monetary Policy," testimony before the Subcommittee on Monetary Policy and Trade, US House of Representatives Financial Services Committee, March 5, 2013.

25. The main financial markets are those for real estate, equities, and bonds. Real estate is unlikely to experience a bubble until the memories of the recent bubble fade, at least 20 years from now.

by halting QE almost surely raises greater risks to financial stability (through higher bankruptcies and loan losses) than are raised by doing more QE.

Finally, the fourth cost is not a cost when viewed appropriately. What matters is not the effect of QE on central bank profits in any given year, but the effect of QE on the burden of the national debt as measured by the ratio of the debt to GDP. There is no plausible scenario in which QE increases the ratio of debt to GDP in the long run. Indeed, QE will almost surely reduce the debt burden.

Seth Carpenter et al. (2013) show that even under an adverse scenario in which the Fed buys an additional $1 trillion of long-term assets at low yields in 2013 and then faces a run-up of bond yields to a sustained level of 5 percent, the reduction of future Fed remittances to the Treasury would not exceed the excess of previous remittances over normal levels. IMF (2013a) also assumes that the Fed buys an additional $1 trillion of long-term bonds at low yields in 2013. In a tail-risk scenario in which interest rates at the short and long ends of the yield curve rise 600 basis points and 375 basis points, respectively, the IMF calculates that the present value of Fed losses would be just over 4 percent of GDP. However, this comes after a period in which excess Fed profits created by QE total about 2 percent of GDP.

Moreover, both of these studies ignore any benefits to the Treasury from locking in lower borrowing costs on massive bond issuance during the period of QE or from higher tax revenues arising from higher nominal GDP made possible by QE. According to Janet Yellen, the Fed's main macroeconomic model suggests that $500 billion of purchases of long-term assets reduces the long-term ratio of federal debt to GDP by 1.5 percentage points.[26] As of December 2012, the Fed had purchased $3 trillion of long-term assets, which would imply a reduction in the debt ratio of 9 percentage points, with purchases continuing in 2013. Even if this overstates the benefits, QE surely does not increase a country's long-run debt burden. Given that the main alternative to QE—fiscal stimulus—would require higher budget deficits worth many percentage points of GDP, it is clear that concerns about the potential budgetary cost of QE are entirely misplaced.

William White (2012) discusses the above risks and raises a few others. In particular, he worries that easy monetary policy removes the incentive for governments to carry out structural reforms and enables the continuation of fiscal profligacy.[27] However, the opposite position seems equally plausible: governments may be unwilling to undertake painful reforms or close budget

---

Equity bubbles are not leveraged and thus pose only minor macroeconomic risks. Bond markets are now under the control of central banks, which have the capacity to guide long-term rates gradually higher and prevent any disruptive crash.

26. Yellen, "Challenges Confronting Monetary Policy."

27. IMF (2013a, 1) also expresses concern that "monetary policy is called on to do too much, and that the breathing space it offers is not used to engage in needed fiscal, structural, and financial sector reforms."

deficits unless monetary policy supports economic growth.[28] In any event, it seems that the best prescription is for specific policymakers to focus on achieving the objectives assigned to them, taking the actions of other policymakers as given. White and others have worried that an environment of ultra-low rates discourages saving and may misallocate capital. However, Bernanke has pointed out that premature monetary tightening would only delay the eventual return to normal interest rates.[29] The ultimate cause of ultra-low interest rates is the unwillingness of businesses and households to invest in new houses, structures, and productive equipment.[30] Raising interest rates will only worsen that problem.

A 2011 working paper by three IMF staffers (Mark Stone, Kotaro Fujita, and Kenji Ishi) provides a good overview of all of the issues raised by central bank responses to the financial crisis. Overall, the paper supports the actions taken but sounds a cautious note concerning the potential costs. In particular, it expresses concern about communicating exit strategies and about political risks arising from future volatility of central bank profits. No evidence is presented on the significance of these risks. Adam Posen argues strongly that central banks should make the case to the public that the risks they are taking on with unconventional monetary policy are small relative to the benefits.[31]

Some have argued that QE in advanced economies causes an increase in capital inflows to developing and emerging-market countries that may be risky. IMF (2011) finds little difference in the effect on capital flow between QE and conventional monetary policy in advanced economies. Moreover, the IMF (2012) has recently put forward recommendations for countries to adopt to protect themselves from potentially risky capital inflows.

Conclusions

Central banks moved aggressively to ease monetary policy, provide liquidity, and calm volatility in financial markets during and after the global financial crisis and the sovereign debt crisis in Europe. Although there are a few dissenters, the overwhelming view of researchers is that both the liquidity programs and the unconventional monetary measures were successful in the sense that they affected conditions in the desired direction. A separate ques-

---

28. Adam Posen, "How to Do More," speech at Wotton-under-Edge on September 13, 2011, www.bankofengland.co.uk/publications/Documents/speeches/2011/speech517.pdf (accessed on July 1, 2013).

29. Bernanke, press conference following the FOMC meeting, Federal Reserve Board, March 20, 2013.

30. Adam Posen, "Making the Most of Doing More," speech at the Barclays Short End Rates Seminar, June 11, 2012, www.bankofengland.co.uk/publications/Pages/speeches/2012/585.aspx (accessed on July 1, 2013).

31. Ibid.

tion is whether the measures were implemented as aggressively as would have been optimal, or perhaps were implemented too aggressively.

With respect to the liquidity programs and emergency support, some would argue that the Fed should not have allowed Lehman Brothers to fail. However, Chairman Bernanke has said that the Fed lacked the authority to save Lehman because it did not have sufficient collateral to support a loan of the size needed.[32] No other systemically important institution was allowed to fail and markets continued to function through the crisis, albeit under strain. Others have argued that too much support was given and that this has created a long-run moral hazard because large banks know they will not be allowed to fail and other market participants will expect extraordinary liquidity to be provided in future emergencies. Assessing the balance between doing too much and doing too little is beyond the scope of this chapter, but it is at least clear that rules and limits to prevent moral hazard must be agreed upon before a crisis hits. During the panic of a crisis, policymakers should use all available tools to their maximum legal extent. Over the past four years, legislators and financial supervisors have taken steps to address the moral hazard problem and to reduce the risk of future crises. Time will tell whether enough has been done.

With respect to the unconventional monetary policies, known broadly as quantitative easing, there is also disagreement. Some argue that the weak recovery, and in some cases double-dip recessions, are evidence that monetary policy has not been sufficiently easy. Others counter that QE has not been effective. The evidence surveyed here refutes the latter view. Still others are worried that the costs of QE may exceed the benefits. The costs may or may not prove to be significant, but there is little evidence for them as yet. In our view, the solid evidence of the benefits of QE vastly outweighs the weak evidence of the costs.

References

Admati, Anat, and Martin Hellwig. 2013. *The Bankers' New Clothes*. Princeton, NJ: Princeton University Press.

Adrian, Tobias. Karin Kimbrough, and Dina Marchioni. 2011. The Federal Reserve's Commercial Paper Funding Facility. *Economic Policy Review* 17, no. 1 (May): 25–39.

Agell, Jonas, and Mats Persson, and Benjamin Friedman. 1992. Does Debt Management Matter? In *Does Debt Management Matter?* ed. Jonas Agell, Mats Persson, and Benjamin Friedman. Oxford, UK: Clarendon Press.

Aït-Sahalia, Yacine, Jochen Andritzky, Andreas Jobst, Sylwia Nowak, and Natalia Tamirisa. 2012. Market Response to Policy Initiatives during the Global Financial Crisis. *Journal of International Economics* 87, no. 1: 162–77.

Aizenman, Joshua, and Gurnain Kaur Pasricha. 2010. Selective Swap Arrangements and the Global Financial Crisis: Analysis and Interpretation. *International Review of Economics and Finance* 19, no. 3 (June): 353–65.

---

32. Bernanke, "Federal Reserve's Response to the Financial Crisis."

Ashcraft, Adam, Nicolae Garleanu, and Lasse Heje Pedersen. 2011. Two Monetary Tools: Interest Rates and Haircuts. *NBER Macroeconomics Annual 2010 Volume* 25. Chicago: University of Chicago Press.

Baba, Naohiko, and Frank Packer. 2009. From Turmoil to Crisis: Dislocations in the FX Swap Market Before and After the Failure of Lehman Brothers. *Journal of International Money and Finance* 28, no. 8 (December): 1350–74.

Bauer, Michael, and Christopher Neely. 2012. *International Channels of the Fed's Unconventional Monetary Policy*. Working Paper 2012-028A. Federal Reserve Bank of St. Louis.

Bauer, Michael, and Glenn Rudebusch. 2011. *The Signaling Channel for Federal Reserve Bond Purchases*. Working Paper 2011-21. Federal Reserve Bank of San Francisco.

Baumeister, Christiane, and Luca Benati. 2010. *Unconventional Monetary Policy and the Great Recession*. Working Paper No. 1258. Frankfurt: European Central Bank.

Beirne, John, Lars Dalitz, Jacob Ejsing, Magdalena Grothe, Simone Manganelli, Fernando Monar, Benjamin Sahel, Matjaz Susec, Jens Tapking, and Tana Vong. 2011. *The Impact of the Eurosystem's Covered Bond Purchase Programme on the Primary and Secondary Markets*. ECB Occasional Paper 122. Frankfurt: European Central Bank.

Breedon, Francis, Jagjit Chadha, and Alex Waters. 2012. The Financial Market Impact of UK Quantitative Easing. *Oxford Review of Economic Policy* 28, no. 4: 702–28.

Bridges, Jonathan, and Ryland Thomas. 2012. *The Impact of QE on the UK Economy–Some Supportive Monetarist Arithmetic*. Working Paper 442. London: Bank of England.

Campbell, Sean, Daniel Covitz, William Nelson, and Karen Pence. 2011. Securitization Markets and Central Banking: An Evaluation of the Term Asset-backed Securities Loan Facility. *Journal of Monetary Economics* 58, no. 5: 518–31.

Campbell, Jeffrey, Charles Evans, Jonas Fisher, and Alejandro Justiniano. 2012. Macroeconomic Effects of Federal Reserve Forward Guidance. *Brookings Papers on Economic Activity* Spring: 1–80. Washington, DC: Brookings Institution.

Carpenter, Seth, Selva Demiralp, and Jens Eisenschmidt. 2012. The Effectiveness of the Non-Standard Policy Measures during the Financial Crises: The Experiences of the Federal Reserve and the European Central Bank. Board of Governors of the Federal Reserve System. Photocopy.

Carpenter, Seth, Jane Ihrig, Elizabeth Klee, Daniel Quinn, and Alexander Boote. 2013. *The Federal Reserve's Balance Sheet and Earnings: A Primer and Projections*. Finance and Economics Discussion Series 2013-01. Board of Governors of the Federal Reserve System.

Chen, Han, Vasco Cúrdia, and Andrea Ferrero. 2012. The Macroeconomic Effects of Large-Scale Asset Purchase Programmes. *Economic Journal* 122, no. 564: F289–315.

Cheun, Samuel, Isabel von Köppen-Mertes, and Benedict Weller. 2009. *The Collateral Frameworks of the Eurosystem, the Federal Reserve System and the Bank of England and the Financial Market Turmoil*. ECB Occasional Paper 107. Frankfurt: European Central Bank.

Christensen, Jens, and Glenn Rudebusch. 2012. The Response of Interest Rates to US and UK Quantitative Easing. *Economic Journal* 122, no. 564: F385–414.

Christensen, Jens, Jose Lopez, and Glenn Rudebusch. 2009. *Do Central Bank Liquidity Facilities Affect Interbank Lending Rates?* Working Paper 2009-13. Federal Reserve Bank of San Francisco.

Chung, Hess, Jean-Philippe Laforte, David Reifschneider, and John Williams. 2011. *Have We Underestimated the Likelihood and Severity of Zero Lower Bound Events?* Working Paper 2011-01. Federal Reserve Bank of San Francisco.

Claessens, Stijn, Ceyla Pazarbasioglu, Luc Laeven, Marc Dobler, Fabian Valencia, Oana Nedelescu, and Katharine Seal. 2011. *Crisis Management and Resolution: Early Lessons from the Financial Crisis*. IMF Staff Discussion Note 11/05. Washington, DC: International Monetary Fund.

Daines, Martin, Michael Joyce, and Matthew Tong. 2011. *QE and the Gilt Market: A Disaggregated Analysis*. Working Paper 466. London: Bank of England.

D'Amico, Stefania, and Thomas King. 2013. Flow and Stock Effects of Large-Scale Treasury Purchases: Evidence on the Importance of Local Supply. *Journal of Financial Economics* 108, no. 2: 425–48.

D'Amico, Stefania, William English, David López-Salido, and Edward Nelson. 2012. The Federal Reserve's Large-Scale Asset Purchase Programmes: Rationale and Effects. *Economic Journal* 122, no. 564: F415–46.

Duygan-Bump, Burcu, Patrick Parkinson, Eric Rosengren, Gustavo A. Suarez, and Paul Willen. 2013. How Effective Were the Federal Reserve Emergency Liquidity Facilities? Evidence from the Asset-Backed Commercial Paper Money Market Mutual Fund Liquidity Facility. *Journal of Finance* 68, no. 2: 715–37.

Eser, Fabian, Marta Carmona Amaro, Stefano Iacobelli, and Marc Rubens. 2012. *The Use of the Eurosystem's Monetary Policy Instruments and Operational Framework since 2009.* ECB Occasional Paper 135. Frankfurt: European Central Bank.

Fawley, Brett, and Christopher Neely. 2013. Four Stories of Quantitative Easing. *Federal Reserve Bank of St. Louis Review* 95, no. 1: 51–88.

Fleming, Michael. 2012. *Federal Reserve Liquidity Provision during the Financial Crisis of 2007–2009.* Staff Report 563. Federal Reserve Bank of New York.

Fleming, Michael, and Nicholas Klagge. 2010. The Federal Reserve's Foreign Exchange Swap Lines. *Current Issues in Economics and Finance* 16, no. 4 (April): 1–7.

Fleming, Michael, Warren Hrung, and Frank Keane. 2009. The Term Securities Lending Facility: Origin, Design, and Effects. *Current Issues in Economics and Finance* 15, no. 2 (February): 1–11.

Fleming, Michael, Warren Hrung, and Frank Keane. 2010. Repo Market Effects of the Term Securities Lending Facility. *American Economic Review: Papers & Proceedings* 100: 591–96.

Frank, Nathaniel, and Heiko Hesse. 2009. *The Effectiveness of Central Bank Interventions during the First Phase of the Subprime Crisis.* IMF Working Paper 09/206. Washington, DC: International Monetary Fund.

Frankel, Jeffrey. 1985. Portfolio Crowding-Out, Empirically Estimated. *Quarterly Journal of Economics* 100, no. 5: 1041–165.

Friedman, Benjamin. 1981. *Debt Management Policy, Interest Rates, and Economic Activity.* NBER Working Paper 830. Cambridge, MA: National Bureau of Economic Research.

Fuster, Andreas, and Paul Willen. 2010. *$1.25 Trillion Is Still Real Money: Some Facts about the Effects of the Federal Reserve's Mortgage Market Investments.* Public Policy Discussion Paper 10-4. Federal Reserve Bank of Boston.

Gagnon, Joseph. 2011. Central Bank Responses to the 2007-08 Financial Crisis: The Case for Further Action. In *An Ocean Apart: Comparing Transatlantic Responses to the Financial Crisis*, ed. Jean Pisani-Ferry, Adam Posen, and Fabrizio Saccomani. Brussels: Bruegel and Peterson Institute for International Economics.

Gagnon, Joseph, and Matthew Raskin. 2013. Quantitative Easing and the Term Premium: Evidence of a Portfolio Balance Channel. Peterson Institute for International Economics. Photocopy.

Gagnon, Joseph, Matthew Raskin, Julie Remache, and Brian Sack. 2011. The Financial Market Effects of the Federal Reserve's Large-Scale Asset Purchases. *International Journal of Central Banking* 7, no. 1: 3–43.

Gambacorta, Leonardo, Boris Hofmann, and Gert Peersman. 2012. *The Effectiveness of Unconventional Monetary Policy at the Zero Lower Bound: A Cross-Country Analysis.* BIS Working Paper 384. Basel: Bank for International Settlements.

Gerlach-Kristen, Petra, and Peter Kugler. 2010. *Central Bank Liquidity Measures: An International Perspective.* University of Basel Working Paper. Available at http://wwz.unibas.ch/fileadmin/ wwz/redaktion/makro/Papers/CB_Liquidity_Measures.pdf (accessed on July 1, 2013).

Giannone, Domenico, Michele Lenza, and Lucrezia Reichlin. 2012. *Money, Credit, Monetary Policy and the Business Cycle in the Euro Area*. CEPR Discussion Paper 8944. London: Centre for Economic Policy Research.

Glick, Reuven, and Sylvain Leduc. 2012. Central Bank Announcements of Asset Purchases and the Impact on Global Financial and Commodity Markets. *Journal of International Money and Finance* 31, no. 8: 2078–101.

Goldberg, Linda, Craig Kennedy, and Jason Miu. 2011. Central Bank Dollar Swap Lines and Overseas Dollar Funding Costs. *Economic Policy Review* 17, no. 1 (May): 3–20.

González-Páramo, José Manuel. 2013. Innovations in Lender of Last Resort Policy in Europe. In *Handbook of Safeguarding Global Financial Stability: Political, Social, Cultural, and Economic Theories and Models*, ed. Gerard Caprio. London: Elsevier.

Greenwood, Robin, and Dimitri Vayanos. 2008. *Bond Supply and Excess Bond Returns*. NBER Working Paper 13806. Cambridge, MA: National Bureau of Economic Research.

Gürkaynak, Refet, Brian Sack, and Jonathan Wright. 2007. The US Treasury Yield Curve: 1961 to the Present. *Journal of Monetary Economics* 54, no. 8: 2291–304.

Hamilton, James, and Cynthia Wu. 2012. The Effectiveness of Alternative Monetary Policy Tools in a Zero Lower Bound Environment. *Journal of Money, Credit, and Banking* 44, no. 1 (Supplement, February): 3–46.

Hancock, Diana, and Wayne Passmore. 2011. Did the Federal Reserve's MBS Purchase Program Lower Mortgage Rates? *Journal of Monetary Economics* 58, no. 5: 498–514.

Ihrig, Jane, Elizabeth Klee, Canlin Li, Brett Schulte, and Min Wei. 2012. *Expectations about the Federal Reserve's Balance Sheet and the Term Structure of Interest Rates*. Finance and Economics Discussion Series no. 2012-57. Board of Governors of the Federal Reserve System.

IMF (International Monetary Fund). 2011. *The United States: Spillover Report—Article IV Consultation*. IMF Country Report 11/203. Washington, DC.

IMF (International Monetary Fund). 2012. *The Liberalization and Management of Capital Flows: An Institutional View* (November 14). Washington, DC.

IMF (International Monetary Fund). 2013a. *Unconventional Monetary Policies—Recent Experience and Prospects* (April 18). Washington, DC.

IMF (International Monetary Fund). 2013b. *Unconventional Monetary Policies—Recent Experience and Prospects*. Background Paper (April 18). Washington, DC.

Johnson, Simon, and James Kwak. 2010. *13 Bankers: The Wall Street Takeover and the Next Financial Meltdown*. New York: Pantheon Books.

Joyce, Michael, Ana Lasaosa, Ibrahim Stevens, and Matthew Tong. 2011. The Financial Market Impact of Quantitative Easing in the United Kingdom. *International Journal of Central Banking* 7, no. 3: 113–61.

Kaminska, Iryna, Dimitri Vayanos, and Gabriele Zinna. 2011. *Preferred-Habitat Investors and the US Term Structure of Real Rates*. Working Paper 435. London: Bank of England.

Kapetanios, George, Haroon Mumtaz, Ibrahim Stevens, and Konstantinos Theodoridis. 2012. Assessing the Economy-Wide Effects of Quantitative Easing. *Economic Journal* 122, no. 564: F316–347.

Kim, Don, and Athanasios Orphanides. 2007. The Bond Market Term Premium: What Is It and How Can We Measure It? *BIS Quarterly Review* (June). Basel: Bank for International Settlements.

Kozicki, Sharon, Eric Santor, and Lena Suchanek. 2011. Central Bank Balance Sheets and Long-Term Forward Rates. In *Interest Rates, Prices and Liquidity*, ed. Jagjit Chadha and Sean Holly. London: Cambridge University Press.

Krishnamurthy, Arvind, and Annette Vissing-Jorgensen. 2011. The Effects of Quantitative Easing on Interest Rates. *Brookings Papers on Economic Activity* (Fall): 3–43. Washington, DC: Brookings Institution.

Kuttner, Kenneth. 2006. *Can Central Banks Target Bond Prices?* NBER Working Paper 12454. Cambridge, MA: National Bureau of Economic Research.

McAndrews, James, Asani Sarkar, and Zhenyu Wang. 2008. *The Effect of the Term Auction Facility on the London Inter-Bank Offered Rate.* Staff Report 335. Federal Reserve Bank of New York.

Meaning, Jack, and Feng Zhu. 2011. The Impact of Recent Central Bank Asset Purchase Programmes. *BIS Quarterly Review* (December). Basel: Bank for International Settlements.

Meaning, Jack, and Feng Zhu. 2012. The Impact of Federal Reserve Asset Purchase Programmes: Another Twist. *BIS Quarterly Review* (March). Basel: Bank for International Settlements.

Neely, Christopher. 2010. *The Large-Scale Asset Purchases Had Large International Effects.* Working Paper 2010-018D. Federal Reserve Bank of St. Louis.

Posen, Adam. 2011. Monetary Policy, Bubbles, and the Knowledge Problem. *Cato Journal* 31, no. 3: 461–71.

Rosa, Carlo. 2012. *How "Unconventional" Are Large-Scale Asset Purchases? The Impact of Monetary Policy on Asset Prices.* Staff Report 560. Federal Reserve Bank of New York.

Rose, Andrew, and Mark Spiegel. 2012. Dollar Illiquidity and Central Bank Swap Arrangements during the Global Financial Crisis. *Journal of International Economics* 88, no. 2 (November): 326–40.

Rose, Andrew, and Tomasz Wieladek. 2012. *Too Big to Fail: Some Empirical Evidence on the Causes and Consequences of Public Banking Interventions in the United Kingdom.* Working Paper 460. London: Bank of England.

Stolz, Stéphanie Marie, and Michael Wedow. 2010. *Extraordinary Measures in Extraordinary Times: Public Measures in Support of the Financial Sector in the EU and the United States.* ECB Occasional Paper 117. Frankfurt: European Central Bank.

Stone, Mark, Kotaro Ishi, and Kenji Fujita. 2011. *Should Unconventional Balance Sheet Policies Be Added to the Central Bank Toolkit? A Review of the Experience So Far.* IMF Working Paper 11/145. Washington, DC: International Monetary Fund.

Stroebel, Johannes, and John Taylor. 2012. Estimated Impact of the Federal Reserve's Mortgage-Backed Securities Purchase Program. *International Journal of Central Banking* 8, no. 2: 1–42.

Swanson, Eric. 2011. Let's Twist Again: A High-Frequency Event-Study Analysis of Operation Twist and Its Implications for QE2. *Brookings Papers on Economic Activity* (Fall): 151–207. Washington, DC: Brookings Institution.

Taylor, John, and John Williams. 2008. *A Black Swan in the Money Market.* Working Paper 2008-04 (April). Federal Reserve Bank of San Francisco.

Thornton, Daniel. 2011. The Effectiveness of Unconventional Monetary Policy: The Term Auction Facility. *Federal Reserve Bank of St. Louis Review* 93, no. 6: 439–53.

Thornton, Daniel. 2012a. Verbal Guidance and the Efficacy of Forward Guidance. *Economic Synopses* 26. Federal Reserve Bank of St. Louis.

Thornton, Daniel. 2012b. *Evidence on the Portfolio Balance Channel of Quantitative Easing.* Working Paper 2012-015A. Federal Reserve Bank of St. Louis.

US Department of the Treasury. 2012. *Fiscal Year 2012 Q1 Report.* Washington, DC: Office of Debt Management. Available at www.treasury.gov/resource-center/data-chart-center/quarterly-refunding/Documents/TBAC%20Discussion%20Charts%20Feb%202012.pdf (accessed on July 1, 2013).

US Department of the Treasury. 2013. *Fiscal Year 2013 Q2 Report*. Washington, DC: Office of Debt Management.

Vollmer, Uwe, and Ralf Bebenroth. 2012. The Financial Crisis in Japan: Causes and Policy Reactions by the Bank of Japan. *European Journal of Comparative Economics* 9, no. 1: 51–77.

White, William. 2012. *Ultra Easy Monetary Policy and the Law of Unintended Consequences*. Working Paper 126. Federal Reserve Bank of Dallas, Globalization and Monetary Policy Institute.

Wright, Jonathan. 2012. What Does Monetary Policy Do to Long-Term Interest Rates at the Zero Lower Bound? *Economic Journal* 122, no. 564: F447–66.

Wu, Tao. 2011. The US Money Market and the Term Auction Facility in the Financial Crisis of 2007-2009. *Review of Economics and Statistics* 93, no. 2: 617–31.

Appendix 3A

Table 3A.1 Timeline of central bank responses to the financial crisis

Date	United States	Japan	United Kingdom	Euro area
August 2007	Increased liquidity and expanded term loans to banks, narrowed spread on discount window loans			Increased liquidity and expanded term loans to banks
September through December 2007	Increased term liquidity to banks, lowered policy rate 100 basis points		Frontloaded bank reserves, widened reserve target range, increased term liquidity to banks, gave loan to Northern Rock, lowered policy rate 25 basis points	Frontloaded bank reserves, increased term liquidity to banks, provided dollar liquidity through Fed swaps
January through April 2008	Increased term liquidity to banks, began term loans to primary dealers, established term securities lending, gave loan to Bear Stearns, lowered policy rate 225 basis points		Established term securities lending, lowered policy rate 50 basis points	Increased dollar liquidity through Fed swaps
May through August 2008				Raised policy rate 25 basis points

(continues on next page)

Table 3A.1 Timeline of central bank responses to the financial crisis *(continued)*

Date	United States	Japan	United Kingdom	Euro area
September through December 2008	Increased term liquidity to banks, supported commercial paper market, broadened collateral accepted, began outright purchases of agency securities, gave loans to AIG, Bank of America, and Citigroup, lowered policy rate 185 basis points and guided down future expectations	Increased term liquidity to banks, supported commercial paper market, provided dollar liquidity through Fed swaps, increased Japanese government bond purchases, lowered fee on security lending, lowered policy rate 40 basis points	Increased term liquidity to banks, provided dollar liquidity through Fed swaps, broadened collateral accepted, lowered policy rate 250 basis points	Increased term liquidity to banks, increased dollar liquidity through Fed swaps and provided Swiss franc liquidity through Swiss National Bank swaps, broadened collateral accepted, narrowed corridor between standing facilities, lowered policy rate 125 basis points
January through June 2009	Began purchasing longer-term Treasury securities and expanded purchases of agency securities, began to support the asset-backed securities market	Began outright purchases of commercial paper and short-term corporate bonds	Began purchasing longer-term gilts, corporate bonds, and commercial paper, suspended reserve targets, lowered policy rate 150 basis points	Offered unlimited term liquidity to banks, began purchasing covered bonds, lowered policy rate 150 basis points
July 2009 through April 2010	Wound down extraordinary liquidity facilities	Increased term and year-end liquidity to banks, broadened collateral accepted	Increased purchases of longer-term assets	
May through December 2010	Began to reinvest maturing longer-term assets, started a new program of purchases of longer-term bonds (QE2)	Reactivated currency swaps, increased credit facilities for financial institutions, reduced target for overnight rate to a range of 0 to 10 basis points, created fund to purchase long-term bonds, equity, and real estate	Reactivated currency swaps	Began purchases of longer-term government and private bonds, reactivated unlimited term liquidity to banks, reactivated currency swaps, relaxed credit rating thresholds for collateral

January through July 2011	August through December 2011	January through June 2012	July through December 2012
Raised policy rate 50 basis points	Made further purchases of covered and government bonds, expanded and extended term liquidity for banks, lowered pricing on Fed swaps, loosened collateral requirements, reduced required reserve ratio, lowered policy rate 50 basis points	Broadened eligible collateral	Reduced policy rate 25 basis points, announced new program of purchases of government bonds conditional on fiscal consolidation and structural reforms (not yet implemented)
	Made further long-term asset purchases, provided term dollar liquidity through Fed swaps, created a new contingency lending facility	Made further purchases of longer-term assets	Made further purchases of longer-term assets, began new program to encourage bank lending by targeted reduction in funding costs
Provided emergency lending in disaster areas, increased size of asset purchase fund	Increased asset purchase fund	Adopted an inflation goal of 1 percent, increased asset purchase fund, extended maximum maturity of bonds purchased to three years	Increased asset purchase fund
	Stated that policy rate is likely to remain near zero until mid-2013, began to extend average maturity of asset holdings, mortgage-backed securities redemptions to be reinvested in those securities	Stated that policy rate is likely to remain near zero at least until late 2014, adopted inflation goal of 2 percent, started to publish committee member expectations of future policy rate, extended program to increase maturity of assets	Began open-ended program of purchases of longer-term Treasury and mortgage-backed securities (QE3) until labor market improves substantially

Source: Based on the public record as documented in newspapers and on the websites of the four central banks and various issues of *OECD Economic Outlook.*

4

Why Did Asian Countries Fare Better during the Global Financial Crisis than during the Asian Financial Crisis?

DONGHYUN PARK, ARIEF RAMAYANDI, AND KWANHO SHIN

The global financial crisis that started in 2008 marked a momentous turning point in the global financial and economic landscape. In contrast to most crises, which originated in developing countries, the global crisis originated in the advanced economies. Its immediate origins lay in market failures in the US housing and financial markets. The crisis had a disproportionate impact on the advanced economies and less of an impact on developing countries.[1] More significantly, while the advanced economies still remain mired in stagnation and uncertainty, developing countries have largely shrugged off the effects of the crisis and are recovering with a healthy dose of certainty and momentum. The outbreak of the euro area sovereign debt crisis has further held back the stuttering recovery of the advanced economies.

From the viewpoint of developing Asia, the global crisis heralds a new era of diminished growth expectations. Despite the large and growing relative weight of developing countries in global output, advanced economies still exert an outsized influence on Asia's external environment. In particular, advanced economies continue to absorb a large share of the region's exports, especially final goods. The weakness of advanced economies is likely to persist beyond the short term in light of the wide range of structural problems they face. This has negative ramifications for Asia's growth prospects, since exports

Donghyun Park is principal economist at the Economics and Research Department of the Asian Development Bank. Arief Ramayandi is an economist at the Economics and Research Department of the Asian Development Bank. Kwanho Shin is professor of economics at Korea University. They thank Ilsoo Han and Aleli Rosario for their excellent research assistance and the Asian Development Bank for financial support.

1. See Blanchard, Faruqee, and Das (2010) for the relatively manageable impact of the global financial crisis across emerging-market economies. Morris Goldstein and Daniel Xie (2009) also find that for Asia the impact of the global financial crisis was less severe than that of the Asian crisis.

continue to be a major driver of growth for the region. In addition to a slower growth rate, Asian countries are likely to face greater external instability in the postcrisis period. The traditional bedrocks of global financial and economic stability—that is, the advanced economies—have increasingly become the sources of global instability since the crisis. The advanced economies are large enough to systematically matter, and they affect Asia and the rest of the world.

Notwithstanding its substantial adverse implications for Asia's medium-term growth prospects and global stability, the global crisis has had a relatively limited short-term impact on Asia and other developing countries. Indeed, Asia's surprising resilience is one of the most striking stylized facts about the global crisis. This is by no means to suggest that Asia was completely immune from the global crisis, even in the short run. In particular, the crisis left a tangible mark on the region's real economy, primarily through the trade channel. Asia's exports and growth plummeted in the fourth quarter of 2008 and first quarter of 2009 due to the severe recession in the advanced economies and the consequent collapse of global trade. However, massive fiscal and monetary stimulus enabled the region to mount a robust recovery. More fundamentally, the region was largely spared the financial turmoil and seizing up of credit markets that devastated the United States and the European Union. Contrary to widespread fears, Asia never suffered a financial crisis, although it did suffer a trade crisis that curtailed its growth.

However, the fact that Asia largely averted financial instability in the face of a full-blown global financial crisis is no cause for hubris or overconfidence. In fact, in 1997–98 Asia had suffered a devastating financial crisis of its own. That crisis brought the region's financial markets to their knees as stock markets and currencies collapsed. The crisis soon spread to the real sector, pushing the economy into a deep recession and putting millions of Asians out of work. Although the region staged a V-shaped recovery in 1999, the crisis was a game changer that put a rude stop to the vaunted "East Asian miracle."

The central objective of this chapter is to analyze and compare the macroeconomic performance of East Asian countries during the global financial crisis with their performance during the Asian financial crisis of 1997–98. East Asian countries fared much better during the global crisis than they did during the Asian crisis. East Asia's resilience in the face of the global crisis is all the more surprising in light of the sheer magnitude of the shock and the region's high level of integration into the world economy. From the region's perspective, the immediate catalyst of both crises was the sudden outflow of foreign capital. During the Asian crisis, the region suffered a massive reversal and withdrawal of capital inflows as investor confidence in the region evaporated. During the global crisis, US and European financial institutions withdrew their funds from Asia to support their badly damaged balance sheets at home. Yet, despite the common central role of foreign capital in both crises, the Asian crisis had a more markedly deep impact on East Asia than the global crisis. This chapter seeks to shed some light on why this is the case.

In the section that follows, we examine and compare the macroeconomic empirical stylized facts of the Asian and global financial crises. We then lay out the empirical framework used to perform a more in-depth comparative analysis of the two crises and discuss key findings from our analysis, before concluding with some final observations.

Macroeconomic Performance of Five Asian Countries: The Asian versus the Global Financial Crisis

This section examines the macroeconomic performance of Indonesia, the Republic of Korea, Malaysia, the Philippines, and Thailand during the Asian financial crisis and the global financial crisis. We selected those East Asian countries—referred to as the EA-5—because they were the most severely affected by the Asian crisis, which was triggered by the forced devaluation of the Thai baht in July 1997. The crisis spread like wildfire to Indonesia and the Republic of Korea, which suffered a similar collapse of their currencies. All three countries turned to the International Monetary Fund (IMF) for large bailout packages. Malaysia instead imposed capital controls, while the Philippines, which was not as severely affected as the other four countries, did not have to undergo similar extreme policy responses. Before we can meaningfully analyze and compare the causes and impacts of the two crises in the context of the five countries, we have to first understand the stylized facts of the crises in those countries. The next subsections look at the countries' aggregate performance during the two crises and then examine in more depth the behavior of some key macroeconomic indicators prior to each crisis. The aim is to seek possible descriptive explanations of the stylized facts.

Macroeconomic Performance of the EA-5 during the Two Crises: Stylized Facts

In this subsection, we examine the macroeconomic performance of the EA-5 as a whole. Figure 4.1 compares the behavior of some key macroeconomic indicators during the two crises. Panel A compares the average real GDP growth rate of the five countries before and after the Asian financial crisis and the global financial crisis. It is evident that the recession was much milder and the recovery much quicker during the global crisis. Depreciation of the exchange rate against the US dollar was also much smaller during the global crisis (panel B), with only Indonesia and the Republic of Korea suffering a currency crisis in 2008, according to Carmen Reinhart and Kenneth Rogoff's (2011) classification.

External demand was much stronger after the Asian crisis. While the five countries enjoyed an export boom after the Asian crisis, exports dropped sharply after the global crisis (panel C). This is intuitively plausible, since exports to the advanced economies, and in particular the United States, were the primary driver of Asia's V-shaped recovery in 1999. In contrast, during the global crisis

Figure 4.1 Key macroeconomic indicators around the two crises, East Asia-5 average

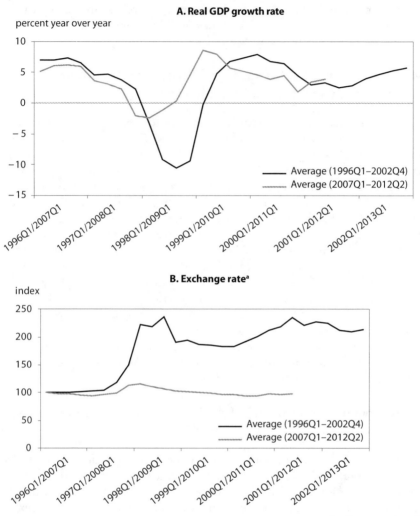

A. Real GDP growth rate

percent year over year

Average (1996Q1–2002Q4)
Average (2007Q1–2012Q2)

B. Exchange rate[a]

index

Average (1996Q1–2002Q4)
Average (2007Q1–2012Q2)

(continues on next page)

the advanced economies were the epicenters of the crisis and contributed to the collapse of global trade.

Investment fell after the Asian crisis but held up well after the global crisis (panel D). Fiscal policy moved in opposite directions during the two crises (panel E). While Asia witnessed strong fiscal expansion after the global crisis, deep fiscal contraction was the norm after the Asian crisis. On the basis of the IMF's policy prescriptions, during the Asian crisis the Asian countries pursued fiscal contraction, which deepened the recession. On the other hand, large fiscal stimulus programs quickly and decisively implemented by the Asian countries

C. Real export growth rate

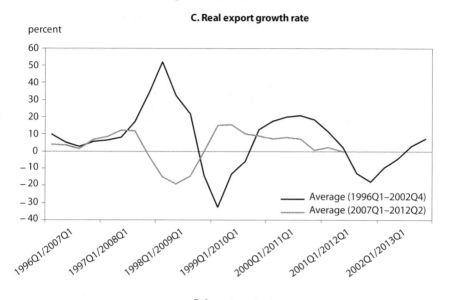

D. Investment rate

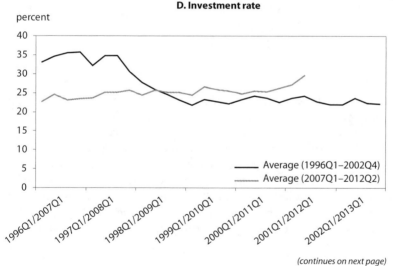

(continues on next page)

supported aggregate demand and laid the foundation for recovery. Taken together, panels D and E indicate that the five countries were in much better shape during the global crisis. In particular, domestic demand was stronger.

Finally, panel F suggests that monetary policy quickly turned expansionary during the 2008 crisis as central banks sought to support growth by providing liquidity for their financial systems. In contrast, during the Asian crisis, central banks raised interest rates. While higher interest rates were intended to stem

Figure 4.1 Key macroeconomic indicators around the two crises, East Asia-5 average *(continued)*

E. Growth rate of government expenditure

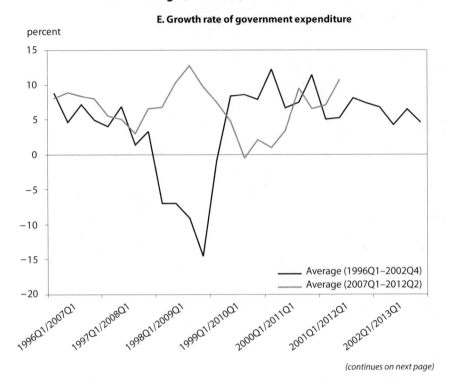

percent

Average (1996Q1–2002Q4)
Average (2007Q1–2012Q2)

(continues on next page)

capital outflows and restore the confidence of financial markets, they had an adverse impact on the real economy.[2]

Overall, internal structural problems contributed considerably to the outbreak of the Asian crisis and robust external demand helped the five countries export their way out of the crisis.[3] In contrast, the global crisis was largely an external crisis from the viewpoint of the five countries, which enjoyed relatively strong internal fundamentals in 2007–08.[4] Another important difference between the two crises was the stance of fiscal and monetary policy. Whereas both policies were clearly countercyclical during the global crisis, they amplified

---

2. The high interest rates during the Asian crisis were heavily criticized by, among others, Jason Furman and Joseph E. Stiglitz (1998) and Steven Radelet and Jeffrey Sachs (1998). More recently, Hangyong Lee and Changyong Rhee (2012) also emphasize that, during the global financial crisis, advanced economies did not use the prescriptions given to Asia in 1997.

3. We investigate internal structural problems during the Asian crisis in greater depth later in this chapter.

4. Dongchul Cho (2012) also emphasizes that the Republic of Korea managed to recover quickly thanks to relatively sound fundamentals achieved as a result of the restructuring process following the 1997–98 crisis.

F. Short-term interest rate

percent

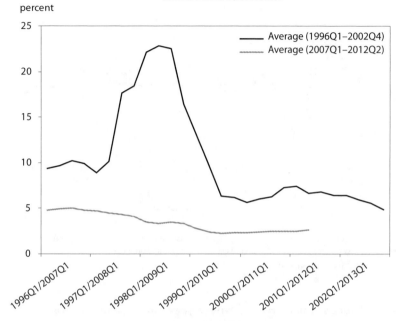

a. The exchange rate is the nominal exchange rate against the US dollar.

Note: East Asia-5 comprises Indonesia, the Republic of Korea, Malaysia, the Philippines, and Thailand.

Source: Authors' calculations based on data from IMF, *International Financial Statistics.*

the downturn during the Asian crisis. These issues are examined more rigorously later in this chapter. The next subsection, however, takes a closer look at the macroeconomic situation of the individual EA-5 countries in the years prior to the two crises.

Behavior of Key Macroeconomic Indicators Prior to Both Crises in the EA-5

In this subsection, we take a more in-depth look at the macroeconomic performance of the EA-5 by dissecting the performance of individual countries to seek possible explanations for their different reactions during the two crises. In the years leading up to both crises, output in the EA-5 countries outpaced their trend, opening up growing output gaps before output plunged during the crisis (shaded areas in figure 4.2). Although qualitatively similar, the output gaps prior to the global crisis are much smaller than those prior to the Asian crisis. Rapid growth prior to both crises pushed actual output far above its potential, creating macroeconomic imbalances and high inflationary pressures. Those imbalances were especially evident in the buildup to the Asian crisis.

Figure 4.2   Output deviation from trend in the five East Asian countries, 1994–2012

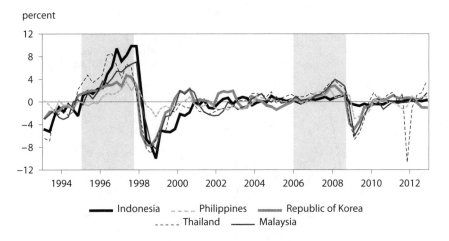

percent

Note: The gap is measured as the log difference between the seasonality adjusted quarterly output and its Hodrick-Prescott filtered trend. The shaded areas indicate a 3-year window prior to each crisis.

Source: Authors' calculations based on data from the CEIC.

Table 4.1   Average quarterly (year-over-year) inflation in the five East Asian countries, 1993–2012 (percent)

Year	Indonesia	Republic of Korea	Malaysia	Philippines	Thailand
1995–96	8.2	4.7	3.5	7.6	5.8
2006–07	9.7	2.4	2.8	4.2	3.5
Noncrisis years	7.9	3.5	2.4	5.4	3.3

Notes: "Noncrisis years" indicates the average quarterly inflation for 1993–2012, excluding the period of the Asian financial crisis (1997–99) and the global financial crisis (2008–09).

Source: Authors' calculations based on data from the CEIC.

Average inflation in the years leading up to the two crises was generally higher than the average of noncrisis years during the last two decades (table 4.1). Since aggregate demand pressures prior to the global crisis were much weaker than before the Asian crisis, the average inflation rate was lower.[5] In the

---

5. Indonesia appears to be an exception due to a jump in inflation as the government dramatically increased its domestically administered fuel prices in March and October 2005. Adjusting for the direct impact of this increase on the consumer price index inflation rate produces lower inflation figures for 2006, which are more consistent in reflecting the price movements that are due to demand pressures faced by the economy (Ramayandi and Rosario 2010). Average inflation for 2006-07 after adjusting for this direct impact of the domestic fuel price increase is much lower, at about 6.9 percent.

Figure 4.3 Share of investment in GDP in the five East Asian countries, 1994–2012

percent

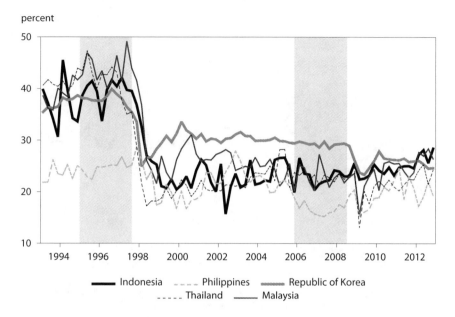

Note: The shaded areas indicate a 3-year window prior to each crisis.

Source: Authors' calculations based on data from the CEIC.

Republic of Korea and the Philippines, inflation prior to the global crisis was even lower than the noncrisis average, suggesting that it was not a major issue during this time.

The behavior of investment plays an important role in the EA-5's economic performance during the two crises. The share of investment in GDP prior to the Asian crisis was much higher than that prior to the global crisis (figure 4.3). This share dropped sharply during the Asian crisis and has not fully recovered since then. In turn, the lower share of investment reversed the saving-investment gap into positive territory, making room for lower interest rates after the Asian crisis.

The massive surge in investment prior to the Asian crisis was accompanied by high rates of imports that led to current account deficits despite the EA-5's export-led growth strategy. Figure 4.4 shows that the current account balance turned negative prior to the Asian crisis and turned positive afterward. The deficit widened in the period leading up to the Asian crisis, but narrowed somewhat in the period leading up to the global crisis. Rapid growth in exports, coupled with falling imports, reversed the current account balance of the EA-5 after the Asian crisis.

The exchange rate seems to play a significant role in explaining the different behavior of investment and the current account during the two

Figure 4.4   Current account balance as a share of GDP in the five East Asian countries, 1994–2012

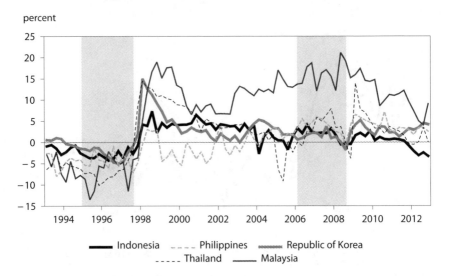

percent

Note: The current account includes the balance of trade in goods and services as well as the net foreign income and transfers. The shaded areas indicate a 3-year window prior to each crisis.

Source: Authors' calculations based on data from the CEIC.

crises. Prior to the Asian crisis, EA-5 exchange rates tended to be overvalued and their movements were limited. In 1997–98, the currencies went through a massive correction in all these countries. Indonesia and Thailand abandoned their heavily managed exchange rate regime and moved to a more flexible regime. Overvalued currencies had made imports cheaper to the EA-5 economies in the pre–Asian crisis years. Expectations of continuous appreciation of the exchange rate also lowered the cost of borrowing overseas, which further fueled a boom in investment that relied on external debt and imported capital goods. External debts grew rapidly, reaching their peak in 1998 (figure 4.5), mainly due to private and short-term external borrowing. As a result of very high investment rates, the current account balance turned negative despite healthy export performance.

The Asian crisis saw a sharp depreciation of currencies, which represented a massive correction of misaligned exchange rates. This made imports and loans from abroad much more expensive for the EA-5 countries. Exchange rate corrections initially overshot their new but much weaker equilibrium values. The Indonesian rupiah in terms of the US dollar was about four times weaker than in 1996. Other countries saw their currencies depreciate by more than 50 percent relative to the US dollar (figure 4.6). Following these large corrections, investments plunged and exports jumped as the EA-5 gained exchange rate competitiveness amid strong global demand. On the other hand, though

Figure 4.5 Total external debt relative to GDP in the five East Asian countries, 1992–2011

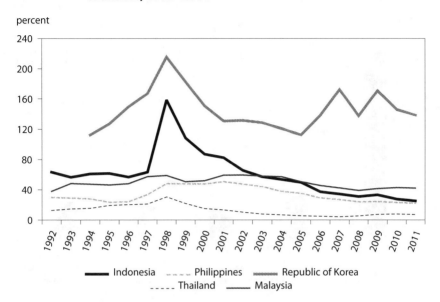

percent

Source: Authors' calculations based on data from the CEIC.

all countries except Thailand experienced currency depreciation between 2006 and 2008, the magnitude of the depreciation was muted relative to the Asian crisis.[6]

Haunted by the exchange rate collapse during the Asian crisis, the EA-5 countries have been building up international reserves despite more flexible exchange rate regimes. Partly helped by current account balance surpluses, gross international reserve holdings have accelerated rapidly since 2004 (figure 4.7). Ample international reserves provided the five countries with more ammunition to defend their currencies during the global crisis.

A more flexible regime adopted after the Asian crisis also limited pressures for exchange rate correction during the global crisis. To illustrate the point further, table 4.2 provides a measure akin to an exchange rate premium based on a residual from the uncovered interest parity condition. A negative value indicates that the maintained interest differential fell short of the actual currency depreciation and a positive value indicates the opposite. In other words, a negative value suggests that the domestic interest rate was too low to maintain the exchange rate value, and hence the country may have been prone to capital outflows. Except for the Philippines—the country least affected by

---

6. The only exception is the Republic of Korea, which experienced significant exchange rate depreciation after the global financial crisis.

Figure 4.6   Nominal exchange rate depreciation in the five East Asian countries, 1997–98 and 2008–09

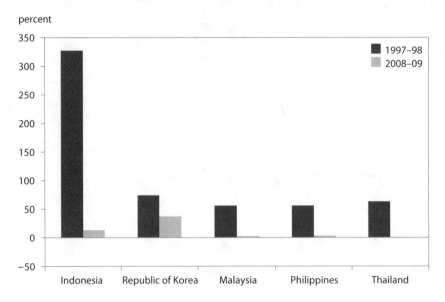

percent

Source: Authors' calculations based on data from the CEIC.

Figure 4.7   Gross international reserves in the five East Asian countries, 1992–2012

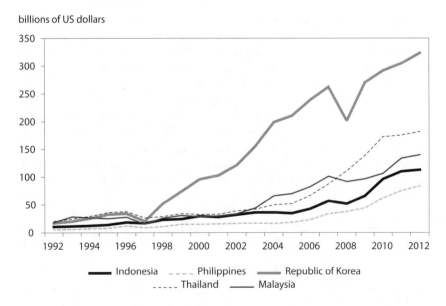

billions of US dollars

Source: Authors' calculations based on data from the CEIC.

Table 4.2   Residual from the interest parity condition, 1993–2012
          (percent)

Year	Indonesia	Republic of Korea	Malaysia	Philippines	Thailand
1995–96	−3.63	−3.6	−5.02	2.05	−7.03
2006–07	2.52	−7.21	3.19	11.68	5.69
Noncrisis years	4.52	3.56	0.83	8.82	0.49

Notes: The residuals are computed as the difference between the domestic-US short-term interest rate differential and a change in the one-year-lead actual domestic currency versus the US dollar exchange rate. A zero value indicates the fulfillment of the interest parity condition. A negative value suggests that the domestic interest rate is too low to match changes in the exchange rate, and vice versa. "Noncrisis years" indicates the average for 1993–2012, excluding the periods of the Asian financial crisis (1997–99) and the global financial crisis (2008–09).

Source: Authors' calculations based on data from the CEIC.

the Asian crisis—all EA-5 economies had a negative value prior to the crisis. As a result, these countries were prone to capital outflows during this time. Prior to the global crisis, the situation was reversed. Except for the Republic of Korea, other EA-5 countries had a positive value, and hence tended to attract capital inflows rather than outflows.

The condition faced by the domestic banking sector in the EA-5 also differs between the two crises. The growth of bank credit to the private sector around the global crisis episode is more in line with its trend relative to that around the Asian crisis. But does this imply more benign domestic financial imbalances during the global crisis? Claudio Borio and Philip Lowe (2002a, 2002b) argue that rapid cumulative growth in credit to the private sector and asset prices are often good leading indicators to gauge a buildup in domestic financial sector imbalances. Following their arguments, figure 4.8 examines domestic financial conditions of selected EA-5 countries.[7] The figure show the credit and asset price behavior around the Asian and global crises. All panels plot the percentage deviation (gap) of each of the indicators from their trend. Buildups of a positive gap in private sector credit prior to the Asian crisis were more obvious than those before the global crisis (panel A). In both cases, credit to the private sector continued to swell after the crisis started and tumbled at the peak impact of each crisis. The size of the gap, however, is somewhat smaller during the global crisis and was preceded by more stable credit conditions.

Increasing gaps in stock prices can also be seen prior to each crisis (panel B). Unlike credit, however, these buildups tumbled immediately once the crisis started. Although the sampled countries' real economies were hardly affected by the dot-com crisis in the early 2000s, a similar buildup in stock prices was also evident prior to the dot-com bust. This suggests that the swings in stock prices in these countries may be driven more by the global market situation and

---

7. The Philippines is excluded from figure 4.8 due to the unavailability of consistent time series data throughout the sample.

Figure 4.8   Credit and asset price behavior in four East Asian countries around the two crises, 1994–2012

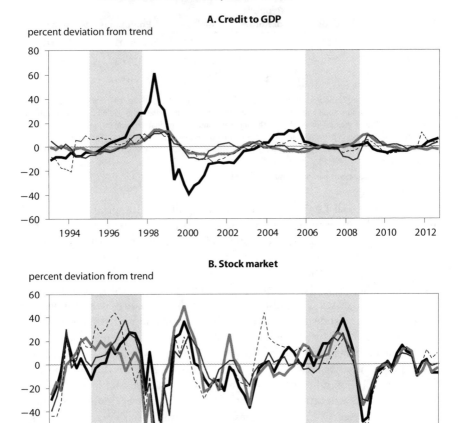

A. Credit to GDP

percent deviation from trend

B. Stock market

percent deviation from trend

———— Indonesia   ———— Republic of Korea   – – – – Thailand   ———— Malaysia

(continues on next page)

the sentiment of global investors. Unfortunately, data on property prices prior to the Asian crisis are available only for the Republic of Korea. Except for that country, however, there was no clear indication of property market stress in the other countries prior to the global crisis (panel C). This last panel supports the argument that the stress in the domestic financial sector in the run-up to the global crisis was much less than that in the run-up to the Asian crisis.

By extension, different pressures for exchange rate correction and different domestic financial sector conditions explain the situation that the EA-5 central banks faced during the two crises. Prior to the Asian crisis, there was practically

Figure 4.8   Credit and asset price behavior in four East Asian countries around the two crises, 1994–2012 *(continued)*

C. Property prices

percent deviation from trend

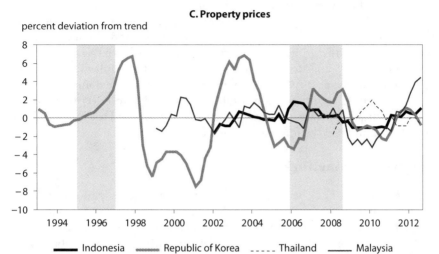

━━━ Indonesia   ▰▰▰ Republic of Korea   ----- Thailand   ━━ Malaysia

Note: Gaps are measured as a percentage deviation from the Hodrick-Prescott filtered trend. The shaded areas indicate a 3-year window prior to each crisis.

Sources: Panel A: Authors' calculations based on Bank for International Settlements (BIS) data. Panel B: Authors' calculations based on data from the CEIC. Panel C: Authors' calculations based on data from the central banks of Indonesia, Malaysia, and Thailand, and from the private sector for the Republic of Korea, as compiled by the BIS. All data were downloaded on June 6, 2013.

no scope for easing interest rates. In fact, higher interest rates were needed to stem capital outflows. This interest rate hike, however, had an adverse effect on the real economy. In contrast, prior to the global crisis, there was plenty of scope for lowering interest rates, which in turn helped boost aggregate demand. This difference offers an intuitive explanation for why interest rates behaved differently in the two crises. Monetary policy was well positioned for an expansion at the onset of the global crisis, while the opposite was true in the case of the Asian crisis.

Another major difference between the two crises was the reaction of fiscal policy. Fiscal consolidation became inevitable after the Asian crisis, when governments were forced to absorb contingent fiscal liabilities as they bailed out bankrupt firms. For example, a nationalization of major domestic banks in Indonesia reduced fiscal space and hence the scope for fiscal stimulus. Mounting external debts due to exchange rate depreciation also reduced the fiscal space available to the EA-5 governments. In contrast, the governments faced no such constraints during the global crisis. They were not forced to bail out bankrupt firms this time around. In addition, public debts were either declining or stable at relatively low shares of GDP in the EA-5 countries (Ferrarini and Ramayandi 2012). Under these conditions, the governments were equipped with enough fiscal space to decisively implement large fiscal stimulus programs. The stimulus helped to support aggregate demand and growth at a time when private demand and external demand were imploding.

In sum, the EA-5 economies were in completely different conditions prior to the two crises. A number of structural domestic problems lay at the heart of the regional financial crisis of 1997–98. On the other hand, domestic fundamentals were sound during the global crisis, which was thus largely an external crisis for the EA-5 countries. Structural reforms and more flexible exchange rate regimes in the post-Asian-crisis period strengthened the domestic fundamentals of those countries. As a result, they were able to effectively pursue countercyclical monetary and fiscal policy, which cushioned the impact of the global crisis and laid the foundation for recovery.

Empirical Framework

This section lays out the empirical framework we use to perform a more in-depth comparative econometric analysis of the Asian currency crisis and the global financial crisis. More specifically, using quarterly data from 1990Q1 to 2011Q4, we perform three exercises in order to identify factors contributing to the different responses of the five Asian countries to the two crises.

First, we run a panel probit regression on the likelihood of a crisis. By investigating the economic fundamentals that are responsible for a crisis, we examine whether Asian countries' fundamentals were sounder during the global crisis than during the Asian crisis. The crisis is defined as a currency crisis as identified by Reinhart and Rogoff (2011).[8]

Second, we identify economic factors determining the depth of a crisis and investigate what economic fundamentals are responsible for the less severe slowdown of Asian countries around the global financial crisis.

Third, we identify what economic fundamentals determine recovery from a crisis and analyze how Asian countries could rapidly recover from the global financial crisis.

How Can the Depth of a Crisis and Recovery from It Be Measured?

Figure 4.9 illustrates the measurement of the depth of a crisis and recovery from a crisis. Suppose that a crisis occurs at time T_1. The depth is measured by the fall in real GDP from a peak before a crisis (a local maximum) to a trough after the crisis (a local minimum). The peak is a local maximum level of real GDP between $T_1 - 4$ and $T_1 + 1$ quarters. In the figure, the maximum is attained at time T_0. The trough is a local minimum level of real GDP within three years (T_1 and $T_1 + 12$ quarters) after the crisis. The minimum is attained at time T_2. The depth of a crisis is defined as the difference between the local maximum

---

8. We also defined a crisis dummy that takes one if either a currency crisis or a banking crisis as identified by Reinhart and Rogoff occurred. The results are qualitatively very similar. Results are available upon request.

Figure 4.9   Graphical representation of depth of and recovery from a crisis

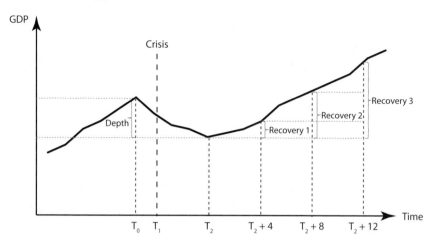

Notes: A crisis occurs at time T_1. The depth is a decrease in real GDP from a local maximum to a local minimum around the crisis. The local maximum is the maximum level of real GDP between $T_1 - 4$ and $T_1 + 1$ quarters. The local minimum is the minimum level of real GDP within three years (T_1 and $T_1 + 12$) after the crisis. In the figure, the local minimum is attained at time T_2. The depth of a crisis is defined as the difference between the local maximum and the local minimum. We also measure three recoveries: one-, two-, and three-year recoveries. One-year recovery is an increase in real GDP for one year after the minimum (Recovery 1). Two-year recovery is an increase in real GDP for two years after the minimum (Recovery 2). Three-year recovery is an increase in real GDP for three years after the minimum (Recovery 3).

Source: Authors' illustration.

and the local minimum. We also measure one-, two-, and three-year recoveries, as described in the figure.

How Do We Choose Explanatory Variables for a Crisis?

There are a number of economic variables considered in the early warning literature that signal a crisis. For purposes here, we consider economic variables that are identified to be most significant in recent studies. Pierre-Olivier Gourinchas and Maurice Obstfeld (2012, 226), based on a discrete-choice panel analysis using 1973–2010 data, found that "domestic credit expansion and real currency appreciation have been the most robust and significant predictors of financial crises, regardless of whether a country is emerging or advanced." By reviewing more than 80 papers, Jeffrey A. Frankel and George Saravelos (2010) find that foreign exchange reserves, the real exchange rate, and the growth rate of credit are the most frequent statistically significant indicators. The next most significant variables are GDP and the current account.

Based on the above two studies, we choose the following seven explanatory variables for probit analysis of a crisis: (1) foreign reserves/GDP, (2) five-year average of real exchange rate appreciation, (3) credit/GDP, (4) five-year average growth rate of real GDP, (5) current account/GDP, (6) five-year average

Table 4.3   Summary statistics: Full sample, 1990–2011

Variable	Observations	Mean	Standard deviation	Minimum	Maximum
Dummy for crisis	1,631	0.15	0.36	0	1
Foreign reserves/GDP	3,278	0.49	6.49	0	197.89
5-year real exchange rate depreciation	2,250	0	0.1	−1.42	0.97
5-year real GDP growth	2,944	0.02	0.04	−0.23	0.41
Credit/GDP	2,230	0.46	0.42	−0.16	3.29
Current account/GDP	3,082	−0.18	5.71	−164.57	105.41
5-year inflation rate	2,455	0.09	0.14	−0.05	1.72
Export share of GDP	3,082	0.4	0.26	0	2.35
Depth of crisis	135	0.08	0.07	0	0.27
1-year recovery	140	0.05	0.04	−0.03	0.15
2-year recovery	136	0.1	0.05	0.01	0.23
3-year recovery	129	0.13	0.07	−0.08	0.31
1-year money growth	303	0.2	0.28	−0.13	3.77
2-year money growth	286	0.2	0.21	−0.1	2.69
3-year money growth	267	0.2	0.17	−0.02	1.86
1-year interest rate difference	87	−3.5	7.82	−48.67	18.32
2-year interest rate difference	86	−3.59	8.22	−48.3	14.59
3-year interest rate difference	82	−3.85	8.41	−45.79	14.59
1-year government expenditure growth	146	0	0.14	−0.64	0.55
2-year government expenditure growth	143	0.02	0.1	−0.37	0.32
3-year government expenditure growth	135	0.02	0.08	−0.27	0.18

Source: See text for explanation.

of the inflation rate, and (7) export share of GDP. The summary statistics are reported in table 4.3 for the full 1990–2011 sample and in table 4.4 for the global crisis sample.

The real exchange rate is the real effective exchange rate against OECD countries where trade shares are used as weights. Following Gourinchas and Obstfeld (2012), domestic credit measured in domestic currency comes from the IMF's *International Financial Statistics*. Domestic credit is obtained by subtracting net claims on the central government (IFS line 32an) from total domestic claims of depository corporations (central banks and other deposi-

Table 4.4   Summary statistics: Global financial crisis

Variable	Observations	Mean	Standard deviation	Minimum	Maximum
Dummy for crisis	527	0.06	0.23	0	1
Foreign reserves/GDP	874	0.2	0.19	0	1.44
5-year real exchange rate depreciation	902	−0.02	0.11	−1.42	0.35
5-year real GDP growth	1,122	0.03	0.03	−0.09	0.18
Credit/GDP	626	0.64	0.52	0.03	3.29
Current account/GDP	808	−0.03	0.12	−0.5	0.48
5-year inflation rate	979	0.06	0.05	−0.04	0.58
Export share of GDP	794	0.44	0.28	0.01	2.3
Depth of crisis	22	0.06	0.04	0.01	0.16
1-year recovery	22	0.05	0.03	0.01	0.12
2-year recovery	19	0.09	0.05	0.01	0.23
3-year recovery	11	0.12	0.07	0.02	0.25
1-year money growth	62	0.15	0.11	−0.06	0.53
2-year money growth	45	0.14	0.09	−0.01	0.36
3-year money growth	26	0.15	0.07	0.02	0.33
1-year interest rate difference	21	−3.75	2.71	−10	2.07
2-year interest rate difference	20	−3.47	3.54	−15	0.68
3-year interest rate difference	16	−2.42	3.22	−11.5	0.62
1-year government expenditure growth	22	0.03	0.08	−0.13	0.26
2-year government expenditure growth	19	0.03	0.05	−0.07	0.15
3-year government expenditure growth	11	0.04	0.04	−0.01	0.12

Source: See text for explanation.

tory corporations, IFS line 32). Exceptions are as follows: Brazil (claims on the private sector and other financial corporations of other depository institutions, IFS lines 22d + 22g); Australia (claims on the private sector and other financial corporations of depository institutions, IFS lines 32d + 32g); and Argentina (claims on the private sector, IFS line 32d). The credit-to-GDP ratio is calculated by dividing domestic credit by nominal GDP in domestic currency. Export share of GDP is exports divided by GDP.

Table 4.5 Coefficients of bivariate regressions on each independent variable: Full sample

Variable	Dummy for currency crisis	Depth of crisis	1-year recovery	2-year recovery	3-year recovery
	(1)	(2)	(3)	(4)	(5)
Foreign reserves/GDP	−5.04***	−0.07	−0.02	−0.06	0.01
	(0.84)	(0.06)	(0.03)	(0.07)	(0.07)
5-year real exchange rate appreciation	1.93*	0.21	0.09	0.15	0.18
	(1.09)	(0.13)	(0.06)	(0.1)	(0.13)
Credit/GDP	−2.79	−0.05	−0.01	−0.04	−0.24
	(2.58)	(0.25)	(0.11)	(0.2)	(0.27)
5-year real GDP growth	2.04***	0.02	0.01	0.02	0.01
	(0.52)	(0.03)	(0.02)	(0.04)	(0.05)
Current account/GDP	−2.52***	−0.18	0.03	0.04	−0.01
	(0.92)	(0.13)	(0.07)	(0.12)	(0.16)
5-year inflation rate	2.76***	0.16***	0.06***	0.08***	0.10***
	(0.41)	(0.02)	(0.01)	(0.02)	(0.03)
Export share of GDP	−3.02***	−0.06	−0.04*	−0.03	−0.03
	(0.56)	(0.04)	(0.02)	(0.03)	(0.04)
Money growth		0.00	0.13***	0.17***	0.23***
		(0.01)	(0.02)	(0.03)	(0.04)
Interest rate changes		−0.00*	−0.07*	−0.18***	−0.18*
		(0.00)	(0.04)	(0.07)	(0.09)
Real government expenditure growth		−0.08***	0	0.14***	0.34***
		(0.03)	(0.02)	(0.04)	(0.07)

Notes: Column (1) is a panel probit estimation with random effects. All other columns are pooled ordinary least squares regressions. Depth and recoveries are defined only for countries that experienced a crisis between 1990 and 2011. *, **, and *** represent statistical significance at the 10, 5, and 1 percent level, respectively. Standard errors are in parentheses.

Source: Authors' calculations.

Empirical Results

This section reports and discusses key findings from our econometric comparative analysis. We look at the determinants of a crisis, the depth of a crisis, and recovery from a crisis.

Determinants of a Crisis

We report both bivariate (tables 4.5 and 4.6) and multivariate panel regression results (tables 4.7 to 4.11). First, we look at the bivariate results, reporting the results for panel probit regressions with random effects for the entire sample

Variable	Dummy for currency crisis	Depth of crisis	1-year recovery	2-year recovery	3-year recovery	Depth of crisis, 2008	1-year recovery, 2008	2-year recovery, 2008	3-year recovery, 2008
	(1)	(2)	(3)	(4)	(5)	(6)	(7)	(8)	(9)
Foreign reserves/GDP	-1.3	0.12	0.02	0.01	0.53*	0.08	0.12***	0.17***	0.16***
	(0.95)	(0.1)	(0.06)	(0.13)	(0.28)	(0.29)	(0.02)	(0.03)	(0.05)
5-year real exchange rate appreciation	5.25**	0.45	0.12	0.23	0.79	2.81*	-0.09	-0.18	-0.1
	(2.3)	(0.31)	(0.19)	(0.43)	(1.05)	(1.55)	(0.12)	(0.2)	(0.31)
Credit/GDP	15.14***	1.03**	0.33	0.84	3.75***	-0.18	-0.03	-0.19**	-0.14
	(4.51)	(0.41)	(0.27)	(0.54)	(0.88)	(0.38)	(0.02)	(0.09)	(0.16)
5-year real GDP growth	2.65**	0.05	-0.01	-0.23	0.14	0.17	0.76***	1.65***	3.12***
	(1.16)	(0.04)	(0.02)	(0.29)	(0.67)	(2.13)	(0.18)	(0.3)	(0.53)
Current account/GDP	-0.64	-0.05	0.06	0.23	0.56	0.05	0.13***	0.18***	0.41**
	(1.33)	(0.14)	(0.08)	(0.22)	(0.53)	(0.51)	(0.04)	(0.07)	(0.16)
5-year inflation rate	2.4	0.83***	0.28*	0.62*	1.79***	2.77	0.23	0.54*	1.01
	(2.36)	(0.22)	(0.16)	(0.33)	(0.5)	(1.85)	(0.17)	(0.32)	(0.71)
Export share of GDP	-1.93**	-0.11	-0.10*	-0.11	-0.05	0.02	0	0	0.01
	(0.84)	(0.1)	(0.06)	(0.13)	(0.28)	(0.17)	(0.01)	(0.02)	(0.03)
Money growth		0.13	0.08	0.23	1.60***	2.29	0.27***	0.52***	0.60*
		(0.1)	(0.06)	(0.17)	(0.59)	(3.18)	(0.08)	(0.17)	(0.36)
Interest rate changes		0.75**	-0.26	-0.64**	-0.01	-0.87**	0.33	0.22	-0.11
		(0.31)	(0.22)	(0.37)	(0.7)	(0.34)	(0.26)	(0.45)	(0.73)
Real government expenditure growth		0.09	0.1	0.75***	1.38***	-0.17	0.13**	0.58***	2.08***
		(0.17)	(0.07)	(0.21)	(0.45)	(0.12)	(0.06)	(0.17)	(0.38)

Notes: Column (1) is a panel probit estimation with random effects. All other columns are pooled ordinary least squares regressions. In columns (2) to (5), depth and recoveries are defined only for countries that actually experienced a crisis in 2008. In columns (6) to (9), depth and recoveries are defined for all countries assuming that they experienced a crisis in 2008. *, **, and *** represent statistical significance at the 10, 5, and 1 percent level, respectively. Standard errors are in parentheses.

Source: Authors' calculations.

in column (1) in table 4.5. The dependent variable is a crisis dummy. We use each variable one by one as an explanatory variable. All the dependent variables are one-year lagged to obtain precrisis values.

The first three variables are statistically significant at the 1 or 10 percent level, consistent with the previous literature. The more foreign reserves a country has, the less likely it will experience a crisis. The more the exchange rate appreciates before a crisis, the more likely a country will experience a crisis. The more domestic credit expands before a crisis, the more likely a country will experience a crisis. The second and third variables are closely related to capital inflows. A typical symptom of capital inflows is real exchange rate appreciation and domestic credit expansion. Except for the five-year real GDP growth rate, the other three remaining variables—the current account, inflation rate, and export share—are also statistically significant at the 1 percent level. The larger the current account surplus, the less likely a crisis. The higher the inflation rate, the more likely a crisis. Finally, the larger the export share, the less likely a crisis.

In order to see any difference in the causes of the global financial crisis, we restrict our sample in column (1) of table 4.6 to that crisis by setting the dependent variable to be a crisis dummy that takes the value of one if a currency crisis occurs between 2008 and 2011. We used the sample period of 2006–11. In this case, only four variables are significant: real exchange rate appreciation, domestic credit, real GDP growth rate, and export share of GDP. The results suggest that the impact of the global crisis seems to be more closely related to foreign capital inflows. Real exchange rate appreciation, a domestic credit boom, and real GDP typically surge follow foreign capital inflows.

Table 4.7 shows the results for panel probit regressions with random effects when all the explanatory variables are included together—i.e., multivariate analysis. The dependent variable is a crisis dummy that takes the value of one if a currency crisis occurs between 1990 and 2011. All explanatory variables are lagged by one year. The first three main explanatory variables are included in all columns. The remaining four variables are then included one by one. Finally in the last column, all the seven explanatory variables are included together. In this multivariate set-up, all the other variables are still significant except the real exchange rate appreciation, five-year real GDP growth rate, and current account.

Table 4.8 restricts the sample again to the global crisis and performs multivariate panel probit regressions where all the explanatory variables are included together. The dependent variable is a crisis dummy that takes the value of one if a currency crisis occurs between 2008 and 2011. We used the sample period of 2006–11. All explanatory variables are lagged by one year.

Now foreign reserves and the inflation rate are no longer significant. Instead, real exchange rate appreciation is highly significant at the 1 or 5 percent levels. The five-year real GDP growth rate and the current account are not significant. Again, the results in table 4.8 strongly suggest that the impact of the global crisis is closely related to foreign capital inflows. Real exchange

Table 4.7 Random effects panel probit regression for a currency crisis: Full sample

Variable	(1)	(2)	(3)	(4)	(5)	(6)
Foreign reserves/GDP	-3.94***	-4.12***	-3.69***	-2.46**	-3.24**	-2.21**
	(1.23)	(1.23)	(1.23)	(0.99)	(1.27)	(1.00)
5-year real exchange rate appreciation	1.42	2.07	1.4	1.06	1.19	1.93
	(1.32)	(1.42)	(1.33)	(1.26)	(1.34)	(1.39)
Credit/GDP	1.65***	1.58***	1.57**	1.96***	1.75***	1.96***
	(0.61)	(0.6)	(0.62)	(0.63)	(0.62)	(0.65)
5-year real GDP growth		0.45				2.73
		(4.02)				(3.88)
Current account/GDP			-0.64			0.39
			(1.4)			(1.24)
5-year inflation rate				2.43***		2.41***
				(0.49)		(0.5)
Export share of GDP					-1.28**	-0.89*
					(0.58)	(0.47)
Pseudo R²	0.05	0.05	0.05	0.09	0.06	0.11
Observations	610	600	597	610	604	581
Countries	91	90	88	91	86	82

Notes: The dependent variable is a crisis dummy that takes a value of one if a currency crisis occurs between 1990 and 2011. All the explanatory variables are lagged by one year. The estimation is based on a panel probit regression with random effects. *, **, and *** represent statistical significance at the 10, 5, and 1 percent level, respectively. Standard errors are in parentheses.

Source: Authors' calculations.

Table 4.8 Random effects panel probit regression for a currency crisis: Global financial crisis

Variable	(1)	(2)	(3)	(4)	(5)	(6)
Foreign reserves/GDP	-1.16	-2.13	-1.26	-1.31	-0.69	-2.12
	(1.56)	(1.75)	(1.57)	(1.56)	(1.52)	(1.92)
5-year real exchange rate appreciation	9.93***	7.93**	10.12***	8.49**	9.56***	7.45**
	(3.73)	(3.42)	(3.79)	(3.74)	(3.7)	(3.79)
Credit/GDP	2.39**	2.53**	2.51**	2.48**	2.45**	2.96**
	(1.13)	(1.15)	(1.17)	(1.12)	(1.14)	(1.29)
5-year real GDP growth		19.03**				22.29**
		(7.42)				(9.45)
Current account/GDP			0.93			2.04
			(2.07)			(2.22)
5-year inflation rate				4.47		-0.11
				(3.83)		(4.39)
Export share of GDP					-1.88*	-1.94*
					(1.11)	(1.18)
Pseudo R^2	0.11	0.16	0.11	0.12	0.14	0.2
Observations	286	286	283	286	280	277
Countries	90	90	87	90	85	82

Notes: The dependent variable is a crisis dummy that takes one if a currency crisis occurs in 2008 or afterwards. *, **, and *** represent statistical significance at the 10, 5, and 1 percent level, respectively. Standard errors are in parentheses.

Source: Authors' calculations.

rate appreciation, a domestic credit boom, and strong GDP growth are typically associated with a surge in foreign capital inflows. While only significant at the 10 percent level, the export share coefficient is negative.

Determinants of the Depth of a Crisis

First, we examine bivariate regression results for the depth of a crisis, which are reported in column (2) of table 4.5 for the entire sample and column (2) of table 4.6 for the global crisis sample. In addition to the same seven explanatory variables as in the probit equation, we incorporate monetary and fiscal policy measures. Monetary policy is measured by (1) M2 growth rate or (2) interest rate changes one year after the peak defined in figure 4.9. Fiscal expansion is measured by the growth rate of real government expenditures one year after the peak.

In table 4.5 (column 2), only the inflation rate and the two policy variables are significant at the 1 or 10 percent level. The higher the inflation rate before the crisis, the deeper the crisis. If the interest rate increases during the crisis, then the crisis becomes deeper. If the growth rate of real government expenditures increases, then the crisis becomes less deep.

In table 4.6 (column 2), credit/GDP is significant. Hence the larger the domestic credit expansion before a crisis, the deeper the crisis. While the coefficient of monetary policy measured by interest rate changes continues to be statistically significant, the coefficient of fiscal policy is no longer significant.

Column (6) of table 4.6 examines determinants of the depth of a crisis under the assumption that all countries experienced the global crisis in 2008. In other words, we calculated the depth of crises for all countries whether or not they are classified as crisis countries. In this case, the real exchange rate appreciation is significant; the greater the precrisis appreciation of the real exchange rate, the deeper the crisis. In addition, interest rate increases during the crisis deepen the crisis.

Multivariate regression results for the depth of the crisis are shown in table 4.9, which reports three cases. Columns (1) to (3) consider all the crises experienced between 1990 and 2011. Columns (4) to (6) restrict the sample to the countries that experienced a crisis in 2008. Finally, in columns (7) to (9), the dependent variable is the depth of the global crisis given that all countries are assumed to experience a crisis in 2008. The estimation is based on pooled ordinary least square regressions.

According to column (1), precrisis domestic credit expansion, the precrisis real GDP growth rate, and the precrisis inflation rate are positively related to the depth of crisis. Columns (2) and (3) suggest that government policies during the crisis also affect its depth. Consistent with the results in table 4.2, column (3) indicates that if the interest rate increases during the crisis, then the crisis becomes deeper. In addition, if the growth rate of real government expenditures increases, then the crisis becomes less deep.

Table 4.9 Determinants of depth of crisis

Variable	All crises (1)	All crises (2)	All crises (3)	Global financial crisis (4)	Global financial crisis (5)	Global financial crisis (6)	All countries in 2008 (7)	All countries in 2008 (8)	All countries in 2008 (9)
Foreign reserves/GDP	−0.01	0.02	−0.04	−0.21	−0.13	−0.19	0.24	0.01	−0.09
	(0.08)	(0.12)	(0.1)	(0.14)	(0.2)	(0.16)	(0.78)	(0.14)	(0.09)
5-year real exchange rate appreciation	0.02	0.15	0.15	0.23	−0.24	−0.27	3.77*	−0.19	−0.11
	(0.12)	(0.13)	(0.13)	(0.43)	(0.75)	(0.47)	(2.17)	(0.31)	(0.28)
Credit/GDP	0.09**	0.02	0.07	0.08**	0.06	0.05	−0.24	0.03	0.04
	(0.04)	(0.04)	(0.04)	(0.04)	(0.07)	(0.07)	(0.41)	(0.06)	(0.04)
5-year real GDP growth	0.93***	0.4	0.78**	0.49	0.7	0.42	−5.9	1.91***	1.32**
	(0.32)	(0.37)	(0.39)	(0.72)	(0.96)	(0.84)	(4.38)	(0.74)	(0.67)
Current account/GDP	0	0.05	−0.02	0.13	0.13	0	−0.1	−0.02	−0.03
	(0.15)	(0.17)	(0.18)	(0.19)	(0.27)	(0.28)	(0.9)	(0.16)	(0.13)
5-year inflation rate	0.20***	0.03	0.24***	1.35**	1.13	1.35**	3.81	−0.18	−0.11
	(0.03)	(0.06)	(0.04)	(0.56)	(0.86)	(0.62)	(2.92)	(0.46)	(0.43)
Export share of GDP	0	−0.01	0	0.1	0.09	0.13	0.26	0.01	0.04
	(0.04)	(0.05)	(0.05)	(0.16)	(0.25)	(0.18)	(0.39)	(0.07)	(0.05)
Money growth		0.15***			0.08			0.16	
		(0.05)			(0.21)			(0.14)	
Interest rate changes			0.15**			0.29			0.31*
			(0.06)			(0.64)			(0.18)
Real government expenditure growth		−0.11	−0.14**		0.12	0.15		−0.14	−0.02
		(0.08)	(0.07)		(0.24)	(0.18)		(0.15)	(0.13)
Adjusted R²	0.433	0.3	0.465	0.473	0.119	0.395	−0.011	0.278	0.329
Observations	66	44	55	16	14	16	54	28	35

Notes: The dependent variable is depth of crisis. All the explanatory variables are values one year before the crisis. Column (1) includes all crises experienced between 1990 and 2011. Column (2) includes only the global crisis in 2008 and afterwards. For column (3), the dependent variable is depth of the global financial crisis given that all countries are assumed to experience a crisis in 2008. The estimation is based on a pooled ordinary least square regression. *, **, and *** represent statistical significance at

However, for the global crisis, as shown in columns (4) to (6), the precrisis real GDP growth and government policy variables are no longer significant. In columns (7) to (9), when we assume that all the countries experienced a crisis in 2008, only real exchange rate appreciation, the real GDP growth rate, and interest increases are significant.

Overall, the depth of a crisis is determined by both economic fundamentals and policy variables. The findings thus suggest that unsound fundamentals such as excessive credit expansion and high inflation rates, as well as policy mistakes, might have been responsible for the severe recession inflicted upon Asian countries in 1997.

Determinants of Recovery from a Crisis

First, we examine bivariate regression results in tables 4.5 and 4.6. We also consider two policy variables as additional explanatory variables. Monetary policy is measured by the (1) M2 growth rate or (2) interest rate changes during the period for which each recovery is measured. For example, we used the one-year M2 growth rate for the one-year recovery equation, the two-year M2 growth rate for the two-year recovery equation, and so on. Fiscal expansion is measured by the growth rate of real government expenditure during each recovery period. Again, we used the one-year growth rate of real government expenditure for the one-year recovery equation, the two-year growth rate for the two-year recovery equation, and so on.

We consider the entire sample in columns (3), (4), and (5) in table 4.5 for one-, two-, and three-year recoveries. For recovery, policy variables are much more significant.[9] The higher the money growth rate (or the lower the interest rate level), or the higher the growth rate of real government expenditures, the faster the recovery. In addition, the inflation rate and sometimes the export share are significant.

We consider the recovery from the global crisis in columns (3), (4), and (5) in table 4.6 for one-, two-, and three-year recoveries. Again, policy variables are quite significant.

In columns (7), (8), and (9) in table 4.6, assuming that all countries experienced a crisis in 2008, we consider the recovery of all countries in 2008. Policy variables continue to be significant. Interestingly, other economic variables are also significant. For example, higher foreign reserves, a higher real GDP grow rate, and a current account surplus lead to faster recovery. These results suggest that Asian countries' quick and robust recovery from the 2008 crisis may have been due to their sounder fundamentals as well as better policies.

Next, we examine the results when we use multivariate regressions in tables 4.10 to 4.13. Table 4.10 considers all recoveries from crises between 1990 and 2011; table 4.11 restricts the sample to the countries that experienced a

---

9. Yong Chul Park and Jong Wha Lee (2003) also emphasize that expansionary macroeconomic policies were critical for Asian countries after the Asian financial crisis.

Table 4.10   Determinants of recoveries from crisis: Full sample

Variable	1-year recovery			
	(1)	(2)	(3)	(4)
Money growth	0.12***		0.13***	
	(0.02)		(0.02)	
Interest rate changes		−0.06		−0.06
		(0.04)		(0.04)
Real government expenditure growth	−0.01	−0.04	−0.01	−0.06
	(0.04)	(0.04)	(0.04)	(0.04)
Real GDP			0	−0.01
			(0.01)	(0.00)
Export share of GDP			0.02	0.05***
			(0.02)	(0.02)
Adjusted R^2	0.414	0.024	0.401	0.119
Observations	75	72	75	72

	2-year recovery			
	(5)	(6)	(7)	(8)
Money growth	0.17***		0.18***	
	(0.03)		(0.03)	
Interest rate changes		−0.19***		−0.19***
		(0.07)		(0.07)
Real government expenditure growth	0.15	0.33***	0.14	0.26**
	(0.11)	(0.12)	(0.12)	(0.12)
Real GDP			0	0
			(0.01)	(0.01)
Export share of GDP			0.04	0.08**
			(0.04)	(0.03)
Adjusted R^2	0.327	0.161	0.324	0.204
Observations	73	70	73	70

(continues on next page)

crisis in 2008; and table 4.12 considers the recovery of all countries in 2008 under the assumption that all countries experienced a crisis in 2008.

Table 4.10 reports determinants of recovery from crises in a multivariate setup for the entire sample. The dependent variable is one-year recovery (columns 1 to 4), two-year recovery (columns 5 to 8), and three-year recovery (columns 9 to 12) from crises between 1990 and 2011—i.e., the entire sample. We found earlier in a bivariate setup in tables 4.5 and 4.6 that policy variables are mainly responsible for recovery. Therefore, we use our two policy variables as the main explanatory variables. We use the money growth rate as a proxy for monetary expansion in columns (1) and (3) and interest rate increases in

Table 4.10   Determinants of recoveries from crisis: Full sample
                 (continued)

| | 3-year recovery | | | |
	(9)	(10)	(11)	(12)
Money growth	0.18***		0.19***	
	(0.04)		(0.04)	
Interest rate changes		−0.18*		−0.18**
		(0.09)		(0.09)
Real government expenditure growth	0.62***	0.43**	0.66***	0.22
	(0.16)	(0.19)	(0.17)	(0.2)
Real GDP			0.01	−0.01
			(0.01)	(0.01)
Export share of GDP			0.01	0.11**
			(0.05)	(0.04)
Adjusted R²	0.412	0.098	0.404	0.171
Observations	65	62	65	62

Notes: The dependent variable is 1-year recovery (columns 1 to 4), 2-year recovery (columns 5 to 8), and 3-year recovery (columns 9 to 12) from crises between 1990 and 2011. The estimation is based on a pooled ordinary least squares regression. *, **, and *** represent statistical significance at the 10, 5, and 1 percent level, respectively. Standard errors are in parentheses.

Source: Authors' calculations.

columns (2) and (4). In columns (3) and (4) we add additional control variables: per capita real GDP and export share of GDP. We repeat the same estimation for a two-year recovery in columns (5) to (8) and for a three-year recovery in columns (9) to (12). Generally, money growth is highly significant. If we use interest rate changes, it always has the right sign and is significant for two- and three-year recoveries. The growth rate of real government expenditures is also generally significant for two- and three-year recoveries. There is some evidence that the recovery is faster when the export share is higher.

Table 4.11 reports determinants of recovery from the global crisis by restricting the sample to the countries that experienced a crisis in 2008. When we compare the results in table 4.11 with those in table 4.10, the money growth rate is less significant, while real government expenditure is more significant.[10] For example, the money growth rate is significant only for the three-year recovery in table 4.11. On the other hand, the growth rate of real government expenditure is always significant for any specification for the two-year recovery. The evidence that the recovery is fast when the export share is higher is much weaker. This is intuitively plausible because global trade collapsed during the

---

10. IMF (2009, chapter 3) also found that while countercyclical monetary policy can help shorten recessions, its effectiveness is limited in financial crises. By contrast, the IMF argued that expansionary fiscal policy is particularly effective in shortening recessions associated with financial crises and in boosting recoveries.

Table 4.11   Determinants of recoveries from crisis: Global financial crisis

Variable	1-year recovery			
	(1)	(2)	(3)	(4)
Money growth	0.08		0.05	
	(0.06)		(0.07)	
Interest rate changes		−0.32		−0.37
		(0.21)		(0.22)
Real government expenditure growth	0.06	0.12*	0.11	0.05
	(0.09)	(0.07)	(0.12)	(0.09)
Real GDP			0.02	−0.01
			(0.02)	(0.01)
Export share of GDP			−0.12	−0.03
			(0.09)	(0.06)
Adjusted R²	−0.008	0.116	−0.031	0.135
Observations	17	21	17	21

	2-year recovery			
	(5)	(6)	(7)	(8)
Money growth	0.17		0.13	
	(0.15)		(0.19)	
Interest rate changes		−0.56**		−0.60**
		(0.28)		(0.3)
Real government expenditure growth	0.77**	0.72***	0.89**	0.57**
	(0.31)	(0.2)	(0.42)	(0.28)
Real GDP			0.02	−0.02
			(0.03)	(0.02)
Export share of GDP			−0.09	0.03
			(0.18)	(0.1)
Adjusted R²	0.317	0.479	0.206	0.435
Observations	15	19	15	19

(continues on next page)

global crisis. As a result, in contrast to the Asian crisis, Asian countries could not export their way out of the recession.

Finally, we examine recovery for every country under the assumption that all countries experienced a crisis in 2008, and report the determinants of recovery in tables 4.12 and 4.13. Compared with the results in table 4.11, we find that the money growth rate is much more significant, while the evidence for interest rate changes is much weaker. The evidence for fiscal policy continues to be highly significant. There is some evidence that the recovery is faster when the export share is higher.

Table 4.11 Determinants of recoveries from crisis: Global financial crisis *(continued)*

	3-year recovery			
	(9)	**(10)**	**(11)**	**(12)**
Money growth	1.44**		2.33***	
	(0.62)		(0.38)	
Interest rate changes		−0.35		−0.58
		(0.52)		(0.61)
Real government expenditure growth	0.64	1.45***	2.85***	1.18
	(0.69)	(0.48)	(0.73)	(1.25)
Real GDP			0.11***	−0.02
			(0.03)	(0.05)
Export share of GDP			0.24*	0.19
			(0.13)	(0.24)
Adjusted R²	0.502	0.418	0.882	0.324
Observations	7	11	7	11

Notes: The dependent variable is 1-year recovery (columns 1 to 4), 2-year recovery (columns 5 to 8), and 3-year recovery (columns 9 to 12) from the global financial crisis. The estimation is based on a pooled ordinary least squares regression. *, **, and *** represent statistical significance at the 10, 5, and 1 percent level, respectively. Standard errors are in parentheses.

Source: Authors' calculations.

Summary of Findings and Their Implications for the Five Asian Countries

A number of interesting and significant results emerge from the econometric analysis. Some of the most salient findings are the following:

- All seven explanatory variables are statistically quite significant as early indicators of a crisis.

- For the global crisis, only four variables—real exchange rate appreciation, domestic credit expansion, the real GDP growth rate, and the export share of GDP—are significant. This suggests that the impact of the global crisis seems to be more closely related to capital inflows.

- In general, a crisis is deeper if the precrisis inflation rate is higher, precrisis domestic credit expansion is larger, the precrisis real GDP growth rate is higher, the interest rate increases during the crisis, and/or the growth rate of real government expenditures decreases during the crisis.

- For the global crisis, besides the policy variables, higher credit expansion, higher real exchange rate appreciation before a crisis, and a higher precrisis real GDP growth rate make the recession deeper.

- In general, policy variables such as monetary and fiscal expansions are quite significant in explaining quick recovery from a crisis. There is some evidence that the recovery is faster when the export share is higher.

Table 4.12 Determinants of recoveries from the global financial crisis: All countries

Variable	1-year recovery			
	(1)	**(2)**	**(3)**	**(4)**
Money growth	0.25***		0.22***	
	(0.08)		(0.08)	
Interest rate changes		0.07		−0.06
		(0.25)		(0.2)
Real government expenditure growth	0.04	0.15**	−0.04	0.04
	(0.09)	(0.07)	(0.08)	(0.06)
Real GDP			0	−0.02**
			(0.01)	(0.01)
Export share of GDP			0.02	0.02
			(0.02)	(0.01)
Adjusted R²	0.16	0.074	0.208	0.13
Observations	37	45	36	44

	2-year recovery			
	(5)	**(6)**	**(7)**	**(8)**
Money growth	0.49***		0.49***	
	(0.19)		(0.15)	
Interest rate changes		0.23		−0.06
		(0.41)		(0.27)
Real government expenditure growth	0.46**	0.66***	0.13	0.25*
	(0.23)	(0.19)	(0.16)	(0.13)
Real GDP			0	−0.03***
			(0.01)	(0.01)
Export share of GDP			0.03	0.04*
			(0.02)	(0.02)
Adjusted R²	0.233	0.193	0.292	0.325
Observations	34	43	33	42

(continues on next page)

- For the global crisis, policy variables continue to be significant in explaining the fast recovery. We also found some evidence that higher foreign reserves, a higher real GDP grow rate, and a current account surplus led to a faster recovery.

Table 4.14 compares the average values of seven fundamental economic variables and policy variables for the five countries in the Asian crisis versus the global crisis. It shows that the fundamentals were much stronger during the global crisis than during the Asian crisis in the sense that the ratio of foreign

Table 4.12   Determinants of recoveries from the global financial crisis: All countries *(continued)*

	3-year recovery			
	(9)	**(10)**	**(11)**	**(12)**
Money growth	−0.25		0.15	
	(0.64)		(0.59)	
Interest rate changes		−0.72		−0.51*
		(0.5)		(0.3)
Real government expenditure growth	2.48***	2.28***	0.94	1.22***
	(0.76)	(0.41)	(0.84)	(0.46)
Real GDP			0.01	0
			(0.04)	(0.02)
Export share of GDP			0.02	0.04*
			(0.04)	(0.02)
Adjusted R^2	0.434	0.561	−0.053	0.49
Observations	18	24	17	23

Notes: The dependent variable is 1-year recovery (columns 1 to 4), 2-year recovery (columns 5 to 8), and 3-year recovery (columns 9 to 12) from the global financial crisis. We assume that all countries experienced a crisis in 2008. The estimation is based on a pooled ordinary least squares regression. *, **, and *** represent statistical significance at the 10, 5, and 1 percent level, respectively. Standard errors are in parentheses.

Source: Authors' calculations.

reserves to GDP was higher, precrisis real exchange rate appreciation was lower, credit expansion was lower, the current account surplus was larger, the precrisis inflation rate was lower, and the export share was larger. This helps to explain why Asian countries responded better to the shocks during the more recent global crisis. Policy variables were more appropriate for reviving aggregate demand and growth, and the interest rate fell and real government expenditure rose after the 2008 crisis. Monetary and fiscal policy thus reduced the severity of the recession and laid the foundation for recovery. Recovery was faster and more robust as a result of aggressive fiscal expansion, particularly in the first year (as shown in the fourth line from the bottom of table 4.14). This was possible because the Asian countries were in a healthy budget situation.

Concluding Observations

Asia fared much better during the global financial crisis than during the Asian financial crisis. The central question this chapter has tried to address is why. There is a limit to the usefulness of such a comparative analysis because no two crises are completely alike and each crisis has its own unique set of underlying causes. Given the uniqueness of each crisis, an exhaustive comparative analysis is not feasible and cannot be comprehensive. Nevertheless, it is possible to meaningfully analyze and compare the performance of the East Asian coun-

Table 4.13   Determinants of recoveries from the global financial crisis: All countries, additional specifications

Variable	1-year recovery			
	(1)	**(2)**	**(3)**	**(4)**
Money growth	0.21***		0.20***	
	(0.06)		(0.07)	
Interest rate changes		−0.13		−0.28
		(0.2)		(0.2)
Real government expenditure growth	−0.04	0.07	−0.04	−0.02
	(0.07)	(0.05)	(0.08)	(0.06)
Real GDP			0	−0.02**
			(0.01)	(0.01)
Export share of GDP			−0.01	−0.01
			(0.02)	(0.02)
Foreign reserves/GDP	0.06**	0.07**	0.08*	0.06
	(0.03)	(0.03)	(0.04)	(0.05)
Current account/GDP	0.07	0.08	0.07	0.12**
	(0.05)	(0.05)	(0.06)	(0.05)
Adjusted R^2	0.374	0.172	0.34	0.249
Observations	36	44	36	44

	2-year recovery			
	(5)	**(6)**	**(7)**	**(8)**
Money growth	0.44***		0.43***	
	(0.11)		(0.14)	
Interest rate changes		0.04		−0.18
		(0.3)		(0.29)
Real government expenditure growth	0.05	0.30*	0.05	0.15
	(0.16)	(0.15)	(0.16)	(0.16)
Real GDP			0	−0.03***
			(0.01)	(0.01)
Export share of GDP			0	0.03
			(0.03)	(0.04)
Foreign reserves/GDP	0.08	0.11**	0.08	0.02
	(0.05)	(0.05)	(0.07)	(0.08)
Current account/GDP	0.12	0.03	0.12	0.11
	(0.09)	(0.09)	(0.09)	(0.09)
Adjusted R^2	0.404	0.172	0.359	0.316
Observations	33	42	33	42

(continues on next page)

Table 4.13   Determinants of recoveries from the global financial crisis: All countries, additional specifications (*continued*)

	3-year recovery			
	(9)	**(10)**	**(11)**	**(12)**
Money growth	0.17		0.28	
	(0.41)		(0.5)	
Interest rate changes		−0.59**		−0.75**
		(0.27)		(0.32)
Real government expenditure growth	0.63	1.18***	0.67	0.66
	(0.58)	(0.25)	(0.88)	(0.54)
Real GDP			0.01	−0.02
			(0.04)	(0.02)
Export share of GDP			−0.06	−0.03
			(0.05)	(0.06)
Foreign reserves/GDP	0.08	0.08	0.16	0.12
	(0.1)	(0.06)	(0.14)	(0.13)
Current account/GDP	0.26	0.18	0.24	0.33
	(0.29)	(0.15)	(0.35)	(0.2)
Adjusted R^2	0.279	0.547	0.245	0.527
Observations	17	23	17	23

Notes: The dependent variable is 1-year recovery (columns 1 to 4), 2-year recovery (columns 5 to 8), and 3-year recovery (columns 9 to 12) from the global financial crisis. We assume that all countries experienced a crisis in 2008. The estimation is based on a pooled ordinary least squares regression. *, **, and *** represent statistical significance at the 10, 5, and 1 percent level, respectively. Standard errors are in parentheses.

Source: Authors' calculations.

tries during the global crisis and the Asian crisis by limiting the analysis to a common set of factors that play a major role in explaining any crisis. This was the analytical approach adopted in this chapter. While the empirical approach cannot address all dimensions of the countries' performances during the two crises, it does help to shed light on perhaps the most significant dimensions for which a comparison is feasible.

Overall, the empirical analysis yields a number of important and interesting findings. First, economic fundamentals exert a significant influence on the likelihood of crisis. Foreign exchange reserves, real exchange rate appreciation, domestic credit, precrisis real GDP growth, the current account, inflation, and export shares all help to explain the likelihood of a crisis. Second, economic fundamentals significantly affect the depth of a crisis. The fundamentals that seem to matter the most are the inflation rate, domestic credit expansion, and the precrisis GDP growth rate. Third, the policy stance during the crisis matters. While monetary and fiscal tightening have an adverse impact, countercyclical expansionary monetary and fiscal policy can mitigate the impact of a crisis and

Table 4.14 Average values of economic variables for the five Asian countries around the two crises

Variable		Asian financial crisis	Global financial crisis
Crisis	Foreign reserves/GDP	0.12	0.26
	Five-year real exchange rate appreciation	0.02	0.01
	Credit/GDP[a]	0.37	–0.1
	5-year real GDP growth	0.05	0.04
	Current account/GDP	–0.03	0.04
	5-year inflation rate	0.06	0.04
	Export share of GDP	0.5	0.59
Depth	Money growth	0.24	0.09
	Interest rate difference	0.29	–1.94
	Real government expenditure growth	–0.13	0.05
Recovery	1- year money growth	0.12	0.11
	2-year money growth	0.1	0.1
	3-year money growth	0.09	0.1
	1-year interest rate difference	–5.18	–1.18
	2-year interest rate difference	–5.34	–1.35
	3-year interest rate difference	–4.42	–0.76
	1-year real government expenditure growth	0.07	0.12
	2-year real government expenditure growth	0.08	0.05
	3-year real government expenditure growth	0.08	0.05
	Per capita real GDP	8.71	8.93

a. Detrended value.

Source: Authors' calculations.

contribute to a more robust recovery. To sum up, the evidence strongly suggests that economic fundamentals and macroeconomic policy matter a lot in staving off a crisis, cushioning its blow, and laying the foundation for recovery.

The overarching policy implication for Asian policymakers is to do more of the same—pursue the sound policies and robust fundamentals that have served the region well in the past. Asia's fundamentals have strengthened further as a consequence of the painful lessons learned during the Asian crisis. Asia's healthy current account balances and foreign exchange reserve levels are a response to the severe shortage of US dollar liquidity, which crippled the region during the Asian crisis. Other fundamentals have also improved since the Asian crisis. Furthermore, the expansionary stance of both fiscal and monetary policy during the global crisis was far more appropriate than the contractionary stance during the Asian crisis. So the central answer to the central question is that Asia fared much better during the global crisis due to stronger fundamentals and better macroeconomic policies.

References

Blanchard, Olivier, Hamid Faruqee, and Mitali Das. 2010. The Initial Impact of the Crisis on Emerging Market Countries. *Brookings Papers on Economic Activity* (Spring): 263–307. Washington, DC: Brookings Institution.

Borio, Claudio, and Philip Lowe. 2002a. *Asset Prices, Financial and Monetary Stability: Exploring the Nexus.* BIS Working Paper 114 (July). Basel: Bank for International Settlements.

Borio, Claudio, and Philip Lowe. 2002b. Assessing the Risk of Banking Crises. *BIS Quarterly Review* (December). Basel: Bank for International Settlements.

Cho, Dongchul. 2012. Responses of the Korean Economy to the Global Crisis: Another Currency Crisis? In *Global Economic Crisis: Impacts, Transmission, and Recovery,* ed. Maurice Obstfeld, Dongchul Cho, and Andrew Mason. Cheltenham, UK: Edward Elgar.

Ferrarini, Benno, and Arief Ramayandi. 2012. Public Debt Sustainability Assessments for Developing Asia. In *Public Debt Sustainability in Developing Asia,* ed. Benno Ferrarini, Raghbendra Jha, and Arief Ramayandi. London: Routledge.

Frankel, Jeffrey A., and George Saravelos. 2010. *Are Leading Indicators of Financial Crises Useful for Assessing Country Vulnerability? Evidence from the 2008-09 Global Crisis.* NBER Working Paper 16047. Cambridge, MA: National Bureau of Economic Research.

Furman, J., and J. E. Stiglitz. 1998. Economic Crises: Evidence and Insights from East Asia. *Brookings Papers on Economic Activity* 2: 1–135. Washington, DC: Brookings Institution.

Goldstein, Morris, and Daniel Xie. 2009. *The Impact of the Financial Crisis on Emerging Asia.* Working Paper 09-11. Washington, DC: Peterson Institute for International Economics.

Gourinchas, Pierre-Olivier, and Maurice Obstfeld. 2012. Stories of the Twentieth Century for the Twenty-First. *American Economic Journal: Macroeconomics* 4 (January): 226–65.

IMF (International Monetary Fund). 2009. *World Economic Outlook* (April). Washington, DC. Available at www.imf.org/external/pubs/ft/weo/2009/01/pdf/c3.pdf (accessed on July 1, 2013).

Lee, Hangyong, and Changyong Rhee. 2012. Lessons from the 1997 and the 2008 Crises in Korea. *Asian Economic Policy Review* 7, no. 1: 47–64.

Park, Yong Chul, and Jong Wha Lee. 2003. Recovery and Sustainability in East Asia. In *Managing Currency Crises in Emerging Markets,* ed. Michael P. Dooley and Jeffrey A. Frankel. Chicago: University of Chicago Press.

Radelet, S., and J. D. Sachs. 1998. The East Asian Financial Crisis: Diagnosis, Remedies, Prospects. *Brookings Papers on Economic Activity* 1: 1–74. Washington, DC: Brookings Institution.

Ramayandi, Arief, and Aleli Rosario. 2010. *Monetary Policy Discipline and Macroeconomic Performance: The Case of Indonesia.* ADB Economics Working Paper 238. Manila: Asian Development Bank.

Reinhart, Carmen M., and Kenneth S. Rogoff. 2011. From Financial Crash to Debt Crisis. *American Economic Review* 101, no. 5: 1676–706.

5

Policy Advice and Actions during the Asian and Global Financial Crises

SIMON JOHNSON AND JAMES KWAK

It is certain that a healthy financial system cannot be built on the expectation of bailouts.
—US Treasury Secretary Lawrence Summers, January 2000

For at least a decade, few people thought that the "emerging-market" crises of 1997-98 had something to teach the United States, the world's richest economy and flagship democracy. The differences between Indonesia or the Republic of Korea and the United States are obvious: income level, financial system, political track record, and so on.

US policymakers did draw a number of important lessons from those emerging-market crises—for other emerging markets. Treasury Secretary Lawrence Summers outlined the main points in a high-profile lecture at the 2000 conference of the American Economic Association. Financial crises were the result of fundamental policy weaknesses: "Bank runs or their international analogues are not driven by sunspots: Their likelihood is driven and determined by the extent of fundamental weaknesses." It was more important to look at the soundness of the financial system than to simply count the total amount of debt: "When well-capitalized and supervised banks, effective corporate governance and bankruptcy codes, and credible means of contract enforcement, along with other elements of a strong financial system, are present, significant amounts of debt will be sustainable. In their absence, even very small amounts of debt can be problematic" (Summers 2000).

Companies should not be allowed to expect government support in a time of crisis: "It is certain that a healthy financial system cannot be built on the expectation of bailouts." And in a time of crisis, it was critical to take rapid action to clean up failing banks: "Prompt action needs to be taken to maintain

Simon Johnson, senior fellow at the Peterson Institute for International Economics since September 2008, has been the Ronald A. Kurtz Professor of Entrepreneurship at MIT's Sloan School of Management since 2004. James Kwak is associate professor at the University of Connecticut School of Law. This chapter draws on their joint work, including Johnson and Kwak (2011).

financial stability, by moving quickly to support healthy institutions and by intervening in unhealthy institutions" (Summers 2000).

The best advice Summers offered was a principle famously associated with Mexican president Ernesto Zedillo during a crisis earlier in the decade: "Markets overreact, so policy needs to overreact as well."

These were all valid conclusions. In summary, they meant that emerging-market countries should become more like the United States, with strong legal institutions, transparent accounting, elaborate bank regulations, and an independent political system—or, more accurately, they should become more like the conventional image that we held of our own country. The idea that a major financial crisis of the type that ravaged emerging markets in the 1990s could originate in the United States was too preposterous to even be conceived of.

Two of the crucial ingredients—tight connections between economic and political elites and dependence on fickle short-term flows of foreign capital—seemed completely out of the picture.

Despite rising foreign debt due to growing trade imbalances, Summers' argument implied that the US superior financial system made high debt levels sustainable. More fundamentally, the implication was that political economy—the study of interactions between the political and economic systems—was only of first-order importance for developing and emerging-market countries.

In countries that had already "emerged," like the United States, economic questions could be studied without reference to politics. Instead, economic and financial policy presented only technocratic questions, which Summers compared to regulation of air travel: The jet airplane made air travel more comfortable, more efficient, and more safe, though the accidents were more spectacular and for a time more numerous after the jet was invented. In the same way, modern global financial markets carry with them enormous potential for benefit, even if some of the accidents are that much more spectacular. As the right public policy response to the jet was longer runways, better air traffic control, and better training for pilots—and not the discouragement of rapid travel—so the right public policy response to financial innovation is to ensure a safe framework so that the benefits can be realized, not stifle the change.

But in September–October 2008, when Lehman Brothers collapsed and panic seized the US economy, funds flooded out of the private financial system in what resembled aspects of a classic emerging-market crisis. In retrospect, it was clear that the run-up in housing prices of the 2000s was a bubble fueled by overoptimism and excess debt worthy of any emerging market.

The diagnosis of the International Monetary Fund's 1997 Korea letter of intent seemed to apply perfectly to 2008 America (substituting "household" for "corporate"): "Financial institutions have priced risks poorly and have been willing to finance an excessively large portion of investment plans of the corporate sector, resulting in high leveraging. At the same time, the dramatic decline in stock prices has cut the value of banks' equity and further reduced their net worth" (IMF 1997a).

And when the US federal government began rescuing major banks presided over by ultrawealthy executives—while letting smaller banks fail by the dozens—it began to seem as if our government was bailing out a very specific element of the American elite. In similar situations in the 1990s, the United States had urged emerging-market countries to deal with the basic economic and political factors that had created devastating crises. This advice was often perceived as arrogant (especially when the United States also insisted that crisis-stricken countries open themselves up further to American banks), but the basic logic was sound: When an existing economic elite has led a country into a deep crisis, it is time for change. And the crisis itself presents a unique, but short-lived, opportunity for change.

As in the Republic of Korea a decade before, a new president came to power in the United States in the midst of the crisis. And just like Kim Dae-Jung in the Republic of Korea, Barack Obama had campaigned as the candidate of change. Yet far from applying the advice it had so liberally dispensed to others, the US government instead organized generous financial support for its existing economic elite, leaving the captains of the financial sector in place.

What happened and why? This chapter compares and contrasts advice given to Asia during 1997–98 with what the United States actually chose to do in the crisis of 2008–09 and the financial reform phase that followed.

Has best practice for dealing with financial crises changed or is it one set of rules for emerging markets and another for the United States? And if recent actions by the US authorities have increased the degree of moral hazard and enshrined some version of "too big to fail" beliefs, what does that imply for global financial stability—and for Asia—looking forward?

The Asian Financial Crisis

In the mid-1990s, financial crises in less rich parts of the world were only too common. Mexico had a major meltdown in 1994–95, the Russian Federation struggled with volatility caused by financial inflows and outflows through 1996, and banking systems in the Czech Republic, the Ukraine, and other former communist countries struggled with severe shocks. Then in 1997–98, what seemed like the mother of all international financial crises swept from Thailand through Southeast Asia to the Republic of Korea, Brazil, and the Russian Federation. The contagion even spread to the United States via Long-Term Capital Management (LTCM), a relatively large and inappropriately named hedge fund.

In the United States, economists and policymakers took two main lessons from these crises. The first was that other countries needed to become more like the United States. Both directly and through their influence over the IMF, the key architects of US economic policy—Treasury Secretary Robert Rubin, Deputy Treasury Secretary Lawrence Summers, and Federal Reserve Chairman Alan Greenspan—pressed crisis-stricken countries to liberalize their financial systems, increase transparency in their political systems, and model the governance of their corporations on the Anglo-American system (with a greater role for mutual funds and other institutional investors). For their pains, the Rubin-

Summers-Greenspan trio was featured on the cover of *Time* magazine as the "Committee to Save the World."[1]

The second lesson was that while the US economy was not completely immune to financial panics, any real damage could be contained through a few backroom deals. At the urging of the Federal Reserve, LTCM was essentially bought out and refinanced by a group of private sector banks, preventing a major crisis; a series of interest rate cuts by the Fed even kept the stock market bubble growing for another two years. The mature US financial system, it seemed, could withstand any infection that might spread from the developing world, thanks to its sound financial system and macroeconomic management.

Crises were for countries with immature economies, financial systems, and political systems that had not yet achieved long-term prosperity and stability— countries like the Republic of Korea, Indonesia, and the Russian Federation. These countries had three main characteristics that created the potential for serious instability in the 1990s: high levels of debt, cozy relationships between the government and powerful individuals in the private sector, and dependence on volatile inflows of capital from the rest of the world. Together, these ingredients could lead to economic disaster.

Anatomy of a Crisis

In the 1950s, the Republic of Korea was one of the most economically backward countries in the world, ravaged by war and a half-century of Japanese oppression. No outside observer would have regarded it as a candidate for rapid economic development. By 1997, however, the Republic of Korea had arrived— literally, having joined the club of rich countries, the Organisation for Economic Co-operation and Development (OECD), in 1996.[2] The country's leading companies were fast building global reputations in a wide range of technology-intensive sectors, including shipbuilding, computer chips, and consumer electronics. Top family-owned business groups (*chaebol*) such as Samsung, Daewoo, Hyundai, and LG were increasingly prominent global brands. The country also benefited from a stable political system, with relatively open elections dating back to 1987.

However, the Republic of Korea exhibited some of the classic weaknesses that produce emerging-market crises. Economic activity was dominated by the giant *chaebol*, whose weak governance structures did little to constrain the whims of their founders. Hostile takeovers were essentially impossible due to a web of local rules. Institutional shareholders did not effectively monitor or control management (Joh 2003). The *chaebol* were also deeply in debt: Samsung's debt

---

1. *Time*, February 15, 1999, www.time.com/time/covers/0,16641,19990215,00.html (accessed on July 1, 2013).

2. The Republic of Korea was a leading example of what the World Bank famously and perhaps prematurely termed "the East Asian Miracle" (World Bank 1993).

was 3.5 times its equity, Daewoo's was 4.1 times, and Hyundai's was 5.6 times.[3] Leverage (the ratio of debt to equity) in the corporate sector was more than twice that of the United States.[4]

In earlier decades, the *chaebol* had been kept in check by state-owned banks that had carefully allocated credit, limiting the ability of the system to get out of control.[5] By the 1990s, however, the tables had turned. The *chaebol* had grown big enough to become a political force of their own. With their newfound political influence, they could dictate terms to the banks, making it possible to run up debt cheaply. Because the Republic of Korea belonged to the OECD, its banks could easily borrow short-term money overseas and make longer-term loans to the corporate sector. Alternatively, the *chaebol* could borrow directly from foreign banks that were now eager to lend to the Republic of Korea's booming economy.

The availability of cheap short-term debt led the *chaebol* to splurge on long-term capital investments. The founder of Samsung decided that he needed to add an automotive wing to his already far-flung group—an expensive bet that turned out badly. The founder of Daewoo expanded aggressively into the former Soviet bloc, building manufacturing plants from Eastern Europe to Central Asia, and also placed a big bet on cars. Korean manufacturers, led by Samsung and LG, invested heavily in DRAM chip production capacity, driving down margins. These questionable investments, made possible by cheap borrowing, caused returns on capital to fall, making it harder for the *chaebol* to repay their ever increasing debts.

Trouble first appeared in 1996 and early 1997 among smaller *chaebol* that had made risky bets with borrowed money, attempting to move up to the top tier. Hanbo Group (based on a major steel operation), the number 14 *chaebol* in 1995,[6] defaulted on its debts in January 1997. Kia, the carmaker that was investing heavily to break into the US market, was also in serious financial trouble (Kirk 2001, chapter 8). The government stepped in with various rescue packages, typically providing subsidies or other forms of assistance so that a relatively healthy company could take over a failing company (Haggard 2000, 56–57). The largest firms enjoyed implicit government guarantees—the conventional assumption that the government would not let them go under—which helped protect them from failure (Joh 2001). Still, by the summer of 1997, six

---

3. Calculated from National Information Credit Evaluation data in Gormley, Johnson, and Rhee (2010).

4. In 1997 the average debt-equity ratio of Korean firms far exceeded that of other economies (the Republic of Korea, 396 percent; United States, 154 percent; Japan, 193 percent; and Taipei, China, 86 percent). Se-Jik Kim (2000) has slightly different data and puts the debt-equity ratio of Korean firms at 350 percent in 1996, with most of the debt being bank loans. There is no disagreement that the Korean corporate sector was one of the most highly indebted in the world.

5. See Krueger and Yoo (2002). For more background on *chaebol* development, see Kim (1997).

6. Joh (2003, table 10) reports *chaebol* rankings for each year from 1993 through 1997 from the Korea Fair Trade Commission. Based on total assets belonging to firms in the same *chaebol*, Hanbo was number 14 in 1995, up from number 28 in 1994.

of the 30 largest business groups had gone bankrupt (Joh 2001; Baek, Kang, and Park 2004).

The Korean model and its high short-term debt levels seemed sustainable as long as economic prospects looked strong and investors thought that companies could pay them back. But financing long-term investments with short-term foreign debt creates a major vulnerability: If investors start to worry about getting repaid, they will try to pull out their money (refusing to roll over loans), but because companies put that money in long-term investments they will not be able to pay it back on demand. In this situation, fears that a country is in trouble can become self-fulfilling as foreign investors scramble to pull their money out first, triggering the defaults that they were afraid of.

For the first nine months of 1997, the Korean economy grew at an impressive rate of around 6 percent.[7] In July, however, the Asian financial crisis broke out in Thailand as a crisis of confidence caused a collapse in the local currency, the baht. Overleveraged companies saw their debts double practically overnight—because their debts were in foreign currencies, the amount they owed doubled when the value of the Thai baht fell in half—and were forced to default, causing mass bankruptcies and layoffs. Indonesia followed in August as its currency also collapsed and domestic companies failed.

At first, investors assumed that the Republic of Korea was sufficiently developed to withstand the storm, but nervousness was spreading outward from Southeast Asia. On October 23, 1997, the Hong Kong, China stock market declined sharply, rattling investors. Then Standard & Poor's downgraded Korean sovereign and corporate debt, stoking fears that the Republic of Korea would be the next country to be hit by the crisis.[8] Financial markets started to think again of the Republic of Korea as an emerging market subject to high economic volatility, which made its short-term debt levels seem excessive. Foreign banks became reluctant to roll over their loans and new international financing became hard to obtain. The currency depreciated sharply, falling from 886 won per dollar in July to 1,701 won per dollar in December. Everyone with dollar debts was hit hard, since now it took twice as many won to cover the same dollar debt payments.[9]

The Government of the Republic of Korea attempted to stabilize the situation, using its foreign exchange reserves to help state-owned banks pay off their foreign debts and to slow down the depreciation. But it could not stop the downward spiral—as the currency fell, it became harder for companies to repay foreign debts, and as some fell behind on repayments, creditors became

---

7. See IMF (1997a) for details of the Republic of Korea's economic performance immediately prior to the crisis.

8. Standard & Poor's and other credit rating agencies rate bonds issued by governments and companies. The ratings are supposed to reflect the likelihood that the issuer will pay off its debts. A rating downgrade indicates that the agency is losing confidence in the issuer.

9. For a timeline of events, see Congressional Research Service (1998). For more detail on the banking dynamics, see Delhaise (1998).

more reluctant to roll over the debts of others.[10] The stock market declined sharply and credit collapsed as banks, unable to pay their own foreign debts, reacted by cutting off loans to domestic companies, which made it harder for companies to produce the exports they needed to pay off their debts.[11] The economy declined sharply, leading to layoffs and street protests.

In this kind of situation, the IMF is supposed to help orchestrate a rescue, and the Fund did provide financial support with some sensible conditions. The IMF emergency lending program put limits on bailouts to the corporate sector, insisted that support to the banking system become transparent and that insolvent banks themselves be taken over, and outlined changes in the governance of *chaebol* to limit overinvestment. Many of these ideas were strongly supported by Korean reformers working under new President Kim Dae-Jung, who wanted to take advantage of the *chaebol's* weakness to push through reforms that would make future growth more sustainable, in part by undermining the *chaebol's* economic clout in order to constrain their political power.[12]

But the IMF program also contained three striking and controversial dimensions. First, consistent with the view of the US Treasury, it insisted on tightening monetary policy and, despite the strength of the government's balance sheet, did not condone an increase in government spending to offset the contraction in the private sector.[13] As a result, the Republic of Korea was unable to cushion its economic downturn with the type of stimulus package and low interest rates deployed by the United States and most developed countries in 2008–09.

Second, in the debt renegotiations with foreign lenders, in which the US Treasury was closely involved (Blustein 2001, chapter 7), there was no write-down of the amount owed by Korean banks; although the United States did help force creditors to roll over their loans, the amount they were owed did

---

10. According to Joh (2003, 292): "By the end of 1997, 6.7 percent of all loans were nonperforming loans, totaling 64.7 trillion won (over \$45.6 billion).... By June 1998, over 10 percent of all loans were nonperforming loans. These nonperforming loans severely weakened many banks and eventually provoked the liquidity crisis."

11. See the IMF's first letter of intent (IMF 1997a). Further reforms affecting the financial sector were included in a second letter of intent on December 24, 1997, which allowed the Republic of Korea to access further IMF funding (IMF 1997b). Paul Blustein (2001, chapter 7) explains the US role in arranging this additional support, which included official loans and an agreement that foreign banks would not demand immediate repayment of their loans to the Republic of Korea.

12. The IMF agreement was negotiated in the run-up to the presidential election, but the incoming president clearly expressed his support at critical moments and his team implemented the reforms. See Blustein (2001, chapter 7).

13. In such situations it is hard to determine where US suggestions leave off and IMF advice begins. The first deputy managing director of the IMF at the time, Stanley Fischer, was appointed at the behest of the Clinton administration. Fischer, a leading academic authority on macroeconomics, was in charge of economic strategy at the IMF and in that capacity consulted on a frequent basis with Larry Summers of the US Treasury Department. On this relationship and other connections between Treasury and the IMF, see Blustein (2001, chapter 7).

not change. So while Korean companies were left to struggle, foreign investors were effectively bailed out of their poor lending decisions, giving them no incentive to avoid the same mistakes in the future.[14]

Third, the IMF insisted that the Republic of Korea needed to become more open to foreign capital, quickly. Paragraph 31 of the letter of intent between the Republic of Korea and the IMF reads:

> To increase competition and efficiency in the financial system, the schedule for allowing foreign entry into the domestic financial sector will be accelerated. Foreign financial institutions will be allowed to participate in mergers and acquisitions of domestic financial institutions in a friendly manner and on equal principles. By mid-1998, foreign financial institutions will be allowed to establish bank subsidiaries and brokerage houses. Effective immediately foreign banks will be allowed to purchase equity in domestic banks without restriction, provided that the acquisitions contribute to the efficiency and soundness of the banking sector. (IMF 1997a)

The premise was that the crisis had not occurred because the Republic of Korea was too exposed to volatile flows of foreign capital, but because it was not open enough. To many observers, it looked like the IMF and the United States were taking advantage of the crisis to push forward their program of global financial liberalization.[15]

While every crisis is unique, the Republic of Korea was in many ways typical of the experiences of emerging markets in the 1990s. Big, well-connected companies expanded rapidly by taking on large amounts of cheap debt, unconstrained by the forces that should prevent irresponsible corporate behavior in a capitalist economy. Outside shareholders had little influence over powerful founders, and creditors lent money freely, assuming that the leading *chaebol* were too important for the government to let them go bankrupt.[16] Even though state-owned banks nominally controlled the flow of capital, tight relationships between the private sector and the government meant that the *chaebol* had little to fear. Ultimately political factors lay behind the economic crisis.

---

14. See Louis Uchitelle, "Crisis in South Korea: The Lenders; A Bad Side of Bailouts: Some Go Unpenalized," *New York Times*, December 4, www.nytimes.com/1997/12/04/business/crisis-in-south-korea-the-lenders-a-bad-side-of-bailouts-some-go-unpenalized.html (accessed on July 1, 2013).

15. Jagdish Bhagwati (1998) argues that a Wall Street–Treasury complex pushed countries into liberalizing their capital inflows in a way that created excessive risks. Rawi E. Abdelal (2006) argues that leading European politicians and bureaucrats also pushed this line—including Michel Camdessus, IMF managing director at the time of the Korean crisis. Blustein (2001), based on extensive interviews with the protagonists, concludes that the United States pushed the Republic of Korea directly and through the IMF to open up to direct investment by foreign investors in financial services.

16. Specific ways in which *chaebol* faced fewer financing constraints are explored in Shin and Park (1999).

Friends and Oligarchs

This central role of politics is common to many emerging-market crises. Political connections were even more central in Indonesia, where the late President Suharto's goals were some combination of maintaining order, improving the economic welfare of ordinary people, and enriching his own inner circle.

Suharto adopted neither a communist-style planned economy nor an "anything goes" free-market system. Instead, he cultivated a small group of private business associates whose family businesses became the backbone of the economy. Aided by the president and his family, who opened doors for their friends (and shut them for their competitors), these entrepreneurs built factories, developed cities, and learned how to export raw materials, agricultural products, and simple manufactured items to the rest of the world. As in many other low-income countries in the past half-century, economic development was dominated by a small economic elite selected because of their personal ties to the ruling family, which traded favors for both political support and cold, hard cash—a system known as "crony capitalism."[17] For example, Indofood became one of the largest conglomerates in the country, largely because of a long-time personal friendship between its founder, Liem Sioe Liong, and Suharto.[18] Suharto's wife, Siti Hartinah Suharto, known as Madame Tien, was involved in so many business deals that she was referred to by critics as "Madame Tien Percent" for her alleged fees.[19] Suharto's children also cut themselves into many major deals. His daughter was involved in the largest taxi company, one son tried to build cars, and another son was a financial entrepreneur.[20]

For a long time, the system worked reasonably well. Annual income per capita grew from $1,235 in 1970, just after Suharto came to power, to just over $4,545 by 1997.[21] Indonesia was still a poor country with pervasive poverty,

---

17. The extent to which families run businesses around the world is documented in La Porta, Lopez-de-Silanes, and Shleifer (1999). For Asia, see Claessens, Djankov, and Lang (2000). For the prevalence of political connections between powerful businesspeople and government, see Faccio (2006). Specific countries for which we have detailed data on the role of powerful business interests and their political clout include Thailand (Bertrand et al. 2008); Malaysia (Johnson and Mitton 2003, Gomez and Jomo 1997); and Pakistan (Khwaja and Mian 2005).

18. Liem headed the Salim Group. Bob Hasan, head of the Numsamba group, was another longtime Suharto friend and business ally. See George J. Aditjondro, "Suharto & Sons (And Daughters, In-Laws, & Cronies)," *Washington Post*, January 25, 1998, C1, www.washingtonpost.com/wp-srv/business/longterm/asiaecon/stories/sons012598.htm (accessed on July 1, 2013).

19. Marilyn Berger, "Suharto Dies at 86; Indonesian Dictator Brought Order and Bloodshed," *New York Times*, January 28, 2008, www.nytimes.com/2008/01/28/world/asia/28suharto.html (accessed on July 1, 2013).

20. Ray Fisman (2001) reports on the nature and value of political connections in Indonesia. Michael Backman (2001, chapter 14) details how the Suharto regime interacted with the private sector. On how subsidies were provided, see McIntyre (2000). See also Schwarz (1994, chapter 6).

21. Real GDP per capita (Constant Prices: Chain Series) are from Penn World Table Version 6.3 (Heston, Summers, and Aten 2009). This measure adjusts incomes for their purchasing power, a

but 30 years of economic growth had created higher standards of living for millions of people. The country was regarded as a development success story by the World Bank and by foreign investors, who supplied much of the capital needed to build factories, roads, and apartment buildings. Everyone knew that the flow of capital was controlled by Suharto's family and friends, but this was actually attractive to investors, who quite reasonably thought it safer to lend money to people with strong political connections. The increasing availability of foreign capital fueled economic growth.

But easy credit also fueled overinvestment and increasing risk taking, especially by well-connected businesspeople who assumed they would be bailed out by their powerful friends if things turned out badly. And over time, success in business became less a question of innovation and sound management than of using political connections to obtain government favors and subsidies. The result was an economic boom that could be sustained only by ever increasing amounts of foreign debt, which came crashing down in 1997.

The Russian Federation provided another example of the dangers created by a well-connected economic elite with easy access to foreign capital. With the collapse of communism in 1991, many former Soviet republics attempted to build capitalist economies with independent private sectors. In the Russian Federation, with its vast reserves of oil and gas, privatization of state enterprises provided a direct route to creating the major companies that would be the foundation of the economy. The reformers in the government of President Boris Yeltsin initially planned to create companies with a large number of relatively small shareholders. But in 1995, with Yeltsin facing a difficult reelection campaign the next year, they allowed a small group of powerful businessmen to buy large stakes in major state enterprises cheaply. In return, the businessmen provided crucial financial and media support to Yeltsin during the campaign. This was the creation of the Russian oligarchs, who dominated the economy in the 1990s.[22]

The new power of the oligarchs, however, did not translate into strong economic growth or fiscal stability for the government, whose tax revenues depended heavily on the volatile price of oil. With the Russian Federation needing to keep social spending at a reasonable level to avoid widespread protests, the IMF (and the United States) encouraged the Russian government to open up the country to capital so that foreigners could lend enough money to bridge the government into more prosperous times—the idea being that the Russian Federation could pay back those loans with future economic

---

method that has limitations but is reasonably accurate for assessments over long periods of time (Johnson et al. 2009).

22. On Russian reform and the oligarchs, see Åslund (2007), Freeland (2000), and Hoffman (2002). For early accounts of privatization and other reforms before the rise of the oligarchs, see Blasi, Kroumova, and Kruse (1997) and Gustafson (1999). For a broader assessment of Russian reform, emphasizing that there were no good alternatives, see Treisman (2000). On powerful groups controlling the state in the former Soviet Union, see Hellman, Jones, and Kaufmann (2003).

growth.[23] Private capital could also help restructure the oil and gas industry, develop new fields, and fund other productive investment projects that had been neglected under communism.

Although foreign investors were initially skeptical, their fears diminished as the managers of the big Russian companies demonstrated that they could run companies and service debts. This allowed their companies to raise more capital, acquire other companies, and embark on ambitious investment plans that generated jobs, increasing their political importance. Growing political support meant better access to lucrative contracts, tax breaks, and subsidies. And as in other emerging markets, foreign investors were perfectly happy to lend money to people with the implicit backing of their national governments, even if that backing had the faint whiff of corruption.

However, the Russian Federation's fragile economy was vulnerable to the financial crisis that began in Asia in 1997. The resulting slowdown in global economic growth caused drops in the prices of the commodities that the Russian Federation exported, most notably oil, hurting both company profits and government tax revenues. By mid-1998, both the private sector and the government were in serious trouble because they had large short-term debts to global banks and foreign investors, and those debts were magnified by the falling value of the ruble. Even an emergency IMF loan in July 1998 could not bail the government out of its problems, and in August the Russian Federation was forced to default on its foreign debts, causing massive capital flight out of the country (Åslund 2007, chapter 5).

Seats on the Lifeboat

Financial crises have political roots. Although severe crises are generally preceded by a large buildup of debt, that appetite for debt is the product of political factors, most often including close relationships between the economic and political elites.

The downward spiral that occurred in the Republic of Korea, Indonesia, the Russian Federation, and other countries hit by the 1997–98 crisis was remarkably steep. When foreign credit disappears, economic paralysis ensues; the government is forced to use its own foreign-currency reserves to pay for imports, service debt, and cover losses in the private sector. If the country cannot right itself before defaulting on its own government debts, it risks becoming an economic pariah.

---

23. It is difficult to separate the influence of the IMF and the US Treasury Department. The senior IMF staff member responsible for the Russian Federation makes it clear that the G-7 (the group of seven large industrial nations, within which the United States has a leading voice) agreed with the IMF's overall direction. If anything, the G-7 preferred a bigger budget deficit and, by implication, more capital inflows to the short-term government debt market. See Odling-Smee (2004). The general US preference for capital account liberalization is clear in its subsequent free trade agreements with Singapore and Chile, as well as in its negotiations over the People's Republic of China's accession to the World Trade Organization.

As the currency collapses, companies suspend payments on their debts, unemployment rises sharply, and the reality on the ground becomes nasty. Leading businesspeople—often selected for their personal relationships or political skills rather than their management ability—focus on saving their most prized possessions. Facing shorter time horizons, executives care less about the long-term value of their firms and more about their friends and themselves. As George Akerlof and Paul Romer (1993, 2) wrote in their classic paper entitled "Looting," businesspeople will profit from bankrupting their own firms when "poor accounting, lax regulation, or low penalties for abuse give owners an incentive to pay themselves more than their firms are worth and then default on their debt obligations." In the Russian Federation, as in most emerging-market crises, there was a sharp increase in "tunneling"— borderline illegal ways for managers and controlling shareholders to transfer wealth from their businesses to their personal accounts.[24] Boris Fyodorov, a former Russian minister of finance who struggled against corruption and the abuse of authority, argued that confusion only helps the powerful[25]—when there are complicated government bailout schemes, multiple exchange rates, or high inflation, it becomes difficult to monitor the real market prices of assets and protect the value of firms.[26] In the extreme confusion caused by a crisis, insiders can take the money (or other valuables) and run, leaving banks, industrial firms, and other entities to collapse. Alternatively, confusion means that government officials have extraordinary discretion to save firms or let them fail. Describing an earlier financial crisis, Carlos Diaz-Alejandro (1985, 12) wrote,

> The ad hoc actions undertaken during 1982–83 in Chile to handle the domestic and external financial crisis carry with them an enormous potential for arbitrary wealth redistribution.... Faith in orderly judicial proceedings to clear up debts and claims on assets appeared to be quite low; stories abounded of debtors fleeing the country, and of petty and grand financial chicanery going unpunished.

From a macroeconomic perspective, the government needs to restore the confidence of foreign investors. Large government deficits (the Russian Federation) require cuts in government spending and higher taxes; large private sector debts (the Republic of Korea and Indonesia) need to be resched-

---

24. The classic techniques involve managers transferring assets (below market price) to, or buying inputs (above market price) from, companies they control. See the discussion of Gazprom in Atansov, Black, and Conticello (2008). These phenomena are also seen in high-income countries (Johnson et al. 2000a).

25. See Boone and Fyodorov (1996). Johnson et al. (2000b) presents more general evidence of tunneling during the 1997–98 emerging-market crises.

26. On the appropriation of state property upon the fall of the Soviet Union, see Johnson and Kroll (1991). There was a great deal more theft under the smokescreen created by very high inflation (Åslund et al. 1996).

uled; and to attract capital, interest rates need to be higher, even though this hurts the local economy.

But responding to crises also has a political dimension. The IMF is ready to lend money, but only if it (along with its backers among the major industrial countries) believes that the government is cutting back on the cozy relationships with economic elites that helped produce the crisis.[27] This means less use of national reserves to cover the private sector's debts, less bailout money for the banking system, and fewer subsidies all around. Essentially, the government needs to choose whom to save; it has to squeeze at least some of the oligarchs. Of course, this is rarely the strategy of choice among emerging-market rulers, whose reflex is to be generous to their old friends (and supporters) when the going gets rough, even coming up with innovative forms of subsidies, such as guaranteeing the debts of private companies. Instead, it is politically easier, at least in the short term, to inflict pain on the working class through layoffs, reduced government services, and higher taxes.

Eventually, however, at least some in the elite have to lose out, both because there are not enough foreign-currency reserves to cover everyone's debts and because external lenders (first among them the IMF) demand some sign that the excessive risk-taking that produced the crisis is being punished. In both Thailand and Indonesia in 1997, the real fight was over which powerful families would lose their banks. In Thailand, the issue was handled relatively smoothly: More than 50 Thai "finance houses" (lightly regulated financial intermediaries) were shut down and some of the country's largest banks were taken over by the government. In Indonesia, however, the question was whether the parliamentary government would close the banking operations belonging to one of President Suharto's sons. In the struggle that ensued, the son's bank first lost its license to operate, but then appeared to have obtained another license with the suspected aid of the presidential palace. In the end, the administration did not have sufficient political will or power to stand up to the ruling family, undermining IMF (and US) support and deepening the economic crisis.[28] In

---

27. The IMF's voting structure is determined by countries' quotas (their potential financial commitments to the IMF), which imperfectly reflect their economic and financial power. The G-7 and its close allies control a majority of the votes at the IMF and the United States is the only country that has an effective veto over any major policy decision. It is practically impossible for the IMF to make a loan to any country without the support of the US administration.

28. The Indonesia letter of intent, dated October 31, 1997, promised to clean up the banking system (IMF 1997c). In its retrospective study, the IMF's Independent Evaluation Office stressed that closing 16 banks in November 1997 was supposed to "imply a new way of doing business. However, several factors undermined the credibility of this policy. Most importantly, the President's family challenged the closures. His son arranged for the business operations of Bank Andromeda to be shifted to another bank in which he had acquired an interest. The President's half-brother initiated a legal challenge to the closure of his bank. The public also saw some inconsistency in the closure of the 16 banks when it was widely—and correctly—believed that many other banks were in similar condition.... Under pressure from the President, the Minister of Finance soon reversed his previously announced tough position, saying there would be no more bank closures" (IMF 2003, 75). See also Haggard (2000, 66–67). In January 1998, the Indonesian government was supposed

the Republic of Korea, the confrontation was between the government and the largest *chaebol*, some of which had quite blatantly broken the law. After a series of showdowns—in which Daewoo threatened to default and political forces rallied to its assistance—the government won, and the hugely powerful Daewoo group went through bankruptcy and restructuring.

It is unheard of that all the oligarchs lose out, since the government can easily claim that they are essential to the domestic economy; some typically become even more powerful by absorbing their rivals, as happened in the Republic of Korea, where Hyundai acquired the failing Kia. As the oligarchs in Yeltsin's Russian Federation found out in 1998, it's a game of musical chairs; the postcrash government has enough foreign exchange reserves to help some big companies pay their debts, but not all of them. Usually the biggest of the big—the top *chaebol*, Suharto's close business allies (under the protection of Bacharuddin Jusuf Habibie, who succeeded Suharto as president), and the large Russian natural resource companies (such as Gazprom)—survive and prosper thanks to generous bailouts and other forms of government support. It's their smaller competitors that are cut adrift, while ordinary people suffer through government austerity measures. Of course, the "dispossessed" oligarchs fight back, calling in political favors or even trying subversion—including calling up their contacts in the American foreign policy establishment, as the Ukrainians did with some success in the late 1990s (IMF 2005). But the aftermath of an emerging-market crisis typically leads to a shakeout of the oligarchy, with political power often concentrated in a smaller number of hands.

However, another common feature of emerging-market crises is that they do not last forever. Even while outside observers are still despairing over corporate governance, macroeconomic management, and crony capitalism, growth picks up again. In 1999, the Korean economy grew by 11.1 percent; the Russian recovery took slightly longer, with growth of 4.5 percent in 1999 and 11 percent in 2000; and while growth took longest to resume in Indonesia, by 2000 its economy was expanding at close to 4 percent per year.[29] A depreciated real exchange rate boosts exports, widespread unemployment reduces the cost of labor, and companies with rescheduled debts or new companies with clean books can take advantage of both higher sales and lower costs. Surviving businesses can use their increased market shares and reaffirmed political connections to grow bigger and stronger. The oligarchs who run them can become even wealthier; Carlos Slim bought up companies on the cheap after the 1982

---

to pass a budget that had a surplus equal to 1 percent of GDP. Instead it proposed a budget that appeared to be balanced (with no surplus), which was interpreted as a further sign that Suharto was not willing to take resources away from his family and associated patronage networks. The initial critical reaction from the IMF and the United States helped trigger a further depreciation of the Indonesian rupiah (Reisenhuber 2001, 207). More companies struggled to pay their debts and had to cut costs, contributing to social unrest.

29. Growth rate of real GDP chain per capita from Penn World Table Version 6.3 (Heston, Summers, and Aten 2009).

crisis in Mexico and used the boom-bust cycle of the early 1990s (and his strong political connections) to consolidate his dominant position in telecommunications—becoming one of the world's richest men in the process.[30]

Reform?

Growth can come back even without any real fundamental reforms. Foreign investors learn exactly the wrong lessons from a crisis: They learn that when push comes to shove, the IMF will protect them against the consequences of their bad investments; and they learn that it's always best to invest in the firms with the most political power (and hence the most assurance of being bailed out in a crisis), perpetuating the pattern of crony capitalism. As a result, foreign capital flows back, and emerging markets can repeat the boom-bust-bailout cycle (or what has been called the "doom loop"[31]) for a long time, perhaps indefinitely.

But such economies can also reform. When economic elites capture disproportionate political power—the definition of an oligarchy—it is not just bad for democracy, it is also bad for long-term economic growth. Although oligarchies may be consistent with episodes of growth, they are not good at supporting the development of new entrepreneurs and the commercialization of new technologies (Acemoglu 2008), and they contribute to exaggerated economic cycles that end in debilitating crises. Societies with highly unequal power structures did not industrialize early in the 19th century and generally did not catch up to the income levels of the more prosperous countries in the 20th century.[32] Nor did they become more democratic. This is not surprising—entrenched economic elites have an interest in limiting competition from new ideas and new people and no incentive to level any playing fields. Political elites, dependent on those economic elites for support, are unlikely to adopt policies to increase competition. Without a business environment that promotes innovation and competition from new entrants—like the one enjoyed by the United States early in the 19th century—periodic episodes of debt-fueled expansion do not add up to sustained economic growth.

Fundamental reform requires more than rearranging the seats on the government lifeboat; it requires weakening the economic and political power of the oligarchs and creating a healthier, more competitive economic system. This is only possible for a government with an independent base of support and legitimacy strong enough for it to challenge the economic elites.

---

30. See David Luhnow, "The Secrets of the World's Richest Man: Mexico's Carlos Slim Makes His Money the Old-Fashioned Way: Monopolies," *Wall Street Journal*, August 4, 2007, http://online.wsj.com/article/SB118615255900587380.html (accessed on July 1, 2013).

31. The term "doom loop" is from Piergiorgio and Haldane (2009).

32. See Acemoglu et al. (2008) and Acemoglu, Johnson, and Robinson (2005). Weaker institutions are also associated with greater macroeconomic instability, including more crises and worse crises. See also Acemoglu et al. (2003).

The Republic of Korea had the advantage of a serious reformer, Kim Dae-Jung, winning the presidency just as the crisis hit. Kim had fought for years against the previous regime and its backers and was deeply skeptical of the *chaebol* and the claim that they needed special treatment. He had numerous allies, including the prominent People's Solidarity for Participatory Democracy, which lobbied hard for corporate governance reform as a way to constrain the *chaebol*, strengthen the economy, and protect democracy.[33] Big companies such as SK Telecom and Samsung Electronics were forced to become more transparent to protect minority shareholders against looting. The government also pushed through reforms limiting the power of the *chaebol*: They were no longer allowed to cross-guarantee debts within groups, investments across companies within a *chaebol* were curtailed, large companies were required to have outside directors, financial disclosure requirements were strengthened, and *chaebol* control over the nonbank financial sector was restricted.[34]

Although the reforms did not solve all of the problems presented by economic concentration, they did lead to a solid economic recovery. The rapid expansion of 1999 and 2000 was followed by annual growth of 4 to 5 percent in the early 2000s—a respectable rate for a country as developed as the Republic of Korea, though slower than during the pre-1997 period. There is an active debate in the Republic of Korea over whether the postcrisis corporate and political reforms went far enough, because the largest *chaebol*, including Samsung, LG, and SK, still dominate the economic landscape. But the reforms were a step in the right direction, because they addressed the core problem that led to the crisis—concentration of economic power in an elite with the ability to influence the political system.

Ultimately, ending the doom loop of debt-fueled bubbles and wrenching crises takes more than an IMF bailout package and a new minister of finance with a PhD from an American university.[35] Since emerging-market crises are the result of political conditions, sustained growth requires an end to the close relationships between economic and political elites that distort the competitive environment and encourage the misallocation of capital. Making this transition successfully is one of the central challenges for all emerging-market economies.

---

33. See "Jang Ha Sung, Shareholder Activist, South Korea," *BusinessWeek*, June 14, 1999, www.businessweek.com/1999/99_24/b3633089.htm (accessed on July 1, 2013).

34. See Haggard (2000, chapter 4), Yanagimachi (2004), and Mishkin (2006). Mishkin, a governor of the Federal Reserve from 2006 to 2008, argues that further capital market liberalization is the key to growth in emerging markets.

35. In the 1990s, Argentina tried a version of the Russian strategy—capital inflows that supported a budget deficit and allowed a boom in private sector investment. This was the brainchild of Domingo Cavallo, a distinguished economist with a PhD from Harvard, and it received strong support from the IMF (and the United States) even as the approach ran into trouble. Failure to deal with underlying political issues, including the inability to effectively tax powerful business elites, ended in a collapse of the currency, a banking crisis, and defaults on Argentina's public and private debt in 2001–02. See Blustein (2005) and Mussa (2002).

The United States Is Different

But what does any of this have to do with the United States, the world's richest economy and oldest advanced democracy? Our most ingrained beliefs run directly counter to the idea that a rich, privileged oligarchy could use government relationships in the United States to enrich itself in the good times and protect itself in the bad times. Our economic system is founded on the notion of fair competition in a market free from government influence. Our society cherishes few ideals more than the notion that all Americans have an equal opportunity to make money or participate in government. There is no construct more important in American political discourse than the "middle class."

The United States was not untouched by the emerging-markets crisis of 1997–98. In 1998, the most prestigious hedge fund in the world was Long-Term Capital Management, founded only four years before in Greenwich, Connecticut, by a legendary trader, two Nobel Prize–winning economists, and a former vice chair of the Federal Reserve, among others.[36] When the crisis broke out, LTCM had about $4 billion in capital (money contributed by investors), which it had leveraged up with over $130 billion in borrowed money (Lowenstein 2000, 159). It bet that money not on ordinary stocks or bonds but on complex arbitrage trades (betting that the difference between the prices of two similar assets would vanish) and directional trades (for example, betting that volatility in a given market would decrease).

However, LTCM's models were based on data gathered under ordinary market conditions. When the financial crisis spread and various markets seized up, it began losing money on many of its major trades, and its capital fell to less than $1 billion. But the real problem was that with LTCM on the verge of becoming insolvent, the banks and hedge funds that had lent it money (either directly or through derivatives transactions) were at risk of losing billions of dollars of their own. Fearing the damage an LTCM failure could do to the financial system as a whole, the Federal Reserve Bank of New York brought together representatives from the largest New York banks and pressured them to find a solution. In September 1998, the banks put in $3.6 billion of new money in exchange for a 90 percent ownership stake in the fund, largely wiping out the existing partners. With the new money, LTCM was able to ride out the storm without causing any collateral damage.

LTCM proved that in the new, globalized world, contagion from faraway emerging markets could spread to the United States. However, it also seemed to prove that any damage could be contained through effective intervention and sound macroeconomic management, without requiring taxpayer money or slowing down the real economy. As the long boom of the 1990s continued and the stock market continued to go up, LTCM soon faded into memory.

And when a serious financial crisis hit the United States, the policy response could not have been more different than what was experienced in Asia in 1997–98.

---

36. On the LTCM crisis, see Lowenstein (2000).

The US Financial Crisis

The US (or global) financial crisis first became clearly evident in mid-2007, when problems with subprime mortgages began causing major losses at specific hedge funds and structured investment vehicles with large exposures to securities backed by subprime debt. However, the crisis grew rapidly in severity over the spring and summer of 2008. The first major scare was the collapse of Bear Stearns in March 2008, which was brought on by a liquidity panic—essentially, the wholesale version of a bank run.

Bear Stearns was ultimately sold to JPMorgan Chase in a deal brokered by the Treasury Department and the Federal Reserve in which the principal government roles were played by Treasury Secretary Henry Paulson, Federal Reserve Chairman Ben Bernanke, and then–New York Fed President Timothy Geithner.

Increasing losses on mortgage-backed securities prompted the government takeover of Fannie Mae and Freddie Mac in early September 2008. But full-blown panic set in during the week of September 15. Lehman Brothers—then the fourth-largest Wall Street investment bank—was facing a liquidity run similar to the one that had brought down Bear Stearns; however, a weekend of negotiations did not lead to a rescue plan, and Lehman declared bankruptcy on Monday the 15th. On the same day, Bank of America announced that it was buying Merrill Lynch—then the third-largest investment bank. On Tuesday, American International Group (AIG), the world's largest insurance company, received a government bailout in the form of an $85 billion senior credit line to prevent it from defaulting on its portfolio of credit default swaps.[37]

In response to the Lehman bankruptcy, the Reserve Primary Fund, a major institutional money market fund, was considered likely to have suffered substantial losses and experienced a wave of withdrawals by large investors. The Reserve Primary Fund had total assets of $62.6 billion on the Friday before Lehman failed. By the end of Tuesday, its assets were down to just over $20 billion and it had suspended redemptions.[38] It consequently "broke the buck"—that is, it failed to maintain a net asset value of $1 per share (the first time this had happened in a fund open to the general public). This led to a flight out of money market funds and a freeze-up of the commercial paper market, on which both financial and nonfinancial companies depended for raising money. These developments prompted Paulson and Bernanke to propose the bill that eventu-

---

37. Such a default would have caused large losses at other financial institutions, both US and foreign, that had taken out this form of "insurance" with AIG.

38. The Reserve Primary Fund had only 1.25 percent of its total assets in the form of Lehman commercial paper but its net asset value fell to 97 cents before the suspension. It eventually paid investors 98 cents on the dollar. See Sam Mamudi and Jonathan Burton, "Money Market Breaks the Buck, Freezes Redemptions," *MarketWatch*, September 17, 2008, http://articles.market-watch.com/2008-09-17/finance/30738259_1_peter-crane-reserve-primary-fund-money-market (accessed on July 1, 2013).

ally became the Emergency Economic Stabilization Act (EESA), the centerpiece of which was the $700 billion Troubled Assets Relief Program (TARP).

On Thursday, September 18, Paulson and Bernanke provided a dramatic briefing to congressional leaders. According to Senator Chris Dodd (D-CT), then chair of the Senate Banking Committee, the leaders were told "that we're literally maybe days away from a complete meltdown of our financial system, with all the implications here at home and globally."[39]

The initial Treasury proposal was published on September 20—it was a short three pages and did not specify any independent oversight mechanisms.[40] This was not the sort of approach that would pass muster with the IMF or other outside scrutiny and, not surprisingly, the initial legislative proposal was rejected by the House of Representatives on September 29. An amended version passed, with more safeguards, and was signed into law on October 3, 2008. In terms of TARP funding, $350 billion was available immediately, while accessing the remaining $350 billion required a reapplication to Congress.

Measured by the cost of interbank lending and the prices of credit default swaps on bank debt—both indicators of the likelihood that banks will fail—the crisis in the financial sector only deepened into early October, first over fears that the rescue bill would not pass, and then over confusion over how it would be applied. On October 14, Treasury, the Federal Reserve, and the Federal Deposit Insurance Corporation (FDIC) announced two measures that finally began to calm the markets. The first measure was that $250 billion of TARP money was available to recapitalize financial institutions, and $125 billion had already been accepted by nine major banks. The second was a program under which the FDIC would guarantee new debt issued by banks.[41]

The goal of both programs was to give banks sufficient access to both equity capital and debt to reduce the risk that they would be unable to fund their operations (liquidity risk) and that their assets would become worth less than their liabilities (solvency risk). Although these measures temporarily brought down the fever in the financial sector, temperature spikes would recur several times over the succeeding months as various events created new reasons for panic. One of these episodes occurred in mid-November, when a crisis of confidence in Citigroup necessitated a second bailout over the weekend of November 22–23, 2008.[42]

39. See David M. Herszenhorn, "Congressional Leaders Stunned by Warnings," *New York Times,* September 19, 2008, www.nytimes.com/2008/09/20/washington/19cnd-cong.html (accessed on July 1, 2013).

40. See "Text of Draft Proposal for Bailout Plan," *New York Times,* September 20, 2008, www. nytimes.com/2008/09/21/business/21draftcnd.html?_r=0 (accessed on July 1, 2013).

41. Treasury Department, "Joint Statement by Treasury, Federal Reserve and FDIC," press release, October 14, 2008, www.federalreserve.gov/newsevents/press/monetary/20081014a.htm (accessed on July 1, 2013).

42. The first bailout was the Treasury injection of capital, announced on October 14. As Vikram Pandit, CEO of Citigroup, said when told the terms of that injection, "This is cheap capital" (Bair 2012, 5; Barofsky 2012, 26).

Obama was elected to the presidency during this period of intense uncertainty and unprecedented government intervention into the financial system. One question, as the United States faced its financial crisis, was whether the federal government would apply the lessons that it had so earnestly preached to Asian countries a decade before.

The Discretionary Power of the Government

From March 2008, the government—in the form of Treasury, the Federal Reserve Board of Governors (acting largely with and through the New York Fed), and occasionally the FDIC—had intervened in the fates of Bear Stearns, Fannie Mae and Freddie Mac, Lehman Brothers (by not intervening), AIG, Washington Mutual, and Wachovia. At the very least, these transactions showed the vast discretionary power of the government, with Treasury taking the lead. In the case of Bear Stearns, the government essentially decided to punish Bear shareholders and make what seemed like a gift of the bank's assets to JPMorgan Chase, with the New York Fed guaranteeing up to $29 billion of potential losses.[43],[44] Fannie Mae, Freddie Mac, and Lehman all showed what could happen if the government decided not to support a financial institution in its current form; the first two were placed in government conservatorship, and the last was allowed to fail. Washington Mutual and Wachovia demonstrated the government's role in brokering sales of failing institutions, potentially to the benefit of their acquirers.

Finally, the government was already the majority owner of AIG, which provided another lever of influence over the financial sector. In September, when AIG was first bailed out, there were already reports that major institutions such as Goldman Sachs had significant exposures to AIG.[45]

In these emergency rescues, the government was primarily represented by Paulson and Bernanke, who presented a united front in public. Geithner, as the Fed's point man in New York, was generally perceived as playing an impor-

---

43. Bear Stearns' shareholders were able to insist on a somewhat higher stock price than originally proposed—$10 rather than $2. But the government was still deciding on a potentially significant wealth transfer from Bear Stearns shareholders to JPMorgan shareholders, as well as from taxpayers to JPMorgan shareholders. In the final deal, JPMorgan agreed to take the first $1 billion in losses, with the New York Fed on the hook for the next $29 billion in losses.

44. Jamie Dimon, JPMorgan's CEO, was at the time a director of the Federal Reserve Bank of New York—an early indication that the political governance of the financial crisis would become controversial. The official position is that Dimon had no direct involvement in the decisions that allowed and encouraged JPMorgan Chase to buy Bear Stearns. However, on the basis of information available to outsiders, it is not possible to confirm exactly what happened. Under the circumstances, some observers expected Dimon to step down from the New York Fed Board of Directors. This did not happen—he remained on the board until his term ended on December 31, 2012.

45. See Gretchen Morgenson, "Behind Insurer's Crisis, Blind Eye to a Web of Risk," *New York Times*, September 27, 2008, www.nytimes.com/2008/09/28/business/28melt.html?pagewanted=all&_r=0 (accessed on July 1, 2013).

tant behind-the-scenes role. Before the passage of the EESA, the Fed provided most of the money—such as the $29 billion guarantee for Bear Stearns' assets and the $85 billion credit line for AIG—since it was authorized to provide emergency lending under Section 13(3) of the Federal Reserve Act.[46]

Because Treasury did not have an insurance fund, it also needed the FDIC to guarantee newly issued bank debt in mid-October. Paulson, himself a deal-maker from Wall Street, played a central role in deciding what deals would get done or not done.[47] Paulson was also the front man in the campaign to pass the EESA, which included TARP. TARP explicitly granted broad powers to Treasury to intervene in the financial sector, and Paulson had used it to pressure nine major banks into accepting $125 billion of new government capital on one day.[48]

TARP was especially significant because it gave the Treasury Department a direct role in determining which banks succeeded or failed. First, although the Capital Purchase Program distributed capital on relatively generous terms, all applicants had to be approved by Treasury. Most notably, the dividends on preferred shares were only 5 percent per year.

Access to TARP capital was not guaranteed; in late October, for example, National City was acquired by PNC after learning that its application might not be approved.[49]

At the time, there was little transparency about how applications were being reviewed and what criteria were being used to determine which banks received capital. Pietro Veronesi and Luigi Zingales (2010) calculate that, among the first banks to receive capital, the terms were favorable for Citigroup and the three investment banks but less favorable for JPMorgan Chase.

TARP also demonstrated the ability of the government to channel major subsidies to financial institutions—one reason it was initially a popular program among banks. The investment terms were considerably more favorable than those available from the private sector, such as in Warren Buffett's investment in Goldman Sachs. According to Bloomberg analysis, the government received warrants worth $13.8 billion in connection with its 25 largest equity injections; under the terms Buffett got from Goldman, those warrants would have been worth $130.8 billion.[50] In addition, TARP received a lower

---

46. The Fed's ability to provide such support was severely curtailed—and, some legal experts argue, eliminated—by the Dodd-Frank Financial Reform Act of 2010. Most likely, the form of Fed support has morphed, with the next forms becoming clear only when we encounter another crisis episode.

47. Broadly speaking, this is confirmed by Bair's account, including of how Paulson brought in the FDIC (Bair 2012, chapter 9).

48. Damian Paletta, Jon Hilsenrath, and Deborah Solomon, "At Moment of Truth, U.S. Forced Big Bankers to Blink," *Wall Street Journal*, October 15, 2008.

49. Dan Fitzpatrick, David Enrich, and Damian Paletta, "PNC Buys National City in Bank Shakeout," *Wall Street Journal*, October 25, 2008.

50. Mark Pittman, "Paulson Bank Bailout in 'Great Stress' Misses Terms Buffett Won," Bloomberg

interest rate (5 percent) on its preferred stock investments than did Buffett (10 percent), which cost taxpayers $48 billion in aggregate over five years, according to Bloomberg.[51]

The TARP Congressional Oversight Panel made a similar assessment, estimating in early 2009 that TARP had so far exchanged $254 billion for $176 billion worth of assets, implying a cash subsidy of $78 billion.[52]

Although there were justifications for this subsidy—in particular, Treasury wanted broad participation in order to avoid stigmatizing particular banks—it still constituted potential expected value that the government was willing and able to transfer to specific financial institutions.

In addition, the Capital Purchase Program placed significant holdings of preferred stock in the hands of the Treasury, as well as warrants on common stock. Although the preferred stock was nonvoting and Treasury committed not to vote its shares of common stock, this still left open the prospect of increased government influence. Among other things, the investment terms restricted the ability of the financial institution to pay dividends on or buy back preferred or common shares and also subjected it to the executive compensation and corporate governance requirements of the EESA (although these requirements were considerably less stringent than those implemented in February 2009).[53]

At the time, there was considerable uncertainty about how and to what degree Treasury would attempt to exercise influence over banks that had received TARP money. The mechanics of implementing TARP were housed in Treasury and managed by people appointed by Paulson, who was a former head of Goldman Sachs. Neel Kashkari, a Goldman Sachs alumnus, was named interim head of TARP. Reuben Jeffrey, another Goldman alumnus, was named interim chief investment officer, and several other ex-Goldman executives played important roles in the Paulson Treasury, as profiled in contemporaneous articles.[54]

News, January 10, 2009, www.bloomberg.com/apps/news?pid=newsarchive&sid=aAvhtiFdLyaQ (accessed on July 1, 2013).

51. Nobel Prize–winning economist Joseph Stiglitz is quoted by Bloomberg: "Paulson said he had to make it attractive to banks, which is code for 'I'm going to give money away,'" and "If Paulson was still an employee of Goldman Sachs and he'd done this deal, he would have been fired." See Pittman, "Paulson Bank Bailout in 'Great Stress' Misses Terms Buffett Won."

52. See TARP Congressional Oversight Panel, "February Oversight Report: Valuing Treasury's Acquisitions," www.gpo.gov/fdsys/pkg/CPRT-111JPRT47178/html/CPRT-111JPRT47178.htm (accessed on July 13, 2013).

53. Treasury Department, "TARP Capital Purchase Program: Senior Preferred Stock and Warrants," press release, www.treasury.gov/press-center/press-releases/Documents/document5hp1207.pdf (accessed on July 1, 2013).

54. Julie Creswell and Ben White, "The Guys from 'Government Sachs'," New York Times, October 17, 2008, www.nytimes.com/2008/10/19/business/19gold.html (accessed on July 1, 2013); Deborah Solomon, "The Financial Crisis: Amid Turmoil, Tireless Team of Advisers Backed Paulson," Wall

In short, the crisis situation in general and TARP in particular gave the Treasury Department unprecedented power to use taxpayer money to select winners and losers in the financial sector, a point highlighted by the Congressional Oversight Panel:

> Treasury may have determined that granting the subsidies described above to a group of banks, regardless of their condition, on essentially the same terms was necessary, for one or more reasons, to preserve the integrity of the financial system. Whether the subsidy provided by Treasury to financial institutions represents a fair deal for the taxpayers is a subject for policy debate and judgment, not one that can be answered in a purely quantitative way.[55]

For its part the Treasury Department did not acknowledge these subsidies, instead describing its investments of taxpayer money as "at or near par." To this the Congressional Oversight Panel responded, "if TARP is to garner credibility and public support, a clear explanation of the economic transaction and the reasoning behind any such expenditure of funds must be made clear to the public."[56]

The position of special inspector general for TARP (SIGTARP) was created by Congress to help prevent fraud in TARP-related programs. Neil Barofsky, a former prosecutor, was appointed SIGTARP in December 2008. In retrospect, he writes of the Capital Purchase Program, "We were dismayed by the complete absence of oversight and compliance conditions in the CPP contracts that we received" (Barofsky 2012, 71).

Citigroup, Bank of America, and AIG

In principle, the government is supposed to apply the law without considering the identity of the parties that it is dealing with. During the financial crisis, this became difficult if not impossible because the financial system depended crucially on a handful of large, well-connected financial institutions. In late 2008 and early 2009, Citigroup and Bank of America faced crises requiring extraordinary measures from the government, while AIG needed additional assistance following its initial bailout in September.

The Citigroup bailout in November 2008 and Bank of America bailout in January 2009 both represented major emergency subsidies from Treasury. In each case, the bank received additional TARP capital, but the government also agreed to guarantee a pool of assets against declines in value. These guarantees were effectively a nontransparent and underpriced form of insurance

---

Street Journal, September 17, 2008. There were reportedly eight or nine former Goldman people at Treasury during this time, but we have not been able to confirm their precise identities. Treasury does not publish a complete list of its employees and outside advisers.

55. TARP Congressional Oversight Panel, "February Oversight Report: Valuing Treasury's Acquisitions."

56. Ibid.

(compared with what such guarantees would have cost in the free market). As a result, according to the TARP Congressional Oversight Panel, these bailouts contained an implicit subsidy percentage of 50 percent, compared with a subsidy of 22 percent in the TARP Capital Purchase Program.[57]

There was some debate among government officials over the terms of the Citigroup bailout. Sheila Bair, chair of the FDIC, thought they were overly generous to the bank and its executives but claims that she encountered opposition from Geithner: "Tim seemed to view his job as protecting Citigroup from me, when he should have been worried about protecting the taxpayers from Citi" (Bair 2012, 170).

In contrast, Bair portrays Bernanke as having played a positive role. "Throughout the difficult negotiations with Citi and the regulators, Ben, more than anyone, helped us secure some meaningful management and other changes to that institution" (Bair 2012, 171; see also 39).

While the Citigroup bailout (November 2008 edition) was always understood as a means of saving the bank, it was reported in January 2009 that the Bank of America bailout had been promised in exchange for the bank agreeing to complete its acquisition of Merrill Lynch, then the third-largest investment bank on Wall Street. In April 2009, an investigation by New York Attorney General Andrew Cuomo further revealed that Paulson had threatened to replace Ken Lewis as CEO of Bank of America if he refused to complete the Merrill acquisition.

These interventions clearly benefited Citigroup, which otherwise might have failed, and Merrill Lynch, which otherwise would almost certainly have failed. Whether they benefited Bank of America is another question that is almost impossible to answer. As losses mounted at Merrill in December 2008, it may have become rational for Bank of America to walk away from the planned acquisition; the subsidy provided by the government in the form of the January bailout may or may not have compensated it for those additional losses. Paulson and Bernanke, in applying pressure on Lewis, certainly believed that a failure of Merrill could have serious systemic implications; the net effect, however, was to pressure a North Carolina–based retail bank (with relatively small investment banking operations) to complete its acquisition of a New York–based investment bank (Barofsky 2012, 103–104).

In late February 2009, there were signs that Citigroup was facing another wholesale bank run, most evident in its declining stock price, the falling price of its subordinated bonds, and the rising price of credit default swap protection on its senior bonds. Geithner's initial proposal was to split Citi into a "good bank" and a "bad bank." According to Bair (2012, 167),

> initially, he raised the idea of the FDIC setting up and funding a bad bank, without imposing any loss absorption on shareholders and bondholders. I

---

57. Ibid. The 50 percent figure is for the Citigroup bailout; the Bank of America bailout was not included in the panel report, which only covered transactions through the end of 2008.

was flabbergasted. Why in the world would the FDIC take all of the losses and let Citi's private stakeholders take all of the upside with the good bank?

The government's eventual response was to engineer a preferred-for-common swap including both the Treasury Department and several large investors in Citigroup.

Treasury converted $25 billion of taxpayer-held preferred securities to common shares, while allowing a substantial share of Citi's nongovernment preferred shareholders, as well as subordinated-debt holders, to keep their priority position. The FDIC argued that all the preferred and subordinated-debt holders should have to convert to common stock before the government converted any of its shares. In Bair's assessment (Bair 2012, chapter 15), the deal was generous to Citigroup and its current shareholders.[58] However, the bank's common stock price fell on the news, so presumably the market was expecting an even more generous bailout.

The AIG bailout of March 2009, in which the government improved the terms on its existing preferred stock, invested more cash in exchange for more preferred stock and improved the terms on AIG's credit line. It was engineered in response to a disastrous fourth quarter of 2008 that threatened AIG's viability as an ongoing concern.[59]

By this point, AIG was largely owned by the US government, so the bailout was not intended to benefit AIG's shareholders; instead, its goal was to keep AIG afloat in order to minimize collateral damage to other firms. Because it was still supposedly solvent, AIG was able to honor its commitments to its counterparties, largely credit default swap protection it had sold to other financial institutions. When those counterparties were revealed in March, the top names (excluding European banks) were Goldman Sachs, Merrill Lynch, Bank of America, Citigroup, Wachovia, Morgan Stanley, and JPMorgan Chase.[60]

Because AIG was able to make its counterparties whole, these banks—including the three largest Wall Street investment banks—received more cash than they would have if AIG had failed.[61]

---

58. Treasury also issued a Deferred Tax Asset exemption to Citigroup—another benefit for Citi shareholders. This decision is still being audited by SIGTARP, www.sigtarp.gov/Audit%20 Engagement%20Memorandums/Engagement%20Memo%20-%20Review%20of%20the%20 Section%20382%20Limitation%20Waiver%20for%20Financial%20Instruments%20Held%20 by%20Treasury.pdf (accessed on July 1, 2013).

59. Treasury Department, "U.S. Treasury and Federal Reserve Board Announce Participation in AIG Restructuring Plan," press release, March 2, 2009, www.federalreserve.gov/newsevents/press/ other/20090302a.htm (accessed on July 1, 2013).

60. "AIG Discloses Counterparties to CDS, GIA and Securities Lending Transactions," AIG press release, March 15, 2009, www.aig.com/aigweb/internet/en/files/Counterparties150309RELonly_ tcm385-155648.pdf (accessed on July 1, 2013). For attachments, see www.aig.com/aigweb/internet/ en/files/CounterpartyAttachments031809_tcm385-155645.pdf (accessed on July 1, 2013).

61. Goldman Sachs claimed that even if AIG had collapsed, its positions with AIG were fully hedged. Peter Edmonston, "Goldman Insists It Would Have Lost Little If A.I.G. Had Failed," *New*

Barofsky (2012, 186–87) argues that AIG did not need to pay 100 cents on the dollar, but there was no serious attempt to negotiate a reduction in payments, either when the government rescue was first implemented or when the government closed out these positions.

Rescue Program Design

After taking power in January 2009, the Obama administration, led by the Treasury Department, undertook a number of systemic programs to combat the crisis. The programs were packaged as a Financial Stability Plan, the broad contours of which were announced in a high-profile speech by Geithner on February 10, 2009.[62]

Geithner told CNBC, "We're being exceptionally careful that the taxpayer is being protected, that we're taking risks we understand, and that we're using these resources in a way that's going to give the maximum benefit in getting these markets going again."[63]

The February 10 speech was followed on February 23 by a more dramatic—and ultimately effective—joint statement by the Department of the Treasury, Federal Reserve, FDIC, Office of the Comptroller of the Currency (OCC), and Office of Thrift Supervision (OTS). It included the following statement of principle:

> The US government stands firmly behind the banking system during this period of financial strain to ensure it will be able to perform its key function of providing credit to households and businesses. The government will ensure that banks have the capital and liquidity they need to provide the credit necessary to restore economic growth. Moreover, we reiterate our determination to preserve the viability of systemically important financial institutions so that they are able to meet their commitments.[64]

York Times, March 20, 2009, www.nytimes.com/2009/03/21/business/21goldman.html (accessed on July 1, 2013).

62. See full text of speech via subscription at www.ft.com/intl/cms/s/0/4ff706b4-f78b-11dd-81f7-000077b07658.html#axzz2a5Tm4JoC.

63. On this and the broader market reaction, see Deborah Solomon, "Market Pans Bank Rescue Plan," *Wall Street Journal*, February 11, 2009, http://online.wsj.com/article/SB123427167262568141.html (accessed on July 1, 2013).

64. For the full text of the statement, see "Joint Statement by the Treasury, FDIC, OCC, OTS, and the Federal Reserve," February 23, 2009, www.federalreserve.gov/newsevents/press/bcreg/20090223a.htm (accessed on July 1, 2013). In the assessment of Dennis Kelleher (2012, 6), then a senior aide in the Senate, this statement marks the moment when the full faith and credit of the US government was put behind the banking system. Bair agrees with Kelleher's assessment, at least as far as the largest institutions subject to stress tests were concerned: "[W]e all joined in another statement that essentially said that the chosen nineteen would be propped up by the government no matter what" (Bair 2012, 159). This February 23 statement was Geithner's idea (Bair 2012, 159).

This declaration helped turn around market perceptions. The federal government, including the Federal Reserve, was putting its balance sheet and its capacity to provide credit behind the country's biggest banks. The implication was that these banks would not go through any form of resolution process—and their creditors would not face losses.

This commitment meant that loss-absorbing equity capital would be available to banks that needed it, so there had to be an official process to determine where capital deficiencies existed.

The Capital Assistance Program (CAP) provided a new source of capital. The terms of CAP were generally favorable to the recipients of capital, but it is not obvious whether the program was more or less favorable than the Capital Purchase Program created by Paulson in October 2008. Investments under the CAP were in convertible preferred stock, which has the potential to dilute existing bank shareholders. However, the conversion option is held by the bank, not by Treasury, which essentially gives the bank a put option that always has some positive value.[65]

At the same time, the CAP was coupled with bank stress tests by Treasury and the Federal Reserve that were announced in February and conducted in March and April 2009. These tests were conducted on 19 major financial institutions, with results disclosed to the public on May 7, 2009. Of the 19 institutions, 10 were found to need additional capital: Bank of America, Citigroup, Fifth Third, GMAC, KeyCorp, Morgan Stanley, PNC, Regions, SunTrust, and Wells Fargo. The nine that did not need capital were American Express, BB&T, Bank of New York Mellon, Capital One, Goldman, JPMorgan Chase, MetLife, State Street, and US Bancorp. On paper, the stress tests were a regulatory action applied equally to all of the institutions. However, the complexity of individual bank balance sheets, and the process by which the test results were released, left significant room for firm-specific negotiation.

At least Citigroup, Bank of America, PNC Financial, and Wells Fargo negotiated with the government over the final stress test results.[66] According to the *Wall Street Journal*, "The Federal Reserve significantly scaled back the size of the capital hole facing some of the nation's biggest banks shortly before concluding its stress tests, following two weeks of intense bargaining."[67] These negotiations created latitude for regulators to take actions that might favor some banks over others. For example, the decision to base capital requirements on

---

65. Treasury Department, "Capital Assistance Program, Summary of Mandatorily Convertible Preferred Stock ('Convertible Preferred') Terms," fact sheet, February 25, 2009, www.treasury.gov/press-center/press-releases/Documents/tg40_captermsheet.pdf (accessed on July 1, 2013).

66. Eric Dash, "Citi Is Said to Require New Capital," *New York Times*, May 1, 2009, www.nytimes.com/2009/05/02/business/02stress.html (accessed on July 1, 2013).

67. David Enrich, Dan Fitzpatrick, and Marshall Eckblad, "Banks Won Concessions on Tests," *Wall Street Journal*, May 9, 2009, http://online.wsj.com/article/SB124182311010302297.html (accessed on July 1, 2013).

Tier 1 common capital rather than tangible common equity affected different banks differently, arguably hurting Wells Fargo the most.[68]

In addition to the CAP and the stress tests, the Public-Private Investment Program (PPIP) delivered on the expectation that Treasury would revive Paulson's original plan to use government money to purchase banks' troubled assets. The PPIP offered nonrecourse government loans and FDIC loan guarantees to private sector investors willing to acquire troubled assets.[69]

This plan effectively provided a subsidy to these investors in order to increase their willingness to pay for the assets and help close the gap that separated bids and asks in the open market. Therefore, the plan aimed to benefit banks holding large amounts of troubled assets, but it particularly helped institutions seeking to buy assets—or to manage assets on behalf of investors. These included hedge funds, private equity firms, and asset management firms that were presumed able to raise private capital to participate in the program; beneficiaries may also have included banks themselves, which were free to sell their own troubled assets at the same time that they bought assets from other institutions.

Top administration officials claimed to the press that Treasury did not consult with Wall Street on the details of the PPIP.[70] This has been contested by Barofsky, then special inspector general for TARP, who claims (2012, 129), "PPIP had been designed by Wall Street, for Wall Street"—with BlackRock, the Trust Company of the West Group, and PIMCO heavily involved.[71]

In Barofsky's view, there were insufficient safeguards against fraud and money laundering in the PPIP and in the administration's actions more generally: "We saw Geithner's Financial Stability Plan for what it was: an unprecedented trillion-dollar playground for fraud and self-dealing" (Barofsky 2012, 132). But Barofsky's efforts to protect the taxpayer against abuse in the PPIP were resisted by the Treasury Department.

---

68. Felix Salmon, "Chart of the Day: Common Capital vs. TCE," Reuters, May 9, 2009, http://blogs.reuters.com/felix-salmon/2009/05/09/chart-of-the-day-common-capital-vs-tce (accessed on July 1, 2013).

69. Treasury Department, "Treasury Department Releases Details on Public Private Partnership Investment Program," press release, March 23, 2009, www.treasury.gov/press-center/press-releases/Pages/tg60.aspx (accessed on July 1, 2013).

70. "The Obama team also steered clear of consulting Wall Street about its plan in an effort to avoid being seen as joining with a much-maligned industry, officials say. Top bank executives have been complaining in recent days of being frozen out as the administration crafted its plan." As quoted in Deborah Solomon, "Market Pans Bank Rescue Plan," *Wall Street Journal*, February 11, 2009, http://online.wsj.com/article/SB123427167262568141.html (accessed on July 1, 2013).

71. BlackRock and TCW were selected as fund managers for the PPIP. Other managers included Wellington Management Company, Invesco, AllianceBernstein, and Angelo, Gordon & Co. (Barofsky 2012, 167), as well as Oaktree Capital Management, Marathon Asset Management, and RLJ Western Management. See David Ellis, "9 Firms to Run Toxic Rescue Plan," CNN Money, July 8, 2009, http://money.cnn.com/2009/07/08/news/companies/ppip/index.htm (accessed on July 1, 2013). PIMCO applied to run a fund but later withdrew its application (Barofsky 2012, 129).

The Treasury Department also clashed with the FDIC over the PPIP. In concept, there was one program for securities (which Treasury controlled and did not involve the FDIC) and another for loans, which was supposed to be run by the FDIC.[72]

Both programs were structured the same way, with auction pricing and government-backed financing provided to bidders to help overcome the liquidity discount prevalent in the market at that time. Unlike the securities program, however, the PPIP for loans would have forced banks to take losses on their toxic mortgages, as those assets were being held at inflated "book value" (in contrast to legacy securities, which were mostly marked to market). The FDIC supported the PPIP for loans, with Bair arguing that officials should do more to force banks to sell off their legacy mortgages—but encountered opposition from Treasury.

Treasury and the Fed jointly announced a plan to expand the Term Asset-Backed Securities Loan Facility (TALF), originally announced in November 2008, to a wider range of securities (including mortgage-backed securities) and to $1 trillion in total lending. This plan was designed to greatly increase liquidity in these markets, making it easier for banks to lend money and giving all financial institutions a new market for their assets. In Barofsky's assessment, insufficient safeguards were built into the way that TALF could be used in conjunction with the PPIP—again, raising the specter of potential self-dealing and illegal profits for asset managers, investors, or the banks themselves. In this instance, Treasury was again skeptical, but the Federal Reserve was much more responsive and eventually declined to participate in the way that had been proposed by Treasury (Barofsky 2012, 169–70; see also 122).[73]

In retrospect, it appears that several programs of both the Bush and Obama administrations were designed to get as much support out to banks as fast as possible. This meant distributing money with relatively few strings attached and little concern for whether well-connected bankers or asset managers could exploit the programs for their own ends. Confirming these concerns, Ran Duchin and Denis Sosyura (2012) find that firms with connections to politicians were more able to obtain TARP funds. Moreover, according to their findings, investments in such firms underperformed investments in unconnected firms.

---

72. The FDIC needed a "systemic risk exception" to launch the PPIP for bank loans. This required the Fed's approval, which it provided, and Treasury's approval, which never happened.

73. The New York Fed's chief of compliance, Martin Grant, met with the Treasury's PPIP team and told Barofsky that "they just didn't get it"—meaning that Treasury refused to put adequate safeguards into PPIP (Barofsky 2012, 68). On one occasion, Barofsky quoted Treasury's Herb Allison on an issue, and Grant responded, "'It sounds like Larry Fink [the CEO of BlackRock] is talking, and their mouths are moving'" (Barofsky 2012, 168).

Subsidies for Banks, Not Homeowners

Geithner's February 10 speech included a housing plan with expanded refinancing options for homeowners and cash incentives to lenders, borrowers, and servicers for each mortgage modification.[74]

Arguably, by helping to unblock economically rational loan modifications that would reduce monthly payments, reduce the risk of costly foreclosure, and increase expected payment streams to investors, these incentives aided all parties involved. Insofar as the plan had differential effects within the financial sector, however, its main impact was probably to aid loan servicers, which received new cash bonuses for modifications, and banks that owned whole mortgages, which now had one more option for how to deal with those mortgages. Investors in securitized mortgages, by contrast, could lose some of their existing rights under the plan.

Barofsky (2012, 125–26) was concerned that servicers would gain, potentially at the expense of both investors in mortgages and homeowners. The Treasury Department, however, was not willing to strengthen safeguards in the program and there were subsequent problems with servicer behavior—for example, with the mishandling of trial modifications (Barofsky 2012, 152).

As a practical matter, the housing plan received relatively little attention and few resources from the Treasury Department; apparently Geithner saw it primarily as a way to "help foam the runway" for banks, meaning that it would give the banks more time to absorb losses (Barofsky 2012, 156). Herb Allison, a senior financial services executive brought in to Treasury, referred to "helping them [the banks] earn their way out of this" (Barofsky 2012, 157). By the end of 2011, only $3 billion out of the $50 billion allocated to the Home Affordable Mortgage Program (HAMP) had been spent (Barofsky 2012, 199). Both Bair and Barofsky criticized the lack of attention to housing (Bair 2012, chapters 11 and 13; Barofsky 2012, chapter 8).

This was not an important priority of the Treasury Department, which preferred to provide direct support to the financial sector.[75] In the opinion of journalist Noam Scheiber, the Geithner doctrine was to apply so-called overwhelming force, but this meant primarily subsidies for large firms in the financial sector.[76] This brought Geithner into conflict with other administration officials, such as Christina Romer, chair of the Council of Economic Advisers. "When Tim Geithner imagined the uses of overwhelming force, it was always

---

74. Treasury Department, "Making Home Affordable: Updated Detailed Program Description," fact sheet, March 4, 2009, www.treasury.gov/press-center/press-releases/Documents/housing_fact_sheet.pdf (accessed on July 1, 2013).

75. The *New York Times* reports that, "In one bailout instance, Mr. Geithner fought a proposal to levy fees on banks that would help protect taxpayers against losses." See Jo Becker and Gretchen Morgenson, "Geithner: Member and Overseer of Finance Club," *New York Times,* April 26, 2009.

76. This doctrine originated with the Rubin Treasury and was also articulated by Summers. See Scheiber (2011, 30).

to save the system. When Christy Romer imagined the uses of overwhelming force, it was to save human beings" (Scheiber 2011, 38). In addition, when scandals later erupted regarding how banks had treated borrowers—including the "robosigning" of foreclosure papers—Treasury again sided with the banks. In the assessment of Bair, this undermined the authorities' ability to seek redress from those banks: "If [Treasury and the OCC] had put pressure on the big banks to reach a settlement, the banks would have been more willing to agree to meaningful reforms and financial redress. But without a clear signal from their two chief protectors, Geithner and Walsh, they were reluctant to give much" (Bair 2012, 256; see also 251).

Treasury also refused to pursue action against banks that violated the terms of the HAMP. There were well-documented abuses by servicers of these loans, which included prominent banks. "Treasury, however, demonstrated no interest in taking even the most modest steps to punish them" (Barofsky, 2012, 154; see also 133).

Oversight Concerns

Relative to market expectations in November 2008, oversight of government rescue efforts and TARP in particular was stronger than would have seemed likely. The TARP Congressional Oversight Panel, chaired by Harvard Law School professor Elizabeth Warren, was created as part of the original EESA legislation, but the panel proved more effective than most observers initially expected.

Similarly, while the EESA also created a special inspector general for TARP, this office also proved to have more teeth than seemed likely in November 2008. Barofsky consistently pressed Treasury to provide better supervision of TARP funds than would otherwise have been the case. He also brought a high-profile successful prosecution for fraud against one TARP recipient—and the executives involved were sentenced to jail. Other cases were still pending when he left office in early 2011.

Overall, Barofsky's assessment of the process within Treasury is not positive (Barofsky 2012, 174): "The hurried decisions, lack of transparency, and unquestioning deference to Wall Street that characterized the approach to the PPIP, HAMP, and CPP programs were hardly isolated incidents; it became clear to us that they were part of an emerging pattern that no secretary would want exposed."

For example, SIGTARP found that the process of selling warrants acquired under TARP was flawed because the criteria for pricing were not documented in a consistent manner. This makes it impossible to know with any certainty if taxpayer interests were protected adequately or if some financial institutions received better treatment than others.[77]

---

77. See SIGTARP, "Assessing Treasury's Process to Sell Warrants Received from TARP Recipients," May 10, 2010, www.sigtarp.gov/Audit%20Reports/Assessing%20Treasury%27s%20Process%20 to%20Sell%20Warrants%20Received%20From%20TARP%20Recipients_May_11_2010.pdf (accessed on July 1, 2013).

Financial Reform

In addition to attempting to restore financial stability, the Obama administration, led by Treasury, was deeply involved in shaping the proposals that eventually became the Dodd-Frank Financial Reform Act in 2010.

Financial reform legislation initially passed the House of Representatives in 2009. There were moves to strengthen the restrictions on big banks when the debate moved to the Senate, in part because of several complementary factors: perceived large bonuses paid by Wall Street firms for 2009; a March 2010 report by the Lehman bankruptcy examiner that shed unfavorable light on Wall Street practices and the ability of regulators to keep these in check; and the Securities and Exchange Commission's filing of a high-profile lawsuit against Goldman Sachs in April.

The Dodd-Frank Act is complex and reflected input from people favoring reform in the administration, the House, and the Senate, as well as a great deal of resistance from the industry, some of which was channeled through the administration. Among the huge amount of lobbying against the reforms was that from the "end users" coalition, which was organized in part by JPMorgan Chase, a leading player in the over-the-counter derivatives market.

Treasury requested new powers from Congress to take over systemically important nonbank institutions, including bank holding companies.[78] Such powers are not generally in the interests of large financial institutions and their shareholders because they strengthen the government's hand in negotiating with those banks and potentially make it easier for the government to seize control of them.

According to Bair (2012, chapter 17), Treasury's original idea was to keep a legal mechanism that would have made it easier for the government to provide support to specific financial sector firms, while keeping them in business. Bair's proposal was to allow FDIC resolution for nonbanks, putting them out of business in an orderly fashion (as the FDIC could already do for banks with insured deposits). However, her scheme was altered by Treasury to make it more favorable to banks (and their shareholders) in any future crisis.[79]

Indeed, a number of participants have documented that Treasury also pushed back, mostly behind the scenes, against proposals that would have further restricted the size and activities of very large financial firms and to defeat measures Treasury regarded as unduly onerous for big banks. Most notably, Senators Sherrod Brown (D-OH) and Ted Kaufman (D-DE) proposed

---

78. Tim Geithner, testimony to the House Financial Services Committee, March 24, 2009, www.treasury.gov/press-center/press-releases/Pages/tg67.aspx (accessed on July 1, 2013).

79. Writing of a meeting in the Oval Office in March 2009, in which she proposed expanded resolution powers, Bair states, "You would have thought they would be grateful, and for a time Treasury did embrace empowering the FDIC with powers to close down large nonbank firms. But later Tim would backtrack from the understanding we reached in the Oval Office that morning" (Bair 2012, 182–83).

the SAFE Banking Amendment, which would have imposed a binding size limit on banks. It failed on the floor of the Senate by a vote of 33 to 61, and a senior Treasury official subsequently remarked, "If enacted, Brown-Kaufman would have broken up the six biggest banks in America. If we'd been for it, it probably would have happened. But we weren't, so it didn't."[80]

In December 2009, Paul Volcker, former chairman of the Federal Reserve, proposed to prevent banks from proprietary trading or the similarly risky activity of investing heavily in hedge funds and private equity funds. The version taken forward by Treasury was significantly weaker and senatorial efforts to strengthen significantly what became known as the "Volcker Rule" did not succeed, in part because of a lack of support from Treasury.[81]

A new Office of Financial Responsibility (OFR) was included in the legislation, reportedly at the initiative of Senator Jack Reed (D-RI). He wanted to create a body that would track data and look for systemic risks in an integrated manner so that potential dangers would not slip through any regulatory cracks. Treasury was apparently opposed to this initiative. However, once it became clear that the OFR would be created, the administration insisted that it become part of Treasury. No head of the OFR was appointed for the first 18 months, then the job went to a Wall Street executive (from Morgan Stanley). In the latest development, the OFR has announced a council of outside advisers. According to an assessment by Propublica, an independent news organization, almost all 30 council members are industry insiders or academics with close ties to industry.[82]

There were various proposals to create an independent systemic regulator, including prominent ideas put forward by Bair (2012, 249–51 and 337–39). Treasury opposed these suggestions but, when it became clear that something along these lines would be created, insisted that the new Financial Stability Oversight Council (FSOC) be chaired by the Treasury secretary. To date, the FSOC has not taken any initiatives that could be considered harmful to the interests of big banks, although it did take up the issue of money market reform in fall 2012.[83]

---

80. John Heilemann, "Obama is from Mars, Wall Street is from Venus," *New York Times,* May 22, 2010. This assessment is confirmed by Jeff Connaughton (2012), then chief of staff to Senator Kaufman.

81. Senators Jeff Merkley (D-OR) and Carl Levin (D-MI) proposed a stronger version that was supported by Volcker. Senator Chris Dodd (D-CT), chairman of the Senate Banking Committee, prevented this amendment from being voted on. Presumably he had the support of the administration on this point. See Johnson and Kwak (2011, 229).

82. Jesse Eisinger, "New Financial Overseer Looks for Advice in All the Wrong Places," *Propublica,* November 28, 2012, www.propublica.org/thetrade/item/new-financial-overseer-looks-for-advice-in-all-the-wrong-places (accessed on July 1, 2013).

83. The Securities and Exchange Commission (SEC) is responsible for money market mutual funds. SEC proposals for reform were stalled due to deadlock among commissioners. The FSOC put forward its own proposals for comment. This put pressure on the SEC to act and reform now

The Treasury Department also consistently and successfully opposed proposals to impose assessments on the largest financial institutions that would provide working capital for any subsequent bailout. Bair (2012, 335) writes:

> The assessment would have made the large financial institutions internalize the risks they pose to society and helped level the playing field between small banks and financial behemoths. Funds raised through the assessment would have insulated taxpayers from supporting the liquidation of big financial institutions, even temporarily. Secretary Geithner worked hard to defeat the assessment in the Dodd-Frank bill.

Overall Assessment

In summary, the Treasury Department placed a high priority on helping the financial sector with various forms of explicit and implicit subsidy. In this instance, the general doctrine of "overwhelming force" meant assisting financial firms with subsidies to the greatest extent possible. The most clear case of this strategy is Citigroup, which undeniably received a generous subsidy from the government in early 2009. There was a realistic alternative, which was Bair's preferred course of action:

> ...the preferred shareholders would have been wiped out. This was a high-risk course, granted, but a tool that we could have threatened to use to extract more concessions from shareholders and bondholders.... (Bair 2012, 167)

But this proposal was defeated by the Treasury Department. According to Bair, Citigroup's needs also appear to have guided overall administration policy:

> I frequently wonder whether, if Citi had not been in trouble, we would have had those massive bailout programs. So many decisions were made through the prism of that one institution's needs. (Bair 2012, 125)[84]

Similarly, in the financial reform process, Treasury consistently sided with Wall Street against proposals in the Senate that would have imposed more restrictions on big banks' size and activities. The big New York–based financial firms, in particular, were helped by Treasury efforts to push back against attempts to strengthen the Volcker Rule and on other fronts.

---

seems more likely. This confirms that the FSOC structure can play a useful role in ensuring that systemic risks do not fall between the cracks of the byzantine regulatory structures.

84. The quote is about the November 2008 Citigroup bailout episode, before Geithner became Treasury Secretary, but while he was very much involved in designing policy. Bair expresses this same concern about Citigroup as a recurring theme in her book.

Conclusion

There are two ways to deal with troubled financial firms: put them through some form of resolution process, in which equity is wiped out, debts are converted to equity, and management is typically replaced; or provide various forms of implicit and government financial support. The second approach is known colloquially and not inaccurately as a "bailout."

In the Asian financial crisis, the policy response involved strong elements of the resolution approach. Advice from the US Treasury, both directly and via the IMF, reinforced this approach. And Summers' aforementioned lecture at the 2000 conference of the American Economic Association made a coherent case for why this makes sense (Summers 2000).

The structure of government support during a crisis matters, in part because it establishes expectations regarding how future situations will be handled—including who will bear what kind of costs. This is the heart of the critiques of the US Treasury approach by Bair and Barofsky. Both worked closely with Treasury during the crisis, bailout, and reform period. They both came to the conclusion that Treasury policy was overly favorable to the shareholders and creditors (and management) of particular financial sector firms.

Bair (2012, 120) puts it well: "How many other smaller businesses and households could also have survived intact if the federal government had been willing to give them virtually unlimited amounts of capital investments, debt guarantees, and loans?"

It remains to be seen what will be the full impact of those actions on future financial sector behavior, on the buildup of systemic risk, and on what happens in the next crisis. All crises must end. But the way in which they end affects incentives. We ignore moral hazard issues at our peril.

References

Abdelal, Rawi E. 2006. *Capital Rules: The Construction of Global Finance.* Cambridge, MA: Harvard University Press.

Acemoglu, Daron. 2008. Oligarchic vs. Democratic Societies. *Journal of the European Economic Association* 6, no. 1: 1–44.

Acemoglu, Daron, Simon Johnson, and James Robinson. 2005. Institutions as the Fundamental Cause of Long-Run Growth. In *Handbook of Economic Growth,* ed. Philippe Aghion and Steve Durlauf. Amsterdam: North-Holland.

Acemoglu, Daron, Simon Johnson, James Robinson, and Yunyong Thaicharoen. 2003. Institutional Causes, Macroeconomic Symptoms: Volatility, Crises and Growth. *Journal of Monetary Economics* 50, no. 1: 49–123.

Acemoglu, Daron, Simon Johnson, James Robinson, and Pierre Yared. 2008. Income and Democracy. *American Economic Review* 98, no. 3: 808–42.

Akerlof, George A., and Paul M. Romer. 1993. Looting: The Economic Underworld of Bankruptcy for Profit. *Brookings Papers on Economic Activity* 2: 1–73. Washington, DC: Brookings Institution.

Åslund, Anders. 2007. *Russia's Capitalist Revolution: Why Market Reform Succeeded and Democracy Failed.* Washington, DC: Peterson Institute for International Economics.

Åslund, Anders, Peter Boone, Simon Johnson, Stanley Fischer, and Barry W. Ickes. 1996. How to Stabilize: Lessons from Post-Communist Countries. *Brookings Papers on Economic Activity* 1: 217–313. Washington, DC: Brookings Institution.

Atansov, Vladimir A., Bernard S. Black, and Conrad S. Conticello. 2008. *Unbundling and Measuring Tunneling*. University of Texas Law, Law and Economics Research Paper 117. Available at http://papers.ssrn.com/sol3/papers.cfm?abstract_id=1030529 (accessed on July 1, 2013).

Backman, Michael. 2001. *Asian Eclipse: Exposing the Dark Side of Business in Asia*. Singapore: John Wiley & Sons.

Baek, Jae-Seung, Jun-Koo Kang, and Kyung Suh Park. 2004. Corporate Governance and Firm Value: Evidence from the Korean Financial Crisis. *Journal of Financial Economics* 71, no. 2: 265–313.

Bair, Sheila. 2012. *Bull by the Horns: Fighting to Save Main Street from Wall Street*. New York: Free Press.

Barofsky, Neil. 2012. *Bailout: An Inside Account of How Washington Abandoned Main Street While Rescuing Wall Street*. New York: Free Press.

Bertrand, Marianne, Simon Johnson, Antoinette Schoar, and Krislert Samphantharak. 2008. Mixing Family with Business: A Study of Thai Business Groups. *Journal of Financial Economics* 88, no. 3: 466–98.

Bhagwati, Jagdish. 1998. The Capital Myth. *Foreign Affairs* 77, no. 3 (May-June).

Blasi, Joseph R., Maya Kroumova, and Douglas Kruse. 1997. *Kremlin Capitalism: Privatizing the Russian Economy*. Ithaca, NY: Cornell University Press.

Blustein, Paul. 2001. *The Chastening: Inside the Crisis That Rocked the Global Financial System and Humbled the IMF*, revised edition. New York: Public Affairs.

Blustein, Paul. 2005. *And the Money Kept Rolling In (and Out)*. New York: Public Affairs.

Boone, Peter, and Boris Fyodorov. 1996. The Ups and Downs of Russian Economic Reforms. In *Economies in Transition: Comparing Asia and Europe*, ed. Wing Thye Woo, Stephen Parker, and Jeffrey Sachs. Cambridge, MA: MIT Press.

Claessens, Stijn, Simeon Djankov, and Larry H. P. Lang. 2000. The Separation of Ownership and Control in East Asian Corporations. *Journal of Financial Economics* 58, no. 1–2: 81–112.

Congressional Research Service. 1998. *The 1997-98 Asian Financial Crisis*. Congressional Research Service Report for Congress (February 6). Washington, DC. Available at www.fas.org/man/crs/crs-asia2.htm (accessed on July 1, 2013).

Connaughton, Jeff. 2012. *The Payoff: Why Wall Street Always Wins*. Westport, CT: Prospecta Press.

Delhaise, Philippe F. 1998. *Asia in Crisis: The Implosion of the Banking and Finance Systems*. Singapore: John Wiley & Sons.

Diaz-Alejandro, Carlos. 1985. Good-Bye Financial Repression, Hello Financial Crash. *Journal of Development Economics* 19, no. 1–2: 1–24.

Duchin, Ran, and Denis Sosyura. 2012. The Politics of Government Investment. *Journal of Financial Economics* 106, no. 1: 26–48.

Faccio, Mara. 2006. Politically Connected Firms. *American Economic Review* 96, no. 1: 369–86.

Fisman, Ray. 2001. Estimating the Value of Political Connections. *American Economic Review* 91, no. 4: 1095–102.

Freeland, Chrystia. 2000. *Sale of the Century: Russia's Wild Ride from Communism to Capitalism*. New York: Crown Business.

Gomez, Edmund Terence, and K. S. Jomo. 1997. *Malaysia's Political Economy: Politics, Patronage, and Profits*. Cambridge: Cambridge University Press.

Gormley, Todd, Simon Johnson, and Changyong Rhee. 2010. *"Too Big To Fail:" Government Policy vs. Investor Perceptions* (July 26). Available at http://baselinescenario.files.wordpress.com/2010/08/tbtf-july-26-2010-final.pdf (accessed on July 1, 2013).

Gustafson, Thane. 1999. *Capitalism Russian-Style*. Cambridge: Cambridge University Press.

Haggard, Stephan. 2000. *The Political Economy of the Asian Financial Crisis*. Washington, DC: Institute for International Economics.

Hellman, Joel S., Geraint Jones, and Daniel Kaufmann. 2003. Seize the State, Seize the Day: State Capture and Influence in Transition Economies. *Journal of Comparative Economics* 31, no. 4: 751-73.

Heston, Alan, Robert Summers, and Bettina Aten. 2009. Penn World Table Version 6.3, Center for International Comparisons of Production, Income and Prices at the University of Pennsylvania.

Hoffman, David. 2002. *The Oligarchs: Wealth and Power in the New Russia*. New York: Public Affairs.

IMF (International Monetary Fund). 1997a. *Korea Letter of Intent to the IMF* (December 3). Washington, DC. Available at www.imf.org/external/np/loi/120397.htm (accessed on July 1, 2013).

IMF (International Monetary Fund). 1997b. *[Second] Korea Letter of Intent to the IMF* (December 24). Washington, DC. Available at www.imf.org/external/np/loi/122497.htm (accessed on July 1, 2013).

IMF (International Monetary Fund). 1997c. *Indonesia Letter of Intent* (October 31). Washington, DC. Available at www.imf.org/external/np/loi/103197.htm (accessed on July 1, 2013).

IMF (International Monetary Fund). 2003. *The IMF and Recent Capital Account Crises: Indonesia, Korea, Brazil*. Washington, DC: Independent Evaluation Office.

IMF (International Monetary Fund). 2005. *Ukraine: 2005 Article IV Consultation and Ex Post Assessment of Longer-Term Program Engagement* (November). Washington, DC. Available at imf.org/external/pubs/ft/scr/2005/cr05415.pdf.

Joh, Sung Wook. 2001. Korean Corporate Governance and Firm Performance. Paper presented at the 12th Annual East Asian Seminar on Economics, National Bureau of Economic Research, Hong Kong, China, June 28-30.

Joh, Sung Wook. 2003. Corporate Governance and Firm Profitability: Evidence from Korea Before the Economic Crisis. *Journal of Financial Economics* 68, no. 2: 287-322. Available at http://ideas.repec.org/a/eee/jfinec/v68y2003i2p287-322.html (accessed on July 1, 2013).

Johnson, Simon, and Heidi Kroll. 1991. Managerial Strategies for Spontaneous Privatization. *Soviet Economy* 7, no. 4: 281-316.

Johnson, Simon, and James Kwak. 2011. *13 Bankers: The Wall Street Takeover and the Next Financial Meltdown*. New York: Pantheon.

Johnson, Simon, and Todd Mitton. 2003. Cronyism and Capital Controls: Evidence from Malaysia. *Journal of Financial Economics* 67, no. 2: 351-82.

Johnson, Simon, Rafael La Porta, Florencio Lopez-de-Silanes, and Andrei Shleifer. 2000a. Tunneling. *American Economic Review Papers and Proceedings* 90, no. 2: 22-27.

Johnson, Simon, Peter Boone, Alasdair Breach, and Eric Friedman. 2000b. Corporate Governance in the Asian Financial Crisis. *Journal of Financial Economics* 58, no. 1-2: 141-86.

Johnson, Simon, William Larson, Chris Papageorgiou, and Arvind Subramanian. 2009. *Is Newer Better? Penn World Table Revisions and Their Impact on Growth Estimates*. NBER Working Paper 15455. Cambridge, MA: National Bureau of Economic Research.

Kelleher, Dennis. 2012. The Dodd-Frank Wall Street Reform and Consumer Protection Act: 2 Years Later. Testimony to the Committee on Agriculture, Nutrition and Forestry, July 17.

Khwaja, Asim I., and Atif Mian. 2005. Do Lenders Favor Politically Connected Firms? Rent Provision in an Emerging Financial Market. *Quarterly Journal of Economics* 120, no. 4: 1371-411.

Kim, Eun Mee. 1997. *Big Business, Strong State: Collusion and Conflict in South Korean Development, 1960-1990*. Albany: State University of New York Press.

Kim, Se-Jik. 2000. Bailout and Conglomeration. *Journal of Financial Economics* 71, no. 2: 315–47.

Kirk, Donald. 2001. *Korean Crisis: Unraveling of the Miracle in the IMF Era.* New York: Palgrave.

Krueger, Anne O., and Jungho Yoo. 2002. Falling Profitability, Higher Borrowing Costs, and Chaebol Finances During the Korean Crisis. In *Korean Crisis and Recovery,* ed. David T. Coe and Se-Jik Kim. Washington, DC: International Monetary Fund and Korea Institute for International Economic Policy.

La Porta, Rafael, Florencio Lopez-de-Silanes, and Andrei Shleifer. 1999. Corporate Ownership Around the World. *Journal of Finance* 54, no. 2: 471–517.

Lowenstein, Roger. 2000. *When Genius Failed: The Rise and Fall of Long-Term Capital Management.* New York: Random House.

McIntyre, Andrew. 2000. Funny Money: Fiscal Policy, Rent-Seeking and Economic Performance in Indonesia. In *Rents, Rent-Seeking and Economic Development,* ed. Mustaq H. Khan and Jomo Kwame Sundaram. Cambridge: Cambridge University Press.

Mishkin, Frederic. 2006. *The Next Great Globalization: How Disadvantaged Nations Can Harness Their Financial Systems to Get Rich.* Princeton, NJ: Princeton University Press.

Mussa, Michael. 2002. *Argentina and the Fund: From Triumph to Tragedy.* Policy Analyses in International Economics 67. Washington, DC: Institute for International Economics.

Odling-Smee, John. 2004. *The IMF and Russia in the 1990s.* IMF Working Paper 04/155. Washington, DC: International Monetary Fund.

Piergiorgio, Alessandro, and Andrew G. Haldane. 2009. *Banking on the State.* Consultative Paper for the Bank of England (November). London: Bank of England. Available at www.bankofengland.co.uk/publications/speeches/2009/speech409.pdf (accessed on July 1, 2013).

Reisenhuber, Eva. 2001. *The International Monetary Fund under Constraint: Legitimacy of Its Crisis Management.* New York: Springer.

Scheiber, Noam. 2011. *The Escape Artists: How Obama's Team Fumbled the Recovery.* New York: Simon & Schuster.

Schwarz, Adam. 1994. *A Nation in Waiting: Indonesia in the 1990s.* Boulder, CO: Westview Press.

Shin, Hyun-Han, and Young S. Park. 1999. Financing Constraints and Internal Capital Markets: Evidence from Korean Chaebols. *Journal of Corporate Finance* 5, no. 2: 169–91.

Summers, Lawrence. 2000. International Financial Crises: Causes, Prevention, and Cures. *Papers and Proceedings of the 112th Annual Meeting of the American Economic Association* 90, no. 2: 1–16.

Treisman, Daniel. 2000. *Without a Map: Political Tactics and Economic Reform in Russia.* Cambridge, MA: MIT Press.

Veronesi, Pietro, and Luigi Zingales. 2010. Paulson's Gift. *Journal of Financial Economics* 97, no. 3: 339–68.

World Bank. 1993. *The East Asian Miracle: Economic Growth and Public Policy.* World Bank Policy Research Report. Oxford: Oxford University Press.

Yanagimachi, Isao. 2004. *Chaebol Reform and Corporate Governance in Korea.* Policy and Governance Working Paper Series 18. Graduate School of Media and Governance, Keio University, Japan. Available at http://coe21-policy.sfc.keio.ac.jp/ja/wp/WP18.pdf (accessed on July 1, 2013).

6

Evolution of the Asian and European Financial Crises:
Role of the International Monetary Fund

EDWIN M. TRUMAN

Financial crises are a regrettable but persistent feature of today's global economy and financial system, with economic and financial consequences far beyond the countries immediately involved. Crisis management and prevention thus require international cooperation through the International Monetary Fund (IMF) and other institutions. Each crisis is different, but crises share common characteristics. Policymakers and their advisors and critics should learn from past crises and establish frameworks and procedures not to prevent future crises—a commonly articulated but inherently unrealistic goal—but rather to limit the virulence of crises and their cross-border spillovers. To this end, this chapter compares and contrasts the ongoing European financial crises with the Asian financial crises of the late 1990s. I focus on 15 countries in Asia and Europe that had crises involving substantial engagement of the IMF and programs in support of economic and financial reforms.

The outbreak of the Asian financial crisis is conventionally dated from the flotation of the Thai baht on July 2, 1997, and the spread of the crisis to the Philippines, Malaysia, Indonesia, and the Republic of Korea. The experience of these five countries is reviewed here. Except for Malaysia, each country entered into reform programs supported by the IMF.[1]

Edwin M. Truman has been senior fellow at the Peterson Institute for International Economics since 2001. He thanks Allie E. Bagnall for her dedicated assistance on this project and also acknowledges useful conversations with and comments from Claudio Borio, Gerard Caprio, William Cline, Stewart Fleming, Joseph Gagnon, Timothy Geithner, Hans Genberg, C. Randall Henning, Alberto Musalem, Marcus Noland, Larry Promisel, Garry Schinasi, Brad Setser, Jeffrey Shafer, Shinji Takagi, Jean-Claude Trichet, Steve Weisman, and two reviewers of a previous draft. None should be held responsible for the views expressed.

1. Although the Malaysian authorities ultimately did not request IMF financial support, they broadly embraced an IMF-style program up to the point where Prime Minister Mohamad Mahathir

With respect to Europe, the focus is on 10 countries: Cyprus, Greece, Hungary, Iceland, Ireland, Italy, Latvia, Portugal, Spain, and Romania. The chronology of the European financial crisis is more complicated. A first phase coincided with the global crisis triggered by the collapse of Lehman Brothers in the fall of 2008, followed in 2008–09 by IMF programs with Iceland (which is not a member of the European Union) and Hungary, Latvia, and Romania (which are members of the European Union, but not in the euro area). A second, and still continuing, phase involves euro area countries, which are unique because these countries are bound together in a monetary union. This phase began at the end of 2009 with the Greek crisis, which resulted in an IMF-supported program in May 2010. The Greek program was followed by IMF programs with Ireland, Portugal, and, most recently Cyprus. In addition, in 2011, Spain entered into a de facto program and in 2012 applied for and subsequently received support for its banking system from its euro area partners and the European Stability Mechanism (ESM). The IMF provides technical assistance in monitoring Spain's progress in implementing European financial assistance and developments in the financial sector.[2] Italy also embarked on a de facto stabilization and reform program in the second half of 2011, which was also to be monitored by the IMF. However, the IMF role has been confined to its annual Article IV reviews. The Italian program is more closely monitored by the European Union.

My analysis is divided into three sections: origins, evolution, and lasting lessons.[3] Although there were differences in the details of these crises, the similarities outweigh those differences. Many aspects of the diagnoses and policy responses were also similar, but significant differences stand out. In particular, the European countries received more financial support, despite the fact that their crises involved solvency issues rather than just liquidity issues as in the

---

on September 1, 1998, repegged the ringgit to the US dollar and imposed controls on capital outflows. The Philippines was a central participant in the global debt crisis of the 1980s, and had adopted economic and financial reforms at that time which were intensified in the 1990s. It was operating under an IMF Extended Fund Facility arrangement on July 2, 1997 when Thailand floated the baht. Philippine authorities promptly requested an extension of their program until December 31, 1997, with an augmentation of its size, and in March 1998 established a follow-on Stand-By Arrangement with the IMF. See Noland (2000b) for a detailed account of why the Philippines was less affected in the Asian financial crisis. My choice of these five Asian countries conforms to the choice made by the authors of chapter 4 of this volume.

2. The ESM loan is to Spain, which in turn has used it to support and resolve some of its banks. In the future, the ESM may be used directly to recapitalize banks, breaking the link between a sovereign and its banks, but this procedure is not yet in place, in part because the associated single supervisory mechanism has not been established. and in part because the rules governing such a use of the ESM have not yet been agreed upon. See Veron (2013).

3. In what follows, I employ the framework I have developed elsewhere (e.g., Truman 2011a) for analyzing economic policy coordination: problem identification, diagnosis, policy prescription, policy adjustment, and consequences.

Asian crises. The programs adopted in the European crisis generally have been less demanding and rigorous than those in the Asian crisis. Partly as a result, the negative global impact of the European crisis has been larger.

The three principal lessons of this comparison are, first, that history will repeat itself—the only question is whether the tragedy and farce can be limited; second, the noncrisis countries in the rest of the world have a stake in crisis management, prevention, and preparation; and third, the IMF and its members need to focus their surveillance on monetary unions, such as the euro area, as a whole rather than on the individual countries.

Crisis Origins

Financial crises with significant international ramifications are frequently preceded by credit booms.[4] The booms turn into busts with severe negative consequences for the real economy. In this section I first review the origins of the Asian and European crises—they have shared many common dimensions. The subsequent subsection looks at some differences in the origins of the two crises.

Common Elements of the Crises

One classification of crises includes four types: speculative exchange rate, or currency, crises; sudden-stop crises (also known as capital account or balance sheet crises); debt crises (external debt of the country or the public sector's external or total debt); and systemic banking crises (Claessens and Kose 2013).

The five Asian financial crises were a combination of most of these types. Exceptions were that none of the Asian crisis countries had significant government debt or deficits (table 6.1), and the Philippines did not have problems with its banking system to match its Asian partners.

In Europe, the crises in the non-euro-area countries also involved all four basic crisis types. By definition, the euro area countries did not have foreign exchange crises, though the imposition of capital controls as in Cyprus is a symptom. Ireland and Italy did not have major ex ante external debt problems, though Italy's total government debt was large. Banking systems were not the initial source of crises in Greece, Italy, and Portugal, though their crises tended to bring on such problems.

An alternative way to look at the origins of financial crises is to focus on sources of vulnerability. Nouriel Roubini and Brad Setser (2004) identified seven vulnerabilities that contribute to crises in emerging-market economies: large macroeconomic imbalances, risky financing of budget and current account deficits, doubts about policy credibility, fixed and semifixed exchange

---

4. Truman (2013, forthcoming) elaborates on the discussion in this section.

**Table 6.1   Precrisis macroeconomic indicators in
Asia and Europe** (percent of GDP)

Country	Current account	General government Gross debt	General government Net lending (+)/ borrowing (−)
Indonesia	−2.8	n.a.	0.6
Republic of Korea	−2.1	10	2.5[a]
Malaysia	−7.2	42	1.7
Philippines	−3.5	61	0.0
Thailand	−7.1	15[b]	2.9[c]
Asia average	−4.5	32	1.6
Hungary	−7.8	62	−7.9
Iceland	−17.2	30	3.7
Latvia	−16.0	12	−1.0
Romania	−9.1	17	−1.8
Non-euro-area average	−12.5	30	−1.7
Cyprus	−6.0	69	−2.6
Greece	−8.3	103	−6.4
Ireland	−2.5	27	2.0
Italy	−0.9	105	−3.8
Portugal	−9.8	61	−4.8
Spain	−7.2	43	1.1
Euro area average	−5.8	68	−2.4
Europe average	−8.5	53	−2.2

n.a. = not available.

a. Data are available only for 1995 and 1996.
b. Data are available only for 1995 and 1996.
c. Data are available only for 1996.

Notes: The table shows average 1994 to 1996 for Asian countries and 2004 to 2006 for European countries.

Source: IMF, *World Economic Outlook* database, April 2013.

rates, microeconomic distortions, political shocks, and external shocks.[5] These seven elements are equally applicable to the advanced-country crises in Europe. Roubini and Setser do not provide a ranking of their elements. The emphasis is on the confluence of conditions.

---

5. Then–Treasury Secretary Lawrence Summers (2000), speaking in the wake of the Asian financial crises, presented a similar list. Morris Goldstein (1998), writing while the Asian crises were still in full force, cited similar factors; he also rejected the popular view that the Asian countries were innocent bystanders as a hypothesis that simply doesn't wash.

Table 6.2   Precrisis credit booms in Asia and Europe

Country	Increase in domestic credit (percent)[a]	Domestic credit as a percent of GDP	
		1993/2003	1996/2006
Indonesia	83	48	54
Republic of Korea	61	54	57
Malaysia	95	81	108
Philippines	119	45	67
Thailand	81	81	146
Asia average	88	62	86
Hungary	50	57	68
Iceland	225	130	305
Latvia	249	45	90
Romania	165	16	24
Non-euro-area average	172	62	122
Cyprus	31	191	204
Greece	42	94	106
Ireland	98	116	180
Italy	22	103	113
Portugal	26	143	161
Spain	69	132	177
Euro area average	48	130	157
Europe average	93	110	153

a. Average 1993 to 1996 for Asian countries and 2003 to 2006 for European countries.

Source: IMF, *International Financial Statistics* database, March 2013.

The Asian crisis countries shared most of these vulnerabilities (see tables 6.1, 6.2, and 6.3). Malaysia and the Philippines did not manifest the same level of doubt about the credibility of their policies as in the other countries and did not experience significant political shocks.[6]

With respect to the non-euro-area European countries, they shared almost all of the vulnerabilities. Iceland had a flexible exchange rate and the political situation in Iceland was impressively stable. The six euro area countries shared all seven vulnerabilities with the exception of Italy, which did not manifest a similar degree of ex ante macroeconomic imbalances. Those imbalances in Ireland and Spain were not as severe as in the other four euro area partners.

---

6. Note that in the vulnerability approach, it is exchange rate fixity, as in the euro area, that is identified with a crisis, rather than an exchange rate crisis per se as in the typological approach.

Table 6.3   Real GDP growth in Asia and Europe (percent)

Country	Precrisis[a]	Change from previous three years
Indonesia	7.9	0.7
Republic of Korea	8.3	1.0
Malaysia	9.7	0.2
Philippines	5.0	4.3
Thailand	8.0	−0.1
Asia average	7.8	1.2
Hungary	4.2	0.2
Iceland	6.6	4.4
Latvia	10.0	2.7
Romania	6.8	1.5
Non-euro-area average	6.9	2.2
Cyprus	4.1	1.4
Greece	4.1	−0.5
Ireland	5.2	0.3
Italy	1.6	0.9
Portugal	1.3	0.7
Spain	3.6	0.5
Euro area average	3.3	0.5
Europe average	4.8	1.2

a. Average 1994 to 1996 for Asian countries and 2004 to 2006 for European countries.

Source: IMF, *World Economic Outlook* database, April 2013.

Differences in Origins of the Asian and European Crises

The crises of the individual countries in Asia and Europe were not identical in their origins. Four principal differences stand out: exchange rate regimes, breadth of crises, persistence of crises, and preparedness.

First, in Asia, exchange rates initially were pegged, but those pegs quickly gave way. In contrast, the European crisis countries, with the exception of Iceland, and in principle Latvia, Hungary, and Romania, were locked together in an irrevocable monetary union.[7] The leaders of the euro area countries

---

7. Latvia chose to behave as if it had no choice, which may well have been the best course for that country, and that choice had no significant implications for other countries in the European Union. Hungary and Romania chose not to exploit substantially their potential exchange rate flexibility.

concluded that they had no choice but to stick with the euro. The downside was that after 2009 markets were no longer convinced that participation in the euro was permanent. The monetary element of Economic and Monetary Union (EMU) in Europe had become dysfunctional and the euro itself faced an existential threat, but the threat was not universally recognized by European leaders. It was not until European Central Bank (ECB) President Mario Draghi declared in July 2012 that membership in the euro is irreversible, and added the pledge that the ECB would do whatever it takes acting within its mandate to preserve the euro, that the possibility of euro disintegration was largely put to rest. But tremendous damage to the European integration project had already been done.[8]

Second, the European crises were broader, affecting (by the criteria applied in this chapter) 10 countries with the potential for several more. In contrast, only five countries were caught up in the Asian crises. Other economies in the Asian region were affected, but not to the level of requiring international rescues. Interestingly, the Asian crisis can be said to have had a larger global footprint, as shown in table 6.4. And as also shown in the table, the European crisis countries were not universally wealthier than the Asian crisis countries. The European countries are more economically and financially integrated with each other and with the global economy and financial system, however, with a commensurately greater potential to inflict damage on their immediate partner countries and, consequently, on the world as a whole.[9]

The third difference in the origins of the Asian and the European crises is that the former were rather transitory events measured by the number of years that passed before real GDP regained its precrisis level. In Asia, the gap was a maximum of five years for Indonesia. In the European crisis, only one country (Iceland) is projected to reach that point by 2013 after five years.

The final difference in the origins of the crises in Asia and Europe is that the Europeans were unprepared to deal with their crises, in particular, in the face of their substantially higher degree of economic and financial integration. The lack of European preparedness included an absence of institutions experienced at managing crises for a group of countries bound together in a monetary union. This institutional weakness came on top of the fact that a substantial number of the European countries had deficit and/or debt fiscal problems that meant that they were substantially less well positioned to deal

---

8. In June 2013, the *Financial Times* reported that euro area banks' cross-border holdings of government and corporate debt that had surged after the introduction of the euro from about 20 percent of total portfolios to more than 40 percent—in the process fueling the credit booms across the euro area—had returned to about their 1999 share by early 2012 ("Eurozone Banks Retreat behind National Borders," *Financial Times,* June 11, 2013).

9. Jean Pisani-Ferry, André Sapir, and Guntram B. Wolff (2013) note that the euro area's cross-border assets and liabilities in 2006 were in excess of 500 percent of GDP compared with only slightly more than 200 percent of GDP for the United States.

Table 6.4   Comparison of Asian and European crisis countries

| Country | Precrisis share of world GDP[a] | | GDP per capita 2006, current international dollars (PPP) |
	Current international dollars (PPP)	US dollars	
Indonesia	1.4	0.7	3,400
Republic of Korea	1.8	1.9	24,600
Malaysia	0.5	0.3	12,700
Philippines	0.5	0.3	3,300
Thailand	0.9	0.6	7,700
Asia total/average[b]	5.0	3.8	10,300
Hungary	0.3	0.2	18,000
Iceland	0.02	0.03	37,100
Latvia	0.06	0.04	15,600
Romania	0.4	0.2	10,500
Non-euro-area total/average[b]	0.7	0.6	20,400
Cyprus	0.03	0.04	26,300
Greece	0.5	0.5	27,000
Ireland	0.3	0.4	41,000
Italy	2.8	3.8	29,500
Portugal	0.4	0.4	21,600
Spain	2.1	2.5	28,900
Euro area total/average[b]	6.0	7.7	29,000
Excluding Italy and Spain	1.1	1.4	29,000
Europe total/average[b]	6.8	8.3	25,600
Excluding Italy and Spain	1.9	2.0	24,700

PPP = purchasing power parity

a. Average 1994 to 1996 for Asian countries and 2004 to 2006 for European countries.
b. Total for columns (2) and (3) and average for column (4).

Source: IMF, *World Economic Outlook* database, April 2013.

with their own problems, even if they could have ignored spillover and contagion effects, which they could not. Although the individual Asian countries
were the source and recipients of substantial contagion from their neighbors,
they were not closely locked together economically and financially, and subsequently benefited from the fact that they did not need to closely coordinate
their crisis responses.

Evolution of the Crises in Asia and Europe

Serious financial crises go through seven distinct phases.[10] First is the precrisis phase. The crisis may be brewing, but the authorities are either in ignorance or in denial. Second is the outbreak of the crisis, usually linked to a particular event. Third is the crisis management phase, in which authorities and institutions have little time to chart their next move or ponder the implications of their previous moves. The fourth phase is crisis containment, when the overriding objective is to stop the bleeding.[11] Ultimately, the bleeding does stop and the fifth, mopping-up phase begins. In the sixth phase of a crisis lessons are, or are not, learned. Seventh and finally, preparations are made to prevent or minimize the virulence of the next crisis. Generally, lessons are only partially learned and incompletely applied. The evolution of the crises in Asia and Europe followed this pattern, although it is notable that Europe bungled the crisis containment phase because of inadequate preparation, excessive caution, and inappropriate international forbearance.

Similarities in the Evolution of the Asian and European Crises

Four phrases summarize the similarities in the evolution of the two sets of crises: surprise, denial, and delay; differing diagnoses; nominally comprehensive programs; and frequent restarts and recalibrations.[12]

All crises involve *surprise, denial, and delay* essentially by definition. Because the potential problems in Thailand were well documented, its crisis was less of a surprise to some than normally is the case. IMF Managing Director Michel Camdessus and others at the IMF, starting in 1996, endeavored to convince the Thai authorities to adjust the exchange rate for the baht, reduce the current account deficit, and rein in the financial sector. Those warnings were ignored. However, few anticipated that a crisis in Thailand would be as severe as it proved to be or the extent to which other countries in Asia had their own vulnerabilities and were susceptible to a change in investor appetites.

Similarly, as has been amply documented by the Independent Evaluation Office of the IMF (IEO 2011), warnings about the impending global financial crisis were sparse. There were exceptions, of course, most prominently in papers by Claudio Borio and Philip Lowe (2002) and Borio and William White (2003) and in the pronouncements by Nouriel Roubini.

---

10. On the evolution of crises, see Edwin Truman, "Policy Responses to the Global Financial Crisis," remarks at the Ninth Annual International Seminar on Policy Challenges for the Financial Sector Emerging from the Crisis: Building a Stronger International Financial System, Board of Governors of the Federal Reserve System, World Bank, and International Monetary Fund, June 3, 2009, www.piie.com/publications/papers/paper.cfm?ResearchID=1225 (accessed on July 1, 2013).

11. I owe this phrase to Anna Gelpern (2009).

12. See Truman (2013, forthcoming) for a fuller discussion of similarities in the evolution of the two sets of crises.

On the other hand, Frederic Mishkin and Truggvi Thor Herbertsson (2006) wrote two years before the crisis broke in Iceland that none of the three traditional routes to financial crises had been manifested there: financial liberalization with weak prudential regulation and supervision, severe fiscal imbalances, and imprudent monetary policy. Mishkin and Herbertsson were not alone in their misapprehensions. Jean Pisani-Ferry, André Sapir, and Guntram B. Wolff (2011, 1–2) concluded for the euro area that, overall, "the IMF fell victim to a 'Europe is different' mindset and failed to address issues such as divergence of unit labor costs, capital flows and the resulting large imbalances in country-level current-account."

Errors in identifying crises naturally occur. That is the challenge faced by early warning systems and why they can only be relied upon to indicate a "zone of vulnerability," to use the terminology of Morris Goldstein, Graciela Kaminsky, and Carmen Reinhart (2000), where the probability of a crisis is high but a crisis is not a certainty. The severity of actual crises is a characteristic of crisis syndromes. Even after the crisis breaks, the authorities are in denial and paralyzed from acting decisively; in particular, they delay calling for external support such as from the IMF.

After the baht was finally detached from its peg on July 2, 1997, the Thai authorities did nothing to address the seriousness of the situation via complementary policy actions. They were too much in denial, or too proud, to call on the IMF for further help and advice.

The pattern of surprise, denial, and delay was similar with the European crises. Iceland denied that it faced a crisis until the crisis was fully upon it. Next the authorities sought financial support from the Russian Federation and the Scandinavian countries, wanting to avoid the need for an IMF program. Indeed, the IMF Executive Board completed an Article IV review of Iceland's economy on September 10, 2008, and did not express strong concerns except to note a very high vulnerability to depreciation of its currency.[13] By October 24, Iceland had reached agreement with the IMF staff on a program. The program, approved on November 19, included a nearly unprecedented blessing of comprehensive controls on capital outflows and limited exchange restrictions that required an explicit waiver in Iceland's IMF program.

In Latvia, Hungary, and Romania, denial and delay occurred in adopting reform programs and in asking for support from outside the European Union. Part of the problem was that until the fall of 2008, Europeans tended to think of the global financial crisis as a US crisis with only ripple effects elsewhere. In fact, the European countries had their homegrown crises that almost certainly would have erupted eventually.

Another part of the problem in Eastern Europe was the lack of clarity over whether the European Union would cooperate with or defer to the IMF.

---

13. See "IMF Executive Board Concludes 2008 Article IV Consultation with Iceland," Public Information Notice (PIN) 08/120, September 19, 2008, www.imf.org/external/np/sec/pn/2008/pn08120.htm (accessed on July 15, 2013).

This uncertainty, no doubt, deepened the crises. Dating to the late 1970s, no member of the European Union had required IMF financial assistance because the European Union had its own mechanisms to deal with crises. Before 2008, if one asked European officials whether a member of the European Union in crisis would be "taken care of" by Brussels or the IMF, one got answers ranging from "we will take care of our own" to "we are open to an IMF role."[14] It was quite obvious to observers why over the previous three decades EU countries had turned to Brussels rather than to the IMF: European financing was more abundant and European policy conditionality was more relaxed than the norm in IMF programs.

In the case of the Eastern European EU members, however, European and EU officials quite rapidly came to the conclusion that a role for the IMF was warranted. Given the size of the IMF programs for these countries, and the facts that in two of the three programs more than half of the financing was from the IMF and total financial support was on a nearly unprecedented scale (table 6.5a), one is justified in reaching the conclusion that the Europeans were motivated by the limited size of their own resources as well as by the recognition of the credibility that the IMF's involvement would bring to the countries' reform efforts. Anders Åslund (2010, 7) concludes that "[t]he cooperation between the IMF and the European Commission...worked surprisingly well." He also observes that Poland was granted a flexible credit line by the IMF as a precautionary move "since the ECB was not ready to offer Poland a swap credit."

By the end of 2009, the European debt crisis engulfed the euro area itself, starting with Greece. Denial and delay, again, were the dominant characteristics of the process.[15] Consequently, the December 2009 Greek program involved fiscal adjustment with no external financing. Aided by European dithering, the Greek authorities lost two months of precious time before Europe's leaders in February agreed to help financially. Led initially by the ECB, the Europeans also resisted allowing Greece to go to the IMF.[16] Another two months passed before they agreed in April that the IMF should be involved, and the troika involving the European Commission, the ECB, and the IMF was established.

---

14. I raised this issue in Truman (2005).

15. Pisani-Ferry, Sapir, and Wolff (2013, 81) note the difference in philosophy and style with respect to Europe and the IMF: "[T]he ESM, like its predecessor the EFSF [European Financial Stability Facility], can only grant financial assistance as ultima ratio, i.e., as a last resort. By contrast, the IMF tends to favor early intervention. It is fair to say that in all three euro area programme countries, Greece, Ireland, and Portugal, the late EU-IMF intervention was caused by the European Union, while the IMF sought early intervention in every instance."

16. An alternative interpretation of the position of Jean-Claude Trichet on behalf of the ECB, as reported by Neil Irwin (2013, 206), is that he felt that European governments should shoulder some financial responsibility both for their own actions and for the actions of their partners.

Table 6.5a   Summary of official financial commitments in the European financial crises

Country	International Monetary Fund			Other commitments		Total commitments	
	Billions of US dollars	Percent of quota[c]	Percent of GDP[d]	European institutions[a] Billions of US dollars	Other[b] Billions of US dollars	Billions of US dollars	Percent of GDP[d]
Iceland	2.1	1,190	10.3	0.0	2.7	4.8	23.5
Hungary	15.6	1,015	10.1	8.5	1.3	25.4	16.5
Latvia	2.3	1,200	7.0	4.3	3.8	10.4	31.1
Romania	17.3	1,111	8.4	6.7	2.7	26.7	13.1
Subtotal/average[e]	37.3	1,129	9.0	19.5	10.5	67.3	21.0
Cyprus	1.3	545	5.9	11.7	0.0	13.0	59.0
Greece	63.1	3,750	19.6	255.4	0.0	318.5	98.7
Ireland[f]	30.1	2,322	13.4	53.6	6.4	90.1	40.1
Italy	0.0	n.a.	n.a.	0.0	0.0	0.0	n.a.
Portugal	37.6	2,306	15.8	73.3	0.0	110.9	46.6
Spain	0.0	n.a.	n.a.	121.8	0.0	121.8	8.2
Subtotal/average[e]	132.1	2,231	13.7	515.8	6.4	654.3	50.5
Grand total/average[e]	169.4	1,680	11.3	535.3	16.9	721.6	37.4

n.a. = not applicable

a. European Financial Stability Facility, European Financial Stability Mechanism, European Stability Mechanism, European Investment Bank, and European Balance of Payments Assistance Facility.

b. Bilateral loans and the European Bank for Reconstruction and Development.

c. IMF quota at the time the program was approved, except for Greece in which case its larger quota at the time of its second program is used.

d. GDP in US dollars at market prices and exchange rates for the preprogram year in the cases of Iceland (2007), Greece (2009), Ireland (2009), and Spain (2011).

e. Total for dollar figures and average, excluding Italy and Spain, for percentages, except for total commitments where Spain is included.

f. The tabulation does not include the €17.5 billion in support included in the Irish program to support Irish banks that was drawn from Ireland's own resources including its sovereign wealth fund.

Sources: International Monetary Fund; European Commission, Economic and Financial Affairs, http://ec.europa.eu/economy_finance/assistance_eu_ms/index_en.htm (ac-cessed on July 1, 2013); Henning (2011).

Part of the delay was due to the fact that the Europeans had to cobble together a Greek loan facility mechanism to provide their more-than-two-thirds share of the financing for the first Greek program. The European Financial Stability Facility (EFSF) was devised subsequently as a temporary mechanism to provide a financial firewall against the spread of the Greek crisis to other countries. It was employed in the Irish, Portuguese, and the second Greek programs along with the ad hoc European Financial Stabilization Mechanism (EFSM).[17] In October 2010, agreement was reached on the permanent ESM, but it did not enter into force for another two years, on October 8, 2012. The ESM is being used in Spain and Cyprus.

By any objective standard, the EFSF/EFSM/ESM failed to achieve the objective of preventing the spread of the European debt crisis to other euro area countries, which should be the objective of a firewall. Ireland, Portugal, Italy, Spain, and Cyprus were too deep into their own unfolding crises to be protected from the economic and financial contagion that swept Europe. Each of these countries, of course, offers its own object lessons in denial and delay.

The second term used to describe the evolution of crises, *diagnosis*, is often not widely shared by the authorities of the country, the international organizations called upon to assist, or the other actors (governments, central banks, critics, and markets).

In Asia, it was agreed that Thailand had exhausted its reserves, had an oversized current account, and had a financial system under stress. But there was limited agreement on the priority attached to fixing each of these three elements or on the importance of other issues such as the size of financing packages.[18]

Disagreements about the appropriate stance of fiscal and, in particular, monetary policy in Asia were also a constant, as described below.

In Indonesia, in partial response to European criticism of the size of the Thai program, the composition but not the size of the package of support was altered. In contrast to Thailand, a large portion consisted of a second line of defense that could only be drawn upon once the initial financing was largely exhausted and, therefore, was regarded by some as less credible in establishing confidence in the financing package (table 6.5b).[19]

---

17. The EFSF, established by the euro area countries, was initially authorized to borrow €440 billion. The EFSM, involving all EU members, was authorized to raise an additional €60 billion. The initial announcement of these decisions in May 2010 included the presumption that IMF cofinancing would be one-third of all euro area programs supported by these mechanisms or would be an additional €250 billion. However, the latter figure never received formal endorsement from the IMF Executive Board.

18. Those disagreements continue. Despite the fact that the IMF concluded at the time that the Thai program was more than adequately financed, the Thai authorities disagreed, and Shinji Takagi (2010) repeats the argument that the program was underfinanced.

19. Table 6.5b does not include bilateral assistance from Japan under the New Miyazawa Initiative. For example, Malaysia received $2 billion under this initiative. See Furuoka, Lo, and Kato (2007).

Table 6.5b Summary of official financial commitments in the Asian financial crises

| Country | International Monetary Fund | | | Other commitments | | Total commitments | |
	Billions of US dollars	Percent of quota	Percent of GDP[a]	Multilateral development banks Billions of US dollars	Bilateral Billions of US dollars	Billions of US dollars	Percent of GDP[a]
Indonesia	11.3	557	5.0	8.0	15.0	34.3	15.1
Republic of Korea	21.0	1,938	3.7	14.0	20.0	55.0	9.6
Malaysia	0.0	n.a.	n.a.	0.0	0.0	0.0	n.a.
Philippines	2.0	240	2.2	n.a.	n.a.	2.0	2.2
Thailand	3.9	505	2.1	2.7	10.0	16.6	9.1
Total/average[b]	38.2	810	4.0	24.7	45.0	107.9	9.0

n.a. = not available.

a. GDP in 1996 US dollars at current prices and exchange rates.
b. Total for dollar figures and average, excluding Malaysia, for percentages.

Sources: International Monetary Fund; Henning (2011); Roubini and Setser (2004).

The case of the Republic of Korea raised a number of contentious issues. As a member of the Organisation for Economic Co-operation and Development, it was seen by some as ineligible for IMF assistance. This question was resolved, but surrounding politics led to policy conditions of a quid pro quo type, unrelated, in the view of many, to the crisis itself.

The solution chosen for Korean banks was a mixture of rescues and resolutions. The government made explicit its guarantee of the foreign borrowings of Korean banks. This action was not regarded as fiscally credible; many foreign banks continued not to renew their credit lines. In November 1997, the option of a standstill and renegotiation of such claims was rejected, but that approach was embraced a month later.

A similar pattern of disagreement about diagnoses has played out in Europe. Greece was seen as a classic macroeconomic crisis in its fiscal and external accounts combined with cronyism and a lack of competitiveness. The overwhelming focus of the first Greek IMF program was on the quick reversal of Greece's fiscal position by 10 percent of GDP over three years, a target that Greece has met (IMF 2013c). Structural problems were rampant, but principal attention was given to problems associated with the country's fiscal position.

Ireland and Portugal's problems were diagnosed as similar to those of Greece with an emphasis on their fiscal positions and buildup of government debt. To many informed observers, this was a misplaced emphasis.[20] Ireland's crisis was more closely associated with a housing and credit boom (as in Spain). Portugal's crisis is (as is Italy's) more closely associated with low growth in the precrisis period rather than an unsustainable boom associated with a dramatic acceleration in credit growth. In all cases, a major element of diagnosis was a lack of external competitiveness, but with the exception of Portugal (where its program involved an effort at internal devaluation using tax and compensation policies) and Greece (where the minimum wage was cut), the euro area rescue programs did not contain prominent elements designed to address competitiveness.

As a result of competing diagnoses, *nominally comprehensive programs* are designed to include something to address every issue, particularly the diagnoses of influential skeptics in markets and governments around the world. In the words of Lawrence Summers (2000, 11): "Providing confidence to markets and investors that a credible path out of the crisis exists and will be followed is essential." Summers went on to say that it is necessary to follow the Zedillo dictum: When markets overreact, policy needs to overreact as well.[21]

---

20. See Vitor Constâncio, "The European Crisis and the Role of the Financial System," speech at the Bank of Greece conference on the crisis in the euro area, May 23, 2013, www.ecb.europa.eu/press/key/date/2013/html/sp130523_1.en.html (accessed on July 1, 2013).

21. In addition to transparency with respect to a "consistent and credible commitment to a coherent policy-adjustment package," Summers listed additional important lessons from financial crises: "If lax fiscal policy is a contributor to the crisis, then tightening will be a key part of restoring confidence;...the right monetary policy to restore confidence;...prompt action...to main-

The detailed provisions in the Asian programs produced a backlash. Ten years later, when the European crisis began to unfold, IMF procedures had changed somewhat. The emphasis was on program ownership and narrower, less intrusive conditionality, rather than on many detailed policy commitments that might have to be updated every quarter.

A final crisis similarity is *frequent restarts and recalibrations*, in particular because of the limited agreement on the diagnoses of a crisis and what will work best to limit its depth and spread. When programs are renegotiated because they fail to turn the tide in the crisis, the number of requirements is increased. Programs have to include something new for everyone who criticized the failure of the previous program. One proxy indicator of this common feature of many crises is the number of letters of intent describing their proposed policies and objectives that the country's authorities submit to the IMF in connection with approval of continued disbursements, in particular during the first year. For Indonesia, there were 24 letters of intent, a whopping seven in the first year, and three in the first six months. In the Republic of Korea there were nine letters of intent in total, with six in the first year, but two in the first month (December) in part because the presidential election had occurred; and there were three in the first three months.

The Asian and European crises are not fully comparable because of changes in IMF policies and procedures in the meantime. Nevertheless, delays in reaching agreement on new letters of intent have been common throughout as the troika and the Greek authorities have wrestled with how best to address the Greek tragedy. Two elections also intervened.

Differences in the Evolution of the Asian and European Crises

Financial crises are not identical; they have different economic, financial, and policy environments. In what follows I trace 11 dimensions in which the evolution of the Asian and European crises differed.

The first pair of dimensions concerns the crisis overview. In retrospect, the Asian crises were more about liquidity and the European crises were more about solvency. Nevertheless, the scale of external financial support in the European crises dwarfed that in the Asian crises.

The next six dimensions look at the policy prescriptions or conditionality with respect to fiscal policy, monetary policy, financial sector restructuring, other structural reforms, private sector involvement, and foreign exchange policy. The conclusion is that the European programs have been less demanding than were those in the Asian crisis.

The last three dimensions concern the institutional and economic environment. The global and regional economic environment was more conducive to recovery for Asia than for Europe. But the negative effects of the European

---

tain financial stability;...[and] strong and effective social safeguards." The Zedillo dictum is named for former Mexican President Ernesto Zedillo.

crises on the global economy have been substantially larger than those of the Asian crises.

Crisis Overview

The distinction between liquidity and solvency crises is difficult to establish and not particularly operational in the case of countries and their governments, in particular when taking into account the fact that insolvent banks often have the implicit or explicit guaranty of their governments, which can lead to liquidity problems for governments that may turn into solvency problems. A liquidity crisis, if mishandled, can become a solvency crisis. Striking this difficult balance is one of the rationales for low-cost external financial support from institutions such as the IMF. The Fund provides a blend of financing and adjustment. Conditionality is essential, but all whip and little wampum invites failure.

Viewed through this lens, the Asian financial crises were primarily liquidity crises and the European financial crises involve solvency to a greater degree.

First, the debt and deficit fiscal positions of the Asian governments were sufficiently strong that they could absorb the fiscal effects of recession. Second, these countries were growing fast before their crises and were likely to be able to resume healthy rates of growth after it, which would assist in reducing debt burdens, scaled by GDP, after the crisis had passed.

Contrast the situation in Europe. The average growth rate for the crisis countries was a not-too-shabby 4.8 percent in the three years before the crisis—7.8 percent in the Eastern European countries and 3.3 percent in the euro area countries.[22] But the projected average growth rate for 2013 to 2018 is only 1.5 percent—2.7 percent for the East European countries and 0.9 percent for the euro area countries. These meager growth rates will not contribute much to boosting the denominators of debt ratios going forward. Iceland chose to force its banks to default on their external debts and thereby avoided taking those debts onto the government's balance sheet.

The focus is on numerators. Cyprus is doing the same, and five writedowns of Greek debt have already been arranged so far.[23] More writedowns and stretchouts that objectively reduce the net present value of debt claims are likely before the European crisis is over. Aside from the standstill and refinancing of the debts of Korean banks to foreign banks, a loose pledge of bank support

---

22. In these calculations, I omit Cyprus and include Iceland with the euro area countries.

23. The IMF rejected the first private sector involvement (writedown) for Greece because it provided insufficient debt reduction, with the result that the entire operation took more than eight months, while the Greek program was on hold, and was only completed in February 2012. By the end of that year, another partial writedown was required in the form of a debt buyback as part of a further revision in the Greek program. Meanwhile, there have been three instances of official sector involvement in Greece, reducing interest rates, stretching out maturities, and as a result reducing the net present value of Greek debt. See IMF (2013d).

in Thailand, and the private sector workouts in Indonesia, there was nothing comparable in the Asian financial crisis.

On the other hand, a much larger amount of external financing—the second dimension—has been provided to help overcome the European crises than was provided for the Asian crises (tables 6.5a and 6.5b). The generally wealthier euro area countries, in most cases, have received more external financial support than the Asian countries, but the associated firewalls have been insufficient to stem the spread of the euro area crisis. In light of European complaints about overly generous external financial support for the Asian countries in crisis, this pattern looks like the application of a double standard.

The IMF did not provide a substantially larger share of total commitments of financial support in Asia than in Europe as some claim (see chapter 7 in this volume). But the IMF was a much more dominant player in Asia. From this perspective, concerns about the IMF's minor role in Europe and loss of leverage as a major player (Goldstein 2011) may already have been overtaken by prior events.

Notwithstanding the scale of financial support in the European crises, efforts by the European authorities and the rest of the international community decisively to turn the tide have so far failed, and Europe remains mired in recession. In other words, crisis management in Europe has failed to end the crisis quickly. In the Asian crisis, on average the time required of countries to restore economic activity to the precrisis level was two and a half years. In Europe, only Iceland is projected to reach that point by 2013, five years later. The average for the non-euro-area countries is projected to be seven years, and for most of the euro area countries more than 10 years.[24]

Policy Prescriptions

In this subsection I compare and contrast the Asian and European crisis programs with respect to policy prescriptions regarding fiscal policies, monetary policies, financial sector restructuring, other structural reforms, private sector involvement, and foreign exchange policies.

One of the enduring myths is that the IMF, at the instigation of the advanced countries, imposes on the countries in crisis a one-size-fits-all approach to fiscal policy and that the Asian crises are exhibit A. The Independent Evaluation Office of the IMF (IEO 2003) found essentially no support for the fiscal myth: Fiscal targets are not set on the basis of one size fitting all and they are revised in a flexible manner. On the other hand, programs have often failed to achieve their targets because they were based on overoptimistic growth projections.

Based on the IMF's *World Economic Outlook* (WEO) data for general government net lending or borrowing in the five Asian countries, fiscal policy was less

---

24. Ireland, with the fastest euro area recovery, is projected to reach that point only in 2015, after eight years.

restrained (larger deficits or smaller surpluses) in 1998 than in 1997, and the same in 1999 (except in Indonesia, where fiscal policy tightened in 1999 but the trend toward relaxation resumed in 2000 and 2001). Unfortunately, we do not have consistent data on structural deficits for all of the Asian countries. For the Republic of Korea and Thailand, for which we do have WEO data (IMF 2013e), there was a small fiscal tightening of 0.4 percent of potential GDP in the former in 1998, but in the latter there was a loosening by 2 percentage points. Moreover, government expenditures rose as a percent of actual GDP in all the Asian countries in 1998, with the exception of Indonesia, where they fell by 0.2 percent.

The initial program in Thailand, which is often cited as the poster child for the IMF's fiscal austerity bias in Asia, envisaged a slight tightening to compensate in part for the costs of government rescues of large portions of the Thai financial system.[25] However, the basic critique fails to take into account the fact that programs and letters of intent are negotiated documents and are published. Fiscal policy is based on projections for the economy. In the Thai case, the authorities refused to accept publicly a projection of an economic contraction for 1998 in either of their first two letters of intent with the IMF, in August and November 1997, fearing the impact on confidence.[26] It is difficult to advocate fiscal expansion for an economy when it is in crisis but not in recession. It later emerged that the economy was already contracting in 1997, on a year-over-year basis, and declined by an additional 10 percent in 1998.[27] The Korean story is similar (Truman 2013).

Comparisons with the European crises are difficult because the ex ante fiscal circumstances were different—in particular, the European crises occurred in the aftermath of the global financial crisis and recession. On the same basis as used in the discussion of the Asian cases (general government net lending or

---

25. General government gross debt rose by 15 percentage points of GDP between 1997 and 1999.

26. In the August program, 1997 growth was estimated at 2.5 percent and projected to be 3.5 percent in 1998. The public sector balance was projected to be a deficit of 1.6 percent of GDP in 1997 after a surplus of 2.2 percent in 1996 and then tighten to surplus 1 percent in 1998. See "IMF Approves Stand-by Credit for Thailand," IMF Press Release 97/37, August 20, 1997, www.imf.org/external/np/sec/pr/1997/pr9737.htm (accessed on July 1, 2013).

27. To his credit, then-Treasury Secretary Lawrence Summers expressed strong skepticism about the initial projection of positive growth in Thailand and the tightening of fiscal policy in the program. Two years later (Summers 2000), he and others had recognized, or remembered, that devaluations can be deflationary through expenditure reduction in the short run, weakening the case for promoting domestic expenditure reduction via fiscal restraint to facilitate expenditure switching to external demand. The earlier myopia was not confined to the IMF at the time. At the Federal Reserve (1997) in November 1997, projected average growth in developing economies in 1998 was marked down by only 1.5 percentage points below estimated growth in 1997, and growth was projected to more than recover in 1999. As far as one can discern from the public record, outright recession was not anticipated in any of the Asian crisis countries. A big boost to Asian growth was expected from their real depreciations and consequent improved current account positions.

borrowing), deficits were larger in six of the nine countries (excluding Cyprus) in the first program year than the year before, but only in two countries in the second program year.[28] For the European countries we have a consistent series of general government structural deficits for each country, and on this basis only one country had a larger deficit in the first year of its program: Iceland.

It is also true that, by the late spring of 2010, the international policy mood had shifted to a focus on exiting from the extraordinary stimulus measures adopted in 2008 and 2009 as the global economy appeared to be bouncing back. At the G-20 Summit in Toronto on June 27, 2010, the leaders declared (G-20 2010):

> There is a risk that synchronized fiscal adjustment across several major econo-
> mies could adversely impact the recovery. There is also a risk that the failure to
> implement consolidation where necessary would undermine confidence and
> hamper growth. Reflecting this balance, advanced economies have committed
> to fiscal plans that will at least halve deficits by 2013 and stabilize or reduce
> government debt-to-GDP ratios by 2016.

This mood contributed to the decision by the new government in the United Kingdom aggressively to address that country's fiscal deficit. It is somewhat ironic that according to current projections (IMF 2013a), the only two advanced countries that will fail to fulfill their deficit commitments are Canada, which had a deficit of only 5.2 percent of GDP at its peak in 2010, and the United Kingdom.[29]

Thus, I conclude that the fiscal policy requirements of adjustment programs in Europe were harsher than those in Asia, but with generally good reason, at least for most of the crisis countries, as their fiscal situations were more precarious. Moreover, in Europe, countries faced dual fiscal condition-ality from the IMF and from the European Union's Excessive Deficit Procedure. The latter could be relaxed and has been in some cases, but the longer-term targets remained intact.

The monetary policies prescribed for the Asian crisis countries under their IMF programs also continue to be controversial, but less so. All countries initially sharply increased their interest rates to help stabilize their economies and arrest the free fall of their currencies.[30] Although many agree with the analysis of Jason Furman and Joseph Stiglitz (1998) that the sharp increases in interest rates further weakened banks and the real economy, the truth is that large parts of the financial systems in these economies were already insolvent

---

28. For Italy and Spain, the de facto first program year is 2012. Italy's deficit narrowed that year; Spain's widened.

29. Japan was given a pass at the time.

30. As noted in chapter 4 of this volume, in each of the Asian crisis countries except the Philippines there was a negative foreign exchange premium, suggesting that, in part, the interest rate increases were catching up with the market.

by that time. Moreover, the peaks in interest rates were in either the first or second quarter of 1998, and rates began to decline once conditions stabilized somewhat.[31] The more frequent assessment of this period is that increases in interest rates were associated with some collateral damage to financial institutions and economies, but the alternative of easier policy and continued currency declines would have had worse effects (Noland 2000a, Takagi 2010).

On balance, monetary policy prescriptions were not that different in Iceland and Eastern Europe than they were in Asia. Within the euro area, there was no monetary policy component to the programs. The ECB lowered its policy rate, but then inexplicably raised it twice in 2011 and also adopted nonstandard measures. A case can be made, however, that the IMF was softer on Europe by not insisting that the ECB run an easier policy throughout.

Turning to financial sector restructuring, in the Asian financial crisis, countries chose or were required to undergo a substantial restructuring of their financial systems and promote domestic equity and debt markets.[32] Financial institutions were closed, including more than 25 private banks in Indonesia and more than 50 finance houses in Thailand, or had their operations suspended or merged, including 21 of 30 merchant banks in the Republic of Korea. Some financial institutions were taken over by governments, including two major banks in the Republic of Korea, which the IMF wanted to be closed, and six commercial banks and five finance companies in Thailand. Capital standards were raised. Asset management companies were established in most countries, including Malaysia, which also employed a vehicle under the central bank to recapitalize viable banks and consolidate the banking system. The Basel Core Principles of Effective Banking Supervision were embraced as part of efforts to beef up supervision and regulation.[33]

I dwelt almost exclusively on financial system reform and sequencing in remarks at a conference at the Federal Reserve Bank of Chicago on lessons from the crisis (Truman 1999). Then-Secretary of the Treasury Lawrence Summers (2000, 12, 13) a few months later reviewed the lessons of the Asian crisis from a broader perspective. In a lecture at the 2000 meeting of the American Economic Association, he advocated prompt action "to maintain financial stability, by moving quickly to support healthy institutions and by intervening in unhealthy institutions. The loss of confidence in the financial system and episodes of bank

---

31. Even in Malaysia, without an IMF program, interest rates rose 250 to 300 basis points before declining, and in the Philippines, with its milder crisis, they rose by 300 to 400 basis points. These data are from IMF, *International Financial Statistics* database, 2001.

32. See chapter 5 in this volume for details on policy advice and actions with respect to financial sectors during the Asian financial crises. Marcus Noland (2000a, 222–26) summarizes Korean actions.

33. The Basel Committee on Banking Supervision and Regulation promulgated the Core Principles in September 1997 for all countries, but in particular for those that were not members of the Basel Committee. The principles were developed as a response to problems revealed by the Tequila Crisis in 1994–95.

panics [in Asia] were not caused by necessary interventions in insolvent institutions." They were caused, he continued, by delays in addressing nonperforming loans, implicit bailout guarantees and associated gambles for redemption, deposit guarantees that were not fiscally credible, and political distortions.

In contrast, although banking sector stabilization has been prominent in some European crisis programs, particularly those for Iceland, Ireland, Spain, and Cyprus, comprehensive financial sector restructuring has not figured prominently beyond unavoidable stabilization and rescue operations. In the Irish case, the cleanup started in 2008 with the outbreak of the global financial crisis, but Ireland's IMF and euro area programs, for example, have not settled the issue of unsecured, unguaranteed creditors (Pisani-Ferry, Sapir, and Wolff 2013, 57; Ahearne 2012).

European central bankers and regulators also have participated in efforts centered at the Bank for International Settlements and the Financial Stability Board to reform the global financial system. They instituted EU-wide institutional changes along lines advocated by the group that Jacques de Larosière (2009) chaired on supervisory reforms in the European Union. But not until 2012, five years after the outbreak of the global financial crisis, with failures in financial systems and in supervision and regulation at its core, did the Europeans directly confront issues of banking system supervision and regulation, as they are now doing under the rubric of creating a European banking union. And even those belated efforts have been focused on the prevention and management of future crises rather than on cleaning up after the current crisis.

In the fall of 2011, the IMF sounded the alarm about euro-area-wide weaknesses of banking systems, to the consternation of the European authorities. Then, in 2013 in its *Global Financial Stability Report* (IMF 2013b), the IMF raised concerns about the overhang of corporate debt in the euro area and the implications for financial stability.

It is understandable that, at the start of the global financial crisis, the focus of European authorities was on stabilization of the banking system, initially to prevent a Lehman-style event in Europe. European governments were moved to rescue many banks, often with substantial consequences for their fiscal positions. Subsequently, because of the central role of banks in financial intermediation in Europe, the focus has been on facilitating the resumption of growth and limiting immediate fiscal costs of financial rescues rather than on reform or transformation of the financial system. Compared with the Asian crises, European actions in this dimension have been part of some IMF programs, but not aggressively pursued as advised and analyzed by outside observers such as Morris Goldstein and Nicolas Veron (2011), Adam Posen and Veron (2009), Veron (2007), and Veron and Guntram Wolff (2013).[34]

---

34. Veron (2013) is somewhat more optimistic about prospects for progress in taking the first steps toward establishing a European banking union and breaking the doom loop between banks and the sovereign governments that implicitly or explicitly stand behind them. But it is late in the game.

On balance, although there are some exceptions, I conclude that financial sector reform has been less rigorous and comprehensive in Europe than it was in Asia, even though in Asia it was far from complete.

With respect to promoting structural reform, other than in the financial system, programs in the European crisis countries appear to have been less rigorous than was the case in Asia, where structural conditions were rampant. This type of comparison is difficult to make, however. First, one is comparing feta cheese in Greece with cloves in Indonesia. Second, as noted in Barkbu, Eichengreen, and Mody (2011, 19–21), counting the number of structural conditions is a crude indicator, at best loosely correlated with completed reform even before trying to weigh the importance of those conditions. On the other hand, the euro area crisis countries were subject to a second letter of intent and memorandum of understanding with the European Commission.

The most prominent structural reforms in the programs associated with the European crises have been linked to reform of fiscal systems and reduction of gross government debt via privatization. The apparent overall lack of attention to nonfiscal structural reforms is surprising because one of the principal, putative causes of the European crises was the deteriorating relative competitiveness of the affected economies. One might have thought that IMF-supported and EU structural reform programs would have addressed some of these issues, but aside from a few references to labor market reforms, and cuts in minimum wages in Greece and Portugal, the emphasis has been on pension and other reforms that have fiscal implications. Most summaries of the programs of the European crisis countries do not highlight reforms that are intended to improve relative competitiveness.[35] According to the IMF (2013c), an ex post assessment of the first Greek program, the successive letters of intent contained 21 prior actions and structural benchmarks relating to the fiscal sector, nine relating to competitiveness, and nine relating to the financial sector.

As discussed above, in the context of the liquidity-solvency dimension of these crises, private sector involvement—that is, seeking or imposing financial contributions from private sector investors to help finance or reduce the present or future financial requirements of governments of crisis countries, including with respect to their banks—was limited in the Asian financial crises and already has been more prominent in Europe, though not universal in all cases, with a good chance of more to come.

In Asia, the official sector, without much success, encouraged foreign banks to maintain their exposures in Thailand , and encouraged the settlement of foreign bank claims on Indonesian banks and corporations. But as Roubini and Setser (2004, 153) observe, the latter effort with the banks "was less about avoiding a bad outcome and more about cleaning up the financial mess that

---

35. See Henning (2011) and the website of the European Commission, Economic and Financial Affairs, http://ec.europa.eu/economy_finance/assistance_eu_ms/index_en.htm (accessed on July 1, 2013).

results when an economy and a financial system implode." The one significant element of private sector involvement in Asia was the decision to seek a foreign bank standstill on claims on Korean banks, and the foreign banks' subsequent funding of those claims into longer-term instruments.

In Europe, the question has not been whether, but when and how, to impose losses on private sector creditors via informal understandings, formal negotiations, or unilateral government action. Iceland chose the third route, with capital controls and de facto repudiation of the foreign debts of its major banks as those failed institutions were resolved. The IMF press release on November 19, 2008, about the IMF Executive Board's approval of Iceland's program states that it would include such controls as part of the comprehensive and collaborative strategy for restructuring the banking system, which was already well under way, "ensuring the fair and equitable treatment of depositors and creditors of the intervened banks." Domestic creditors took their losses, and foreign creditors with merit but with little result claim that they did not receive fair and equitable treatment. In the fall of 2008, the issue in the rest of Europe, of course, was preventing a run on the banks that were major holders of sovereign debt. As in the Republic of Korea in November 1997, forcing standstills or stretchouts on banks as creditors was regarded as a sure way to encourage such a run.

The ECB was the principal proponent of caution with respect to aggressive private sector involvement via either negotiation or unilateral government action. Neil Irwin (2013, 290) reports that ECB President Jean-Claude Trichet lobbied long and hard against bailing in government or bank creditors, and that no one was angrier than he at the French-German agreement at Deauville in October 2010, which, as far as markets were concerned, opened the door to this possibility sooner rather than later. One can suspect that the ECB position also was motivated by a desire to protect its own balance sheet. On the other hand, public anger at bailing out governments and banks runs high, which was one of the motivations behind the ill-timed Deauville agreement.

Of course, opinions can differ, these are not easy issues, but I am disinclined to revise my judgment at that time:[36] Any debt reduction would deliver a severe shock to the European economies and it was too early to know how much debt reduction would be appropriate.[37] The contagion argument is the most compelling. If the IMF or non-Europeans had insisted on a deep reduction in the face value of Greece's debt in May 2010, it would have exacerbated the already rampant spread of the euro area debt crises under conditions in which the Europeans had not yet established even the flimsiest of firewalls. In addition, one could not know in May 2010 how much debt reduction was

---

36. Edwin M. Truman, "The Role of the International Monetary Fund and Federal Reserve in the Stabilization of Europe," testimony before the Subcommittee on International Monetary Policy and Subcommittee on Domestic Monetary Policy and Technology, US House Financial Services Committee, May 20, 2010.

37. I was comforted then that Michael Mussa (2010) and I agreed.

required to put Greece back on the road to economic and financial recovery. It was not a pretty picture.

Weaker arguments favoring debt reduction for Greece in May 2010 are that (1) Greece's debt was a burden holding back recovery of the Greek economy, but any added uncertainty was small; (2) the IMF was forced to take on a large part of the total exposure to Greece, that is its job; (3) the Europeans would not have agreed, but if it was the right thing to do, the other members of the IMF should have insisted upon doing it; and (4) generally, as argued in IMF (2013d), debt reduction is too little and too late—without a dramatic change in approach to private sector involvement issues, early debt reductions will almost always be too small and need to be repeated. Without defaulting, Greece in 2010 could not have achieved the two-thirds reduction in face value of its debt that Barry Eichengreen (2013) argues was appropriate.

Finally, in Europe, there has been the mismanaged private sector involvement in the restructuring of Cypriot banks. True, the final solution on its surface is structured to be private-sector-to-private-sector, but no one is fooled, in particular because one of the banks is already in government hands and another one or more banks, as of this writing, may soon follow.

Thus, we have already observed more extensive private sector involvement in the European crisis than was the case in Asia. More is likely to come, and a case can be made for its happening sooner rather than later.

The final dimension of difference between policy prescriptions in the Asian and European crises concerns exchange rate policies, which are the jealously guarded prerogative of governments. Of course, markets do force events, at least with respect to devaluations, and the IMF has some capacity to do so as well once a country has taken the decision to turn to it for assistance, which often happens after, not before, a decisive change in exchange rate policy has already occurred.

Thus, in Asia, Thailand, Malaysia, the Philippines, Indonesia, and the Republic of Korea had already abandoned their pegs before turning to the IMF for advice or financial assistance (or renewed assistance in the case of the Philippines). Once a country has a program with the IMF, the institution can encourage or discourage a particular policy approach. The normal bias is in the direction encouraging exchange rate flexibility, in particular downward so as not to dissipate international reserves.

In the policy community, there were extensive debates about exchange rate regimes during the Asian crisis. The debate featured a number of people who advocated corner solutions, sometimes with no preference between one and the other: an absolutely fixed exchange rate, such as with a currency board, or a regime of an essentially freely floating rate. However, the Asian economies, except for Malaysia, which reverted to a fixed rate in September 1998, chose ad hoc regimes of managed floating, but with less heavy management than before their crises. That management has permitted somewhat greater exchange rate flexibility, but it also has been directed at sustaining competitive (some would say hypercompetitive) exchange rates to support current account surpluses and the substantial accumulation of international reserves as insurance against future crises.

In Europe, the principal shortfall on exchange rate policies was before the crisis. The IMF and outside countries did not engage on the issue of euro memberships and surveillance of the euro area was essentially nonexistent until 2008.

The question is whether the IMF and non-European countries should have forced exchange rate adjustments within the euro area; in other words, should they have advocated the departure from the euro of one or more euro area countries in crisis? This is not an easy question to answer. They should have discussed euro exit, and probably did, but I doubt that either the IMF or its principal non-European shareholders seriously considered advising exit from the euro for any of the crisis countries.

It is clear that several of the countries that joined the euro were not fully prepared for the consequences of giving up their monetary and exchange rate independence, even though both were already highly constrained at the time, as was the case with Hungary and Romania during their crises. However, mulligans are not available to policymakers. The choice of leaving the euro would have been consequential for these economies (Åslund 2012). Once one country exits or is forced to exit, the pressures and contagion are likely to be overwhelming on the remaining candidates to leave. The arguments that there could be an amicable disengagement or temporary exit are naïve; markets and/ or domestic politics will force an exit, and neither governments nor the market will have the leisure for any negotiation that lasts longer than a weekend.

In summary, my assessment is that the programs adopted in the European crisis generally have been less demanding and rigorous than those in the Asian crisis. But the debate is far from over.

In addition to the fact that Europe has received more financing, which may be a program improvement, and that fiscal policies have been more stringent in Europe, which may be a mistake, the euro crisis programs have fallen short relative to the Asian standard. On monetary policy, the ECB could have been required to have been easier. On financial sector restructuring, despite some program content, the core issues have not been fully addressed, in particular on a euro-area-wide basis, to the extent that they were in Asia. On other structural policies, although again there are exceptions, the content has been less than in Asia, which operationally was a different environment with respect to these policies. Private sector involvement has been more prominent in Europe than it was in Asia, but it probably should have been. On exchange rate policies, the failures in Europe were before the euro was introduced and in surveillance of the euro area after the introduction of the common currency.

Institutional and Economic Environment

With respect to institutions, the Asian crisis countries had only loose consultative associations, for example in the form of the Association of Southeast Asian Nations, Asia-Pacific Economic Cooperation forum, and the Executives'

Meeting of East Asia Pacific Central Banks. During the crisis, the Japanese authorities proposed the creation of an Asian Monetary Fund, which was rejected on policy and practical grounds.

After the Asian crises had largely passed, the Chiang Mai Initiative (CMI) was established in 2000. The CMI has since evolved into the Chiang Mai Initiative Multilateralization (CMIM) but it has never been tested in a crisis.[38] Thus, although the Asian countries were linked in crisis, frequently consulted together, and their crises were treated sequentially (learning by doing), their responses were not coordinated. The world was able to respond forcefully to the Asian crises with substantial financial support even as the countries themselves, after a few false starts, responded promptly with policy reforms, despite the view of some of their leaders that the international financial support was inadequate and the IMF was heavy handed.

In Europe, with the exception of Iceland, the preferred approach was lockstep cooperation but with a separate negotiation before taking each step and with little in the way of robust supporting institutions. The EU Balance of Payments Facility was not sufficient to handle the crises in Hungary, Latvia, and Romania, though it played a major role along with the IMF. The euro area had no structures, aside from the ECB and the eurogroup of finance ministers, to address the euro area crises. The ECB lacked an executive branch or government counterpart, and the eurogroup was only a partial substitute. As many warned before 1999 when the ECB began its operations and the euro was first introduced, the institutional architecture of the EMU was incomplete.

Starting in 2007, but with increasing virulence as of late 2009, the need for coordination and for effective euro area institutions became painfully apparent. The euro itself was not sufficient to protect countries as each plunged into crisis or to protect their partners from being pulled down as well. As a result, the Europeans have been playing catchup. Most serious, the lack of institutions and procedures for crisis management prevented the Europeans from following the Powell Doctrine of "overwhelming force" in the application of financial support and policy actions. The firewall was insufficient and policy actions were tentative and less than comprehensive. Much was accomplished in a short period of time, but it was insufficient.

The euro area countries finally agreed, more or less, on one objective: keeping the euro together. But members of the euro area have been pushed further apart economically, financially, and politically. A comprehensive euro area crisis management strategy was never formulated and adopted. I blame the management and staff of the IMF and other major countries, as well as the euro area countries themselves, for this failing.

The members of the euro area wanted to preserve the euro, but they were not prepared to accept conditionality applied to the euro area as a single entity. The rest of the world, to its regret, allowed the Europeans to have it both ways—

---

38. This experience sparked an ongoing international discussion of proposals for global financial safety nets; see chapter 7 in this volume and Truman (2010 and 2011b).

save the euro but by imposing all the policy conditions only on the countries in crisis—another example of a European double standard.

The IMF should have insisted, as part of the first program for Greece, that the other members of the euro area adopt a complementary strategy as a condition for its approval of the Greek program. The IMF (2013c) ex post evaluation of the first Greek program notes the lack of IMF experience in operations with individual countries that are members of monetary unions.

At the outset of the Greek crisis the IMF should have required the ECB immediately to cut its policy interest rate close to zero. The ECB also should have agreed, as an exceptional measure, to exclude the contribution to euro area inflation of value-added tax rate increases by countries in crisis. It was also a mistake not to require the ECB to absorb losses on its holdings of Greek debt when it was restructured in early 2012.

With respect to fiscal policy, given the level of its sovereign debts, Greece had little choice but to tighten its fiscal belt, though with more financing or on better terms the timetable could and should have been stretched out. The scope for gradual adjustment was even more defensible in other euro area crisis countries. In any case, the better-placed countries in the euro area should have compensated for the effects of fiscal restraint in the crisis countries on the area as a whole. A timetable should have been set, in the form of policy conditions, for the comprehensive euro-area-wide restructuring of financial institutions. A similar condition should have been the establishment of a European banking union, which now, three years later, is being discussed. The banking union should have been developed as an immediate crisis management tool with all three crucial elements quickly put in place: supervision, resolution, and deposit protection at least covering systemically important institutions.

Finally, IMF support should have been conditioned on the creation of a structure of euro-area-wide financial assistance in which fiscal commitments from governments provided the equity backstop for the ECB to leverage into overwhelming liquidity support. In other words, what was needed, but was not to be, was an instant ad hoc fiscal union with at least de facto eurobonds.

The European authorities lacked the leadership and cohesion to act decisively once they had rejected a pure euro area rescue and a pure IMF rescue of crisis countries in the euro area without European involvement. The IMF was too timid, paralyzed, or conflicted to require such steps as a condition for its participation in the Greek or subsequent programs.

The Europeans did face at least one environmental factor that was largely not of their own making. Their crises were a component, or an extension, of the global financial crisis and recession, the worst global downturn since the Great Depression. The recovery was likely to be tepid because of the combination of recession with banking crises in most countries (Claessens, Kose, and Terrones 2011).

However, that same interaction was present in Asia as well. Economic growth slowed in developing Asia from an average rate of 8.9 percent over 1994–96 to 5 percent over 1997–98 with a pickup only to 6.9 percent in 1999–

Table 6.6   Estimated effects of the Asian and European crises on global growth (percent)

Country group	Cumulative growth		Difference: postcrisis minus precrisis
	Precrisis estimate	Postcrisis estimate	
Asian crisis			
World	11.9	11.3	−0.6
Advanced	7.9	10.6	2.7
Emerging-market and developing	17.5	12.5	−5.0
Developing Asia	20.6	17.0	−3.6
European crisis			
World	14.1	10.8	−3.3
Advanced	7.6	4.2	−3.5
Emerging-market and developing	20.9	17.7	−3.2
Euro area	5.3	0.5	−4.8
European Union	6.1	1.4	−4.8

Notes: For Asia, 1997 to 2000, and for Europe, 2010 to 2013.

Sources: Precrisis Asia: IMF, *World Economic Outlook* database, May 1997, May 1998, and May 1999; precrisis Europe: IMF, *World Economic Outlook* database, April 2011; postcrisis Asia and Europe: IMF, *World Economic Outlook* database, April 2013.

2003.[39] Consequently, for the world as a whole, growth was 3.5 percent in both the precrisis and postcrisis periods and, in fact, rose to 3.8 percent in the crisis years of 1997–98.

Europe was not so fortunate. Global growth slowed from 4.9 percent on average over 2004–06 (5.1 percent over 2004–07). Of course, during 2008 and 2009, global growth averaged an anemic 1.1 percent, growth in the emerging-market and developing countries was 4.4 percent, and the advanced-country and European-country groups were in recession. Global growth recovered to average only 3.9 percent over 2010–14.[40]

The euro area has failed to implement a growth agenda (Darvas, Pisani-Ferry, and Wolff 2013). Growth agendas are slow acting, but five years is plenty of time if the programs had been well designed and had paid attention to the needs of supporting the EMU.

The question is, Which way does the growth causality run: from the rest of the world to Asia and Europe or vice versa? And was the nature of the causality the same in both periods? Table 6.6 provides estimates of the effects, or correlations if one prefers, of the management of the two crises and contempora-

39. The data and forecasts in this and the following paragraphs come from the IMF's *World Economic Outlook* database, April 2013.

40. The higher global growth in the second crisis period is due to the higher contemporaneous weight on faster-growing emerging-market and developing countries.

neous global growth. The comparison is complicated by the fact, as already noted, that the crises in the euro area occurred in the aftermath of the global financial crisis. But the collective management of the global financial crisis, with its epicenter in the United States, was on the whole quite successful; for example, global growth in 2010, the first full postrecession year, was better than the IMF expected.

The data presented in table 6.6 indicate a relatively small link between the Asian crises and contemporaneous global growth.[41] Cumulative growth of real GDP from 1997 to 2001 produced a level of global GDP in 2001 that was only 0.6 percent less than originally projected; real GDP was 2.7 percent higher for the advanced countries as a group. It was lower not only for developing countries in Asia but also for the larger group of emerging-market and developing countries. They were affected, of course, by the Russian, Brazilian, Turkish, and Argentine crises of 1998–2000, which are often treated as extensions of the Asian crisis.

In contrast, the negative link between the European crises and global growth appears to have been larger and more widespread. The 3.3 percent shortfall in the level of economic activity for the world translates in 2013 into a loss of $2.9 trillion of global GDP (on a purchasing power parity basis) or about $400 for each of the 7 billion residents of the world today.[42] Even at half this size these effects are consequential.

How should one assess blame for this estimated damage? I am inclined to credit the mishandling of the European crises with most of the global shortfall. But should we blame just the Europeans or their partners in the rest of the world as well? My answer is both. The rest of the world exercised forbearance on the Europeans by providing more financing than in earlier crises (though not enough to ring-fence other euro area countries) and, more importantly, by not requiring more forceful policy actions. At the same time, the Europeans proved institutionally unprepared and insufficiently imaginative to supply the financial and policy actions on the needed scale.

Lasting Lessons?

This review of the Asian crisis in comparison with the ongoing European crisis has argued that the two crises are more similar than different. It follows that there will be more crises. The principal lesson from this review is that policies should emphasize not only crisis prevention but also crisis preparedness and management.

As the world becomes more integrated economically and financially, crises are becoming more frequent and have broader effects. The epicenter of the 2008 global financial crisis was not the emerging-market and developing coun-

---

41. See Truman (2013, forthcoming) for more details on these calculations.

42. The loss for the euro area is $550 billion and for the European Union it is $780 billion, implying a loss of $2.1 trillion outside the European Union.

tries, but they were affected. They also have been affected by the European crises even if the causality does not all run one way. The global economy and financial system are parts of a general equilibrium system with many moving parts in terms of institutions and public and private actors. We can limit the virulence of future crises by learning some of the lessons of crisis preparedness as well as crisis prevention to facilitate better crisis management.

The global financial crisis was not fundamentally different from other crises in my experience over the past 40 years. Any student of crises would conclude that there were no real surprises, just amplified variations on the basic theme of excesses that get out of hand, investors who think they can pull out before the crash but end up being victims of the crash, and policymakers in denial. Collectively and consequently, they in turn delay taking corrective actions, disagree on diagnoses, and therefore disagree on short-term and longer-term policy prescriptions with respect to crisis prevention and management.

The fact that crises are inevitable does not mean that countries cannot be better prepared and should not be concerned about their vulnerabilities. IMF Managing Director Christine Lagarde was right in April 2013 to warn that corporations in emerging-market and developing countries may be relying excessively on foreign-currency borrowing, thinking it is cheap and can easily be repaid.[43] Vigilance and reform will be rewarded even if this is not the source of the next crisis.[44] One reason why Asia was less adversely affected by the global financial crisis is that countries in that region had learned some lessons and, consequently, were less vulnerable, i.e., less ill prepared (see chapter 4 in this volume). The same holds for Latin America. Policies are important, growth models matter, and adequate amounts of external financial assistance on appropriate terms are crucial.

Countries can make the wrong choices for themselves and for the system. In hindsight, some countries in the euro area should not have joined the euro. Many countries in and outside the euro area have paid for the hubris of European leaders and their decision to launch the euro with a broad membership. The jury is still out as to whether, and in what economic and financial shape, the EMU will survive. My judgment is that the European integration project and the euro will survive, but the Europeans will pay a high price in terms of economic stagnation for many years to come. The rest of the world already has paid a high price in terms of lost growth.

Thus, I conclude that the European crisis is more severe than the Asian crisis. It follows that outsiders should care more about what groups of countries do. Leaders and institutions outside Europe did not care enough about

43. Christine Lagarde, "The Global Policy Agenda Actions Needed to Stay Ahead of the Crisis," speech at the Economic Club of New York, April 10, 2013, www.imf.org/external/np/speeches/2013/041013.htm (accessed in July 2013).

44. For a broader warning, see Claudio Borio, "On Time, Stocks and Flows: Understanding the Global Macroeconomic Challenges," lecture in Munich, October 15, 2012, Bank for International Settlements, www.bis.org/speeches/sp121109a.pdf (accessed on July 1, 2013).

what was going on in Europe before the outbreak of the crisis there or during the global financial crisis. In the future, IMF surveillance and programs must focus primarily on the euro area as a whole and only tangentially on its individual members. The IMF should let the euro area institutions focus on the individual countries.

References

Ahearne, Alan. 2012. Political-Economic Context in Ireland. In *Resolving the European Debt Crisis*, ed. William R. Cline and Guntram B. Wolff. Special Report 21. Washington, DC: Peterson Institute for International Economics.

Åslund, Anders. 2010. *The Last Shall Be the First: The East European Financial Crisis*. Washington, DC: Peterson Institute for International Economics.

Åslund, Anders. 2012. *Why a Breakup of the Euro Area Must Be Avoided: Lessons from Previous Breakups*. Policy Brief 12-20. Washington, DC: Peterson Institute for International Economics.

Barkbu, Bergljot, Barry Eichengreen, and Ashoka Mody. 2011. *International Financial Crises and the Multilateral Response: What the Historical Record Shows*. NBER Working Paper 17361. Cambridge, MA: National Bureau of Economic Research.

Blustein, Paul. 2003. *The Chastening: Inside the Crisis That Rocked the Global Financial System and Humbled the IMF*. New York: Public Affairs.

Borio, Claudio, and Philip Lowe. 2002. *Asset Prices, Financial and Monetary Stability: Exploring the Nexus*. BIS Working Paper 114. Basel: Bank for International Settlements.

Borio, Claudio, and William White. 2003. Whither Monetary and Financial Stability? The Implications of Evolving Policy Regimes. Paper presented at the Federal Reserve Bank of Kansas City Symposium, Jackson Hole, Wyoming, August 28–30.

Claessens, Stijn, and M. Ayhan Kose. 2013. *Financial Crises: Explanations, Types, and Implications*. IMF Working Paper 13/2. Washington, DC: International Monetary Fund.

Claessens, Stijn, M. Ayhan Kose, and Marco Terrones. 2011. *How Do Business and Financial Cycles Interact?* IMF Working Paper 11/88. Washington, DC: International Monetary Fund.

Darvas, Zsolt, Jean Pisani-Ferry, and Guntram Wolff. 2013. *Europe's Growth Problem (And What to do About It)*. Bruegel Policy Brief 2013/03 (April). Brussels: Bruegel.

de Larosière, Jacques, Leszek Balcerowicz, Otmar Issing, Rainer Masera, Callum McCarthy, Lars Nyberg, José Pérez, and Onno Ruding. 2009. *Report of the High-Level Group on Financial Supervision in the EU*. Brussels: European Commission.

Eichengreen, Barry. 2013. *Lessons of a Greek Tragedy*. Project Syndicate (June 13). Available at www.project-syndicate.org (accessed on July 15, 2013).

Federal Reserve Board. 1997. *Greenbook Part I* (November 12). Available at www.federalreserve.gov/monetarypolicy/fomchistorial1997 (accessed on July 15, 2013).

Furman, Jason, and Joseph E. Stiglitz. 1998. Economic Crises: Evidence and Insights from East Asia. *Brookings Papers on Economic Activity* 2:1–135.

Furuoka, Fumitaka, May Chiun Lo, and Iwao Kato. 2007. Japan's Foreign Aid Policy Towards Malaysia: Case Studies in the New Miyazawa Initiative and the Kelau Dam Construction. *Electronic Journal of Contemporary Japanese Studies* 1 (March 1). Available at www.japanesestudies.org.uk/articles/2007/FuruokaLoKato.html (accessed on July 1, 2013).

G-20 (Group of Twenty). 2010. The G-20 Toronto Summit Declaration (June 27). Available at www.g20.utoronto.ca/2010/to-communique.html (accessed on July 15, 2013).

Gelpern, Anna. 2009. Financial Crisis Containment. *Connecticut Law Review* 41, no. 4 (May): 493–549.

Goldstein, Morris. 1998. *The Asian Financial Crisis*. Policy Brief 98-1. Washington, DC: Institute for International Economics.

Goldstein, Morris. 2011. The Role of the IMF in a Reformed International Monetary System. Paper presented to the Bank of Korea's Research Conference, May 26-27. Photocopy.

Goldstein, Morris, and Nicolas Veron. 2011. *Too Big To Fail: The Transatlantic Debate*. Working Paper 11-2. Washington, DC: Peterson Institute for International Economics.

Goldstein, Morris, Graciela Kaminsky, and Carmen Reinhart. 2000. *Assessing Financial Vulnerability: An Early Warning System for Emerging Markets*. Washington, DC: Institute for International Economics.

Henning, C. Randall. 2011. *Coordinating Regional and Multilateral Financial Institutions*. Working Paper 11-9. Washington, DC: Peterson Institute for International Economics.

IEO (Independent Evaluation Office). 2003. *Fiscal Adjustment in IMF-Supported Programs*. Washington, DC: International Monetary Fund.

IEO (Independent Evaluation Office). 2011. *IMF Performance in the Run-Up to the Financial and Economic Crisis: IMF Surveillance in 2004-07*. Washington, DC: International Monetary Fund.

IMF (International Monetary Fund). 2008. *Iceland: 2008 Article IV Consultation* (December). Washington, DC.

IMF (International Monetary Fund). 2012. *2012 Spillover Report* (July). Washington, DC.

IMF (International Monetary Fund). 2013a. *Fiscal Monitor* (April). Washington, DC.

IMF (International Monetary Fund). 2013b. *Global Financial Stability Report* (April). Washington, DC.

IMF (International Monetary Fund). 2013c. *Greece: Ex Post Evaluation of Exceptional Access Under the 2010 Stand-By Arrangement* (May). Washington, DC.

IMF (International Monetary Fund). 2013d. *Sovereign Debt Restructuring: Recent Developments and Implications for the Fund's Legal and Policy Framework* (April). Washington, DC.

IMF (International Monetary Fund). 2013e. *World Economic Outlook* (April). Washington, DC.

Irwin, Neil. 2013. *The Alchemists: Three Central Bankers and a World on Fire*. New York: Penguin Press.

Mishkin, Frederic S., and Tryggvi Thor Herbertsson. 2006. *Financial Stability in Iceland*. Reykjavik: Chamber of Commerce.

Mussa, Michael. 2010. *Beware of Greeks Bearing Debts* (May 17). Available at www.piie.com/publications/papers/mussa201005.pdf (accessed on July 1, 2013).

Noland, Marcus. 2000a. *Avoiding the Apocalypse: The Future of the Two Koreas*. Washington, DC: Institute for International Economics.

Noland, Marcus. 2000b. The Philippines in the Asian Financial Crisis: How the Sick Man Avoided Pneumonia. *Asian Survey* 40, no. 3: 401-12.

Posen, Adam, and Nicolas Veron. 2009. *A Solution for Europe's Banking Problem*. Policy Brief 09-13. Washington, DC: Peterson Institute for International Economics.

Pisani-Ferry, Jean, André Sapir, and Guntram B. Wolff. 2011. *An Evaluation of IMF Surveillance of the Euro Area: Final Report*. Bruegel Blueprint 14. Brussels: Bruegel.

Pisani-Ferry, Jean, André Sapir, and Guntram B. Wolff. 2013. Financial Assistance in the Euro Area: An Early Evaluation. Presentation at the Peterson Institute for International Economics, Washington, DC (April 19). Available at www.piie.com/publications/papers/pisani-ferry20130419ppt.pdf (accessed on July 1, 2013).

Roubini, Nouriel, and Brad Setser. 2004. *Bailouts or Bail-Ins? Responding to Financial Crises in Emerging Economies*. Washington, DC: Institute for International Economics and Council on Foreign Relations.

Summers, Lawrence H. 2000. International Financial Crises: Causes, Prevention, and Cures. *American Economic Review Papers and Proceedings* 90, no. 2: 1–16.

Takagi, Shinji. 2010. *Applying the Lessons of Asia: The IMF's Crisis Management Strategy in 2008.* ADBI Working Paper 206 (March). Tokyo: Asian Development Bank Institute.

Truman, Edwin M. 1999. Lessons from the Asian Crisis. In *The Asian Financial Crisis: Origins, Implications, and Solutions,* ed. William C. Hunter, George G. Kaufman, and Thomas H. Krueger. Boston: Kluwer Academic Publishers.

Truman, Edwin M. 2005. The Euro and Prospects for Policy Coordination. In *The Euro at Five: Ready for a Global Role?* ed. Adam S. Posen. Special Report 18. Washington, DC: Institute for International Economics.

Truman, Edwin M. 2009. Policy Responses to the Global Financial Crisis. Remarks presented at the Ninth Annual International Seminar, on Policy Challenges for the Financial Sector Emerging from the Crisis: Building a Stronger International Financial System, Board of Governors of the Federal Reserve System, World Bank, and International Monetary Fund, June 3. Available at www.piie.com (accessed on June 15, 2013).

Truman, Edwin M. 2010. *The G-20 and International Financial Institution Governance.* Working Paper 10-13. Washington, DC: Peterson Institute for International Economics.

Truman, Edwin M. 2011a. Asian Regional Policy Coordination. In *Asia's Role in the Post-Crisis Global Economy,* ed. Reuven Glick and Mark Spiegel. San Francisco: Federal Reserve Bank of San Francisco.

Truman, Edwin M. 2011b. Three Evolutionary Proposals for Reform of the International Monetary System. Extension of remarks at the Bank of Italy's Conference in Memory of Tommaso Padoa-Schioppa (December 16). Available at www.piie.com/publications/papers/truman12162011.PDF (accessed on July 1, 2013).

Truman, Edwin M. 2013 (forthcoming). *The Asian and European Financial Crises Compared.* Working Paper. Washington, DC: Peterson Institute for International Economics.

Veron, Nicolas. 2007. *Is Europe Ready for a Major Banking Crisis?* Bruegel Policy Brief 2007/03 (August). Brussels: Bruegel.

Veron, Nicolas. 2013. *A Realistic Bridge towards European Banking Union.* Policy Brief 13-17. Washington, DC: Peterson Institute for International Economics.

Veron, Nicolas, and Guntram B. Wolff. 2013. *From Supervision to Resolution: Next Steps on the Road to European Banking Union.* Policy Brief 13-5. Washington, DC: Peterson Institute for International Economics.

7

Global and Regional Financial Safety Nets: Lessons from Europe and Asia

CHANGYONG RHEE, LEA SUMULONG, AND SHAHIN VALLÉE

The failings of the international monetary system in the 1970s and the rise of financial globalization may well have increased the volatility of economic cycles (Rodrik 1997, Scheve and Slaughter 2001, Krugman 1991). In the last 20 years, the Asian crisis in 1997, the global financial crisis in 2008, and the European crisis in 2009 stand out as having been particularly deep and widespread, causing considerable loss in output in a number of countries. As a result, the demand for insurance against these shocks has grown and the shortcomings of the existing insurance mechanisms have been exposed. The Bretton Woods institutions, and in particular the International Monetary Fund (IMF), met these demands imperfectly, and as a result alternative insurance mechanisms—both national and regional—have been developed over the years.

Even though this process of regionalization of monetary cooperation started in the 1970s, in recent years both the Asian crisis and more recently the European crisis have decisively contributed to the establishment of regional safety net arrangements as a necessary complement to international arrangements. The 2008 global financial crisis has substantially improved the preexisting international financial safety net architecture to address financial crises with liquidity tools designed for preemptive actions. In addition, the central banking community has shown a remarkable ability during the crisis, albeit in

Changyong Rhee is the chief economist of the Asian Development Bank. Lea Sumulong is senior economics officer at the Economics and Research Department of the Asian Development Bank. Shahin Vallée was appointed to the Cabinet of European Council President Herman Van Rompuy as economic advisor in July 2012. He was visiting fellow at Bruegel from October 2010 to June 2012. They thank C. Randall Henning, Yoichi Nemoto, Mark Sobel, Edwin Truman, and two anonymous reviewers for their comments on an earlier draft, and Ryan Jacildo for excellent research assistance The views expressed in this chapter are those of the authors and do not necessarily reflect the views and policies of the Asian Development Bank or its Board of Governors or the governments they represent. Neither does the chapter reflect the views or policies of the European Council.

ad hoc fashion, to coordinate currency swap arrangements in order to improve liquidity conditions and ensure appropriate circulation of key international reserve currencies when the financial system was failing to do so. Yet, those initiatives have by no means discouraged regionalization.

Coexistence and joint interventions between regional financial safety nets and global financial safety nets, whether they be central bank currency lines or more standard IMF instruments, pose a number of important questions about their combined efficiency and effectiveness in ensuring the stability of the international monetary system. In particular, the actual cooperation between different levels of surveillance and financial assistance, conditionality frameworks, analytical perspectives, accountability structures, and sometimes political objectives can lead to tensions that might undermine the potency of these safety nets and leave fragilities in the monetary system.

This chapter reviews the evolution of the existing regional safety nets and compares their institutional framework and modes of operation. The aim is to identify challenges and highlight the existing and potential fault lines in their nascent architecture. The chapter proposes changes to both regional and international safety nets in order to improve their complementarity and subsidiarity and thereby maximize their effectiveness.

Rise of Regional Arrangements

The history and political economy of regional financial arrangements allow the establishment of two clear categories of regional arrangements that respond to two distinct but complementary sets of shortcomings in the international monetary system and global financial safety net architecture.

Two Generations of Regional Financial Cooperation

The first generation of regional arrangements rose in response to the emergence of cracks in the international monetary system (figure 7.1). The end of the gold standard in 1971 and the economic shakeup created by the oil shock in 1973–74 raised new doubts and fears across the world about the ability of the Bretton Woods institutions to fulfill their role. They had indeed not been designed to deliver financial safety nets in a world of acute monetary instability. The creation of regional arrangements is clearly tied to this. In Europe, the Werner Plan, for example, was first and foremost designed to respond to global monetary instability and ended up with the creation of the "European currency snake" and the European Medium-Term Financial Assistance in 1971. Such regional responses emerged across the world, with the Arab Monetary Fund created in 1976, the Association of Southeast Asian Nations (ASEAN) Swap Arrangement in 1977, and the Latin American Reserve Fund (established as the Andean Reserve Fund) in 1978.

In many ways, regional monetary cooperation was first and foremost a response to global monetary instability and was primarily designed to contain

Figure 7.1   Evolution of regional arrangements to date

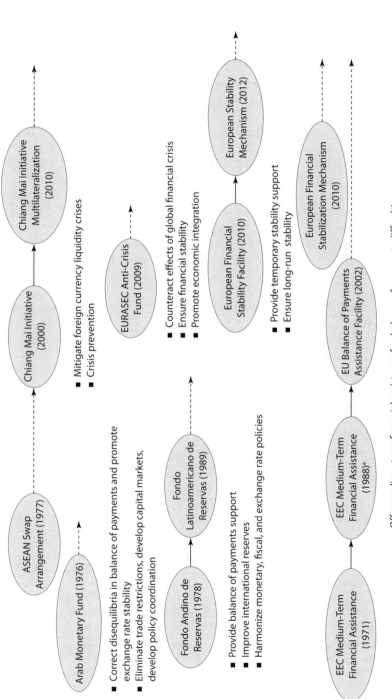

ASEAN = Association of Southeast Asian Nations; EEC = European Economic Community; EURASEC = Eurasian Economic Community

a. In 1988 the Medium-Term Financial Assistance and Community Loan Mechanism were merged into a single Medium-Term Financial Assistance Facility.

Source: Authors' illustration.

its effect on the European continent (James 2013, Mourlon-Druol 2012). Several waves of devaluations, the Werner Report, the Exchange Rate Mechanism, and the Committee of Central Bankers eventually kick-started the process that effectively embedded monetary cooperation in the monetary unification process. However, the 2009–10 European crisis would come to challenge the idea that a single currency would allow monetary stability without the need for regional financial arrangements outside a common central bank.

In Latin America, the creation of the Latin American Reserve Fund (Fondo Latinoamericano de Reservas, or FLAR), established initially in 1978 as the Andean Reserve Fund (Fondo Andino de Reservas or FAR), was gradually expanded to a greater number of members. However, it is interesting to note that it never really evolved into a full-fledged arrangement encompassing all of Latin America and in particular large countries like Mexico, Brazil, or Argentina.[1]

The Arab Monetary Fund (AMF), which was initially the monetary incarnation of the Arab League, was established in 1976 with the political objective of gradually creating a single currency, which never happened. As Pierre Van den Boogaerde (1991) showed, the initial objective and the central financing role of the AMF were largely diluted by a number of alternative financing vehicles that provided other forms of balance of payments assistance to countries of the region.

The second generation of regional financial arrangements—which includes the Chiang Mai Initiative (CMI), the Eurasian Economic Community (EURASEC) Anti-Crisis Fund (ACF), and the European regional financial safety nets—was the result of regional financial crises after the 1980s in a number of places, starting with Latin America. The regionalization wave of the late 1990s was largely driven first by the precedent created by the IMF program for Mexico in 1995 and then by the consequences of the Asian crisis in 1997. Mexico planted an important seed with the North American Framework Agreement (NAFA), which made an important contribution to the overall Mexican program.[2] In reality, this was more of a bilateral support than a truly regional initiative, but it established the need to go beyond standard IMF support and explains at least

---

1. Several conjectures can be made owing to both politics and economics. Mexico probably became so integrated with the United States that it came to enjoy, especially after the conclusion of the North American Free Trade Agreement, a special relationship with the United States that ensured a form of bilateral solidarity that would surely surpass any regional arrangement. Brazil and Argentina always entertained somewhat rival relations, which didn't help a joint initiative, and they were both large enough to be the natural anchor of the regional system but potentially economically too fragile to risk the undertaking. As a result, FLAR remained a relatively limited initiative for small countries. But this is slowly changing and there are increasing discussions for Mexico and others to now join and expand it (Lombardi 2012).

2. NAFA was established in April 1994, enlarging prior bilateral swap agreements among Canada, Mexico, and the United States. The agreement serves as the rubric for the separate bilateral agreements. The Exchange Stabilization Fund, an intervention device of the US Treasury, also maintains a credit line with Mexico that requires a letter of comfort by the IMF managing director when used.

partially why the Latin American crises of the 1980s didn't lead to a deepening and broadening of the regional arrangement in Latin America itself.

This had important consequences globally and in Asia in particular, where dependence on the IMF, and the goodwill of the United States as the key power-broker on its Executive Board, became evident and of concern. According to Phillip Lipscy (2003), the idea of an Asian Monetary Fund was first floated by Japanese authorities in late 1996. Doubtful about the US commitment to Asia, Japanese authorities took the lead in forging an "Asian consensus" on the issue. The plan then was to set up a fund with resources amounting to $100 billion to be shared by the 10 interim member economies.[3] In reality, this was not very consensual until the Asian crisis hit in 1997 and profoundly changed the terms of the debate. The political rejection of the IMF programs and deep-seated criticism of its program conditionality (IMF 2003) contributed to increasing the focus on the liquidity dimension of the Asian crisis, which motivated the establishment of preemptive and regional instruments.

Asia's sour experience with the IMF created an economic and political shock that called for a bold initiative to strengthen supplementary and alternative methods of cooperation in addressing financial crisis outside of the IMF. The original Asian Monetary Fund proposal didn't prosper because of political concerns surrounding the role of the yen in this regional arrangement. Instead, a series of bilateral swap arrangements was originally formed among the ASEAN-5—Indonesia, Malaysia, the Philippines, Singapore, and Thailand—and the Plus Three countries—Japan, the Republic of Korea, and the People's Republic of China (PRC).[4] This was the beginning of a more ambitious and competing form of regionalization that would come to be expanded quite meaningfully not only in Asia but also, in another form, and at a later stage, in Europe.

The Asian and European Experiences

Asia

The embryo of an Asian regional safety net arrangement has existed since 1977, when the five founding members of the ASEAN signed the ASEAN Swap Arrangement (ASA).[5] Following the Asian crisis and after aborted discussion on the creation of an Asian Monetary Fund, Japan launched the New Miyazawa Initiative in October 1998 amounting to about $35 billion, which was targeted at stabilizing the foreign exchange markets of Indonesia, the Republic of Korea,

---

3. The PRC; Hong Kong, China; Japan; the Republic of Korea; Australia; Indonesia; Malaysia; Singapore; Thailand; and the Philippines.

4. Brunei Darussalam, Cambodia, the Lao People's Democratic Republic, Myanmar, and Viet Nam joined the regional arrangements with the other ASEAN countries in 2000 and with the Plus Three countries with the establishment of the Chiang Mai Initiative Multilateralization in 2008.

5. The founding members are Indonesia, Malaysia, the Philippines, Singapore, and Thailand.

Malaysia, the Philippines, and Thailand.[6] The initiative was particularly valuable in containing instability in Malaysia's financial sector, since that country had refused an IMF Stand-By Arrangement. The Japanese maneuver was deemed somewhat mutinous, since the IMF was very critical of Malaysia's approach. But it also cemented the idea that Asia could gather enough resources to sandbag itself during a crisis period so long as Asian countries were united and managed to roll out timely and credible support mechanisms.

In Asian countries under IMF programs, the conditionality associated with the loans included severe fiscal cuts, deep structural reforms, and substantial increases in interest rates to stabilize currency markets. The economic and social cost of the adjustment was so high and abrupt that it provoked social unrest in a number of countries. This would reverberate strongly in the months that followed and leave a lasting scar in relations between Asian countries and the IMF.[7]

This experience fueled both a willingness to self-insure through accelerated reserve accumulation and to strengthen regional arrangements to reduce the reliance on global financial safety nets. Building on this lesson, the CMI was formalized in May 2000 during the ASEAN+3 Finance Ministers Meeting.[8] It largely built on the original ASA and bilateral swap agreements involving the PRC, Japan, and the Republic of Korea but was grounded in a broader program that also included developing Asia's local currency bond market and introduced a regional economic review and policy dialogue to enhance the region's surveillance mechanism (Kawai and Houser 2007). The initiative included the new ASEAN members, increasing the total number of parties to the arrangement from 5 to 10. Table 7A.1 in appendix 7A highlights the evolution of the CMI.

The question of cooperation between the CMI and the IMF quickly became quite heated, with a number of countries arguing that strong ties to the Fund would defeat the initial purpose of the initiative (Korea Institute of Finance 2012), but the ties were kept nonetheless both to mitigate moral

---

6. The "old" Miyazawa initiative was a 1987 proposal by Japan's Minister of Finance Miyazawa Kiichi to resolve the debt crisis in Latin America that involved expanding the roles of the IMF and the World Bank in international financial affairs. While the Brady Plan was favored over Miyazawa's, some of its vital provisions were patterned after the latter (Horisaka 1989).

7. In the case of Indonesia, the government's tight fiscal position forced it to cut back on subsidies on food and fuel. But with the reduction in government price support, food and fuel costs skyrocketed, resulting in weeks of social unrest in the country and the eventual resignation of President Suharto, who had held power for over three decades.

8. Earlier in 1997, the Manila Framework Group was established by 14 Asia-Pacific and North American economies: Australia; Brunei Darussalam; Canada; the PRC; Hong Kong, China; Indonesia; Japan; the Republic of Korea; Malaysia; New Zealand; the Philippines; Singapore; Thailand; and the United States. The purpose of the framework was information exchange and surveillance, with support from the IMF, the World Bank, and the Asian Development Bank. But since it had no formal status and included both Asian and non-Asian economies, the framework proved to be ineffective as a regional surveillance forum and was terminated in 2004. ASEAN+3 meetings superseded the Manila Framework Group meetings (Moon and Rhee 2012).

hazard (Sussangkarn 2011) and to ensure some consistency with conditionality attached to the IMF's own programs.

After the formal creation of the CMI in 2000, the era of Great Moderation that followed to some degree doused further ambitions to strengthen regional arrangements. As a result, when the global financial crisis hit in 2008, the Asian regional financial safety net proved too modest to play a meaningful role. Indeed, instead of seeking support under CMI, the Bank of Korea and the Monetary Authority of Singapore sought a swap agreement with the US Federal Reserve for some $30 billion each. The Republic of Korea concluded bilateral agreements with Japan and the PRC that were not related to the CMI. Similarly, Indonesia established separate bilateral swap lines with Japan and the PRC to shore up its crisis buffer and did not resort to the CMI for credit support (Sussangkarn 2011).

The plan to consolidate the bilateral swap arrangements and form a single, more solid, and effective reserve pooling mechanism—which had initially been put forward by the finance ministers of the ASEAN+3 in May 2007 in Kyoto— was accelerated and evolved in several iterations before the final version was laid out more than two years later. In December 2009, the CMI was multilateralized and the ASEAN+3 representatives signed the Chiang Mai Initiative Multilateralization (CMIM) Agreement, which effectively became binding on March 24, 2010 (BSP 2012). These successive transformations have strengthened the initiative, but it remains largely untested. In addition, other aspects of any credible regional financial arrangement, such as surveillance capacity and coordination of some basic economic policies, remain relatively embryonic.

Europe

The history of European financial safety nets cannot be dissociated from the history of European monetary integration. With this perspective in mind, it dates back to the late 1960s and has been an ongoing debate to this day. The history of European political integration at every turn is marked by failed projects or actual mechanisms of financial solidarity, ranging from loose exchange rate arrangements to the project of a full-fledged European Monetary Fund. The advent of the monetary union was precisely designed to reduce the need for financial safety nets within the euro area. But the architectural deficiencies of the euro area and the lack of internal transfers have required the establishment of alternative mutual insurance mechanisms since the onset of the euro crisis in 2010.

In 2008, when the global financial crisis hit, Hungary had accumulated important external imbalances and large foreign exchange exposures. It had to seek financial assistance almost immediately and initiated contacts with the IMF. The total absence of coordination with European authorities came as an initial shock because it showed that despite decades of intense economic, political, and monetary integration, EU countries could still come to require international financial assistance. The experience pushed European institutions to unearth a forgotten provision of the Maastricht Treaty to provide financial assistance through the Balance of Payments Assistance Facility.[9] This created preliminary and at first ad hoc coordination between the IMF and the European Commission, which was then rediscovering design and monitoring of macroeconomic adjustment programs.

Despite the rapid use of this facility and the emergence of a framework of cooperation with the IMF, contagion from the global financial crisis continued for months and prompted some Eastern European leaders to seek broader and more preemptive support,[10] which failed. However, beyond official sector participation, there was a relatively rapid realization that cross-border banking and financial retrenchment could become a major source of financial disruption and effectively propagate the crisis further—including back to the core of Europe, as large European banks were heavily exposed to Eastern Europe through vast and dense networks of branches and subsidiaries. In response, in late February 2009, under the leadership of the European Bank for Reconstruction and Development (EBRD), the European Investment Bank (EIB) and the World Bank decided to establish what was known as the Vienna Initiative. This was designed as a joint multilateral and private sector coordination and enforcement mechanism to reduce the risk of banking sector sudden stops. In particular, it compelled cross-border European banks to continue to provide appropriate liquidity to their branches and subsidiaries in Central and Eastern Europe. The formalization of such an arrangement[11] quite early in the crisis has certainly proven the case for coordination of financial institutions in emerging-market economies, especially when a relatively small number of institutions have a disproportionate impact on capital flows.

But with the crisis spreading to the euro area, starting with Greece in the fall of 2010, new regional arrangements proved necessary. The lack of instruments forced European officials to first consider bilateral assistance from member states. The idea of involving the IMF was initially violently rejected

---

9. The possibility of granting mutual assistance to a member state with difficulties with its balance of payments is laid down in Article 143 of the treaty. The facility to provide medium-term financial assistance was established by Council Regulation (EC) No. 332/2002. The maximum amount of the facility was increased to €25 billion in December 2008 and further to €50 billion in May 2009 (from €12 billion originally).

10. The Hungarian prime minister, in particular, tried to draw his peers and European leaders together to set up large international support for Eastern Europe. His proposal was eventually turned down by an informal European Council meeting on March 1, 2009, for lack of support by his peers. (The Czech Republic and Poland in particular feared the stigma associated with such an initiative.) See Balazs Penz and Agnes Lovasz, "Hungary Seeks $230 Billion Eastern Aid; World Bank Raises Funds," Bloomberg News, February 27, 2012, www.bloomberg.com/apps/news?pid=newsarchive&refer=home&sid=aPVyz3WPsLZw (accessed on July 13, 2013).

11. The Joint International Financial Institutions initiative was announced on February 25, 2009, with a combined commitment of €25 billion. It was subsequently increased, but only a small portion of these funds were actually committed and disbursed. For a final report on the initiative, see De Haas et al. (2012).

on intellectual and political grounds[12] but proved inevitable. In a number of successive iterations, more solid regional arrangements were designed (Bijlsma and Vallée 2012). Table 7A.2 in appendix 7A shows the evolution of European regional financial safety nets.

The New International and Regional Safety Net Architecture

Following the momentum created by the Asian crisis and the bold call for the establishment of an Asian regional financial safety net, the Group of Seven (G-7) tried in 1998 to reform the monetary system by improving the provision of liquidity ex ante. This brought deep changes at the IMF, following what was called the Summers Call.[13] It led to the creation of a set of new facilities that specifically addressed capital account crises (the Supplemental Reserve Facility and the Contingent Credit Line, for instance), which for lack of use were retired in 2004. These instruments were sorely missed in 2008 when the crisis hit, but the intellectual work had been done in the late 1990s and therefore under emergency conditions the approach to global financial safety nets was quickly and profoundly overhauled. This included two essential but somewhat independent moves: a profound redesign of the IMF toolkit and an extraordinary extension of global currency swap lines between central banks. These instruments could have largely addressed shortcomings of the international monetary system that the regional arrangements were striving to overcome, but they did not.

Revamped Global Financial Safety Nets

Central Bank Currency Swap Arrangements. Central banks played an important role very early during the financial crisis, overcoming their dramatic hesitations dating to the 1930s. They not only acted with rapid nonstandard expansionary actions but also displayed a high degree of cooperation and coordination that clearly helped in allaying market stress by ensuring that widespread access to liquidity contained the worst effects of financial distress. Without determined action, it is not clear that IMF facilities, given the resources available then, could have prevented full-blown banking and balance of payments crises in a number of advanced and emerging economies.

Because of the central role of the dollar in the international financial system, the US Federal Reserve played a pivotal role in the establishment and expansion of these agreements. It agreed to a first temporary reciprocal currency arrangement with the European Central Bank (ECB) and the Swiss

---

12. European Central Bank President Jean-Claude Trichet and Executive Board member Lorenzo Bini Smaghi were among those most opposed to involving the IMF in the euro area.

13. Lawrence Summers, "Priorities for a 21st Century Global Financial System," remarks at Yale University, New Haven, CT, US Department of the Treasury press release, September 22, 1999, www.treasury.gov/press-center/press-releases/Pages/ls111.aspx (accessed on July 1, 2013).

National Bank (SNB) in December 2007 for $20 billion and $4 billion, respectively. Access to dollar liquidity in Europe had become difficult as early as the summer of 2007 following the decision by a large European bank to freeze assets on some funds it could not value properly for lack of liquidity in the US mortgage market. This first arrangement was gradually expanded in size and scope as market stress deepened and eventually covered 14 central banks and represented some $620 billion in outstanding volumes. Note that after October 2008, the Federal Reserve agreed to full allotment auctions for the four leading central banks: ECB, SNB, Bank of Japan (BOJ), and Bank of England (BOE), effectively giving unlimited dollar liquidity to these counterparties.

Interestingly, these swap arrangements were extended to some key emerging-economy central banks (Banco de Mexico, Banco Central do Brasil, Monetary Authority of Singapore, and Bank of Korea) prior to the creation of the IMF's Flexible Credit Line (FCL). The countries were selected on the basis of their economic fundamentals because these arrangements had no conditionality, and considering their importance as regional financial hubs capable of playing an important role in the financial stability of their respective regions.

Linda Goldberg, Craig Kennedy, and Jason Miu (2010) have demonstrated the effectiveness of these arrangements in allaying funding pressures internationally. William Allen and Richhild Moessner (2010) have also shown the extent to which these arrangements were targeted precisely to those countries that were facing the biggest challenges, as indicated by currency mismatches in their financial systems' balance sheets. However, little has been said of other bilateral swaps like those provided by the ECB or the PRC. The ECB's foreign exchange swaps were remarkably modest and in some cases (e.g., Poland and Hungary) replaced by liquidity operations against eligible euro collateral rather than real unsecured foreign exchange swap arrangements like those the Federal Reserve extended. The PRC's bilateral swap arrangements came later but became substantial in size and scope. However, they quickly appeared to be designed to serve the more medium-term objective of promoting the use of the renminbi in bilateral trade rather than addressing short-term liquidity and financial stability concerns (Rhee and Sumulong 2013).

IMF Lending Toolkit. Broadly speaking, the overhaul of the previous IMF credit support system was driven by two new important events. The first was the realization that financial crises not only were affecting emerging economies but also could wreak havoc in large advanced economies. As a result, the financial support needed could be extremely large and could test the limits of IMF lending programs. Second, it became clear that global imbalances and reserve accumulation for the purpose of self-insurance were a sign of defiance of the global financial safety net architecture that needed to be confronted. This doesn't mean that excess reserve accumulation was only a response to deficiencies in the international monetary system as in many places it certainly served a mercantilist undertaking, but it forced to address global imbalances that would otherwise remain a permanently threatening feature of the global economy.

In April 2009, the London Group of Twenty (G-20) Summit jump-started a debate about a complete redesign of the IMF's policies and crisis instruments. Further extensive deliberations were held during 2010 and concluded with the G-20 Summit in Seoul. The Republic of Korea proposed the strengthening of global safety nets as one of its key priorities under its presidency (Rhee 2011). Unlike in 1997, the recent liquidity crisis episode emanated from liquidity shortages in global banks, starting with those in the United States. Ironically, it was the Republic of Korea's bilateral swap arrangement with the US Federal Reserve that eventually stabilized the domestic financial market. The Republic of Korea recognized the importance of having an ex ante crisis prevention mechanism and initially proposed the institutionalization of swap lines as a major goal of strengthening the global safety net. Given the resistance it met, however, the Republic of Korea shifted its focus to strengthening the IMF lending toolkits.

The process of strengthening IMF lending toolkits and moving in the direction of ex ante crisis prevention instruments instead of an ex post crisis resolution mechanism unearthed a number of political and economic challenges, including moral hazard considerations, stigma, credibility, and financing constraints. Despite these challenges, the IMF and the G-20 were able to agree, in a relatively short period of time, to triple the IMF's lending capacity from $250 billion to $750 billion; devise and establish instruments that profoundly changed the existing IMF toolkit, particularly the creation of the FCL and then the Precautionary Credit Line (PCL), which was eventually replaced with the Precautionary and Liquidity Line (PLL); extend high access programs; and extend special drawing rights (SDR) allocation of $250 billion. These combined measures were thought to clearly lay out the eligibility criteria and make them sufficiently stringent to reduce risks of moral hazard while also supporting potential "crisis bystanders."

The FCL was made available in March 2009 mainly to serve member countries' actual and imminent financing needs. The PCL, on the other hand, was only formally offered in August 2010 to deal with the contingent financing requirements of member countries (IMF 2011). The PLL was introduced in November 2011 to replace and broaden the scope of the PCL (IMF 2012). However, in the IMF's own assessment, members using the new credit lines remained fairly limited, potentially because of the remaining stigma associated with their use (IMF 2011).

Regional Financial Safety Nets

This substantial strengthening of global financial safety nets, which addressed a number of shortcomings that regional arrangements had been trying to solve since the 1970s, could well have weakened the case for regional arrangements. But this did not happen and the distinctly European crisis that started in 2010 confirmed maybe once and for all the need for a more decentralized safety net architecture relying on regionalism. Indeed, despite the many improvements to the global financial safety nets, their economic and political limitations justified stronger regional mechanisms. Table 7.1 presents some key characteristics of existing regional financial safety nets.

Although the European Stability Mechanism (ESM) was a latecomer, it appears to be the strongest of all existing regional arrangements in terms of legal basis, fund size, paid-in capital, and leverage capacity. Together with the ACF, European financial arrangements hold the distinction of being based on treaties, compared with the other regional arrangements that are based simply on agreements. The European financial arrangements also are the biggest, with the ESM and European Financial Stability Facility (EFSF) having a combined lending ceiling of €700 billion as of July 2013, €80 billion of which is pledged by member states and the balance to be raised from capital markets. In terms of GDP, the ESM accounts for over 5 percent of members' GDP, compared with less than 1 percent for the other regional financial arrangements (IMF 2013a). Except for the ACF and CMIM, all the other regional arrangements have the option to issue bonds.

In terms of lending instruments, most regional financial arrangements offer loans, guarantees, and swaps. Maturities vary from short-term instruments (e.g., 30 days for the treasury credit offered by the FLAR) to very long-term ones (up to 20 years for the low-income stabilization credit offered by the ACF), depending on the objective and type of lending instrument. Interest rates are either fixed or floating. Meanwhile, only the CMIM and ESM have ex ante crisis prevention facilities. In all regional financial safety nets, conditionality is usually mentioned, but not specified in detail. In fact, except for the CMIM and the European regional financial arrangements, linkage with the IMF is optional. For the CMIM, the IMF delinked portion was increased to 30 percent in 2012 with a view to increasing it to 40 percent in 2014 subject to review should conditions warrant.

The mandate and capacity for surveillance also differ widely. The AMF undertakes no surveillance but has periodic consultations with members on their economic conditions. The FLAR introduced a macroeconomic surveillance program in July 2011, which is in the process of being fully implemented. It includes monitoring of financial and banking stability conditions for use in providing advice to member countries. The CMIM, after incorporating the surveillance mechanism of ASEAN+3 Economic Review and Policy Dialogue in May 2005, established the ASEAN+3 Macroeconomic Research Office (AMRO) in April 2011 as an independent regional surveillance unit to monitor economic conditions of member economies, which will in turn have input into CMIM decision making. Similarly, the ACF has outsourced the surveillance function to the Eurasian Development Bank, which manages ACF funds. In the European Union, ESM surveillance complements the new framework for reinforced economic surveillance, which includes a stronger focus on debt sustainability and more effective enforcement measures, and focuses on prevention that should substantially reduce the probability of a crisis emerging in the future.

Table 7.1 Key characteristics of existing regional financial arrangements

Regional financial arrangement	Number of members	Legal basis	Fund size	Paid-in capital/pledge	With option to issue bonds?	Instruments
Arab Monetary Fund (Middle East)	22	Agreement	$2.7 billion	600 million Arab dinars	Yes	▪ Automatic loan ▪ Ordinary loan ▪ Extended loan ▪ Compensatory loan ▪ Structural Adjustment Facility ▪ Short-term liquidity
Latin American Reserve Fund (Fondo Latinoamericano de Reservas, FLAR)	7	Agreement	$3.28 billion	$2.28 billion	Yes	▪ Balance of payments credit ▪ Foreign debt restructuring ▪ Liquidity credit ▪ Contingent credit ▪ Treasury credit
European Union Balance of Payments Facility	27	Treaty	€50 billion	€50 billion	Yes	▪ Loan/credit line
Chiang Mai Initiative Multilateralization (ASEAN+3)	13	Agreement	$240 billion	Pledge	No	▪ Swap, precautionary line ▪ Swap, stability facility
EURASEC Anti-Crisis Fund (Central Asia)	6	Treaty	$8.513 billion	$8.513 billion	No	▪ Stabilization credit ▪ Sovereign loans

(continues on next page)

225

Table 7.1 Key characteristics of existing regional financial arrangements *(continued)*

Regional financial arrangement	Number of members	Legal basis	Fund size	Paid-in capital/pledge	With option to issue bonds?	Instruments
European Stability Mechanism (euro area)	17	Treaty	€500 billion	€80 billion	Yes	■ Loan ■ Credit line (PCCL and ECCL) ■ SMSF
European Financial Stabilization Mechanism (European Union)	27	Agreement	€60 billion	Backed by EU budget	Yes	■ Loan ■ Credit line
European Financial Stability Facility (euro area)	17	Agreement	€440 billion[a]		Yes	■ Loan ■ Credit line (PCCL and ECCL) ■ SMSF

ASEAN+3 = Association of Southeast Asian Nations plus the People's Republic of China, Japan, and the Republic of Korea; SMSF = Secondary Market Support Facility; PCCL = Precautionary Conditioned Credit Line; ECCL = Enhanced Conditions Credit Line; EURASEC = Eurasian Economic Community

a. Combined lending ceiling of the European Stability Mechanism and European Financial Stability Facility will be €700 billion in July 2013 with €80 billion pledged by member states and the balance to be raised from the capital markets.

Source: Authors' compilation.

As regards fund utilization, the CMIM remains the only arrangement untapped since its inception. The AMF has provided structural loans to Jordan, Morocco, and Mauritania. The FLAR has extended financial credit to Bolivia, Colombia, Costa Rica, Ecuador, Peru, Uruguay, and Venezuela. The ACF has provided financial credit to Belarus and Tajikistan. The ESM is to be used in Cyprus for the first time, but the EFSF has been used for programs in Greece, Ireland, Portugal, and Spain.

Cooperation Challenges and Policy Prescriptions

The evolving landscape of regional arrangements combined with profound changes to global financial safety nets poses the important question of cooperation. Indeed, both the IMF and the G-20 endorsed the use of regional arrangements and made them an integral, if shaky and uncertain, part of the global financial architecture. The International Monetary and Financial Committee first spoke of the importance for the IMF to cooperate with regional arrangements in October 2010. In November 2010, G-20 leaders asked G-20 finance ministers and central bank governors to explore "ways to improve collaboration between regional financial arrangements and the IMF across all possible areas" (G-20 2010). A set of broad and nonbinding principles were effectively delivered and endorsed during the Cannes G-20 Summit in the fall of 2011.[14] Further work is under way and expected in the context of the Russian presidency of the G-20 with more concrete guidelines to be agreed upon during the G-20 meeting of the leaders in St. Petersburg in the fall of 2013.

C. Randall Henning (2011) explained that the rationale for cooperation between regional and global arrangements essentially rested on the need to (1) limit risks of arbitrage between arrangements, especially in cases where they overlap; (2) avoid redundancy over and above what competition can justify; (3) align interest to ensure that resources are additive; and (4) organize some form of division of labor between institutions both in the conduct of surveillance and in program monitoring and financing. Building on these issues, we discuss key challenges related to cooperation and highlight a few policy prescriptions.

Strengthening Existing Global and Regional Arrangements

Before improving collaboration between global and regional financial safety nets, strengthening both regional and global arrangements might be an important prerequisite to ensure the stability of the international monetary system.

---

14. The G-20 Cannes Communiqué states: "We have agreed on actions and principles that will help reap the benefits from financial integration and increase the resilience against volatile capital flows. This includes coherent conclusions to guide us in the management of capital flows, common principles for cooperation between the IMF and Regional Financial Arrangements, and an action plan for local currency bond markets" (G-20 2011).

The global financial crisis brought important lessons to bear so as to improve tools and policies for global financial safety nets. The European crisis in particular, and the developments of its own safety nets through the crisis, also provides a testing case for regional safety nets globally.

Global Arrangements

The divergences in approaches, purposes, and network and second-order effects of these foreign exchange swap arrangements beg the question of their governance. Indeed, they can be seen either as a substitute for the more ambitious high-access instruments provided by the IMF, or as a complement. But in both cases, devising effective global financial safety nets requires a degree of predictability that these ad hoc and discretionary arrangements do not offer. In addition, if the sense of emergency and responsibility was clearly present during the global financial crisis, one cannot rule out that under political pressure from the US Congress, for instance, the Federal Reserve would have been far more parsimonious, with potentially significant consequences for financial stability globally.

In 2011, in preparation of the G-20 Seoul Summit, the IMF tried to argue that these bilateral and ad hoc foreign exchange swap lines should be multilateralized in order to increase their effectiveness and improve their governance. But these ideas have been met with great skepticism by the central banking community, which expressed reluctance and concern over seeing such operations with potential important implications for domestic monetary expansion handed over to governments sitting on the board of the IMF. However, this debate might not necessarily be closed forever, and alternative arrangements for coordinating these swap arrangements, while respecting the autonomy, independence, and discretion of central banks, could be promoted.

Regional Arrangements

Improve the Legal and Financial Structure. Legally, the CMIM is an institution based on agreements by member countries and has no identity under corporate law. As such, it is marred with legal uncertainty. The recent commitment by the ASEAN+3 economies to strengthen the CMIM, which was announced at the ASEAN+3 Finance Ministers' meeting in May 2013 in Delhi, is a welcome development. The agreement to involve central bank governors in CMIM decision making and to ensure the CMIM's operational readiness is a positive development. In addition, work will continue "to consider ways to seek an effective cooperative relationship with the IMF and other multilateral financial institutions in the areas of surveillance, liquidity support arrangement and capacity development" (ASEAN 2013). Financially, CMIM funding is based on pledges with no paid-in capital, unlike the case of the ESM, which is an intergovernmental treaty and has significant paid-in capital. Due to this inherent weakness, the CMIM has been criticized as being untested, and there is constant suspicion that pledges may not be honored promptly enough to prevent spillovers when a crisis starts. Securing a strong financial structure backed by meaningful paid-in capital seems to be the urgent step necessary to secure market confidence in the CMIM.

Improve Precautionary and Multicountry Lending Capacity. The stigma effect is not necessarily a unique problem for IMF loans. Even if swaps under the CMIM can have more flexible conditionality, best efforts should be made to reduce the stigma effect, particularly on ex ante programs. A few options have been considered to mitigate stigma, such as via a multicountry lending offer. By making unilateral and simultaneous offers of financial assistance to several countries with good policy track records (but with the capacity to propagate shocks), the CMIM could communicate to the public that the credit lines are provided for an ex ante crisis prevention purpose. The swap lines extended by the US Federal Reserve on October 29, 2008, to four countries—Brazil, Mexico, the Republic of Korea, and Singapore—are good examples. The IMF also introduced the multicountry FCL in 2011. Multicountry swap offers could play a complementary role to that played by large central banks, but would have the advantage of being formally institutionalized compared with the ad hoc nature of central bank swap lines. They would also be able to address more flexibly members' needs beyond central banks' narrow mandates.

Improve Predictability. Once a crisis has started and the market is in panic, it will be difficult to reverse market perceptions even by saying that programs offered by regional financial safety nets are for prevention purposes. Markets are likely to focus only on negative news, and any indication that the CMIM is considering extending credit lines to a specific country could itself propagate a vicious circle. To avoid this, a prequalification system can be considered using a set of transparent "Maastricht-like" criteria particularly for the CMIM's Precautionary Credit Lines. The prequalification criteria and the resulting list of eligible countries need not be made public. Assessing whether countries meet the prequalification criteria can be done regularly and privately within the institution. A rule-based prequalification mechanism would improve the effectiveness of the qualification process and reduce the stigma effect.

Predicating qualification for the multicountry swap offer on systemic importance and strong fundamentals, as well as on having offers of liquidity extended unilaterally and simultaneously to all qualified countries, would address the first-mover problem and reduce the stigma effect associated with accessing resources from the IMF.

Build Capacity for Surveillance. Surveillance capacity is critical for well-functioning regional financial arrangements. The AMRO was created to undertake surveillance that will support CMIM decision making. However, the organization is still in an incipient stage. Currently, it needs more human capital and stronger research and monitoring capacities. These will take time. In the interim, the CMIM should tap the resources of international financial institutions in the areas of surveillance and capacity development.

Collaboration between the IMF and Regional Financial Arrangements

If anything, the most recent global crisis, and in particular the European experience, has underscored the difficulties associated with cooperation between regional and global safety nets. There was initially a clear reluctance to involve the IMF in Europe in general and in the euro area in particular. However, the lack of immediately actionable instruments, the slow political and institutional response in Europe, and the superior expertise of the IMF in addressing balance of payments crises and designing policy conditionality made its involvement inevitable. This collaboration has now been formally institutionalized.

In Asia, at the onset of the financial crisis, the CMI was also not in a position to play its role alone, therefore making other forms of support necessary, which could certainly have led to the involvement of the IMF had the economic situation warranted.

Similarly, in Latin America, Domenico Lombardi (2012) described how the case of Peru from 1978 to the 1990s illustrated alternatively a high degree of cooperation between the FLAR and the IMF (1978–84), then a situation of conflict when the former became the only lender as Peru accumulated arrears vis-à-vis the IMF, and finally a new phase of cooperation in the 1990s under President Alberto Fujimori.

Cooperation Challenges

In Europe, cooperation challenges and divergences have in reality been more widespread than is often reported.

In Latvia, the IMF quickly reached the conclusion that the program would not be sustainable without a currency devaluation, which the European Commission opposed for economic but probably also for political reasons. The IMF effectively suspended disbursement for six months, which could have completely derailed the economics of the program.

In Ireland, the IMF had recommended and supported the Irish government in its willingness to bail in banks' bondholders to strengthen the capital position of the banks without stretching public finances excessively. This time it was the ECB, another key stakeholder in program design and monitoring (although not a financial contributor), that resisted bail-in on financial stability grounds for the rest of the euro area.

In Greece, the IMF realized relatively quickly that the first Greek program would not be sustainable and that a form of debt reduction would be necessary. European authorities resisted it for a long time until a private sector involvement deal was reached in July 2011 and eventually augmented twice. The IMF then went on to press a form of debt forgiveness by official lenders in order to bring debt back to a more sustainable position, which was granted imperfectly in November of 2012.

In Spain, the IMF was considering the extension of the precautionary program for a long time at the end of 2011 and early in 2012, but this did not gain enough political support in Europe. The situation deteriorated so rapidly that the suitability of a precautionary program vanished, making way for a financial sector assistance program with macroeconomic conditionality in which the IMF was not a formal party, although it accepted to play a role in the monitoring.

Finally, in Cyprus, the IMF and European authorities had quite divergent views in terms of both the definition of a sustainable debt trajectory for a small economy like Cyprus and the best way to restructure a banking system that for the most part had become insolvent. Hence, disagreements and tensions in program design and monitoring were in reality much more the rule than the exception, and they were not exactly benign because they sometimes compounded divergences of views between European member states.

These numerous examples illustrate the inherent complexity in organizing interinstitutional cooperation in an ad hoc fashion. The IMF (2013b, 22) itself recognizes that "differences of views that arise from fundamentally differing institutional mandates and priorities will continue to pose challenges." Despite these tensions and disagreements, the experience of cooperation between the IMF and European authorities has generally been operationally effective. But it is unclear the extent to which it can be replicated in other regions.

Policymakers outside Europe, and in Asia in particular, remain of the view that the degree of cooperation attained in Europe can hardly be replicated in other parts of the world and would lead to much more confrontational situations. The experiences of the Latin American and Asian crises leave the overwhelming impression that regional views would not be heard in particular because of the governance of the IMF, in which emerging economies are in a minority and are largely absent from senior management. In addition, because emerging economies cannot print a global reserve currency to finance their adjustment process, their dependency on global financial safety nets would always be far greater than that of Europe. The challenges standing before effective cooperation are multidimensional. They range from conditionality to program financing by way of surveillance. In this sense Europe has enjoyed a relatively unique set of economic and political circumstances that have probably provided a lot of room for negotiation and made cooperation between regional safety nets and the IMF far smoother and more balanced than it can be in any other region of the world.

Conditionality and Program Design

Conditionality is at the heart of every adjustment program. It is also essential to devise effective and credible qualification criteria for ex ante liquidity support. In most cases, it is perceived as both a deterrent meant to steer governments away from unsustainable economic policies and as a corrective instrument to adjust economic imbalances. Yet the rise of regional arrangements can be explained by tensions surrounding conditionality—which was rightly or wrongly regarded as inadequate. The Independent Evaluation Office of the IMF (2003) itself highlighted a number of deficiencies of IMF conditionality, in particular its expansion into policy areas that were neither critical nor directly linked to the success of the adjustment program. On the other hand, the introduction of regional actors with competing conditionality should not be an occasion to weaken and distort IMF conditionality to a point that it undermines the effectiveness and success of associated programs.

This calls for a real clarification of the division of labor between the global and regional arrangements. The early evaluation by the IMF (2013c) of the Greek program and the objections it engendered from the European Commission, as well as an early assessment of programs in Greece, Portugal, and Ireland by Jean Pisani-Ferry, André Sapir, and Guntram Wolff (2013), allow for drawing some lessons learned about governance and program design with regional financial arrangements and the IMF. The European experience is also particularly interesting in the sense that the IMF evolved from being a majority lender in Hungary to a relatively small contributor in Cyprus in a framework that, at least formally, did not lead to evident weakening of policy conditionality. The IMF (2013c) also highlighted important lessons learned for program design that could actually justify a stronger engagement with regional arrangements and some complementarity. Indeed, lack of ownership of reforms and institutional weaknesses were considered important sources of program failure—areas where regional arrangements might have a comparative advantage. But this issue of the linkages of conditionality remains very controversial.

In the case of Europe, linkages with IMF conditionality are tight and mandatory, but Europe in principle has important leverage over the IMF because of the latter's governance structure, which creates some symmetry in their relations. This is not the case for other regional groupings. In the case of Asia, for example, the CMIM is gradually reducing the proportion of its lending that requires linkage to IMF programs. Whether the ultimate target for the IMF-delinked portion should be zero is an unsettled issue. Considering that links to IMF programs are generally optional in other regional financial arrangements, the CMIM is also moving in this direction, gradually reducing its formal linkages with the IMF commensurate with its improving surveillance capacity.

Decentralized and Complementary Surveillance

The European crisis has demonstrated the limits of regional as well as international surveillance, both of which by and large missed the importance of the fundamental financial and external imbalances that were building up in a number of economies. A real and comprehensive postmortem of surveillance capacities has not yet been undertaken, although Pisani-Ferry, Sapir, and Wolff (2011) highlighted how IMF surveillance suffered from substantial shortcomings in the years preceding the crisis despite the existence of formal surveillance instruments.

As shareholders of the IMF, countries are subject to regular bilateral IMF surveillance. However, regional arrangements are also developing their own surveillance apparatus. To the extent that surveillance is inextricably linked to program conditionality, regional financial arrangements have to develop strong independent surveillance capacity using local and regional knowledge to complement the IMF's global surveillance. This will in turn prove key to establishing the regional conditionality framework, which can be combined with IMF conditionality in cases of program cofinancing.

At the regional level, over the last decade the European Commission had probably devised the most expansive and intrusive machinery for conducting macroeconomic surveillance combining outcome as well as policy analysis and recommendations. Yet the crisis has shown its relative ineffectiveness, which raises very important questions about the trust and confidence that should be granted to surveillance in general and regional surveillance in particular. Profound ongoing changes to the economic governance framework—including constitutional fiscal rules, a system risk board, and other far-reaching preventive and corrective mechanisms—could significantly improve surveillance and monitoring by the European regional financial arrangements. Whether that will actually happen remains to be seen.

Against the backdrop of the European experience, the nascent surveillance apparatus in Asia appears extremely modest. Having been established only in April 2011, the AMRO is still in the process of building up its capacity. Currently, its relatively small staffing may not seem sufficient to effectively meet its mandate,[15] which is "to prepare quarterly consolidated reports on the overall macroeconomic assessment of the region as well as on individual countries." During a time of crisis the mandate is "to provide an analysis of the economic and financial situation of the CMIM Swap Requesting Country; to monitor the use and impact of the funds disbursed under the CMIM Agreement; and monitor the compliance by the CMIM Swap Requesting Country with any lending covenants to the CMIM Agreement.[16] In the interim, partnering with the IMF in the field of surveillance may be necessary while AMRO continues to strengthen its capacity.

Beyond Europe and Asia, building regional surveillance institutions with very different levels of analytical capacity and political backing raises impor-

---

15. The AMRO is governed by an executive committee composed of deputy finance ministers and central bank heads of member economies. The committee provides the general direction for the entire institution and is responsible for designating the members of the advisory panel and the AMRO director. The advisory panel, on the other hand, comprises six representatives from the member states: one each from the PRC, Japan, and the Republic of Korea, and three from ASEAN. It generally gives technical, strategic, and professional guidance to AMRO but is independent from AMRO staff members (Hill and Menon 2012). The AMRO director is the top technocrat of the institution and is in charge of overseeing specific organization functions that are presently carried out by 12 professional staff, two technical assistants, and five administrative staff (Siregar and Chabchitrchaidol 2013).

16. See the AMRO website at www.amro-asia.org (accessed on July 1, 2013).

tant issues, particularly in terms of the potential division of labor between regional and global surveillance. It is not clear what part of surveillance would be best undertaken at the regional or at the global level.

What appears clear, however, is that surveillance of regional blocs covered by regional financial safety nets should be under scrutiny by the IMF, as is the case with the European Monetary Union. Whether this means that country surveillance should first and foremost be undertaken at the regional level is unclear. One objective of regional surveillance is to introduce checks and balances and alternative views from that of the IMF. One should consider, however, that strong country surveillance at the regional level is a necessary consequence of financial solidarity at the regional level. However, one should establish clearer responsibility for IMF surveillance of regional arrangements in order to ensure their robustness and credibility, especially in a context where the IMF is expected to be a financing partner.

Multilayered and Multistakeholder Lending Framework

In principle, if regional arrangements were solid and effective, they would be able to take care of small shocks that do not have global repercussions. A real multistakeholder lending framework would only become necessary in cases where interregional spillovers are large and financing needs potentially exceed regional capacity. The nature of the crisis, depending on whether the shocks are external or homegrown, could also help determine the extent to which support from global financial safety nets is required from both a financing and confidence point of view. The question is whether the IMF should become a cofinancier in each national program or whether it should instead provide either lending or guarantees to the regional financial arrangement. There are pros and cons to both approaches. One interesting paradox is that even though the development of regional financial safety nets reflects at least in part some dissatisfaction with multilateral assistance as provided by the IMF, all regional arrangements remain more or less tied to the requirements of IMF-supported programs. In particular, the recent European experience has shown that the share of financing was not a decisive factor in the respective weight of institutions in the decision-making process pertaining to program design and monitoring. Indeed, despite the declining share of IMF financing over time—down to being nil in Spain and symbolic in Cyprus—the IMF's judgment and conditionality did not decline in relative importance.

The organization of a real multilayered financing arrangement remains in its infancy, partly because regional financial safety nets have somewhat different structures, resources, and constraints, and partly because the establishment of new instruments by the IMF requires more operational thinking about their imbrication with regional arrangements. As a general rule, regional financial safety nets have limited information on cross-regional linkages and international spillovers that can probably be duly internalized only by the IMF.

There are a couple of ways to pursue joint lending between a global and regional financial safety net. One is through a joint lending system ensuring that each country receiving financial assistance, even if primarily from a regional safety net, sees a portion of financing coming from a global safety net so as to ensure comparable treatment across the world and thereby limit spillovers. The second approach is a much more decentralized system in the form of a reinsurance/guarantee of the regional financial safety net. In this model, responsibility for managing balance of payments or financial crises in a country party to a regional financial safety net would fall squarely on the safety net itself, thereby creating incentives for strong surveillance, credible lending capacity, and effective lending instruments.

These two polar alternatives may not be realistic at least in the current transitory phase. In the medium to long term, one might prefer a scheme of reinsurance/guarantee of regional financial safety nets in order to align incentives and responsibilities. But in the transition period, it is probably more appropriate and realistic to think of a hybrid system that organizes both complementarity and subsidiarity through a financing system that would enable both the IMF and the regional safety net agency to channel capital directly to the country receiving the assistance. This would not preclude a regional financial safety net from lending on its own to a handful of members if the crisis appears small and contained, with no immediate or foreseen regionwide or international consequences. However, if the shock hits the entire region, this would be beyond the capabilities of regional financial safety nets, and global financial safety nets should be called upon to participate alongside the regional ones. The global safety net could lend directly to the regional one, rather than only to member countries. This might reduce the individual stigma effect for each country and increase the leverage of the IMF in the functioning of the regional financial safety nets and associated internal redistributional issues.

The outline of this joint financing system raises a number of potential issues, not the least of which is the fact that the IMF's Articles of Agreement as they are today do not allow lending to any but a shareholding country. Hence, legally speaking, the IMF could only backstop regional arrangements if it lends collectively to individual shareholding countries directly. Lending directly to the regional arrangements would require a change in the Articles of Agreement and would also require the regional financial safety net to establish joint responsibility for such lending.

More importantly, if the regional financial safety net is not an entity with enough centralization of economic prerogatives, the ability to impose conditionality is limited. Even in the context of a relatively integrated monetary union like the euro area, not all policies are sufficiently centralized for conditionality to be applied to the euro area as a whole without the signature of binding letters of intent in all member states. This could probably be even more complex in regional arrangements with lighter degrees of economic and political integration like those covered by the CMIM, the FLAR, or the AMF.

Cooperation with Other Stakeholders

Beyond the issue of coordination between regional and global financial safety net arrangements, history has proven that other stakeholders could be involved in a more systematic manner, especially in the context of precautionary programs where confidence and coordination are as important as the financing and the adjustment policies themselves. Two particular important stakeholders come to mind: central banks, given their involvement in establishing and operating currency swap arrangements, and regional development banks.

Central Banks and Currency Swap Arrangements

As discussed previously, bilateral swaps can be quite effective in restoring financial market confidence and preventing a benign liquidity shortage from becoming a solvency issue. However, such swaps are often carried out on an ad hoc basis, and political uncertainties can hamper their effectiveness. One intuitive way of addressing this issue, as Edwin Truman (2010, 2011) has suggested, would be to have the IMF coordinate swap agreements with major central banks so that it can use the resources in case of a global liquidity shock. This idea was actively promoted by the IMF and the Korean presidency of the G-20, but the central banking community expressed reluctance on grounds of central bank independence and moral hazard.

Another option, beyond the IMF and taking into account the concerns of the central banking community, would be for the Bank for International Settlements (BIS) to ensure coordination to establish a transparent and accountable mechanism to decide on such liquidity assistance. This forum would allow some discretion by central banks while ensuring that international demands and externalities related to global financial stability are duly considered.

Indeed, there is today no framework to ensure that the issuers of global reserve currencies are compelled to deliver temporary and targeted liquidity provisions where and when necessary. The framework for SDR allocation is a more modest second-order option to drive global monetary aggregates, but it does not address very short-term tensions as effectively as currency swap arrangements. One might consider either a more multilateral process involving the IMF for the supply of SDR, considered as medium-term global liquidity, and the BIS for emergency liquidity provisions, or an approach centered on the IMF both for the supply of SDR and coordination of swap agreements.

Regional Development Banks, Program Support, and Coordination Mechanisms

Both the Asian experience in 1997 and, maybe more convincingly, the Eastern European experience in 2009 have showed the importance of actively managing the liquidity/rollover risk.

In response to the Asian crisis, for example, the Asian Development Bank (ADB) resumed its lending to the Republic of Korea and significantly raised the volume of lending to Indonesia and Thailand. About $7.1 billion in total crisis support was approved for these three countries, three-quarters of which was disbursed as program loan tranches over a 14-month period beginning in December 1997. In addition, the release of program loans was accelerated to ensure the availability of funds for liquidity/balance of payments support when most needed, and to help avoid a further deterioration of economic conditions (ADB 2009).

Similarly, in response to the global financial crisis, ADB established the $3 billion Countercyclical Support Facility (CSF) in June 2009 as a time-bound budget support instrument to provide more effective countercyclical aid. This facility is in addition to ADB's regular loan and technical assistance products for crisis response. In 2009, ADB approved $2.5 billion in CSF assistance to five countries: Bangladesh, Indonesia, Kazakhstan, the Philippines, and Viet Nam. Much of the increase in ADB's crisis-related lending of $5.08 billion in 2008–09 came through the CSF. ADB also expanded the Trade Finance Program (TFP) in March 2009 by raising the exposure limit from $150 million to $1 billion to improve access to trade finance. Overall, ADB assistance to sovereign and nonsovereign borrowers (excluding the TFP) grew by 28 percent in 2009 (ADB 2011).

In Europe, the Vienna Initiative played an important role in coordinating European banks' involvement in Eastern Europe and avoiding uncooperative behavior that could have plunged Eastern Europe into dire straits. With external imbalances being completely financed by European banks, withdrawal or reduced commitments by those banks to their branches and subsidiaries could have precipitated a dramatic balance of payments crisis. The European Bank for Reconstruction and Development (EBRD) along with the European Investment Bank initiated an important coordination effort with the private sector to ensure the rollover of commitments to the region. To this end, the EBRD developed both a commitment framework for the private sector and a monitoring mechanism, while mobilizing financial resources to help banks roll over their exposure. This approach became an integral part of program financing in certain countries and proved a very useful way to leverage resources of regional development banks with private sector commitments.

It is unclear, however, whether regional development banks are necessarily the most appropriate institutions to undertake this coordination effort and enforce it globally. And it is not clear whether the relative success of the Vienna Initiative can be replicated in a different context where bank financing does not dominate capital flows. However, the importance of having a forum for negotiating with the financial sector beyond questions of rollover has been demonstrated several times, particularly in a context where no formal sovereign debt restructuring mechanism is in place. Clearly in the case of Greece, the tacit agreement by banks to maintain their exposure to Greece was imperfectly respected and the subsequent private sector involvement was negotiated with an ad hoc bondholders committee effectively spearheaded by the Institute of International Finance (IIF).

Given the importance of these negotiations, either in a purely coordinating context or in the more binding context of an exchange offer with consequences for creditors, it is essential to set out more formal and effective negotiation and coordination devices. Regional development banks along with regional arrangements can surely play an important role in this context.

Conclusion

Financial globalization, driven by liberalization and the internationalization of supply chains, has increased the integration of economies around the world, in both real and financial terms. This very fact increases the need for a strong and effective financial safety net architecture. The shortcomings of global financial safety nets have repeatedly been met by additional regional financial arrangements that have sprouted organically across the globe since the 1970s but take very different shapes and forms. The IMF and the G-20 have now recognized that regional arrangements are a force that can no longer be ignored or avoided, and the European crisis has probably played a decisive role in this new state of affairs. But despite tentative guidelines and principles for effective cooperation, much remains to be done.

The ability of regional and global arrangements to cooperate in a positive and balanced manner appears inextricably linked to two fundamental issues: first, the governance of the IMF and the voting quota of emerging-market economies; and second, the ability to self-insure via recourse to a global reserve currency. In other words, an international monetary system resting on strong regional currencies would allow a form of balance that a unipolar international monetary system can probably not produce even with optimal cooperation between regional and international arrangements.

This links the cooperation debate to two slow-burning issues: IMF governance and the future shape of the international monetary system. The former is being slowly addressed by ongoing quota reform at the IMF, which could be an initial step in the long road toward more balanced governance. The latter is still relatively uncertain and depends on the success of the euro as an alternative international currency or on the potential for the renminbi to establish itself as a regional and then global reserve currency, thereby contributing to an international monetary system less dependent on one or two reserve currencies.

In addition, understanding of financial crises has evolved tremendously since the 1980s. In particular, it is now clear that financial crises can be the result of mismanaged liquidity crises and that they can therefore hit "innocent bystanders." This calls for instruments that are more preemptive in nature and that prevent situations in which relatively benign liquidity shortages spin into full-blown solvency crises. Important steps in this direction have been taken since 2009 by the IMF, but more can be done, particularly by strengthening and widening currency swap arrangements and making them more systematic, predictable, and transparent.

Finally, the recognition that regional financial arrangements are an important feature of the future international monetary order requires bold efforts on both sides to improve cooperation. This probably means revising the IMF's Articles of Agreement to allow lending directly to regional arrangements, provided they can contribute meaningfully to enhanced surveillance and ensure smoother cooperation. It also requires regional financial arrangements to think beyond their regional interest and organize their structures in a way that facilitates cooperation with the IMF, in particular when it comes to surveillance and program design and monitoring. This last point is particularly important to avoid regionalism turning against international cooperation and leading to a form of introversion that would be unhealthy for global economic and monetary cooperation.

References

Allen, William, and Richhild Moessner. 2010. *Central Bank Co-operation and International Liquidity in the Financial Crisis of 2008–9*. BIS Working Paper 310. Basel: Bank for International Settlements.

ADB (Asian Development Bank). 2009. *Lessons from the Asian Development Bank's Responses to Financial Crises*. ADB Evaluation Information Brief 2009-02. Available at www.adb.org/sites/default/files/EIB-2009-02_0.pdf (accessed on July 1, 2013).

ADB (Asian Development Bank). 2011. *Lessons Learned from ADB's Response to the Global Economic Crisis of 2008–2009*. Manila (July). Available at www.adb.org/sites/default/files/LL-Crisis.pdf.

AMRO (ASEAN+3 Macroeconomic Research Office). 2009. *Key Points of CMI Multilateralization Agreement*. Singapore.

ASEAN (Association of Southeast Asian Nations). 1977. Memorandum of Understanding on the ASEAN Swap Arrangement (August 5). Kuala Lumpur.

ASEAN (Association of Southeast Asian Nations). 1978. The Supplementary Agreement to the Memorandum of Understanding on the ASEAN Swap Arrangement (September 26). Washington, DC.

ASEAN (Association of Southeast Asian Nations). 1981. Amendments to the Memorandum of Understanding on the ASEAN Swap Arrangement (January 16). Colombo.

ASEAN (Association of Southeast Asian Nations). 1982. Amendments to the Memorandum of Understanding on the ASEAN Swap Arrangement (February 4). Bangkok.

ASEAN (Association of Southeast Asian Nations). 2006. Memorandum of Understanding on the ASEAN Swap Arrangement, November 17, 2005. ASEAN Document Series 2005 (April). Jakarta: ASEAN Secretariat.

ASEAN (Association of Southeast Asian Nations). 2007. The Joint Ministerial Statement of the 10th ASEAN+3 Finance Ministers' Meeting (May 5). Kyoto.

ASEAN (Association of Southeast Asian Nations). 2008. The Joint Ministerial Statement of the 11th ASEAN+3 Finance Ministers' Meeting (May 4). Madrid.

ASEAN (Association of Southeast Asian Nations). 2009a. The Joint Media Statement of the 12th ASEAN+3 Finance Ministers' Meeting (May 3). Bali.

ASEAN (Association of Southeast Asian Nations). 2009b. The Establishment of the Chiang Mai Initiative Multilateralization. Joint Press Release of the Finance Ministers and Central Bank Governors of the ASEAN Member States (December 28).

ASEAN (Association of Southeast Asian Nations). 2012. The Joint Statement of the 15th ASE-AN+3 Finance Ministers and Central Bank Governors' Meeting (May 3). Manila.

ASEAN (Association of Southeast Asian Nations). 2013. The Joint Statement of the 16th ASEAN+3 Finance Ministers and Central Bank Governors' Meeting (May 3). New Delhi.

Bijlsma, Michiel, and Shahin Vallée. 2012. *The Creation of Euro Area Financial Safety Nets*. Working Paper 2012/09. Brussels: Bruegel.

BSP (Bangko Sentral ng Pilipinas). 2012. Chiang Mai Initiative Multilateralization (September). Manila.

De Haas, Ralph, Yevgeniya Korniyenko, Elena Loukoianova, and Alexander Pivovarsky. 2012. *Foreign Banks and the Vienna Initiative: Turning Sinners into Saints*. IMF Working Paper 12/117. Washington, DC: International Monetary Fund.

Goldberg, Linda, Craig Kennedy, and Jason Miu. 2010. *Central Bank Dollar Swap Lines and Overseas Dollar Funding Costs*. NBER Working Paper 15763. Cambridge, MA: National Bureau of Economic Research.

G-20 (Group of Twenty). 2010. The G-20 Seoul Summit Leaders' Declaration (November 11–12). Available at http://online.wsj.com/public/resources/documents/G20COMMUN1110.pdf (accessed on July 18, 2013).

G-20 (Group of Twenty). 2011. G-20 Principles for Cooperation between the IMF and Regional Financing Arrangements (October 15). Available at www.mofa.go.jp/policy/economy/g20_summit/2011/pdfs/annex04.pdf (accessed on July 18, 2013).

Henning, C. Randall. 2002. *East Asian Financial Cooperation*. Policy Analyses in International Economics 68. Washington, DC: Institute for International Economics.

Henning, C. Randall. 2011. *Coordinating Regional and Multilateral Financial Institutions*. Working Paper 11-9. Washington, DC: Peterson Institute for International Economics.

Hill, Hal, and Jayant Menon. 2012. *Financial Safety Nets in Asia: Genesis, Evolution, Adequacy and the Way Forward*. ADBI Working Paper 395. Tokyo: Asian Development Bank Institute.

Horisaka, Kotaro. 1989. *Japanese Banks and the Latin American Debt Problem*. Georgetown University Center for Latin American Studies Working Paper 4. Washington, DC: Georgetown University.

IMF (International Monetary Fund). 2003. *The IMF and Recent Capital Account Crises: Indonesia, Korea, Brazil*. Report by the Independent Evaluation Office. Washington, DC.

IMF (International Monetary Fund). 2011. Review of the Flexible Credit Line and Precautionary Credit Line (November). Washington, DC.

IMF (International Monetary Fund). 2012. Precautionary and Liquidity Line—Operational Guidance Note (May 31). Washington, DC. Available at www.imf.org/external/np/pp/eng/2012/053112a.pdf (accessed on July 1, 2013).

IMF (International Monetary Fund). 2013a. *Regional Financing Arrangements: Their Role in the International Financial Architecture and Cooperation with the IMF*. Issues Note for G20/IMF Seminar at the World Bank/IMF Annual Meeting (April). Washington, DC.

IMF (International Monetary Fund). 2013b. *Stocktaking the Fund's Engagement with Regional Financing Arrangements*. Washington, DC.

IMF (International Monetary Fund). 2013c. Greece: Ex Post Evaluation of Exceptional Access under the 2010 Stand-By Arrangement (June). Washington, DC. Available at www.imf.org/external/pubs/ft/scr/2013/cr13156.pdf (accessed on July 1, 2013).

James, Harold. 2013. Making the European Monetary Union. Voxeu.org (February 17). Available at www.voxeu.org/article/making-european-monetary-union (accessed on July 1, 2013).

Kawai, Masahiro, and Cindy Houser. 2007. *Evolving ASEAN+3 ERPD: Towards Peer Reviews or Due Diligence?* ADBI Working Paper 79. Tokyo: Asian Development Bank Institute.

Korea Institute of Finance. 2012. *The Role of Regional Financial Safety Nets in Global Architecture.* 2011/2012 ASEAN+3 Research Group Final Report and Summary (March).

Krugman, Paul R. 1991. *Geography and Trade.* Cambridge: MIT Press.

Lipscy, Phillip Y. 2003. Japan's Asian Monetary Fund Proposal. *Stanford Journal of East Asian Affairs* 3, no. 1: 93–104.

Lombardi, Domenico. 2012. *The Relationship between Global and Regional Safety Nets. Papers and Proceedings.* Office of Economic Studies, Latin American Reserve Fund (November). Bogotá.

Ministry of Foreign Affairs of Japan. 2005. *Executive Report: Progress of Implementation of the ASEAN-Japan Plan of Action* (December). Available at www.mofa.go.jp/region/asia-paci/asean/conference/report0512.html (accessed on July 1, 2013).

Moon, Woosik, and Yeongseop Rhee. 2012. *Asian Monetary Integration: Coping with a New Monetary Order after the Global Crisis.* Cheltenham: Edward Elgar.

Mourlon-Druol, Emmanuel. 2012. *A Europe Made of Money.* Ithaca, NY: Cornell University Press.

Pisani-Ferry, Jean, André Sapir, and Guntram Wolff. 2011. *An Evaluation of IMF Surveillance of the Euro Area.* Bruegel Blueprint Series (October). Brussels: Bruegel.

Pisani-Ferry, Jean, André Sapir, and Guntram Wolff. 2013. Financial Assistance in the Euro Area: An Early Assessment. Presentation at the Peterson Institute for International Economics, Washington, DC, April 19. Available at www.piie.com/publications/papers/pisani-ferry20130419ppt.pdf (accessed on July 1, 2013).

Rhee, Changyong. 2011. From Seoul to Cannes: What Has the G20 Delivered So Far? *Harvard International Review* 33, no. 3: 22–26.

Rhee, Changyong, and Lea Sumulong. 2013. *A Practical Approach to International Monetary System Reform: Building Settlement Infrastructure for Regional Currencies.* ADB Economics Working Paper 341. Manila: Asian Development Bank.

Rodrik, Dani. 1997. *Has Globalization Gone Too Far?* Washington, DC: Institute for International Economics.

Scheve, Kenneth F., and Matthew J. Slaughter. 2001. *Globalization and the Perceptions of American Workers.* Washington, DC: Institute for International Economics.

Siregar, Reza, and Akkharaphol Chabchitrchaidol. 2013. *Enhancing the Effectiveness of CMIM and AMRO: Selected Immediate Challenges and Tasks.* ADBI Working Paper 403. Tokyo: Asian Development Bank Institute.

Sussangkarn, Chalongphob. 2011. Chiang Mai Initiative Multilateralization: Origin, Development and Outlook. *Asian Economic Policy Review* 6, no. 2: 203–20.

Truman, Edwin. 2010. *The G-20 and International Financial Institution Governance.* Working Paper 10-13. Washington, DC: Peterson Institute for International Economics.

Truman, Edwin. 2011. Three Evolutionary Proposals for Reform of the International Monetary System. Remarks delivered at the Bank of Italy Conference in Memory of Tommaso Padoa-Schioppa. Available at www.piie.com/publications/papers/truman12162011.pdf (accessed on July 1, 2013).

van den Boogaerde, Pierre. 1991. *Financial Assistance from Arab Countries and Arab Regional Institutions.* IMF Occasional Paper 87. Washington, DC: International Monetary Fund.

Appendix 7A

Table 7A.1 Evolution of the Chiang Mai Initiative, 1977–2012

Date	Form	Size (billions of US dollars)	Member countries	Linked with IMF (percent)	Notes
1977	ASEAN Swap Arrangement (ASA)	0.1	ASEAN-5[a]	0	▪ Contribution: $20 million each ▪ Maximum swap maturity: one, two, or three months, renewable once for three months ▪ Source of swap funds: equal shares by nonrequesting members, except when financially unable to provide their share ▪ Swap amount: based on gearing ratio of 1:2 ▪ Validity: one year
1978–99	ASA	0.2	ASEAN-5	0	▪ Contribution : $40 million each
2000	Chiang Mai Initiative (CMI)[b] -ASA	1.0	ASEAN-10[c]	0	▪ Contribution: $150 million each for Brunei Darussalam, Indonesia, Malaysia, the Philippines, Singapore, and Thailand; $60 million for Viet Nam; $20 million for Myanmar; $15 million for Cambodia; $5 million for the Lao People's Democratic Republic (PDR) ▪ Max swap maturity: six months ▪ Swap amount: twice the contribution ▪ Validity: two years
May 2005	CMI-ASA	2.0	ASEAN-10	0	▪ Contribution: $300 million each for Brunei Darussalam, Indonesia, Malaysia, the Philippines, Singapore, and Thailand; $120 million for Viet Nam; $40 million for Myanmar; $30 million for Cambodia; $10 million for Lao PDR ▪ Swap maturities: one, two, three, or six months; rollover period of not more than six months inclusive of the initial swap period

Date	Name		Group		Details
2002–09	CMI-Bilateral Swap and Repurchase Agreement	17.0–90.0	ASEAN-10+3[d]	90–80[e]	■ 6 to 26 bilateral swap and repurchase agreements, with some bilateral swaps outside the CMIM remaining in place ■ Maximum swap maturity (not IMF-linked): 180 days (90 days, renewable once for another 90 days) ■ IMF-linked swap maximum maturity: two years (90 days, renewable seven times) ■ A review of the CMI resulted in the following enhancements: (a) integration of surveillance mechanism (i.e., the ASEAN+3 Economic Review and Policy Dialogue) into the CMI; (b) adoption of a collective decision-making mechanism as a first step toward multilateralization; (c) significant increase in fund size; and (d) increase in the IMF delinked portion from 10% to 20%.
May 2008	CMI Multilateralization (CMIM)[f]	At least 80.0	ASEAN-10+3	80	■ Agreements reached on contributions, borrowing accessibility, activation mechanism, and other elements ■ Consensus not yet reached on concrete conditions for borrowing eligibility and contents of covenants specified in borrowing agreements
February 2009	CMIM	120	ASEAN-10+3	80	■ Agreement to establish an independent surveillance unit ■ No consensus yet on main components
March 2010	CMIM	120	ASEAN-10+3 and Hong Kong, China	80	■ Commitment: 20 percent by ASEAN and 80 percent by +3 economies ■ Borrowing quota: contribution x borrowing multiplier ■ Maximum swap maturity: 90 days but can be rolled over seven times ■ Coordinating countries: one from ASEAN, one from +3 economies ■ Requirements for drawing request: completion of economic and financial situation review, compliance with periodic surveillance report, and participation in the ASEAN+3 Economic Review and Policy Dialogue ■ Exemption from contributing to a swap request is possible only after approval of an executive-level decision-making body ■ Validity: five years ■ Agreement on all elements of ASEAN+3 Macroeconomic Research Office[g] ■ Agreement to improve Economic Review and Policy Dialogue process

(continues on next page)

Table 7A.1   Evolution of the Chiang Mai Initiative, 1977–2012 *(continued)*

Date	Form	Size (billions of US dollars)	Member countries	Linked with IMF (percent)	Notes
May 2012	CMIM	240	ASEAN-10+3 and Hong Kong, China	70	■ Maturity (full amount): extended from 90 days to one year (with two renewals) ■ Supporting period: extended from two to three years ■ Maturity of the IMF-delinked portion: extended from 90 days to six months (with three renewals) ■ Support period of the IMF-delinked portion: extended from one to two years ■ Crisis resolution function renamed as the CMIM Stability Facility ■ CMIM precautionary line—a crisis prevention facility was introduced

a. ASEAN-5 are Indonesia, Malaysia, the Philippines, Singapore, and Thailand.

b. The CMI was signed in May 2000.

c. ASEAN-10 are the ASEAN-5 plus Brunei Darussalam, Cambodia, Lao PDR, Myanmar, and Viet Nam.

d. Plus Three (+3) are the People's Republic of China, Japan, and the Republic of Korea.

e. The IMF-delinked portion was increased from 10 to 20 percent in May 2005 and to 30 percent in May 2012.

f. The CMIM was signed in December 2009 and took effect in March 2010.

g. ASEAN+3 Macroeconomic Research Office (AMRO) was established and started operation in May 2011.

Notes: The ASA remained in effect even after the operationalization of the CMIM (BSP 2012). Hong Kong, China is a party to the CMIM Agreement but its borrowing capacity is limited to the IMF-delinked portion of the swap line, since it is not a member of the IMF.

Sources: AMRO (2009) (see also the AMRO website at www.amro-asia.org); ASEAN (1977, 1978, 1981, 1982, 2006, 2007, 2008, 2009a, 2009b, 2012, 2013); BSP (2012); Henning (2002); Hill and Menon (2012); Ministry of Foreign Affairs of Japan (2005); and Sussangkarn (2011).

Table 7A.2 European regional financial safety nets, 1970–2012

Date	Form	Size	Member countries	Conditionality	Link with IMF	Other
1970	Short-Term Monetary Support (STMS)	$1 billion	European Economic Community (EEC)	No	No	
1971	Medium-Term Financial Assistance (MTFA)	13.9 billion euros	EEC	Yes	No	Credits are up to two years but the facility was amended and expanded on several occasions through the 1970s and 1980s. It needed a decision of the European Council to be activated and involved policy conditionality.
1973	European Monetary Cooperation Fund (also known by its French acronym, FECOM). The Fund also came to manage the STMS.	Ad hoc	EEC. Note that the central banks of Denmark, Ireland, and the United Kingdom became party to the Fund although they were not part of the EEC yet.	Ambiguous	No	The European Monetary Cooperation Fund was established shortly after the agreement on the "European currency snake" (1972) and was designed to operate the underlying agreement between central banks, in particular its very short-term financing facility, which effectively arranged for the settlement of currency interventions. The Fund, whose secretariat was the Bank for International Settlements, was tasked with coordinating and undertaking concerted interventions and arranging for settlements between the central banks.
1975	Community Loan Mechanism	6 billion ECU expanded to 8 billion ECU in 1985	EEC	Yes	No	Created in response to the first oil shock.

(continues on next page)

Table 7A.2 European regional financial safety nets, 1970–2012 *(continued)*

Date	Form	Size	Member countries	Conditionality	Link with IMF	Other
1979	Exchange Rate Mechanism (ERM)		EEC	Yes	No	With the move toward the European Monetary System, the definition of the ECU became a key feature of monetary cooperation in Europe. This ought to be supported by a strengthening of the FECOM and the development of short-term credit facilities, implying increased and more automatic interventions by central banks to support the agreed central parity.
1992	Balance of Payments Assistance Facility	€12 billion	All EEC countries until the establishment of the euro	Yes	No	This facility was a relic of ERM days but was used once for Italy and left dormant until it was used again in Hungary in 2008.
1994	European Monetary Institute		Countries party to the ERM2	No	No	The European Monetary Institute coordinated foreign exchange interventions and settlements.
2009	Expansion of the Balance of Payments Assistance Facility	€50 billion	Non-euro-area members of the European Union	Yes	Not necessarily	In consideration of expanding needs in Central and Eastern Europe the facility was raised first to €25 billion and then to €50 billion.

Year	Instrument	Amount	Coverage			Comments
2009	Vienna Initiative. Gradually expanded in size and scope to become the European Banks Coordination Initiative (EBCI), which involves the European Commission	€25 billion	EBRD countries of operations—Central and Eastern Europe	No	Not necessarily	The Vienna Initiative was started in February with only €25 billion of commitments from multilateral development banks. The initiative was expanded and renamed in 2010 the European Banking Coordination Initiative.
2010	Bilateral Support Lines (set up for the first Greek program)	€90 billion	From all 17 euro area governments to Greece	Yes	Yes	In the absence of existing instruments to provide balance of payments assistance, euro area countries were forced to resort to bilateral loans in addition to IMF support.
2010	European Financial Stabilization Mechanism (EFSM)	€60 billion	All members of the European Union	Yes	Yes	Given the shortcomings of bilateral loans, it was decided to create a facility backed by the European budget.
2010	European Financial Stability Facility (EFSF)	€440 billion	17 members of the euro area	Yes	Yes	Given the small size of the European budget, euro area member states decided to set up an intergovernmental body to replace bilateral loans. The facility was meant to be temporary and limited to the life of the exceptional loans it was providing.

(continues on next page)

Table 7A.2   European regional financial safety nets, 1970–2012 *(continued)*

Date	Form	Size	Member countries	Conditionality	Link with IMF	Other
2010	Securities Market Programme (unconditional but limited ECB interventions)	Limited (in effect €200 billion)	Only countries of euro area were eligible. In practice, it was only used in Greece, Spain, Ireland, Portugal, and Italy	No	No	Financial distress highlighted the need for the ECB to be able to backstop sovereign debt markets. ECB set this up with this objective but failed to stabilize sovereign debt markets.
2011	European Stability Mechanism (ESM)	€500 billion	All members of the euro area	Yes	Yes	The EFSF was made permanent and this was the permanent version, which allowed for temporarily combining the three facilities and raising the level of total usable resources to almost €1 trillion.
2012	Outright Monetary Transactions (conditional ECB interventions on sovereign debt markets)	Potentially unlimited	All members of the euro area but only applicable to countries under an ESM adjustment program	Yes, indirectly	Yes to the extent that the ESM does	Most of the safety nets created during the crisis were budgetary in nature and had therefore limited resources. Growing financial fragmentation that risked tearing apart the monetary union eventually forced the ECB to announce a plan opening the door to potentially unlimited interventions in sovereign debt markets.

EBRD = European Bank for Reconstruction and Development; ECB = European Central Bank; ECU = European currency unit; ERM2 = Second Phase of Exchange Rate Mechanism

Source: Authors' compilation.

8

Regional Responses to Financial Crises:
The Americas, East Asia, and Europe

STEPHAN HAGGARD

Developments in both Europe and Asia have focused attention on regional lenders of last resort and their relationship to global lenders.[1] Latin America also has a long-standing subregional experiment—the Latin American Reserve Fund (Fondo Latinoamericano de Reservas, FLAR)—with ongoing discussion of its possible expansion into a regionwide fund. This chapter considers these regional financial arrangements through the lens of institutional design and politics: how decision making among the principals affects the provision of liquidity, the extent and nature of delegation to supranational entities for monitoring and enforcement, and the credibility of policy commitments.

Debates about the design of international lender-of-last-resort institutions—including the International Monetary Fund (IMF) itself—always confront the problem of how to provide adequate and timely liquidity while mitigating potential moral hazard problems. There are two ways of addressing these tradeoffs. Ex ante or preventive mechanisms seek to constrain policy so that the risks of crises are reduced in the first place. As the IMF's long experience with surveillance has demonstrated, it is difficult to make these arrangements credible. Creditors as well as debtors have to bind themselves to obligations that are precise—yet simultaneously adequately flexible—so that they can be

Stephan Haggard, visiting fellow at the Peterson Institute for International Economics, is the Lawrence and Sallye Krause Distinguished Professor at the University of California, San Diego, Graduate School of International Relations and Pacific Studies. He thanks Bill Cline, Andrew Moravcsik, Marcus Noland, Christina Schneider, Ted Truman, and two anonymous reviewers for their comments, as well as Andrew Chiang and Kelly Matush for research assistance.

1. See McKay, Volz, and Wölfinger (2010); Henning (2011); Eichengreen (2012); Lombardi (2013); and chapter 7 in this volume.

enforced. Institutions at both the collective and national levels then have to be designed to monitor and constrain those collective and individual choices.

A simple expectation is that the more heterogeneous the membership of any regional organization, the less likely it will be to generate binding ex ante commitments and the more likely it will rely on what international legal scholars call "soft law"—informal understandings and at best peer pressure. Even in Europe, where countries share common democratic political systems and commitments to monetary union, ex ante mechanisms have a turbulent history. Both large creditor countries and the smaller, peripheral debtors have been guilty of derogations; indeed, the credibility of the Stability and Growth Pact (SGP) was initially weakened as much by the behavior of the former than the latter. In Asia and Latin America, such commitments have been even weaker; again, the interests of creditors have been as significant as those of debtors in limiting ex ante commitments. In the regional case studies, I explore some of the sources of regional heterogeneity that limit such commitments. These differences go well beyond the standard distinction between debtors and creditors and encompass political factors such as competing geostrategic and ideological interests and whether regimes are democratic or authoritarian.

The second way of handling the liquidity–moral hazard tradeoff—and the one that has received more attention—is through ex post or corrective measures and the design of crisis lending itself. Since Walter Bagehot's well-known injunctions—to lend freely into crises against good collateral and at penalty rates—the design of lender-of-last-resort institutions has been an object of controversy. First, decisions must be made about the amount of liquidity on offer and its basic terms, such as maturity and lending rates. One way of seeking to join the ex ante and ex post mechanisms is through no bailout rules: to enforce caution by limiting liquidity altogether. As the European case shows clearly, it is virtually impossible to make such commitments credible given the externalities financial crises produce in highly integrated regions. Even supra-national institutions such as the European Central Bank (ECB) have been constrained to act in ways that push up against the limits of the no-bailout commitment, and with good reason (see chapter 3 in this volume).

As with preventive measures, the design and operation of corrective or lender-of-last-resort institutions ultimately rests on intergovernmental processes. This has been shown to be the case with respect to the IMF as well (Stone 2011). The standard way of thinking about the political economy of lender-of-last-resort functions is in terms of the conflict of interest between creditors and debtors. I find that creditor interest in ex ante or preventive measures varies quite substantially across regions: Some have sought tougher commitments while others seek to maintain their own discretion. But preferences with respect to ex post or lending arrangements are more predictable. When creditors favor these institutions at all—and Germany has consistently resisted them—they prefer arrangements that are limited in size and scope and with governance structures that enshrine their formal and informal influence over the provision of liquidity. At the level of both broad policy and of actual lending, a common feature of virtually all lenders of last resort is intergovernmental review processes and weighted voting rules that favor the voice of creditors.

As with preventive approaches, regional agreements require institutions to evaluate requests from borrowers and monitor their performance with respect to loan conditions. The standard argument for delegating these functions to independent administrative bodies is efficiency and effectiveness; monitoring is costly and those costs are reduced by organizational specialization. But the problems are also political: In the absence of delegation, intergovernmental monitoring would occur in bodies in which borrowers are represented—and even strongly represented. These constraints account for the widely observed tendency for regional agreements to rely in whole or in part on the IMF, although the FLAR marks an interesting exception.

Before turning to the cases, two further introductory observations are warranted. First, institutions are not typically designed in good times or all at once. They often evolve as ad hoc, incremental responses to crises. The narratives below are designed to capture the evolutionary nature of institutional change and the compromises that necessarily arise during crisis circumstances. Second, it is important to underline that these regional arrangements are not forged in a political vacuum, but arise on the foundation of wider regional arrangements that shape organizational choice. Path dependence is an important feature of these arrangements.

I begin with Europe, where regional institutions—including commitment to monetary union—were highly developed at the outset of our story. The political foundation of the European Union and the euro area rested on a strong no-bailout rule in the Maastricht Treaty and a reliance on ex ante surveillance mechanisms through the SGP. However, the political institutions of the European Union provided representation to debtors, and the risks to the euro from peripheral defaults were by no means limited to the deficit countries. Difficult and highly contentious political compromises were required to generate a more robust crisis management process in the form of the European Stability Mechanism (ESM), and only in the face of costly delays caused by the inevitable bargaining over terms. Creditor countries expressed strong concerns about the level of liquidity and insisted on institutionalized coordination with the IMF in order to monitor conditionality. Moreover, they advanced an agenda for dramatically strengthening ex ante surveillance through mechanisms with a substantial supranational component.

At the outset of the financial crisis in 1997–98, Asia was much more weakly institutionalized than Europe. Existing political institutions—including the Asia-Pacific Economic Cooperation (APEC) forum, the Association of Southeast Asian Nations (ASEAN), and an emergent ASEAN+3 framework including the People's Republic of China (PRC), Japan, and the Republic of Korea—were thin and the crisis was far beyond their mandate or capacity. The United States played an important role in managing the crisis and strongly resisted ideas for an Asian Monetary Fund (AMF) proposed by Japan, the other major creditor country in the region. The IMF also had doubts about the wisdom of creating a new regional institution. The rapid return of current account surpluses provided the financial foundation for a modest regional crisis management system led by the three largest surplus countries in the region: the PRC, Japan, and the Republic of Korea. The Chiang Mai Initiative (CMI)—a network of bilateral swap arrangements—has subsequently been multilateralized and deepened on the basis of rules that mark a fundamental departure from past ASEAN practice, including weighted voting.

The questions hanging over the new Asian institutions are two. First, will the CMI be supplemented by a surveillance mechanism that would signal closer policy coordination or even first steps toward monetary union? The political as well as economic heterogeneity of the major players and the political weight of potential deficit countries in regional institutions suggest that steps along these lines are likely to remain modest. A larger question is whether the facility is likely to be used at all given the revealed preference in the region for large current account surpluses and reserves.

When the Latin American debt crisis struck, the Americas did not have an institutional framework that could provide lender-of-last-resort functions. As in Asia, the United States played a central political role in crisis management, with the IMF providing liquidity and monitoring conditionality. For quite obvious reasons, the United States showed no subsequent interest in tying its hands through participation in regional financial arrangements, meaning that they had to be constructed entirely of potential borrowers. A small institution attached to the Andean regional integration experiment—the FLAR—sustained modest balance of payments lending for nearly three decades on the basis of a surprisingly informal political structure. For this institution to be scaled up, it would have to bring in the larger economies in the region: Argentina, Mexico, and particularly Brazil. There is some doubt whether they would be willing to play that role in the absence of quite fundamental institutional changes, if at all.

What do these three diverse regional experiences tell us about the design of regional financing arrangements and their relationship with global ones? The experience underlines the extraordinary difficulty of establishing robust ex ante surveillance. Such efforts have faced ongoing challenges in Europe, where political conditions would appear most auspicious, and are even less likely to take root among politically diverse emerging markets. The core questions thus reside in the design of lender-of-last-resort functions. A key finding is that we have surprisingly little experience to actually draw on beyond the European case; the discussion of regional financing arrangements appears to be far outrunning actual experience. The limited experience available suggests that creditors are highly reluctant to commit to such institutions, and that when they do they strongly prefer intergovernmental versus supranational governance arrangements that allow them to retain a powerful voice in lending and monitoring decisions. This reluctance can itself compound crises, however, as parties negotiate not only over short-term responses to distress but longer-run institutional issues and crucial questions of precedent.

The complementary analysis in chapter 7 of this volume provides a more extended treatment of the relationship between global and regional safety nets, but one observation emerges clearly. "Coordination" is the current watchword, and many good ideas exist about how this might be implemented. But it is important to underline that the interests of global and regional institutions necessarily diverge because of the very different composition of their memberships. If this is true even with respect to the relationship between the IMF and Europe—which remains overrepresented at the Fund—it is even truer of the relationship between the IMF and other regional financing arrangements. Given these differences, "division of labor" may be a more appropriate guiding watchword than "coordination" for the relationship between global and regional institutions.

Europe: The Road to the European Stability Mechanism and the Fiscal Compact

Europe has seen the most robust development of regional crisis management mechanisms. However, these developments were not as obvious as they appear with the benefit of hindsight. Although the Treaty of Rome provided for a modest, transitional balance of payments support mechanism, the Maastricht Treaty contained important provisions that limited both EU and ECB lender-of-last-resort activities. Stability was to be maintained not by lending ex post, but by SGP commitments and ex ante macroeconomic policy surveillance. These arrangements faced tests well before the onset of the global financial crisis and the subsequent problems of how to manage Greece.

From 2010 on, however, the European Union was forced to develop new lender-of-last-resort capabilities in the wake of political delays that exacerbated adverse market sentiment and threatened the integrity of the entire euro area. These developments are considered here in three steps: the institutions in place prior to the onset of the global financial crisis; the ad hoc innovations that were forced on Europe as a result of the Greek crisis; and the new institutions—the European Stability Mechanism and Fiscal Compact—that emerged in 2011. Although I note the broader innovations of the ECB—culminating in the Outright Monetary Transactions program of 2012—the focus is primarily on the new intergovernmental institutions. The wider role of the ECB in crisis management is addressed in more detail in chapter 3 in this volume.

The Status Quo Ante: Limited EU and ECB Tools

Prior to the onset of the Greek debt crisis in 2010, the European Union had relatively limited collective ability to lend in the face of crises. These limitations did not reflect sins of omission; they were crucial elements of the design of monetary union. The "no bailout" rule in Article 104 of the Maastricht Treaty in 1992—subsequently incorporated into Articles 123-5 of the Lisbon Treaty in 2007—ruled out member governments using "overdraft facilities or any other type of credit facility" with the ECB as well as direct ECB purchase of national debt instruments. The European Union could also not be held liable or assume the commitments of member governments.

These commitments were given added weight and credibility by the nature of German constitutional law. Under Germany's constitution, the Bundestag has an inalienable responsibility for the budget. Any decision regarding revenues and expenditures—including facilities that would potentially create liabilities of unknown magnitude—required explicit Bundestag approval. Even with this approval—starting with two laws passed in May 2010 in connection with the Greek package—negotiations over new facilities occurred in the shadow of the German constitutional court, and key legal issues were not resolved until crucial rulings in 2011 and 2012.

Several exceptions to the no-bailout rule largely confirm the reticence to create lender-of-last-resort institutions. The founding Rome Treaty (Article 143) permitted balance of payments support for members experiencing temporary difficulties, but this measure was considered transitional to the formation of the common market and no separate facility was initially created. Article 122 permitted financial assistance under exigent circumstances, and later provided the legal foundation for new community lending.[2] But it, too, was never formalized.

Following the Hague summit of December 1969, debate ensued over a proposal by Willy Brandt to establish a European Reserve Fund. A European Monetary Cooperation Fund was ultimately established in 1973. But the most important institution for managing misalignments and crises remained central bank cooperation, organized at the policy level through the Committee of Central Bank Governors and operationally through a network of credit lines (Szasz 1999). These arrangements remained in place following the Central Banks' Agreement of 1979 that established the rules of the road for the European Monetary System that existed from March 1979 through its effective collapse following the financial crises of 1992–93 (Mastropasqua, Micossi, and Rinaldi 1988).[3]

Following the European financial crises of 1992–93, the community moved to implement the Maastricht commitments. These negotiations centered on

---

2. Article 122 permitted the European Council to grant financial assistance to a member state "seriously threatened with severe difficulties caused by natural disasters or exceptional occurrences beyond its control." Clearly, there is significant doubt as to whether subsequent difficulties were truly exogenous, but the article subsequently was cited as legal foundation for the European Financial Stabilization Mechanism created in 2010. See Ryvkin (2012).

3. Under the European Monetary System, interventions were compulsory but foreign exchange for this purpose was made available through the Very Short-Term Financing Facility, a network of central bank credit lines that made foreign exchange available on an automatic basis and without limit. Balances could subsequently be settled in either convertible currencies or newly created European currency units (ECUs). Over the course of the decade, these credit facilities were expanded by rules that raised ECU acceptance limits and provided access for intramarginal as well as marginal interventions.

two institutional pillars: the creation of the European Monetary Institute as the precursor to the ECB—and the simultaneous dissolution of the Committee of Central Bank Governors and the European Monetary Cooperation Fund—and the domestic policy commitments of the SGP.[4] The dissolution of the European Monetary Cooperation Fund raised the question of how medium-term financing for balance of payments purposes would be provided for those outside the euro. When the new facility was formed in 2002 (the Facility Providing Medium-Term Financial Assistance for Member States' Balances of Payments),[5] it fell not under the ECB but under the purview of the inter-governmental council and was administered by the European Commission. The facility mirrored basic IMF procedures, but with more generous interest rates, and borrowing was explicitly linked to a Fund Stand-By Arrangement. The member seeking support would submit an adjustment program first to the Economic and Financial Affairs Council of the European Union (Ecofin), the agenda of which was set by the intergovernmental Economic and Financial Committee with participation by the European Commission (Directorate General for Economic and Financial Affairs) and the ECB. Only then would the proposal go to the IMF.

With high growth and the convergence of private borrowing costs in Europe during the 2000s, the modest facility—limited to €12 billion—was not drawn on until the onset of the global financial crisis. It was increased to €25 billion in December 2008 and to €50 billion in May 2009. These changes were not anticipatory; rather, they followed programs reached with Hungary (November 2008), Latvia (December 2008), and Romania (May 2009 and a second precautionary program in November 2011). As in the Latin American and Asian financial crises, financing was ultimately provided by shifting consortia of lenders that went beyond the fund's initial design: in addition to the European facility and the IMF, the World Bank, European Bank for Reconstruction and Development, European Investment Bank, and (in the case of Latvia) the Nordic countries participated.

The Latvian and Romanian programs revealed differences in the policy approach of the IMF and the European Union that reflected distinctive European political interests. In both programs, the Fund took positions that were more

---

4. To manage relations between euro area and non-euro-area countries, the Exchange Rate Mechanism set a band (15 percent), created a procedure for consideration of adjustment of rates involving the Ecofin Council and the European Commission, and formalized the Very Short-Term Financing Facility as a community institution. But these mechanisms were for those countries initially (or permanently) remaining outside the euro area. See "Summaries of European Legislation: Exchange Rate Mechanism (ERM II) between the Euro and Participating National Currencies," Europa Summaries of European Legislation, September 19, 2011, http://europa.eu/legislation_summaries/economic_and_monetary_affairs/institutional_and_economic_framework/l25082_en.htm (accessed on July 1, 2013).

5. Council of the European Union, Council Regulation No 332/2002 of 18 February 2002 Establishing a Facility Providing Medium-Term Financial Assistance for Member States' Balances of Payments, http://eur-lex.europa.eu/LexUriServ/LexUriServ.do?uri=OJ:L:2002:053:0001:0003:EN:PDF (accessed on July 1, 2013).

permissive with respect to the path of fiscal adjustment. In the Latvian case, the IMF also expressed skepticism about the maintenance of the peg, which the Ecofin Council required for Latvia to ultimately stay on a path to adoption of the euro (Lütz and Kranke 2013).

It is important to emphasize that these financing mechanisms were only made available for those *outside* the euro area. For those on the euro, crises would be avoided through the "preventive" arm of the SGP; the focus here is not on the substantive merits of the SGP but the political process of monitoring and enforcing it. Under the SGP, EU member states were required to submit annual macroeconomic and fiscal projects, called "stability programs" in the case of countries that had adopted the euro and "convergence programs" in the case of aspirants. Monitoring and enforcement were delegated in ways that appeared to create automaticity. Under its "corrective arm," the pact required the European Commission to prepare a report whenever the deficit of a member state exceeded 3 percent of GDP. Under the Excessive Deficit Procedure, recommendations and deadlines were established to bring deficits back in line with SGP requirements, culminating in sanctions for those who remained in serious breach.

The rigidity of the SGP has been an object of contention from its inception (for example, Eichengreen and Wyplosz 1998). However, important political features of the monetary union also undermined its credibility. When the Maastricht Treaty was signed, expectations were that it would be a relatively limited monetary union among a handful of states that had strongly convergent macroeconomic policy preferences and policies: Germany, France, the Netherlands, Belgium, Luxembourg, and Austria (if it joined the European Union; Eichengreen 2008, 220). The politics of the European Union, however, dictated the admission of countries that had not met the convergence criteria, including most notably Greece.

The credibility of the SGP was by no means impaired only by the behavior of the peripheral countries. Contrary to the design favored by Germany, sanctions under the procedure were not as automatic as they looked and required Council scrutiny and approval. Portugal was the first to breach the deficit limits, but Germany and France quickly followed in 2003. These two countries effectively blocked the European Commission's recommendations with respect to required fiscal adjustments at the level of the intergovernmental Council. Although technically legitimate, the management of these two defining cases demonstrated the ability of major powers to finesse commitments. Reforms in 2005 sought to introduce greater precision into country-level commitments through the medium-term budgetary objectives, but the damage had been done. The onset of the crisis in 2008 called the entire edifice into question once again as the demands for countercyclical policy came into conflict with the SGP; not only did Greece, Ireland, and Portugal fall under the Excessive Deficit Procedures, but so did Spain, Latvia, Lithuania, Romania, Poland, Slovakia, Slovenia, and the Czech Republic.

Greek Crisis and Transitional Institutions: European Financial Stability Facility and Mechanism (EFSF and EFSM)

The route to the formation of more robust regional financial institutions was littered with well-known missteps that rattled markets and forced the hands of the major players. In the absence of a functioning architecture, these delays were arguably inevitable. But they resulted in part from a complex intra-European bargaining process not only over the liquidity that would be provided to those on, rather than outside, the euro—starting with Greece—but the broader institutions and rules that would govern emerging lender-of-last-resort functions. The stakes were high. Germany sought to limit both its and the community's exposure. It also sought to ensure that the costs of adjustment would be borne by the deficit country—with Greece as the precedent—and that the broader surveillance and policy mechanism of the SGP would be reformed to forestall such eventualities in the future.

After the victory of the Socialists in the Greek election in October 2009, the fiscal position of the government was revealed to be much worse than had been thought. A joint statement by the European heads of state on February 11, 2010, promised "determined and coordinated action, if needed," but provided no detail on what such action would look like. The statement did nothing to calm markets. Subsequent announcements on March 25 and April 12 promising support continued to reflect deep differences within the community. These differences included the terms of any support, the adjustments required of Greece, and the extent of participation by the IMF. But the statements also emphasized political procedure. The March 25 statement is worth quoting at length:

> This mechanism, complementing International Monetary Fund financing, has to be considered ultima ratio, meaning in particular that market financing is insufficient. Any disbursement on the bilateral loans would be decided by the euro area member states by unanimity subject to strong conditionality and based on an assessment by the European Commission and the European Central Bank. We expect Euro-Member states to participate on the basis of their respective ECB capital key.[6]

The statement resolved the issue of IMF involvement and created a "troika" that included the ECB and European Commission as well. However, the real message was that potential opponents of any program would effectively exercise a veto over it through an intergovernmental mechanism that required unanimity. The role of the Commission was distinctly subordinated to the intergovernmental process. Technically, the May 2 package was not even a European community effort at all. Rather, the eurogroup agreed to provide

---

6. The statement is available at www.consilium.europa.eu/uedocs/cms_data/docs/pressdata/en/ec/113563.pdf.

up to €80 billion in bilateral loans, with the European Commission acting only as coordinator (Pisani-Ferry, Sapir, and Wolff 2013).

The May 2010 crisis quickly generated two new lending vehicles. The first and more modest was the European Financial Stabilization Mechanism (EFSM), which was an extension of the medium-term financing facility model that had been used to assist Hungary, Latvia, and Romania. The EFSM expanded the balance of payments facility by €60 billion in new money, guaranteed through the EU budget by all 27 member states, and dropped the prohibition on its use by euro area members.

The second and more ambitious component of the package was the creation of the European Financial Stability Facility (EFSF). Rather than being created as an EU entity, the EFSF was set up as a special-purpose vehicle incorporated in Luxembourg with the power to issue bonds or other debt instruments to finance its lending operations. The EFSF was by design a temporary organization.[7] Its structure was also decidedly intergovernmental and designed to avoid up-front commitments that would challenge the no-bailout rule. The board was made up of representatives of the 17 euro area states and chaired by the chairman of the EU Economic and Financial Committee. The European Commission and ECB participated in the board as observers only. The governance structure corresponded to the underlying funding model. EFSF issues were backed by €440 billion in guarantees rather than paid-in capital, raised to €780 billion in July. The amount of guarantees was based on the formula for the paid-up capital of the ECB.[8] On the basis of this formula, Germany accounted for 29 percent of guarantees, France 21.8 percent, and Italy 19.2 percent. But the decision-making process operated on the basis of consensus laid down in the March statement, and thus granted an effective veto to any member.

The EFSF was empowered to act on the basis of country programs that were submitted through a complex institutional filter first spelled out in the Greek program. The borrowing country was required to submit an acceptable letter of intent to the intergovernmental Ecofin Council, the European Commission, and the IMF. The ECB was also brought into the review process. If the European Commission, ECB, and IMF—the "troika"—believed funding was required and the letter of intent adequate, then the ministers would specify the amount of EFSF bond issues required, their price and duration, and the number of loan installments to be disbursed.

At the time that the EFSF was negotiated, it was believed that if the Greek problem could be solved by a large-scale but temporary commitment, the crisis

---

7. If no country required a loan within the three-year time frame of its existence, the EFSF would close down on June 30, 2013. If loans were extended, the facility would close with the liquidation of the last obligation.

8. To assure the highest possible credit rating and protect against default risk, bonds were overcollateralized by 20 percent with the excess escrowed, reducing the amount that could be borrowed by a corresponding amount. Once a member state receives funding from the EFSF, it is no longer obliged to guarantee loans. The pool of guarantees was thus vulnerable to shrinkage at the margin, with greater responsibility falling on the larger creditors.

would pass. In November 2010, however, this optimistic expectation proved wrong when Ireland approached the EFSF and was ultimately granted an €85 billion package. Portugal followed in May 2011 with a €78 billion program. In addition, the ECB was forced into a range of discretionary actions that pushed up against the no-bailout rule. With the announcement of each of the three country programs, the ECB suspended rating standards on collateral eligibility requirements for the debt instruments issued or guaranteed by the program country. At the time of the first Greek program in May 2010, the ECB also initiated a Securities Markets Program to purchase securities that it would normally accept as collateral in "dysfunctional market segments." It was hard to see how relaxing ratings standards and purchasing securities in the secondary market was fundamentally different from the direct financing of the government. It was in this context of continuing crisis that negotiations took place over a more permanent facility and a revision of the SGP framework.

The European Stability Mechanism and Tightening of Surveillance

As with initial innovations driven by events in Greece, it was a second round of financial crises centered on Ireland and Portugal, continuing problems in Greece, and fears of further contagion that triggered negotiations over a more permanent crisis-management institution, the ESM. As with the initial creation of the EFSF, difficult bargaining ensued among the EU partners, with German preferences casting a long shadow over the negotiations.[9] Agreement was reached in principle in March 2011 to increase total lending through the EFSF to €440 billion and to relax terms; credit would be extended at rates equal to those on offer from the IMF. At a July 21 summit, following new evidence of missed Greek targets, a new €109 billion package was put together for that country that substantially relaxed the terms of the first package, including through longer maturities, a lowering of earlier penalty rates on borrowing, and a commitment to private sector involvement. As with previous ad hoc interventions, however, the new Greek program did little to alter market sentiment; to the contrary, the second half of 2011 was marked by a steady decline in the major European equity markets and increased volatility. By September it was increasingly apparent that more drastic measures were needed vis-à-vis the European banking system and the growing risk of contagion to the much larger "systemic" cases of Italy and Spain.

Unlike the ad hoc measures contained in the EFSF and ECB actions, the establishment of a permanent lender-of-last-resort-facility faced more significant political hurdles because it ultimately required treaty revision. A first round of negotiations took place at crucial summits in October, focusing on three core issues: the extent and nature of private sector involvement in the

---

9. Just prior to the key European Council Summit of March 24–25, 2011, for example, the Bundestag passed resolutions that would restrict certain operations and "special arrangements" outside of the new facility such as those for Greece. "Germany to Reinforce Tough Stance on Eurozone Bail-outs," *Financial Times*, February 24, 2011.

Greek program; the problem of how to recapitalize European banks; and the design and path from the EFSF to the ESM.[10] By the fall of 2011, the agreement to expand the size of the EFSF that had been reached earlier in the year looked much less potent. The Greek, Irish, and Portuguese bailouts had substantially reduced available EFSF resources and eliminated those countries' commitments to the fund, leaving only about €250 billion in reserve. But the solidity of this funding was called into question by the fact that a substantial share of total EFSF guarantees came from Italy and Spain, which were increasingly seen as potential borrowers. A heated debate ensued about various mechanisms through which the EFSF might be leveraged. Schemes ranged from special IMF facilities to address the problems facing Italy and Spain to the creation of a special-purpose vehicle that would permit investment from major surplus countries, including the PRC, and the conversion of the EFSF into a bank that could borrow from the ECB.

These and other proposals, including the issue of bonds guaranteed by the European Union, faced a combination of German opposition and skepticism from possible lenders. The leveraging proposals all ultimately wilted.[11] The ESM ultimately proved smaller than rival proposals. At €700 billion—but with €200 of that tied up in existing programs—the total capacity of the mechanism was nonetheless equal to 5.4 percent of EU GDP and 7.2 percent of euro area GDP, far larger than any other regional arrangement. But the governance structure and mandate of the ESM strongly reflected creditor interests. At the European Council meeting on December 16–17, the constitutional changes were made by adding a short paragraph to Article 136 of the treaty that is worth quoting in full:

> The Member States whose currency is the euro may establish a stability mechanism to be activated if indispensable to safeguard the stability of the euro area as a whole. The granting of any required financial assistance under the mechanism will be made subject to strict conditionality.[12]

Of interest are the particularly stringent conditions for providing support: not only conditionality, which is required in connection with any lender-of-last-resort support, but also the existence of a threat to the integrity of the euro.

---

10. See Peter Siegal and Alex Barker, "A Weekend to Save the Euro," *Financial Times*, October 19, 2011. For blow-by-blow coverage of the summit, see Simone Foxman, "EU Leaders Announce Plans To Leverage EFSF By 4-5 Times, Recapitalize Banks, And Deal On 50% Bond Haircuts," *Business Insider*, October 26, 2011, www.businessinsider.com/live-coverage-europe-tries-to-save-itself-at-huge-summit-2011-10 (accessed on July 1, 2013).

11. See Stefan Kasner, "Controversial Leverage Plan: Europe Opting for Discredited Tools to Solve Crisis," Spiegel Online, October 26, 2011, www.spiegel.de/international/europe/controversial-leverage-plan-europe-opting-for-discredited-tools-to-solve-crisis-a-794025.html (accessed on July 1, 2013).

12. See the European Council decision at http://eur-lex.europa.eu/LexUriServ/LexUriServ.do?uri=OJ:L:2011:091:0001:0002:EN:PDF (accessed on July 18, 2013).

Like the EFSF, the ESM is an intergovernmental body headed by a board of governors made up of the finance ministers of the eurogroup. As with the EFSF, the European Commission and the ECB participate as observers. An interesting departure from previous institutional designs was a subtle shift away from consensus decision making toward modified majoritarianism. Decisions on a set of core issues, including the terms of lending, the overall size of the facility, and the menu of instruments, were to be taken by a modified consensus in which abstentions would not block lending. Other issues were to be decided on the basis of an 80 percent qualified majority but with weighted voting in proportion to capital shares in the ESM. The intergovernmental nature of the agreement is mirrored in the capital structure of the mechanism, but with one fundamental departure from the EFSF model: The total €700 billion capital of the ESM includes not only €620 in callable capital but €80 billion of paid-in capital as well, provided by members in annual installments phased in from mid-2013.

The main instruments of the ESM are akin to the other European facilities that have been described here. Following a request for funding, the European Commission, IMF, and ECB assess the existence of risk to the euro area and the sustainability of public debt before concluding an adjustment program. In principle, support could be denied on the basis of failure to clear either of the two hurdles. The introduction of the sustainability analysis was associated with new expectations with respect to private sector involvement. If the sustainability analysis suggests the ability to restore access to the markets through an adjustment program, then the ESM would encourage investors to maintain exposure voluntarily. However, when a program reveals that public debt is not sustainable, borrowers will be required to engage with creditors. To facilitate these negotiations, the agreement required the inclusion of standardized collective action clauses that would permit creditors to take qualified majority decisions with respect to standstills, extension of maturities, and outright haircuts.

In parallel with the negotiation establishing new crisis management institutions, the European Union and the eurogroup also moved forward on an ambitious reform of the SGP that ultimately culminated in the Fiscal Compact (formally the Treaty on Stability, Coordination and Governance in the Economic and Monetary Union) signed on March 2, 2012. The first stage of these reforms pertained to the entire European Union, not just the eurogroup, and came in the wake of the Irish crisis in the form of a so-called six-pack of five new community regulations and one directive. The six-pack strengthened the fiscal and public debt components of the SGP, which had been adversely affected both by the German and French decisions in 2003 and by the explosion of countries falling under the Excessive Deficit Procedure after the onset of the global financial crisis. First, the six-pack defined a medium-term budget objective for each country, a more precise quantitative definition of a "significant deviation" from the medium-term budget objectives, and the parameters of the requisite adjustment path. In addition, the six-pack operationalized a more precise debt criterion and allowed the Excessive Deficit Procedure to be triggered on the basis of a debt ratio above 60 percent of GDP if the country was not on a path toward the treaty reference value at a satisfactory pace.[13]

From an institutional perspective, one of the more significant features of the six-pack was the continued move toward greater supranationality—permitted by greater precision in commitments—and qualified majority voting with respect to sanctions. When a country falling under the procedure fails to take steps to reduce fiscal imbalances, interest-bearing deposits of 0.2 percent of GDP are required, but these can turn into fines of up to 0.5 percent of GDP with continued noncompliance. The six-pack introduced reverse qualified majority voting for most sanctions, a procedure under which a proposal from the European Commission is considered adopted in the Council unless a qualified majority of member states votes against it. Reverse qualified majority voting thus increases the likelihood that sanctions will be voted.

Two pieces of legislation in the six-pack further strengthened surveillance through the creation of a Macroeconomic Imbalance Procedure (MIP) that goes beyond the Excessive Deficit Procedure and entails greater supranationality. The MIP rests on an Alert Mechanism Report prepared by the European Commission that identifies countries requiring further scrutiny. Although the European Commission exercises some discretion, the process relies on a set scoreboard of indictors that are used to generate recommendations to guide national policymaking during the course of the so-called European Semester, the annual policy coordination cycle. If imbalances are deemed excessive—on the grounds that they pose risks to the function of the economic and monetary union—the European Commission can invoke the corrective arm of the MIP, which is called the Excessive Imbalance Procedure. The member state concerned is then required to prepare a corrective action plan with a roadmap, deadlines for meeting objectives, and enhanced surveillance by the European Commission. Like the Excessive Deficit Procedure, the Excessive Imbalance Procedure is backed by escalating sanctions.

In parallel with these measures pertaining to the European Union as a whole, the European Commission advanced two additional regulations (the "two-pack") for the euro group.[14] These measures—ultimately finalized in March 2013—did not pose additional requirements on the members of the euro area; to the contrary, they introduced the concept of a structural budget position that provided greater leeway for automatic stabilizers to function. But at the same time, they institutionalized enhanced monitoring requirements that involved not only the European Commission and the European Council but new procedures at the national level as well. Under the two-pack,

---

13. To be precise, members would be required to reduce the debt ratio by 1/20 of the difference between the actual debt-to-GDP ratio and the 60 percent threshold. This rule pertains to a three-year-average and countries are given a three-year grace period after the correction of their current deficit below the 3 percent target before the 1/20 rule comes into effect.

14. "'Two-Pack' Completes Budgetary Surveillance Cycle for Euro Area and Further Improves Economic Governance," European Commission MEMO/13/196, March 12, 2013, http://europa.eu/rapid/press-release_MEMO-13-196_en.htm (accessed on July 1, 2013).

the nature of this monitoring depends on whether the country in question has an ongoing Excessive Deficit Procedure or Excessive Imbalance Procedure in place. If the euro area member state is not involved in either procedure, the additional requirement over the SGP is the submission of a draft fiscal budget to the European Commission for review. Euro area member states that do have an ongoing Excessive Deficit Procedure or Excessive Imbalance Procedure, or are under EFSF/ESM programs, are required under the two-pack to further increase the frequency of reporting to the European Commission in order to put further roadblocks—or at least warning signs—in the way of fiscal derogations. The European Commission does not exercise an actual veto over national fiscal policy; it is not clear how such a veto would even operate. But the procedure involves multiple layers of surveillance. The European Commission can issue warnings in advance of parliamentary consideration if the proposal is deemed to violate SGP (and later Fiscal Compact) commitments. The European Commission can then ask the member state to submit a revised budgetary plan. The surveillance and monitoring process also permits the European Commission to publish a comprehensive assessment of the budgetary outlook for the entire euro area, which is then subject to intergovernmental eurogroup scrutiny and peer review. The two-pack also reaches into national-level budgetary processes by requiring member states to base their draft budgets on independent macroeconomic forecasts and ensure independent bodies are in place to monitor compliance with national fiscal rules.

While the two-pack was being introduced, the European Union moved on a parallel track toward the negotiation of the wider Fiscal Compact that effectively incorporated the six-pack and two-pack innovations in a multilateral treaty. The agreement was signed on March 2, 2012, by all member states of the European Union except the Czech Republic and the United Kingdom. The linkage between the European Union's new lender-of-last-resort functions and the new fiscal arrangements was made quite explicit. The granting of new financial assistance under the ESM was made conditional on ratification of the Fiscal Compact and transposition of the balanced budget rule into national legislation "in due time."

The Fiscal Compact has an odd political structure. Although applicable only to members of the eurogroup—EU members not on the euro would be bound only after adopting it—the pact was initially intended to be a revision of existing EU treaties. But when Britain objected, the Fiscal Compact was negotiated and ratified outside of the EU legal structure altogether. Upon ratification, member states on the euro are not simply required to bring their fiscal policies in line with SGP norms; rather, they are required to have enacted national laws requiring budgets to be in balance or in surplus within one year after the Fiscal Compact enters into force. The treaty does incorporate the innovations of the six-pack by defining a cyclically adjusted balanced budget.[15]

---

15. The pact defines a balanced budget as a general budget deficit less than 3 percent of GDP and a structural deficit of less than 1 percent of GDP if the total public debt level is below 60 percent.

The treaty also institutionalizes the "debt brake" criteria of the SGP and six-pack, which define the rate at which debt-to-GDP levels above 60 percent of GDP should converge to the 60 percent target. These domestic injunctions are then enforced through a major innovation with respect to the European Court of Justice. Under the Fiscal Compact, any member state can bring enforcement proceedings against another member before the court if the required implementation law is not ratified, with fines up to 0.1 percent of GDP for those in continuing breach.

In sum, both the European Union as a whole and the euro area countries were forced to innovate lender-of-last-resort functions in the wake of the financial crisis. Creditor interests, and particularly those of Germany, exercised a strong influence over these negotiations. The facility was more modest than alternative proposals and at least on paper had a particularly strong supranational form. Abandoning the no-bailout rule came in exchange for conditionality enforced not only through the ESM but by the additional filter of the ECB and European Commission, with ultimate accountability back to the Ecofin Council. These innovations were explicitly linked to a supranational surveillance mechanism capable of independent budget recommendations and requirements with respect to national budgetary institutions and process, and backed up by ultimate recourse to the European Court of Justice. However, it is worth underlining two sources of skepticism about these new institutional arrangements. First, their credibility is untested, and given past history there is ample room to doubt that these commitments would necessarily withstand a future crisis (Frankel 2013). Second, as Joseph Gagnon and Marc Hinterschweiger document in chapter 3 in this volume, the ESM did not ultimately solve the many problems that were laid at its doorstep. In the end, ECB operations—the long-term refinancing operations and the "wall of money" in the so-called Outright Monetary Transactions program—played a central role in the overall EU policy mix.

Asia: Intergovernmentalism and Limits of the Chiang Mai Initiative

The standard interpretation of the Chiang Mai Initiative traces its origins to resentment over the region's reliance on the IMF during the Asian financial crisis of 1997–98 and to the heavy hand that the United States exercised in management of the crisis (see chapter 7 in this volume, Amyx 2008, Henning 2009, Grimes 2009, Sussangkarn 2010, Ciorciari 2011). The United States was able to effectively veto a regional alternative advanced by Japan for an Asian Monetary Fund, which would have offered an alternative to the IMF with a relaxed program design more attractive by borrowers. The so-called Manila Framework—hammered out at a meeting of the Asian Finance and Central Bank Deputies in November 1997 that included the United States—made very

---

For those outside the SGP debt targets, structural budget deficits have to fall below 0.5 percent of GDP.

cautious reference to a "cooperative financing arrangement" and surveillance mechanism for the region. But the core message of the Manila Framework was "the central role of the IMF in the international monetary system." Under this interpretation, the CMI marked an effort—albeit initially cautious—to revive the AMF idea for a regional financial mechanism independent from the IMF and its stigma (Ito 2012) and, more broadly, independent of the United States through its location in the emerging ASEAN+3 framework.

The reality is somewhat more complicated. Omitting the United States from the 10 countries that were initially included in the AMF proposal and suggesting that it would operate independently of the IMF generated predictable US opposition (Lipscy 2003). But the PRC's position with respect to the proposal was initially unclear and then publicly soured. Subsequent negotiations revealed other intra-Asian as well as trans-Pacific disagreements on institutional design. The CMI only adopted a common governance structure—so-called Multilateralization (CMIM)—more than a decade after the crisis and following prolonged negotiations between Japan and the PRC. Moreover, the overall institutional setting in which the CMI and CMIM evolved—the ASEAN +3 institutions—potentially favored borrowers and was constrained by ASEAN norms that favored consensus, relatively weak and imprecise formal commitments, and a corresponding absence of delegation to ASEAN-wide institutions (Haggard 2013).

In such a setting, there were clear political as well as administrative limits on ex ante surveillance. It was therefore not surprising that the creditors maintained a high degree of discretion and opted for weighted voting and supermajority provisions in extending credit, even if these rules were a very marked departure from the ASEAN way. Nor is it surprising that the CMI continues to rely on the IMF to provide monitoring functions, even if this link makes it less likely that potential borrowers would draw on the CMI in any other than highly exigent circumstances.

The Chiang Mai Initiative I

For the purposes here, the most significant feature of the original CMI—signed in May 2000—is that it was not really a multilateral agreement in the traditional sense of the term at all. Rather, it was a network of bilateral agreements that were not even extended to all of the organization's purported members. The agreement lacked any supranational structure whatsoever, relying both on creditor discretion and complementary actions on the part of the IMF.

The original CMI had two components, setting aside the related but legally distinct expansion of short-term local-currency swap facilities among the Plus Three countries. The first was an expansion of the extremely modest ASEAN Swap Arrangement (ASA) initiated in 1977.[16] For ASEAN members

---

16. With the CMI, the ASA was expanded from $200 million to $1 billion. Given the modesty of the lines of credit, conditionality was not deemed a problem. Members were able to draw up to

in crisis, however, financing of any significance would only come from the bilateral swap arrangements with the Plus Three. Creditors exercised discretion over these arrangements in two critical ways. First, the arrangements were not fully multilateral. At the onset of the negotiations over multilateralization in 2005, only 16 bilateral swap arrangements (out of 30 of potential significance[17]) had been concluded between the Plus Three and the ASEAN-10, with none extended to the weaker and more vulnerable members: Myanmar, Lao People's Democratic Republic, Cambodia, and Viet Nam. Second, extension of credit under the agreement was not automatic but at the discretion of the creditor and the creditor alone.

Even with these limitations on the risk that creditors would be called on to assume, a debate ensued about conditionality. The Plus Three countries were in the uncomfortable position of either having to turn down funding for a regional partner or assume risks in the absence of a regional institution that could provide monitoring functions (Grimes 2011). The concessions made to potential borrowers were initially cosmetic. Only 10 percent of the bilateral swap arrangements could be disbursed in the absence of an IMF program; this was raised to 20 percent in 2005, when total swap lines were also doubled. But as initially conceived, the CMI would clearly not substitute for IMF resources and oversight, as the AMF had pretensions to do.

The Chiang Mai Initiative II: Multilateralization and Surveillance

Although the collective decision to multilateralize the CMIM was taken in 2005, agreement on the institution was not reached until 2009. The problems in reaching agreement centered in the first instance on leadership of the institution, which was manifest in debates about contributions (Rathus 2009). The ultimate compromise allowed Japan to claim that it was the largest single contributor by allocating the country 32 percent of the CMIM ($38.4 billion of the $120 billion pool), while giving the PRC the exact same share, but divided between the PRC and Hong Kong, China ($34.2 billion and $4.2 billion, respectively). Current swap lines now stand at $240 billion. While only 1.5 percent of CMI GDP, these lines are equal to 11.4 percent of ASEAN GDP.

A closer look at the governance of the CMI suggests a much more modest organization than these numbers might suggest. Three institutional features of the CMIM are noteworthy: the overarching governance structure, continued reliance on the IMF, and the modesty of independent surveillance mechanisms. As with the IMF and the European mechanisms, voting rights were allocated on the basis of contributions and thus implied weighted voting. The ASEAN economies collectively contributed 20 percent of the total funds, while

---

twice their contribution to the ASA for six months—with a further six-month rollover—without conditions.

17. Although in principle there are 78 possible bilateral swap pairs, those among the Southeast Asian countries are not relevant.

the Plus Three economies contributed the remaining 80 percent (split between Japan, 32 percent; the PRC, 32 percent; and the Republic of Korea, 16 percent). Consensus was required for major changes in the rules, but lending decisions were to be made on the basis of a two-thirds supermajority. Given the allocation of votes, none of the creditors had an individual veto over lending. But lending decisions required the support of two of the three major creditors—Japan, the PRC, and the Republic of Korea—assuming that at least some of the ASEAN countries would favor the extension of credit in a crisis.

In a major departure from the bilateral swaps, however, all countries were covered and the capacity to draw was weighted in favor of the most vulnerable. Borrowing was available according to a "purchasing multiple" of underlying contributions, ranging from 0.5 for Japan and the PRC to 2.5 for the ASEAN-5 economies and 5.0 for Brunei Darussalam, Cambodia, Lao PDR, Myanmar, and Viet Nam. As Reza Siregar and Akkharaphol Chabchitrchaidol (2013) point out, these multiples make the non-IMF-linked portion of available funding larger than that available through the IMF's Rapid Financing Instrument, which sought to move toward greater flexibility in the provision of support. The second feature of institutional design, however, was the continued reliance on the IMF. The delinked portion of the quota was raised from 20 to 30 percent in 2012 with a promise to consider raising this further to 40 percent. But the IMF remained an anchoring element of the agreement for any major intervention.

The third component of institutional design has centered on the development of an independent regional surveillance capacity, and has been an issue of lively debate since the launching of the CMI (see chapter 7 in this volume, Institute for International Monetary Affairs 2005, Kawai and Houser 2007, Truman 2011, Siregar and Chabchitrchaidol 2013). The Asian arrangements are much less supranational in design than European institutions and the reasons are fundamentally political. In Europe, the creation of new lender-of-last-resort and surveillance functions took root in a community of democracies that had already committed to monetary union; institutions were pushed along by a coalition of conservative governments strongly committed to tighter surveillance. In the ASEAN+3, by contrast, the membership is politically heterogeneous and even prone to rivalries. The largest economy in the region—the PRC—is an authoritarian regime unlikely to welcome outside surveillance of any significant sort, and certainly none that would tie its hands. To date it has had natural allies on this issue among a majority of the ASEAN countries.

At the very outset of the CMI process in 2001, Japan floated a proposal for a surveillance facility at the CMI that was flatly rejected by the PRC, leading to the creation of the Economic Review and Policy Dialogue (ERPD) in April 2002. The ERPD built on the so-called finance ministers' process that began in the wake of economic crisis in 1999: an annual meeting of the 13 finance ministers supplemented by a semiannual meeting of the ASEAN+3 finance and central bank deputies. At the ERPD sessions of the deputies' meetings, ADB, IMF, and invited outside experts stimulate dialogue and individual country representatives provide overviews of current policy. But the ERPD process was not initially designed as a peer review in which policies would be critically assessed or subject to recommendation. Thus, even though participation in the ERPD process became a condition for borrowing under the CMI, this was pro forma as all countries willingly participated in any case, the ERPD had no formal monitoring role, and the process did not entail any binding commitments.

When the ASEAN+3 launched its Macroeconomic Research Office (AMRO) in 2011, its institutional structure confirmed the relatively tight leash on which any surveillance process would be held. In the absence of an ASEAN+3 secretariat under which the body could be housed, AMRO had its own dedicated institutional arrangements, at the top of which sat an intergovernmental executive committee of deputy finance ministers and central bank governors and an independent advisory panel. AMRO was given three broad responsibilities: to prepare quarterly reports on the macroeconomic situation in ASEAN+3 countries, which have now been through several rounds; to assess macroeconomic and financial vulnerabilities and provide assistance in mitigating risks; and to ensure compliance of CMIM borrowers with lending covenants, presumably under the delinked tranches and in addition to the IMF for borrowing. Given the small staff size, the question remains of how to exploit the advantages of proximity to key policymakers while not duplicating what is already done elsewhere in both the public and private sectors.

The constraints on the AMRO are deeper and go far beyond the lack of administrative capacity. Will a heterogeneous group of this sort support more sustained—and potentially critical—bilateral surveillance or steps toward multilateral policy commitments? Will it even be able to access credible data on issues that remain sensitive, such as with respect to the financial sector? Will AMRO even be able to take on the sensitive task of monitoring program compliance with CMIM drawings, when and if they are ever made? Given the composition of the ASEAN+3 and its institutional structure, there are strong reasons for skepticism and some have even questioned whether the CMIM will ever be used (Hill and Menon 2012).

The Western Hemisphere: American Leadership, Weak Institutions

As in Asia a decade later, when the debt crisis of the 1980s struck in Latin America there were no regionwide institutions in the Americas that had either the mandate or the capacity to address the crisis. The institutional framework consisted of a largely political institution (the Organization of American States), a regional development bank (the Inter-American Development Bank, IDB), and regional integration schemes of limited success among the debtors themselves. Because of the exposure of US banks to the region, the United States had strong incentives to exercise leadership with respect to the initial phase of concerted lending as well as the subsequent program of market-oriented debt forgiveness and reduction (the Volcker, Baker, and Brady Plans).

Conditionality was orchestrated through the international financial institutions, with the IDB playing at best a complementary role in concerted lending efforts (Cline 1995, 203–75). A broadly similar pattern of unilateral US leadership was evident in the second wave of financial crises that hit the region, beginning with Mexico in 1994–95 and spreading as a result of contagion from Asia and the Russian Federation and the onset of the so-called sudden stop in external lending.

The important point is that the United States has shown no interest in formally committing to participation in lender-of-last-resort institutions for the region. The US Exchange Stabilization Fund (ESF) maintained a large number of swap lines with Latin American countries after World War II. But these were gradually eliminated and by 1970 only a swap line with Mexico remained. In 1994, this line of credit was brought under a modest North American Framework Agreement that currently allows for cumulative drawings of up to $2 billion by Canada and $3 billion for Mexico. But this arrangement is clearly the exception that proves the more general rule; although the Framework Agreement was technically triggered, ESF support of the Mexican program of 1995 was unilateral (Henning 1999).

The lack of interest on the part of the United States in such arrangements has critical implications for the design and even viability of lender-of-last-resort institutions for Latin America. In Europe and Asia, institutional arrangements include issuers of currencies that could be of use during crises: the euro, yen, and increasingly the renminbi. In Latin America, by contrast, any reserve fund would have to hold dollars, thus only marginally improving on the self-insurance strategies of reserve accumulation that middle-income countries in the region pursued during the 2003–07 boom.

But the problems of heterogeneous interests are not limited to the differences between the United States and potential borrowers; they are replicated within the existing regional integration schemes and between and among the two competing "new generation" integration efforts: the Union of South American Nations, and the Venezuelan-led Bolivarian Alliance for the Peoples of Our America–People's Trade Agreement. All of the major regional integration agreements—including Mercosur, Central American Common Market, and Andean Community—contained aspirations to macroeconomic policy coordination and even monetary integration. The Central American Common Market even had a stabilization fund that was ultimately shut down. During the turbulence of the late 1990s, both Mercosur and the Andean Community faced serious stresses as a result of divergent macroeconomic policies and shocks and real exchange rate volatility. Both institutions launched high-level efforts to increase macroeconomic policy coordination and both developed modest administrative capacity to monitor developments.[18] But these

---

18. In 2000, the Mercosur presidents issued a joint statement—the Presidential Declaration of Mercosur on Macroeconomic Convergence (Florianopolis, December 15)—that contained precise targets for public debt, fiscal deficits, and inflation with convergence targets. A Macroeconomic Monitoring Group was also established, but these efforts were undone by the Argentine crisis. In

efforts came to naught, in part because the boom rendered them less pressing, and in part because of increasing political and policy divergence within the region. The political turn to the left in a number of countries gave rise to visions of an alternative financial architecture that would decouple the region from the United States and the dollar: the Bank of the South, an alternative payments and currency arrangement called the SUCRE (Sistema Unitario de Compensación Regional), and a regionwide reserve fund, with the FLAR as its possible foundation.

Of these organizations, however, only the FLAR has any track record to consider. Established as an independent legal entity with its own capital in 1991, it grew out of the Andean Reserve Fund, which in turn had been established in 1976 by the central banks of Bolivia, Colombia, Ecuador, Peru, and Venezuela (at that time the remaining members of the Andean Community following Chile's withdrawal in 1973 after Augusto Pinochet came to power). The FLAR's political structure includes an assembly composed of ministers of finance, a board of directors composed of central bank governors, and an executive president overseeing operations. One of its distinctive features compared with the other regional institutions examined here is in voting arrangements. The organization operates on a foundation of paid-in rather than callable capital, with contributions reflecting differences in country size. Colombia, Peru, and Venezuela contribute twice as much as Bolivia, Ecuador, and the two newer entrants, Costa Rica (1999) and Uruguay (2008). Total lines of credit are equal to about 1 percent of regional GDP. Voting at both the assembly and board levels is based on a one-country, one-vote model, although with supermajority provisions. The assembly has ultimate responsibility for capital increases, credit limits, and terms; the board can recommend on these issues and takes decisions on loans.[19] The executive president analyzes the requests for balance of payments lending, which must include a declaration of insufficient reserves, a plan to correct external imbalances, and a commitment not to affect trade with the partners. But in contrast to arrangements in both other regions, there is neither a link to the IMF nor any ideological commitment to

---

1997, the Andean Group set up an Advisory Council of finance ministers, central bank presidents, and economic planning officers, which in 1999 and again in 2001 defined similar convergence criteria. In 2001, a permanent technical monitoring group was created and countries were required to submit convergence reports as of 2003.

19. The FLAR extends five types of loans: balance of payments support, liquidity, contingency lending, lending in support of debt restructuring, and treasury lines of credit. However, the overwhelming number of its operations are balance of payments and liquidity support. The difference between the two is in maturities, terms, and decision making. Balance of payments lending is for up to three years, with an additional grace year for capital contributions. The lending multiple is 2.5 times paid-in capital, but rates are at 400 basis points over three-month Libor. Liquidity support is up to paid-in capital for one year at 150 basis points over Libor; liquidity operations are also at the discretion of the executive. See the FLAR website at www.flar.net/ingles/contenido/default.aspx (accessed on July 1, 2013).

provide an alternative to it, and there is an apparently permissive approach to conditionality.

The FLAR has never denied a loan request but nonetheless has a zero-default history and maintains a credit rating that is superior to that of its members. Given the lack of an IMF link and the erratic debt-servicing history of a number of its members, there has been substantial discussion in the small literature on the FLAR on the conditions that permit it to avoid opportunism (Eichengreen 2006, Agosin and Heresi 2010, Rosero 2011, Levy-Yeyati 2012, Ocampo and Titelman 2012). Some explanations can easily be dismissed. The FLAR's success rests neither on a strong ex ante convergence mechanism nor even on informal policy convergence. Throughout its political history, the political divergence within the organization has been as wide as within Latin America as a whole, and recently the organization has included left-populist governments in Venezuela, Bolivia, and Ecuador and more moderate and even conservative ones in Uruguay, Costa Rica, and Colombia.

As the FLAR's covenants are apparently not readily available to the public (Rosero 2011), it is difficult to judge whether the organization effectively mirrors the IMF in its lending terms. However, several recent loans to Ecuador suggest how conditionality and ex post surveillance operate (Moody's Global Sovereign 2009). Ecuador sought balance of payments support in the midst of substantial political upheaval in 2006, but although the loan was quickly approved it was not disbursed until the new government of President Alfredo Palacio assured the FLAR that a new Central Bank Board was in place (Rosero 2011). In April 2009, FLAR's Board of Directors approved a three-year $480 million balance of payments credit to the Central Bank of Ecuador. Before the credit was approved, the FLAR conducted special consultations to assure the assembly and board that the loan would not subsequently be deemed illegitimate or run afoul of the new constitution. When the Ecuadoran government rejected conditions the FLAR typically attached to the loan, credit was extended only on the requirement that the Central Bank of Ecuador deposit $250 million of reserves with FLAR. Although not a formal guarantee, the funds could only be withdrawn in line with amortizations (Moody's Global Sovereign 2009).

There are two other possibilities as to how the FLAR operates, not altogether mutually exclusive. The first is that joint management of the institution and paid-in capital commitments permit peer pressure to operate in ways that are similar to collective lending in microfinance projects. A second possibility is that the political diversity of the organization may work to its advantage while actually supporting opportunism elsewhere. For leftist governments, the FLAR may be a "lender of very last resort." Borrowers may accord it a kind of senior creditor status even as they are in default on commercial or other multilateral commitments. There is some evidence that this has occurred—as the Ecuador cases suggest—although it hardly augurs well for an expansion of such facilities. There is substantial discussion about using the FLAR as the nucleus of a wider Latin American Monetary Fund, including from the Bolivarian Alliance for the Peoples of Our America, which seeks a sharply defined alternative to the IMF and United States (for example, the Ecuadoran proposal described in Perez 2009–10). To date, however, the substantial difficulties that have been faced in making the Banco del Sur operational suggest that difficult negotiations will be required to move forward. Larger countries such as Brazil are likely to raise questions about both the institutional design and operations of such a fund given their likely creditor status.

Conclusion

Regional arrangements, no less than the IMF, must grapple with the tradeoffs between the timely provision of liquidity and the risks of opportunism and moral hazard. This chapter has considered these issues through the lens of institutional design and governance: how regional arrangements resolve coordination and principal-agent problems.

First, there is ample evidence of the difficulty of managing these tradeoffs through strong ex ante surveillance, even where member countries of the regional arrangement are relatively homogenous in their political form and policy preferences. The European case has seen repeated efforts to tighten ex ante surveillance, including the most recent effort to write a comprehensive fiscal pact. Crises have tended to overwhelm these efforts, however, and not simply for economic reasons. Even in Europe, elaborate supranational mechanisms are ultimately nested in intergovernmental structures that larger powers as well as smaller ones have been able to finesse; not all opportunism is on the side of potential borrowers. In the developing-country groupings of Asia and Latin America, political and policy heterogeneity is even greater and there is less willingness to create strong ex ante surveillance mechanisms. This heterogeneity is not limited to differences in policy preferences narrowly conceived but encompasses geostrategic rivalries (the PRC and Japan), ideological differences (Colombia and Peru versus Ecuador, Venezuela, and Bolivia), and differences in fundamental regime type (within Asia in particular). Such heterogeneity does not rule out gains from weaker agreements that involve information sharing, greater input from outsiders, and peer pressure. But the political limits of ex ante mechanisms should be recognized. Europe is the exception, not the likely model.

In turning to the design of ex post, lender-of-last-resort functions, there is a very limited track record to work with—the debate about regional financing arrangements appears to be running far ahead of the actual experience. The reason is that creditors have exercised strong influence on these arrangements and have tended to limit their ambition. Even in Europe, where there is a commitment to a common political project, creditors (most notably Germany) have shown extreme reluctance to commit to robust regional mechanisms and did so only under duress. When they did, arrangements were more modest and the conditions more stringent than needed, as evidenced by the continual revision of programs. In Asia, the creditor countries managed to devise institutional arrangements that marked a substantial departure over regional norms, including the first weighted voting scheme in the history of the ASEAN institutions. But the facilities have never been used, and given the region's penchant for surpluses it is not clear that they are likely to be used any time soon. In the Western Hemisphere, the FLAR represents the exception that proves the rule. A residual arrangement from a long-standing subregional integration scheme, the FLAR has not expanded to include any of the three major Latin American economies (Argentina, Brazil, and Mexico). Needless to say, the United States has shown little interest in arrangements that would give it an institutionalized lender-of-last-resort function in the Western Hemisphere. Even with its two closest North American trading partners, arrangements are modest and characterized by a high level of discretion.

With respect to institutional design, governance arrangements in all three regions have maintained strongly intergovernmental forms in which creditors have exercised influence through some combination of weighted voting and supermajority provisions; ASEAN is again of interest in this regard given its history of consensus decision making. All three regions also provide evidence of the difficulties of delegating authority to independent bodies to monitor the lending process and oversee conditionality. These problems were not just administrative—the European Commission is one of the largest and most developed international bureaucracies in the world. Rather, delegation to the IMF helped perform functions that the Europeans could not easily undertake themselves. The CMI maintained a link to the IMF. The FLAR is again the exception, but the conclusions that can be drawn from its experience are neither obvious nor heartening, as it appears to have largely financed regional partners with limited access to either international financial markets or international financial institutions. Such lending may be desirable from the perspective of political solidarity, but its economic merits appear mixed at best.

Linking global and regional financial arrangements has a number of theoretical advantages, including the complementarity of both financial resources and information. Yet the interests of global and regional organizations will never perfectly converge, as several of the European programs, including Greece, showed quite clearly. Henning (2011) has offered a useful typology of why coordination is therefore needed between global and regional arrangements, including the needs to limit risks of arbitrage between arrangements, avoid redundancy, ensure that resources are additive, and assure a division of labor in surveillance and monitoring and financing. Yet even these reasons for coordination reflect differences in underlying political purposes between organizations that rest on different constituent bases.

The limited experience we have suggests that an alternative to coordination might be a sharper delineation of spheres of competence, in which regional arrangements handle shocks of regional significance and global institutions take the lead whenever crises have international implications. As the European crisis has shown, even defining those differences is deeply political.

References

Agosin, Manuel R., and Rodrigo Heresi. 2010. *Hacia un Fondo Monetario Latinoamericano*. Economics and Business School, Department of Economics. Santiago: University of Chile.

Amyx, Jennifer. 2008. Regional Financial Cooperation in East Asia since the Asian Financial Crisis. In *Crisis as Catalyst: Asia's Dynamic Political Economy*, ed. Andrew MacIntyre, T. J. Pempel, and John Ravenhill. Ithaca, NY: Cornell University Press.

Ciorciari, John D. 2011. Chiang Mai Initiative Multilateralization. *Asian Survey* 51, no. 5 (September/October): 926–52.

Cline, William. 1995. *International Debt Reexamined*. Washington, DC: Institute for International Economics.

Eichengreen, Barry. 2006. *Insurance Underwriter or Financial Development Fund: What Role for Reserve Pooling in Latin America?* NBER Working Paper 12451. Cambridge, MA: National Bureau of Economic Research.

Eichengreen, Barry. 2008. *Globalizing Capital: A History of the International Monetary System*. Princeton, NJ: Princeton University Press.

Eichengreen, Barry. 2012. *Regional Monetary Arrangements and the International Monetary Fund*. ADBI Working Paper 394 (November). Tokyo: Asian Development Bank Institute.

Eichengreen, Barry, and Charles Wyplosz. 1998. The Stability Pact: More Than a Minor Nuisance? *Economic Policy* 13, no. 26 (April): 65–113.

Frankel, Jeffrey. 2013. Will Europe's Fiscal Compact Work? Project Syndicate (January 18). Available at www.project-syndicate.org/commentary/will-europe-s-fiscal-compact-work-by-jeffrey-frankel (accessed on July 1, 2013).

Grimes, William W. 2009. *Currency and Contest in East Asia: The Great Power Politics of Financial Regionalism*. Cornell Studies in Money. Ithaca, NY: Cornell University Press.

Grimes, William W. 2011. The Asian Monetary Fund Reborn? Implications of Chiang Mai Initiative Multilateralization. *Asia Policy* 9 (January).

Haggard, Stephan. 2013. The Organizational Architecture of the Asia-Pacific: Insights from the New Institutionalism. In *Integrating Regions: Asia in Comparative Context*, ed. Miles Kahler and Andrew MacIntyre. Stanford, CA: Stanford University Press.

Henning, C. Randall. 1999. *The Exchange Stabilization Fund: Slush Money or War Chest?* Washington, DC: Institute for International Economics.

Henning, C. Randall. 2009. *The Future of the Chiang Mai Initiative: An Asian Monetary Fund?* Policy Brief 09-5. Washington, DC: Peterson Institute for International Economics.

Henning, C. Randall. 2011. *Coordinating Regional and Multilateral Financial Institutions*. Working Paper 11-9. Washington, DC: Peterson Institute for International Economics.

Hill, Hal, and Jayant Menon. 2012. Asia's New Financial Safety Net: Is the Chiang Mai Initiative Designed Not to Be Used? Voxeu.org, July 25. Available at www.voxeu.org/article/chiang-mai-initiative-designed-not-be-used (accessed on July 1, 2013).

Institute for International Monetary Affairs. 2005. *Economic Surveillance and Policy Dialogue in East Asia*. ASEAN+3 Research Group Studies, 2004–2005. Tokyo: ASEAN.

Ito, Takatoshi. 2012. Can Asia Overcome the IMF Stigma? *American Economic Review: Papers & Proceedings* 102, no. 3: 198–202.

Kawai, Masahiro, and Cindy Houser. 2007. *Evolving ASEAN+3 ERPD: Towards Peer Reviews or Due Diligence?* ADBI Discussion Paper 79 (September). Tokyo: Asian Development Bank Institute.

Levy-Yeyati, Eduardo. 2012. *Latin American Economic Perspectives: All Together Now*. Washington, DC: Brookings Institution.

Lipscy, Philip. 2003. Japan's Asian Monetary Fund Proposal. *Stanford Journal of East Asian Affairs* 3, no. 1: 93–104.

Lombardi, Domenico. 2013. The Relationship between Global and Regional Safety Nets. Paper presented at FLAR International Conference on Economic Studies. Available at www.flar.net/documentos/5419_Papers_&_Proceedings_2013-V1.0_.pdf (accessed on July 1, 2013).

Lütz, Susanne, and Matthias Kranke. 2013. The European Rescue of the Washington, DC Consensus? EU and IMF Lending to Central and Eastern European Countries. *Review of International Political Economy*. Available at http://dx.doi.org/10.1080/09692290.2012.747104 (accessed on July 1, 2013).

Mastropasqua, Cristina, Stefano Micossi, and Roberto Rinaldi. 1988. Interventions, Sterilisation and Monetary Policy in European Monetary System Countries, 1979-87. In *The European Monetary System*, ed. Francesco Giavazzi, Stefano Micossi, and Marcus Miller. Cambridge: Cambridge University Press.

McKay, Julie, Ulrich Volz, and Regina Wölfinger. 2010. *Regional Financing Arrangements and the Stability of the International Monetary System*. Discussion Paper 13/2010. Bonn: German Development Institute.

Moody's Global Sovereign. 2009. *Credit Analysis: Fondo Latinoamericano de Reservas (FLAR), Rating Rationale and Outlook*. New York and London.

Ocampo, Jose Antonio, and Daniel Titelman. 2012. *Regional Monetary Cooperation in Latin America*. ADBI Working Paper 373 (August). Tokyo: Asian Development Bank Institute.

Perez, Pedro Paez. 2009-10. The Ecuadorian Proposal for a New Regional Financial Architecture. *Journal of Post Keynesian Economics* 32, no. 2 (Winter): 163-72.

Pisani-Ferry, Jean, André Sapir, and Guntram Wolff. 2013. Financial Assistance in the Euro Area: An Early Evaluation. Presentation at the Peterson Institute for International Economics, Washington, DC (April 19). Available at www.piie.com/publications/papers/pisani-ferry20130419ppt.pdf (accessed on July 1, 2013).

Rathus, Joel. 2009. The Chiang Mai Initiative: [The People's Republic of] China, Japan and Financial Regionalism. *East Asia Forum* (May 11). Available at www.eastasiaforum.org (accessed on July 1, 2013).

Rathus, Joel. 2012. ASEAN's Macroeconomic Research Office: Open for Business. *East Asia Forum* (May 23). Available at www.eastasiaforum.org/2012/05/23/aseans-macroeconomic-research-office-open-for-business (accessed on July 1, 2013).

Rosero, Luis Daniel. 2011. Essays on International Reserve Accumulation and Cooperation in Latin America. PhD dissertation, University of Massachusetts, Amherst. Available at http://scholarworks.umass.edu/cgi/viewcontent.cgi?article=1482&context=open_access_dissertations (accessed on July 1, 2013).

Ryvkin, Boris. 2012. Saving the Euro: Tensions with European Treaty Law in the European Union's Efforts to Protect the Common Currency. *Cornell International Law Journal* 45, no. 227: 228-55.

Salines, M., G. Glockler, and Z. Truchlewski. 2012. Existential Crisis, Incremental Response: The Eurozone's Dual Institutional Evolution 2007-2011. *Journal of European Public Policy* 19, no. 5: 665-81.

Siregar, Reza, and Akkharaphol Chabchitrchaidol. 2013. *Enhancing the Effectiveness of CMIM and AMRO: Selected Immediate Challenges and Tasks*. ADBI Working Paper 403. Tokyo: Asian Development Bank Institute.

Stone, Randall. 2011. *Controlling Institutions: International Organizations and the Global Economy*. Cambridge: Cambridge University Press.

Sussangkarn, Chalongphob. 2010. *The Chiang Mai Initiative Multilateralization: Origin, Development, and Outlook*. ADBI Working Paper 230. Tokyo: Asian Development Bank Institute.

Szasz, Andre. 1999. *The Road to European Monetary Union*. London: Macmillan Press.

Truman, Edwin M. 2011. *Asian Regional Policy Coordination*. Working Paper 11-21. Washington, DC: Peterson Institute for International Economics.

9

Sovereign Debt and Asia:
International Lessons and Emerging Issues

WILLIAM R. CLINE

In the past three decades there have been three international debt crises. The first was the Latin American debt crisis of the 1980s. The second was the East Asian crisis in the late 1990s, with its spillover to Argentina, Brazil, and the Russian Federation. The third is the recent and ongoing European debt crisis. There are important similarities but important differences among these three. This chapter seeks to distill the relevant lessons from these international experiences for Asia going forward and examine prospects for sovereign creditworthiness in the region.

The Latin American Crisis in the 1980s

The most severe and protracted sovereign debt crisis of the past three decades is still that of Latin America in the 1980s.[1] This crisis largely reflected the recycling of oil surpluses in the 1970s, as international banks developed syndicated loans at floating interest rates. Large capital inflows fueled large external deficits and budget deficits in Latin America. Three external shocks—the Volcker interest rate surge to halt high inflation at the end of the 1970s, the second surge in oil prices in 1980, and the (until then) deepest global recession in the postwar period in 1982—combined to force first Mexico and later almost the entire region into temporary suspensions of payments on government debt owed mainly to foreign banks. The most acute problem was an external transfer

William R. Cline has been a senior fellow at the Peterson Institute for International Economics since 1981. He thanks Jared Nolan for research assistance. For comments on an earlier draft, he thanks, without implicating, Joseph Gagnon, Marcus Noland, Edwin M. Truman, and two anonymous reviewers.

1. For a contemporary diagnosis of the crisis, see Cline (1984). A retrospective analysis is given in Cline (1995).

problem as export earnings were insufficient to service external debt. But there was also an internal transfer problem, as large fiscal deficits that previously had been financed from abroad now needed to be closed or financed domestically. The problem lent itself to an analogy to the principle of the lender of last resort when a bank is solvent but faces a run and a liquidity problem. Hence, for the first few years the problem was managed through emergency lending, including concerted lending by banks and official support from the International Monetary Fund (IMF) and others.

The large US, European, and Japanese banks accounted for the bulk of the lending and were few enough in number that they could coordinate in lending packages. This approach was incorporated in the Baker Plan of the mid-1980s, which included commitments by Latin American economies to carry out structural reforms and fiscal adjustment. This process proved sufficient for just two countries, however: Colombia, which never resorted even to debt rescheduling (though it did go through three rounds of concerted refinancing); and Chile, which did reschedule but never requested a haircut (a writedown of principal or stretchout at interest rates well below original terms). Concerted lending proved insufficient for the other major debtors, however, including Mexico and Brazil, in part because political leaders perceived the need to demonstrate that the creditors were bearing their share of the responsibility for the economic distress.

The earthquake in Mexico City in 1985 and Mexico's prospectively lower oil revenue as oil prices fell in 1986 marked the turning point at which management of the problem moved toward debt reduction. By then there were significant gaps between the secondary market price and face value that provided a possible mutual gain from reducing principal in exchange for increasing security (as the Brady Plan did by offering US zero-coupon bonds as collateral for exchanged debt). There were also economic theories that sought to demonstrate the need for debt reduction—particularly the "debt overhang" concept postulating that private investment for growth would not occur so long as excessive public debt meant that future private investment returns would be vulnerable to cooptation by the state to pay off debt if there was insufficient forgiveness. As it turned out, however, the amount of the haircut in the Brady Plan, circa 1989–92, that resolved the Latin American crisis was moderate. The benchmark was a 30 to 35 percent reduction in debt for Brazil, Argentina, Mexico, and even Venezuela, which needed it less on economic grounds but sought relief on political grounds.

Lessons from the Latin American debt crisis included, first of all, pursuing fiscal sustainability, including by avoiding losses in state enterprises through privatization. A broader lesson was that domestic fiscal and financial conditions need to be strong enough to withstand external shocks. Another important message was the key role of a cooperative approach between debtors and creditors—ultimately, cooperation on the Brady Plan provided the foundation for a new period of a return to international capital markets and much more normal economic conditions by the early 1990s. Yet another lesson was that realistic exchange rates and interest rates, as well as political stability, are important for avoiding capital flight that aggravates the external debt problem. An additional lesson, which is much more feasible to apply now than then, was that governments should develop domestic debt markets so they are not as vulnerable to valuation shocks when exchange rate depreciation becomes necessary. Similarly, regulators should curb currency mismatches of banks, again to limit balance sheet vulnerability.

The East Asian Crisis of the Late 1990s

The next major round of international debt crises began in Thailand in 1997 and spread to the rest of East Asia as well as the Russian Federation, Brazil, and Argentina. Before that, however, there was a transitory debt problem in Mexico in 1995. Mexico had had huge inflows of capital with the anticipation of the North American Free Trade Agreement. Mexico had a quasi-fixed exchange rate. At the time there was a popular argument—the Lawson doctrine named for UK Chancellor of the Exchequer Nigel Lawson—that if a country did not have a fiscal deficit, the size of its current account deficit did not matter because there could not be an external debt problem without a fiscal problem. That thesis was tested and found wanting. There had to be a major devaluation of the peso, and once again it was necessary to activate the lender-of-last-resort principle. The United States and the IMF made large emergency loans to Mexico, and this time it was possible to resolve the problem without any haircut.

The Mexican episode was thus a precursor for the late 1990s debt problem in East Asia, which also turned out to be a liquidity problem rather than a solvency problem. The East Asian problem once again was related to inadequate adjustment of the exchange rate, and excessive external deficits associated with capital inflows in the form of "hot money" (loans instead of direct investment). The initial epicenter of the crisis was Thailand, which was forced to devalue in July 1997. The crisis then spread to Indonesia, the Republic of Korea, Malaysia (which eventually imposed capital controls in September 1998), and to a lesser extent the Philippines. One of the very clear signals of problems in the area was the high exposure to short-term external debt, measured by the very high ratio of short-term external debt to reserves. Perhaps the single largest lesson that came out of the crisis—and one that even today continues to some extent to distort the international economy—was that countries should accumulate large external reserves to be ready to confront a "sudden stop" crisis. Pursuing this lesson too far, however, tends to lead to excessive trade imbalances and to capital flows from poor countries to rich countries instead of vice versa.

The East Asian crisis did turn out to be one of liquidity. There were no massive haircuts. Where there were bankruptcies, as in Indonesia, they were bankruptcies of private firms rather than of the sovereign. In the Republic of Korea, there was a three-year debt rollover arrangement with the foreign banks, in what was called at the time the last 20th century debt crisis in the sense that it involved large foreign bank creditors rather than dispersed bondholders. The stretchout did not involve a haircut, as the interest rates were set slightly above the original terms in what was a market-friendly arrangement. In retrospect, the Korean crisis of 1998 resembles that of Ireland in 2010 in that the locus of the problem came from domestic banks rather than the sovereign.

Unfortunately, a prominent lesson that emerged from the East Asian crisis in terms of public perceptions in the region was the view that the IMF was overly intrusive and caused much damage. Indeed, in the Republic of Korea the 1999 downturn is still called "the IMF recession."[2] The poster child for the critique of excessive IMF intervention was its inclusion of closing a clove factory in Indonesia as one required measure on a remarkably long list of "performance requirements." The basis for the closure was addressing corrupt practices, but even so the IMF seems to have become considerably more careful to avoid the appearance of overreaching on internal matters. The damage was done, and Asian economic authorities seem to have retained an extreme reluctance to rely on the IMF. This antipathy has no doubt contributed to the drive to build up war chests of reserves. It has also figured in various talks about creating a regional monetary fund, and keen interest in the region in securing swap arrangements such as those of the Republic of Korea and Singapore with the US Federal Reserve during the 2008 global financial crisis. Regional emergency mechanisms do not seem to have gone very far, however, basically because the regional partners are not prepared to issue a blank check for lending to their neighbors without conditions, and in the end would wind up needing the IMF to determine such conditions if such lending were to take place.

The East Asian crisis repeated the experience of the Latin American crisis with respect to the dangers of currency mismatch combined with a sudden stop. The borrowing was in international currency rather than home currency, so banks and firms were subject to huge balance sheet losses if there were a large depreciation of the currency. This came to be called the "original sin" problem. The notion was that somehow emerging-market economies were subject to original sin because they could not borrow in their own currency, only in foreign currency. As discussed below, that has changed very substantially, and one needs to think about the benefits and possible costs of that change. At the time, however, the currency mismatch meant that a fine line had to be walked between pursuing tight monetary policy with high interest rates to keep the currency from falling too far, on the one hand, and suffering needless recession as a consequence of overly tight money, on the other. That debate at one point pitted the chief economist of the World Bank (Joseph Stiglitz) against the first deputy managing director of the IMF (Stanley Fischer).

---

2. In contrast, in an evaluation at the time I judged that the IMF programs "were not outdated austerity recipes inappropriate to the East Asian situations, as some have charged" but were "tailored to the much greater need than in the past for emphasis on structural change, especially strengthening domestic financial sectors and in moving toward corporate transparency" (Cline 1998, 1). I noted, however, that the programs should have been more explicit in paying attention to cyclically adjusted fiscal targets, and that critics of tight monetary policy gave insufficient attention to "the tradeoff between easier monetary policy and overcoming exchange rate collapse, with its punishing impact on firms and banks owing external debt."

The East Asian crisis was fairly short but acute. It had spillover effects on the rest of the emerging markets: contagion to the Russian Federation in 1998 (aggravated by heightened risk after the collapse of Long-Term Capital Management), leading to restructuring with a substantial haircut, and contagion to Brazil and Argentina. It was not until the end of 2001 that Argentina defaulted, however, as it abandoned its currency board and experienced extremely sharp devaluation that had all the usual mismatching balance sheet effects. The Argentine default at the beginning of 2002, and the creditor losses that eventually came out of that (about 70 cents on the dollar), represented at that time the largest default losses in history. In my view, Argentina imposed a far deeper haircut than was necessary (Cline 2003). It pursued a highly unilateral strategy that has had the consequence of making it a pariah in international financial markets ever since. The most recent instance involves a *pari passu* court decision that may force Argentina to seek swaps for domestic law debt or otherwise engineer an end run around an injunction against paying restructured debt while paying nothing to remaining holdouts.

Domestic politics were a driving force in Argentina, and the country's default has been attributed to an "institutional coup" in the view of Finance Minister Domingo Cavallo, whose government was forced to resign at the end of 2001 before the presidential term was complete (Cavallo 2002). Imposing a default and making the creditors share the losses became a rallying cry for the opposition party, and there was a heavy influence of political dynamics, not only in determining the Argentine default but also in subsequent management of the restructuring.

The Argentine case stands out as a monument to mistaken management of debt restructuring, and by itself seems to have achieved transforming the debt restructuring problem from a perceived plague of rogue creditors to a problem of the rogue debtor. It is perhaps no accident that the earlier push in the IMF for a Sovereign Debt Restructuring Mechanism lost momentum as the most conspicuous debt problem became that of Argentina, with its confrontational and unilateralist approach. Ironically, and perhaps not accidentally, contagion from Argentina to Uruguay was much more successfully handled by the latter country in a market-friendly stretchout of debt that initially faced opposition from the IMF on grounds that it did not convey a debt reduction (Steneri 2011).

The Euro Area Debt Crisis since 2010

The world economy now faces its third major historical debt crisis episode in as many decades: the European debt crisis. Two central features make this crisis very different from the two previous ones. First, it is afflicting rich countries instead of emerging-market economies. Second, it is somewhat unique in that it has been aggravated by the lack of flexibility imposed on countries that are members of a currency union.

Consider the implications of the first of these considerations. The notion that a sovereign debt crisis could hit an advanced industrial country is a financial shock of historical proportions. No such economy had defaulted since the 1930s. The European crisis has forced a paradigm shift in which it is no longer appropriate (and no longer safe) to assume that industrial countries cannot default. Ironically, there was a time when the chairman of Citibank believed that Latin America could not default because "countries do not go bankrupt." He was proven wrong. Now it has been shown that not only emerging-market economies can go bankrupt but so can advanced ones. The paradigm that such countries could not default came crashing down with Greece, and the contagion to other countries in the euro area has caused this to be a "Perils of Pauline" crisis that has affected Ireland, Portugal, and Cyprus, and has threatened to spread to the much more important cases of Italy and Spain.

The second of the two distinctive features is also crucial: This crisis has hit countries that do not control their own currency. A government not in control of its own currency cannot resort to the ultimate means of honoring its sovereign commitment: namely, printing more money to pay the debt and thereby inflating away the debt burden. Nor was exit from the euro attractive as an alternative, considering the likelihood of resulting bank runs and balance sheet losses from devaluation for the stressed economy itself and likely shocks of contagion to other euro area countries. The debt problem in Europe really did not take a major turn toward resolution until the middle of 2012, when the chairman of the European Central Bank (ECB), Mario Draghi, stepped in and said the bank would do "whatever it takes" to preserve the euro. He announced the prospective program of Outright Monetary Transactions (OMT) to buy bonds of countries making adjustment efforts if needed to keep their interest rates from surging to exorbitant levels.

The European debt crisis has provided a powerful example of the classic multiple equilibrium problem. At reasonable interest rates, countries such as Italy and Spain can sustain their debt. But if the interest rate surges to panic levels, the result can become a self-fulfilling prophecy of insolvency. What we have seen is that a country's lack of ability to print its own money has caused a unique source of susceptibility to this bad equilibrium. What the ECB did in mid-2012 basically aimed to overcome this vulnerability by pledging in effect to print money to back the sovereigns in response to a market panic, in the context of conditional programs for the countries involved, despite the strictures in euro area documents and commitments against monetary financing of debt.

Before the euro, there was substantial interest rate dispersion that reflected higher inflation in some countries and thus greater expectation of currency depreciation. The formation of the euro area transformed currency risk into sovereign credit risk. At the time this transformation seemed little more than an academic analytical point, because it was broadly assumed that country credit risk was close to zero for these economies. Spreads between sovereign interest rates soon vanished, and did not begin to reemerge until the Great Recession. Once the paradigm shifted and revealed the possibility of advanced-country default, the euro area countries became vulnerable to self-fulfilling adverse debt dynamics because they could indeed default but they could not print money to pay their debt. The sovereign spreads have accordingly widened, at times reaching 500 to 600 basis points even for Italy and Spain above the German bund rate.

The European crisis was arguably facilitated if not triggered by the Great Recession, or what has been called the North Atlantic financial crisis, that started in the United States with the collapse of Bear Stearns and exploded with the collapse of Lehman Brothers. In that financial crisis there was already some widening of country risk spreads in Europe that for the first time suggested that the euro had not totally eliminated sovereign risk.

What are the lessons so far from the European debt crisis? One lesson might be that the effort to attack moral hazard by making private creditors take a haircut went to counterproductive lengths. The Greek workout arguably could have been done in a fashion that did not create as much trouble for Greece and especially for other economies if there had not been so much of an intent to force the private creditors to take a haircut. Thus, by December 2011 the European Council eliminated the previous mandatory inclusion of private sector restructurings for eligibility for support from the new European Stability Mechanism.[3] Even more importantly, in announcing the OMT program that had so crucial a calming effect on markets after mid-2012, the ECB made it clear that bonds purchased under the program would not have seniority over bonds held by the private sector.[4] This structural feature was crucial to avoiding a potentially counterproductive market effect that could have resulted if private holders began to see a risk of subordination.

An even clearer lesson from the European crisis is that the debt problem can go both from domestic banks to sovereigns, and from sovereigns to banks. In the case of Greece, it was very much the sovereign that had become excessively indebted. It had been underreporting the size of its deficits. The domestic banking system held large amounts of sovereign Greek debt, partly because the incentive system of the Basel capital requirements encouraged such holdings thanks to a zero risk weighting. The consequence, however, was that sudden insolvency in public debt also suddenly turned the banking system insolvent. That of course meant that any steps to forgive sovereign debt also meant that large amounts of additional capital would be needed to recapitalize the banks.

---

3. Although the shift to "IMF principles and practice" left room for private sector involvement (PSI) if needed. The president of the European Council acknowledged that "our first approach to PSI...had a very negative effect on the debt markets" (Herman Van Rompuy, remarks by the President of the European Council following the First Session of the European Council, Brussels, December 9, 2011, www.consilium.europa.eu/uedocs/cms_data/docs/pressdata/en/ec/126657.pdf [accessed on July 1, 2013]).

4. "The Eurosystem...accepts the same (pari passu) treatment as private or other creditors with respect to bonds issued by euro area countries..." (ECB 2012, 1).

Conversely, in Ireland the problem went from the banks to the sovereign. Ireland had an increase in its sovereign debt on the order of 40 percent of GDP as a consequence of its bailout of the banks. The banks had been engaged in a classic euphoric expansion in lending into a real estate bubble. The government's decision to support the banks occurred at the most acute phase of the North Atlantic financial crisis, and it is perfectly understandable that the government felt it could not risk having the banking system come crashing down. The result, however, was that the sovereign got stuck with the resulting debt. Cyprus is an even more acute episode in which a severely overdimensioned banking system got into trouble and imposed a serious debt crisis on the sovereign.

What is the relevance of the European debt crisis for Asia, and more generally, going forward? At least one key aspect of the crisis would seem to make it broadly inapplicable as a broader model: the single-currency aspect. So far the crisis seems to have underscored the potential problems of having a single currency shared by governments elected by disparate publics and separate political organizations. In particular, there is the problem of a single currency shared by countries with separate control of their national fiscal matters. Basically, this arrangement is proving to be very problematic and the costs associated with it have been significant. Presumably the political benefits of the unity effort continue to outweigh these costs, however, and moreover the transitional costs of any dissolution would be high.

The other key new feature of the European debt crisis, however, does seem to be particularly relevant to other countries. Namely, the crisis shows that advanced industrial countries can get into problems of public debt. Moreover, it shows that the quite high ratios of public debt to GDP—which have really only been seen in advanced countries, because they are the only ones with low enough interest rates to sustain those high debt ratios—can represent a problem that the international economy has not faced before but may have to face in the future. Of course, the IMF had already been saying that advanced countries needed to bring down their debt ratios after the sharp increase of indebtedness in the Great Recession, even before the euro area debt crisis. The European experience would seem a justifiable basis for sharpening this concern.

Debt Dynamics

The European debt crisis has underscored the inescapable basics of debt sustainability, which turn on fiscal prudence, economic growth, and the interest rate environment. By demonstrating that even rich industrial countries can enter a danger zone if their debt-to-GDP ratios are high enough, their growth prospects poor enough, and capital markets turn against them and bid up the interest rate they have to pay, the crisis has raised the stakes in the game of fiscal rebalancing in the major industrial countries.

Solvency depends on whether the likely evolution of the debt-to-GDP ratio will be an endless upward spiral or a return toward lower levels. There is an important policy equation that has come out of international debt experience that provides a key guide to that question.[5] The debt sustainability equation says that the future path of the debt-to-GDP ratio depends on the initial level of this ratio, the interest rate, the growth rate of the economy, and the size of the primary (noninterest) fiscal surplus. The interest rate affects the rate of growth of the debt because it is the ongoing annual price on debt inherited from the past. Higher growth alleviates the debt burden by increasing the denominator, GDP. The primary surplus provides means for paying the interest burden and keeping it from ballooning debt. If one thinks about the debt problem in these terms, it quickly becomes clear why Japan has in the past been able to support huge debt ratios—about 250 percent for gross debt and 150 percent for net debt—and by implication where vulnerability might lie in the future. These are ratios that would not be manageable for most countries, but the secret in Japan's case is that the country has had an extremely low interest rate on the debt, in part because of what might be thought of as somewhat captive domestic savings (for example, in the form of the postal savings bank).

The European crisis sharply illustrates the need for a debt-sustainability analytical framework and underscores why there can be a multiple equilibrium problem. Italy, with its debt ratio at about 125 percent of GDP, should be able to achieve a declining debt ratio if the interest rate is moderate and the government runs a high primary surplus (especially if it achieves substantial privatization and thereby reduces rollover borrowing otherwise needed). But Italy's debt ratio could easily spiral upward if it were to face a prolonged period of punitive interest rates because the markets became nervous and ECB support proved not to be available.

For Asia it would seem that the principal thrust of the European debt experience should be to sharpen the mind in terms of thinking about Japan's possible future challenges because of the new paradigm in which industrial countries can default and because one does have to think through what would be the conditions for meeting the debt sustainability equation for a country starting from such a high debt ratio.

Debt Sustainability in Asia

The stylized facts are that the Asian emerging-market economies are broadly in a solid debt position, having overcome their problem of illiquidity in the late 1990s and having avoided excessive government debt. A possible exception is India, where the stylized fact is that sizable fiscal imbalances have persisted for a long time.

---

5. For an early development of this by now standard equation, see Cline (2003, annex A). The sustainability equation is applied in the discussion below to arrive at the estimates in table 9.1.

External Debt

Figure 9.1 confirms the perception that the short-term debt squeeze of the late 1990s has been overcome for a long time now. The ratio of short-term external debt to external reserves reached as high as 313 percent in the Republic of Korea in 1997. The debt rollover in 1998 cut that ratio to only 76 percent, and for most of the past decade most East Asian economies have maintained a ratio of 50 percent or lower. As shown in figure 9.2, in considerable part the decline in the short-term debt-to-reserves ratio reflected a major buildup in reserves. For the five East Asian economies, the median ratio of reserves to imports of goods and services fell from 37.9 percent in 1994 to 26.3 percent in 1997, but then rose to 70.5 percent by 2011.

With respect to the traditional metric of debt vulnerability in Latin America, the ratio of total external debt to exports of goods and services, the Asian economies were not in the exposed position reached by Latin America in the 1980s, and have not had high external debt ratios in recent years. One reason has been that there is higher domestic saving and less reliance on external debt, but another reason has been the higher export base relative to GDP and greater reliance on export growth in the growth strategy. Thus, figure 9.3 shows that external debt to export ratios in the major Latin American economies were on the order of 300 to 500 percent of GDP in the mid-1980s, but fell to a range of 200 to 300 percent by the mid-1990s after the Brady Plan. However, the figure also shows a partial resurgence in Argentina and Brazil in the late 1990s associated with the expansion of international bond finance to the emerging-market economies, prior to a major further decline by 2005 and onward as exports surged with strong commodity markets. It is also important to recognize that the easing of interest rates from the early 1980s to later periods means that there was a greater reduction in the external transfer burden than would be inferred solely from the ratios of debt to exports.

Figure 9.4 shows that the Republic of Korea, Malaysia, and Thailand never reached the high levels of total external debt relative to exports that had characterized the Latin crisis, underscoring the fact that the late-1990s crisis was one of liquidity for them, not solvency. The Philippines, in contrast, shows up in figure 9.4 very much as the "honorary Latin" country of the 1980s crisis, another stylized fact. The Philippines was the only East Asian emerging-market economy to obtain debt reduction under the Brady Plan (Cline 1995, 234).[6] India experienced a sharp increase in external debt in the late 1980s and early 1990s, and reached near-crisis fiscal and external balance conditions that prompted adoption of an IMF structural adjustment program in 1991. Even so, India's debt in this period was primarily low-interest, long-term conces-

---

6. In compensation, by the time of the East Asian crisis the Philippines had done relatively more to strengthen its domestic financial system and was less vulnerable than its neighbors. In 1998, real output fell only slightly (0.5 percent), whereas the declines were in the range of 6 to 8 percent in the Republic of Korea, Malaysia, and Thailand, and 13 percent in Indonesia (Noland 2000).

Figure 9.1   Ratio of short-term external debt to reserves in East Asia, 1994–2011

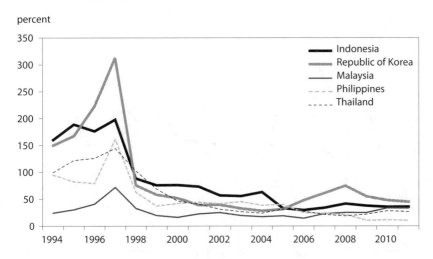

percent

Sources: World Bank (2013a); IMF (2013b); Bank of Korea (2013).

Figure 9.2   Ratio of external reserves to imports of goods and services in East Asia, 1994–2011

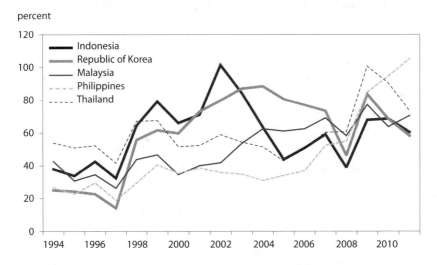

percent

Source: IMF (2013b).

**Figure 9.3   Ratio of external debt to exports of goods and services in
Latin America, 1980–2011**

percent

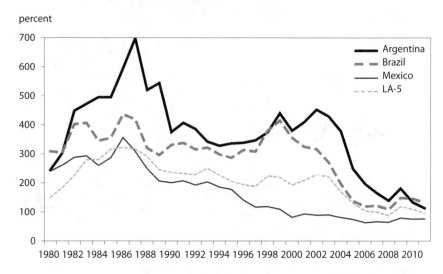

LA-5 = Chile, Colombia, Peru, Uruguay, and Venezuela
Source: World Bank (2013a).

**Figure 9.4   Ratio of external debt to exports of goods and services in
Asia, 1980–2011**

percent

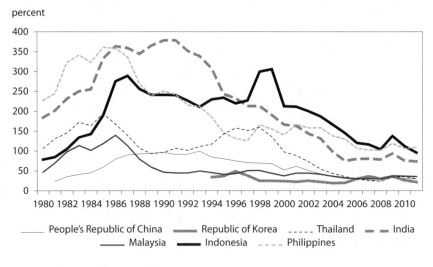

Sources: World Bank (2013a); Bank of Korea (2013).

sional debt from official sources, and hence did not represent the burden that would have been implied by its debt ratio if the debt had been at market terms.[7] Indonesia's debt ratio was also substantial but again reflected a relatively high share of low-burden official financing.[8]

A noteworthy pattern in figures 9.3 and 9.4 is the convergence of the debt-to-export ratios for these principal emerging-market economies by 2010–11. The ratios span about 30 to 100 percent for the Asian countries, and about 75 to 130 percent in the Latin American countries. Considering that the export-to-GDP ratios tend to be higher in Asia, the ratios of external debt to GDP have converged even more.[9] Thus, in 2011, the median ratio of gross external debt to GDP was almost identical for the eight Asian economies reported in figure 9.4 (at 24.2 percent) and the eight Latin American economies reported in figure 9.3 (at 25.1 percent) (World Bank 2013a).

Finally, once external reserves are taken into account, the external debt vulnerability trends for the major Latin American and Asian emerging-market economies are even more favorable. In half of the Asian emerging-market economies, and especially the People's Republic of China (PRC), the buildup in reserves has been so great that these economies have been net creditors rather than net debtors. Figures 9.5 and 9.6 show the paths of net external debt (defined narrowly to deduct only official reserves but not private holdings of credit claims on foreigners) relative to exports. For Latin America, there is a pronounced reduction in the net external debt ratio, from a median of about 200 percent of exports of goods and services in 2002 to about 50 percent by 2011. In Asia, four economies have been net external creditors on this measure dating from as long ago as 2004. The PRC's net creditor position reached 150 percent of exports of goods and services in 2009 before easing somewhat by 2011. Only Indonesia and Viet Nam remained in substantial net external debtor positions by 2011, both at close to 50 percent of exports of goods and services.

Overall, the message from the trends in indicators of external debt relative to exports is that the major emerging-market economies in both Latin America and (especially) Asia have improved in recent years to the point where there should be much less vulnerability to external debt crises than in past decades.

---

7. Thus, in 1990, two-thirds of India's long-term external debt was from official sources (mainly on concessional terms from bilateral donors and the World Bank's International Development Association), whereas in Brazil only 31 percent was from official sources (World Bank 2013a).

8. In 2000, half of Indonesia's long-term debt was from official sources (World Bank 2013a). Note also that Viet Nam is not shown in the figure because its initial debt ratio was off the chart at 1,400 percent in 1989 when exports were close to zero, but by 2000–10 this ratio was down to a relatively low range of about 50 to 70 percent.

9. In 2011, the ratio of gross external debt to GDP was 9 to 20 percent in the PRC, the Republic of Korea, India, and Brazil; 20 to 30 percent in Venezuela, Thailand, Colombia, Indonesia, Mexico, Peru, and Argentina; and 30 to 40 percent in Uruguay, Malaysia, the Philippines, and Chile. The ratio was 47 percent in Indonesia, where the official (largely concessional) component was high (65.5 percent of long-term debt) (World Bank 2013a).

Figure 9.5   Ratio of net external debt to exports of goods and services in Latin America, 2002–11

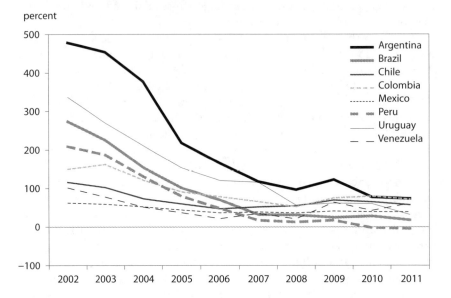

Sources: World Bank (2013a); IMF (2013b).

Figure 9.6   Ratio of net external debt to exports of goods and services in Asia, 2002–11

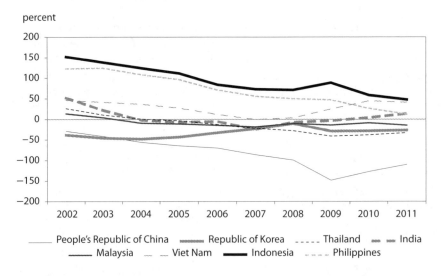

Sources: World Bank (2013a); IMF (2013b); Bank of Korea (2013).

Public Debt and Fiscal Deficits

The Latin American debt crisis of the 1980s was a crisis of both external debt and public debt, with much of the public debt at the time owed to foreign banks. Large fiscal deficits and "discovered debt" (for example, debts incurred by the provinces but assumed by the central government) spurred the run-up in external debt. The East Asian crisis in the late 1990s had much more to do with short-term external debt owed by the banks and the private sector and much less to do with the accumulation of excessive public debt.

The European debt crisis, in contrast, has been first and foremost a crisis of public debt (including that incurred as a consequence of bank bailouts) regardless of the location of its holders. Typically, domestic banks have been among the largest holders. The proximate fuse of a sudden stop of external financing that forces a collapse in the currency has not been an issue in the European experience because the exchange rate has been assured, as the countries in difficulty are members of the single currency. In effect they have automatic "external" financing as needed through the accumulation of balances at central banks of other euro member countries (the "Target2" balances). The European crisis has thus served to focus attention on the sustainability of public debt, rather than the sustainability of external debt. Correspondingly, the principal metric has been the ratio of public debt to GDP, in contrast to the ratio of external debt to exports of goods and services, essentially reflecting focus on the "internal transfer problem" rather than the external one.

A benchmark that has emerged in the crisis is that general government gross debt should not exceed 120 percent of GDP if debt sustainability is to be assured. One suspects that this threshold arose in part because IMF and euro area planners designing the assistance program in the Greek debt crisis would have been in an awkward position to argue that Greek debt had to be substantially lower than this threshold when one of the largest donor economies, Italy, had debt of approximately this scale. There is a certain logic, nonetheless, for a public debt ratio this high in the European debt context. A normal long-term interest rate on public debt in the European context might be 5 percent (3 percent real and 2 percent inflation). Nominal economic growth would be on the order of 3.5 percent (1½ percent real, 2 percent inflation). With a debt-to-GDP ratio of 120 percent, the primary surplus needed to keep that ratio constant would amount to 1.8 percent of GDP, a reasonable objective.[10]

---

10. The debt-ratio-stabilizing primary surplus is $\pi^* = \lambda(r-g)$, where λ is the ratio of debt to GDP, r is the interest rate, and g is the nominal growth rate. With $\lambda = 1.2$, $r = 0.05$, and $g = 0.035$, the primary fiscal target needs to be $\pi^* = 0.018$ in order to stabilize the debt-to-GDP ratio. The adjustment programs in the region have typically sought primary surpluses at least this large (the first Greek program aimed at 6 percent of GDP for the primary surplus, and the most recent programs seek medium-term primary surpluses of 3.5 percent of GDP in Ireland, 3 percent in Portugal, and 4.3 percent in Greece). Italy's primary surplus was 2.3 percent of GDP in 2012 and is projected at 4.3 percent by 2017. Spain has further to go, with a primary deficit of 3.5 percent of GDP in 2013 and still a small deficit of 1.5 percent of GDP by 2018. As a broad consequence, whereas debt ratios

Consideration of trends in the ratio of gross public debt (general government) to GDP for the Latin American and Asian emerging-market economies as well as the euro area periphery countries clearly indicates the emerging problems in the euro area in contrast to progress in limiting public debt burdens in the other two regions.

In figures 9.7 and 9.8, it is striking that the main emerging-market economies in Latin America and Asia, respectively, are all either close to the Maastricht benchmark of public debt at 60 percent (only Brazil and India are a few percentage points higher) or well below it. For eight Latin American economies, the median ratio of government debt to GDP in 2012 was 44 percent; for eight Asian economies, the median ratio was 43 percent. In contrast, for the five stressed euro area periphery economies, the median ratio was 119 percent (figure 9.9). Once again one observes a somewhat uncanny convergence for the emerging-market economies, in that the median is almost identical for the Latin American and Asian economies.

In Asia, among the principal emerging-market economies the most concern about public debt sustainability might be in India. The debt ratio fell from 84 percent of GDP in 2003–04 to 68 percent by 2010–12. It is useful to consider the debt dynamics equation for India. The IMF projects real economic growth at an average of 6.5 percent from 2013–17. Inflation measured by the GDP deflator is projected at a surprisingly high rate of 6.3 percent per year. India's average interest rate on public debt is projected at 7.1 percent.[11] The result is that the IMF projects that India's public debt will remain approximately constant at two-thirds of GDP through 2018, even though India is expected to run a primary deficit averaging 3.6 percent of GDP. Ironically, lack of virtue is being rewarded: A high inflation rate is eroding the debt, because the nominal interest rate on public debt is only slightly higher than inflation (7.1 percent versus 6.3 percent). As a consequence, India does not even need to achieve a primary fiscal balance to keep its debt from rising relative to GDP. Thus, the one country that might appear the most problematical in the region from the standpoint of the debt burden is on track to keep its debt ratio from rising further thanks to extremely high nominal growth (reflecting both high real growth and high inflation) and despite an ongoing primary deficit.

Fiscal Sustainability

At the margin, debt sustainability depends on whether the combined interest rate, primary surplus, and growth dynamics meet the test for stabilizing the ratio of debt to GDP. Namely, the primary surplus as a percent of GDP (defined

---

are planned to converge downward from 130 percent in 2013 to 123 percent by 2018 in Italy, and from 122 percent in 2013 to 106 to 114 percent by 2018 in Ireland and Portugal, they are on track to converge upward from about 85 percent to about 105 percent in Spain (IMF 2013a).

11. As discussed below, this measure is the implicit net interest rate obtained by comparing net interest payments against gross debt at the end of the prior year.

Figure 9.7   Ratio of gross general government debt to GDP in Latin America, 2001–12

percent

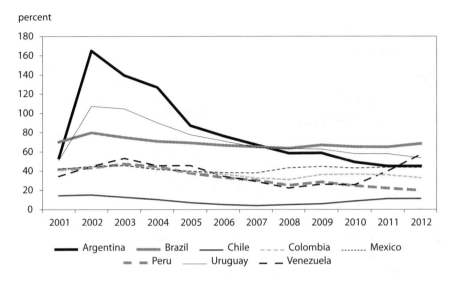

Argentina   Brazil   Chile   Colombia   Mexico
Peru   Uruguay   Venezuela

Sources: IMF (2013a).

Figure 9.8   Ratio of gross general government debt to GDP in Asia, 2001–12

percent

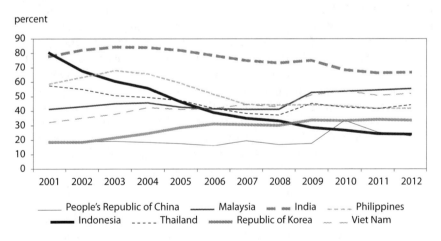

People's Republic of China   Malaysia   India   Philippines
Indonesia   Thailand   Republic of Korea   Viet Nam

Source: IMF (2013a).

as π) must meet the condition $\pi^* = \lambda(r - g)$, where λ is the ratio of debt to GDP, r is the average interest rate on public debt, and g is the nominal growth rate. Table 9.1 applies the IMF's *World Economic Outlook* (WEO) projections for 2013–18 to examine this question for the Latin American and Asian emerging

Figure 9.9   Ratio of gross general government debt to GDP in the euro area periphery, 2001–12

percent

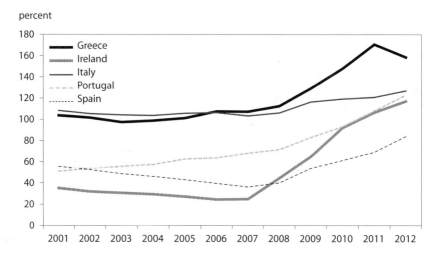

Source: IMF (2013a).

markets, as well as the euro area periphery economies (IMF 2013a). In addition, the table includes for comparison the same information for Australia, Japan, and the United States. The ratio of debt to GDP is the starting level at the end of 2012. All other entries in the table are forward-looking averages for the six-year period. For the interest rate, the estimate used is the implied net interest rate on gross public debt. It is calculated as the ratio of net interest payments (estimated as the difference between the total fiscal balance and the primary fiscal balance) to gross public debt at the end of the previous year. This implicit interest rate turns out to be negative for two countries (the Republic of Korea and Venezuela), apparently reflecting net creditor status of the government, thereby making the debt sustainability target for the primary balance especially easy to achieve.[12] Similarly, the implied net interest rate is quite low for Chile (1.5 percent), Thailand (1.1 percent), and Japan (0.5 percent), apparently reflecting sizable government asset earnings (and in the case of Japan, low interest rates in the face of deflation or low inflation).

---

12. The OECD (2012) estimates that whereas the Republic of Korea's gross general public debt amounted to 36.4 percent of GDP at the end of 2012, its financial assets were twice as large, placing its net financial liabilities at –36.2 percent of GDP. Note, however, that the IMF (2013a) reports the assets of the government of the Republic of Korea as negligible, since it places net debt at only 1.5 percent of GDP less than gross debt. The negative net interest payments in the WEO imply however that the OECD numbers are right and the IMF numbers are wrong regarding net debt. The other country with a negative implied net interest rate is Venezuela, where the primary deficit exceeds the overall deficit, indicating negative net interest payments. However, the IMF (2013a) omits estimates of net debt in the database for Venezuela, and the size of assets is thus ambiguous.

Table 9.1   Public debt dynamics, 2013–18 averages (percent)

Country	Growth	Inflation[a]	Interest rate	Debt/GDP, 2012	Primary surplus	Debt ratio stabilizing primary surplus	Gap to reach debt ratio stabilizing primary surplus	Cyclically adjusted primary surplus
Argentina	3.0	17.5	4.9	44.9	-0.5	-7.2	-6.8	-0.4
Brazil	3.9	5.1	7.3	68.5	3.1	-1.3	-4.4	3.1
Chile	4.7	2.9	1.5	11.2	0.1	-0.7	-0.8	-0.5
Colombia	4.4	2.8	5.8	32.8	0.9	-0.5	-1.4	0.6
Mexico	3.3	3.3	6.1	43.5	-0.2	-0.3	-0.1	-0.2
Peru	6.1	1.9	4.6	19.8	2.6	-0.7	-3.2	2.5
Uruguay	4.0	5.8	6.5	53.7	1.7	-1.9	-3.6	n.a.
Venezuela	2.0	22.1	-4.2	57.3	-10.9	-16.5	-5.6	n.a.
People's Republic of China	8.4	2.9	3.0	22.8	-0.3	-1.9	-1.7	0.4
India	6.5	6.3	7.1	66.8	-3.6	-4.2	-0.6	-3.6
Indonesia	6.4	5.5	6.0	24.0	-0.4	-1.5	-1.1	-0.4
Republic of Korea	3.8	2.4	-3.2	33.7	1.8	-3.2	-5.0	1.8
Malaysia	5.2	2.2	3.8	55.5	-1.6	-2.0	-0.5	-1.6
Philippines	5.5	3.2	6.6	41.9	1.4	-1.0	-2.4	0.3
Thailand	4.7	2.4	1.1	44.3	-1.7	-2.7	-0.9	-1.8
Viet Nam	5.4	7.1	2.3	52.1	-1.9	-5.5	-3.6	n.a.

(continues on next page)

Table 9.1   Public debt dynamics, 2013–18 averages (percent) *(continued)*

Country	Growth	Inflation[a]	Interest rate	Debt/GDP, 2012	Primary surplus	Debt ratio stabilizing primary surplus	Gap to reach debt ratio stabilizing primary surplus	Cyclically adjusted primary surplus
Greece	1.6	0.5	3.0	158.5	3.0	1.5	–1.5	5.2
Ireland	2.4	1.5	3.8	117.1	1.3	–0.2	–1.5	1.5
Italy	0.7	1.4	4.3	127.0	3.6	2.8	–0.8	4.8
Portugal	0.9	1.5	3.4	123.0	1.3	1.2	–0.1	2.4
Spain	0.8	1.2	3.5	84.1	–2.7	1.2	3.9	–1.6
Australia	3.1	1.9	1.6	27.2	0.6	–1.0	–1.5	0.5
Japan	1.3	1.0	0.5	237.9	–5.1	–4.3	0.8	–5.0
United States	3.0	2.0	2.1	106.5	–2.5	–3.2	–0.7	–1.7

n.a. = not available

a. GDP deflator.

Sources: IMF (2013a, 2013c).

The somewhat surprising overall result in table 9.1 is that there are few instances in which sizable gaps exist between prospective primary surpluses and those that would be needed to keep the ratio of debt to GDP constant. Among the more important gaps is that in Spain, where the primary surplus would need to average 1.2 percent of GDP over 2013–18 to keep the debt ratio from rising but instead will average only –2.7 percent; and in Japan, where the debt-stabilizing primary balance would be a deficit of 4.3 percent of GDP, but instead the primary deficit is expected to average 5.1 percent of GDP, placing the debt-stabilizing gap at 0.8 percent of GDP. Part of this seeming pattern of fiscal adequacy is illusory, however, because more ambitious targets are needed than simply avoiding further upward spiraling in already high debt ratios. This is presumably the case for Japan, where even net debt was 134 percent of GDP and gross debt 238 percent at the end of 2012 (IMF 2013a).[13] It is also desirable to reduce the debt ratio in Italy, where the gross debt ratio is about 130 percent of GDP. Although the expected primary surplus of 3.6 percent of GDP is larger than the 2.8 percent needed to stabilize the debt ratio, the excess is highly salutary in view of the need to bring down the debt ratio. The same can be said of the United States, where the essentially disappointing primary balance outcome of an average deficit of 2.5 percent of GDP is larger than the stabilizing deficit of 3.2 percent of GDP, but will not do much to reduce the already high gross debt ratio of 107 percent of GDP.[14]

As suggested above for India, the most surprising cases are those in which high inflation rescues economies from what otherwise would be rapid debt buildups. India's primary deficit of 3.6 percent of GDP is modestly smaller than the 4.2 percent of GDP primary deficit that could be run while still keeping the debt ratio constant, thanks to its high inflation (which boosts nominal GDP growth). This phenomenon of inflationary debt erosion is most pronounced in Argentina and Venezuela, where large primary deficits could be tolerated without increasing the debt ratio. But of course in these cases policy presumably includes the goal of reducing high inflation (at 22 percent in Venezuela), which in turn would imply the need for a higher primary surplus.

For the main emerging-market economies in table 9.1, the message is that not only are public debt ratios moderate, but also the prospective trajectories are favorable because primary balances are somewhat higher than would be needed to keep the debt ratios from rising. For the Asian emerging-market economics shown in the table, all except India have moderate debt ratios (about

---

13. For Japan, both the IMF (2013a) and OECD (2013) report net debt at 134 percent of GDP for end-2012. However, the two sources differ on gross debt, with the IMF estimate at 238 percent but the OECD estimate at 214 percent.

14. Note, however, that IMF estimates of general government debt differ from the main US policy metric, which is federal (as opposed to general government) debt held by the public (and hence excluding, for example, government debt held by the Social Security Administration). This measure stands at about 78 percent of GDP and is projected in the fiscal year 2014 budget to ease to a still-high 73 percent by 2023 (OMB 2013).

50 percent of GDP for Malaysia and Viet Nam, and about 25 to 45 percent for the PRC, Indonesia, Republic of Korea, the Philippines, and Thailand). Moreover, none has a fiscal gap requiring an increase in the primary surplus to stabilize the debt-to-GDP ratio (all entries in the next to last column are negative for the region). It is therefore somewhat surprising that the IMF states that "in many Asian economies, structural deficits that are higher than precrisis levels imply the need for greater effort to rebuild fiscal space" (IMF 2013d, x).

The IMF's call for fiscal restraint is based on a target ceiling of only 40 percent of GDP for public debt, rather than the goal of avoiding further increase. The Fund suggests that "their historically more volatile financial environment suggests more prudent benchmark debt levels [for emerging-market economies] than those used for advanced economies" (IMF 2013c, 17). To meet a ceiling of 40 percent of GDP for the debt ratio by 2020, the Fund identifies a need for a primary surplus increase of 6.7 percent of GDP in India, 3.5 percent in Malaysia, and 1.2 percent in Thailand (IMF 2013c, 73). It even finds a need for a 1.7 percent of GDP fiscal adjustment in Indonesia because there it seeks an even more stringent target: the actual level in 2013, because it is below 40 percent (at 24 percent).[15] As discussed above, the outsized target for a primary surplus increase in India would not seem to take account of the influence of high inflation in eroding the debt burden. But more generally the IMF's implied call for fiscal tightening in these four economies seems questionable in light of the debt sustainability calculations of table 9.1 (especially in Indonesia, which is penalized in the Fund's calculations for starting with a low debt ratio).

Domestic Bond Markets

The discussion above suggests that sharp declines in external debt relative to exports, and especially net external debt relative to exports, have considerably lessened potential vulnerability to external debt problems in the main Asian and especially Latin American economies. Similarly, the discussion of fiscal trends suggests that trends in public debt sustainability were relatively favorable. An important additional dimension of debt vulnerability is the extent to which governments are able to borrow domestically, or instead must borrow abroad in foreign currency because of "original sin." Domestic funding reduces vulnerability to sudden stops.

Table 9.2 reports trends in domestic sourcing of government borrowing in the principal Asian and Latin American emerging-market economies. These

---

15. It is curious that the IMF identifies a need for a rise in the cyclically adjusted primary balance for Indonesia, considering that the calculation of table 9.1 finds no such need, yet the Fund also aims to stabilize debt at the present low ratio. The explanation of the divergence is apparently that the IMF's reported fiscal improvement is against the actual 2013 cyclical primary balance (-1.4 percent of GDP), whereas the estimates of table 9.1 apply the projected average 2013–18 primary balances (for Indonesia, -0.4 percent of GDP).

Table 9.2   Outstanding stocks of domestic government debt securities, 2000 and 2010

	2000		
Country	Billions of US dollars	Percent of GDP	Percent of government debt
Argentina	33	11.6	25.4
Brazil	219	34.0	51.0
Chile	1	1.3	9.7
Colombia	16	16.0	44.1
Mexico	75	11.2	26.2
Peru	4	7.5	17.7
Venezuela	8	6.8	21.4
People's Republic of China	111	9.3	56.3
India	112	23.5	32.3
Indonesia	45	27.3	28.7
Republic of Korea	62	11.6	64.5
Malaysia	28	29.9	84.5
Philippines	20	24.7	42.0
Thailand	16	13.0	22.5

	2010		
Country	Billions of US dollars	Percent of GDP	Percent of government debt
Argentina	31	8.4	17.1
Brazil	949	44.3	68.0
Chile	17	7.9	91.0
Colombia	70	24.6	67.6
Mexico	247	23.9	55.6
Peru	14	9.1	37.1
Venezuela	18	6.1	15.2
People's Republic of China	1,006	17.0	50.6
India	608	37.3	54.8
Indonesia	68	9.6	35.7
Republic of Korea	331	32.6	97.6
Malaysia	125	50.6	99.4
Philippines	62	31.1	71.5
Thailand	86	27.0	63.2

Sources: Mehrotra et al. (2012); IMF (2013a).

data, based on combining Bank for International Settlements (BIS) estimates of domestic debt securities with IMF data on public debt relative to GDP, confirm a substantial trend toward borrowing domestically.[16]

The shifts indicated in table 9.2 are especially impressive in Chile, where domestic public debt reached 91 percent of the total in 2010 in contrast to 10 percent in 2000; in Mexico, where the increase was from 26 to 56 percent; in Colombia, rising from 44 to 67 percent; and in Brazil, increasing from 51 percent in 2000 to 68 percent in 2010.[17] In Asia, the sharp increase in domestic sourcing of government debt is striking in the Republic of Korea, where it has risen from 65 to 98 percent of public debt; in Malaysia, at 99 percent, up from 84 percent; in Thailand, at 63 percent up from 23 percent; and in the Philippines, at 72 percent, up from 42 percent. It is likely no coincidence that all four of these economies were afflicted by the external liquidity crisis of the late 1990s, and hence may have made special efforts to shift borrowing to domestic sources. In short, a shift toward domestic sourcing of government debt, in local currency rather than foreign currency, has further reduced public debt vulnerability in these principal emerging-market economies.

Even as public debt sourced in the domestic market and denominated in local currency (the criteria in the BIS data) has risen as a share of total public debt, the shares of foreigners in the holdings of this domestic debt have also risen. Table 9.3 reports Deutsche Bank (2013) estimates of these shares for six emerging-market economies for three benchmark dates: the first quarter of 2007, the first quarter of 2009, and the third (or fourth) quarter of 2012. For Indonesia, Mexico, Poland, and South Africa, the foreign-held share in domestic debt holdings had risen to a surprisingly high range of 31 to 35 percent by late 2012. Although the shares remained more modest at 10 to 14 percent in the Republic of Korea and Brazil, they have risen substantially from a low initial level of 2 percent in 2007. For the PRC and India, the foreign-held shares remain below 2 percent.

The broad pattern is that there is an encouraging vote of confidence among international investors in the soundness of emerging-market local-currency public debt. This form of debt is presumably safer for the emerging-market economies than debt denominated in foreign currency and held by foreigners because it does not face a potential mismatch between the government's source of income (domestic tax revenue in local currency) and payment obligations.

A further consideration regarding local currency debt, however, concerns the interest rate cost. Traditionally, capital-scarce domestic markets would bear a high interest rate for government debt, whereas capital would be available more cheaply in international capital markets sourced from industrial coun-

---

16. The domestic debt securities data are from Mehrotra, Miyajima, and Villar (2012).

17. The data are puzzling for Argentina, however, where the 2010 domestic share had fallen to 17 percent from 25 percent in 2000, yet the country has largely been cut off from borrowing abroad.

Table 9.3   Share of foreign holdings in domestic government debt, selected emerging-market economies (percent)

Country	2007Q1	2009Q1	2012Q4
Indonesia	15	15	33
Republic of Korea	2	6	10[a]
Brazil	2	6	14[a]
Turkey	15	9	23
Poland	20	11	34
Mexico	9	11	35
South Africa	5	11	31[a]

a. Data are for 2012Q3.

Source: Deutsche Bank (2013).

tries with greater capital abundance. The decision facing the prudent finance minister would then involve a comparison of costs versus risks. As suggested in figure 9.10, the foreign lending rate (in dollars, for example) is lower (at r_f) than the domestic rate (at r_d). The figure shows the fraction of public debt sourced in domestic currency on the horizontal axis, and the interest rate on the vertical axis. The domestic capital supply curve D slopes gently upward as there is crowding out in the domestic market. The foreign source capital supply curve F slopes gently downward as some reduction in the rate is given as the country approaches self-sufficiency in government borrowing. If there were no further considerations, the country would borrow exclusively in foreign currency, because the domestic curve lies entirely above the foreign curve.

However, there is a premium that the prudent finance minister imputes to risk from a sudden stop in foreign lending. This premium, which translates the expected future damages from the sudden stop into an annual interest spread, is represented by the vertical distance σ between the foreign lending curve and the welfare-equivalent foreign lending cost curve, $\hat{F}$. In the figure, the risk premium is high when most debt is in foreign currency, because exposure to the foreign sudden stop is high. As the share of debt owed in domestic currency rises (moving to the right), the risk premium narrows and the $\hat{F}$ curve falls closer to the F curve. The optimal share of foreign versus domestic-currency debt occurs at ϕ_d^*, where the $\hat{F}$ curve intersects the D curve.

Figure 9.10 serves as a reminder that borrowing costs (including crisis risk) should be taken into account in the decision between borrowing in domestic currency and borrowing in foreign currency. The lesser risk of borrowing domestically does not necessarily mean that all borrowing should be done domestically because the domestic interest rate is likely to be higher than the international rate and the extra cost must be weighed against the reduced risk.

Figure 9.11 provides an illustrative comparison of the foreign versus domestic borrowing cost for four emerging-market economies with data readily

Figure 9.10   Foreign borrowing rate, domestic borrowing rate, foreign rate including sudden-stop social risk premium, and optimal share of domestic currency government debt

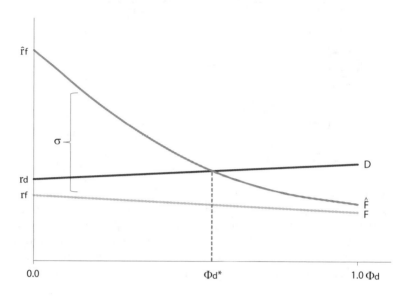

Note: See text for explanation.
Source: Author's illustration.

available. The interest rate for domestic long-term government bonds (*D*) is from IMF (2013b), and is the average for 2011 and 2012. For example, in this period the Republic of Korea was able to borrow domestically (long term) at 3.8 percent and South Africa at 8.2 percent. The "expected foreign" (*EF*) rate is constructed as follows: It equals a risk-free base for the 10-year US Treasury bond (an average of 2.3 percent), plus the inflation differential between the country and the United States (2011–12 average) as a measure of expected annual currency depreciation against the dollar, plus the country-risk spread as measured by the credit default swap (CDS) spread.[18]

In three of the four economies, the domestic borrowing rate exceeded the expected foreign dollar borrowing rate, implying a positive sudden-stop social risk premium (*SSP,* the difference between the first and second columns in the figure). The Republic of Korea, Mexico, and South Africa thus reflected public borrowing decision situations similar to that shown in figure 9.10. In Thailand, however, the implied expected foreign borrowing rate exceeded the domestic borrowing rate, leaving no margin for a sudden-stop premium.

---

18. CDS spreads in the first quarter of 2013 were an average of 67 basis points for the Republic of Korea, 98 for Mexico, 146 for South Africa, and 91 for Thailand (Datastream).

Figure 9.11 Domestic versus expected foreign borrowing cost, Republic of Korea, Mexico, South Africa, and Thailand

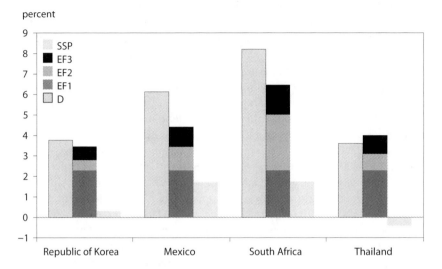

Note: *D* is the interest rate for domestic long-term government bonds. *EF* is the "expected foreign" rate and is constructed as follows: It equals a risk-free base for the 10-year US Treasury bond (*EF1*), plus the inflation differential between the country and the United States (*EF2*), plus the country-risk spread (*EF3*). SSP is the sudden-stop social risk premium.

Sources: Datastream; IMF (2013a, 2013b).

The Japan Problem

Any review of public debt policy issues with special reference to Asia would be incomplete without giving particular attention to the case of Japan. At the end of 2012, Japan's gross public debt stood at 237 percent of GDP and net debt at 134 percent (IMF 2013a). As indicated in table 9.1, Japan has a debt-stabilization fiscal gap of 0.8 percent of GDP. Its nominal growth over 2013–18 is projected to average 2.3 percent annually. It has an exceptionally low nominal net interest rate on its debt (calculated as net interest paid as a fraction of gross debt), averaging only 0.5 percent. It thus enjoys an exceptionally forgiving primary balance of 2.37 × (0.5 − 2.3) = −4.3 percent of GDP to keep the debt ratio from rising. It is on track to achieve an even lower primary balance, averaging −5.1 percent of GDP in 2013–18. Just to stabilize the debt ratio would thus require boosting the primary balance by 0.8 percent of GDP. But of course it would be highly desirable to reduce the debt ratio rather than keep it at its high level, in order to gain fiscal space available to meet future crises if needed.[19] The problem, however, is how to carry out fiscal adjust-

---

19. Thus, in its most recent country study of Japan, the OECD (2013, 107) warns that "With gross government debt surpassing 200% of GDP, Japan's fiscal situation is in uncharted territory. In

ment without curbing growth. The IMF's WEO (2013a) places Japan's average output gap at only 0.61 percent of GDP in 2013–18 (down from 3 percent in 2012). This excess capacity is sufficiently small that the multiplier seems unlikely to be high. If it were, say, 0.5, the 0.8 percent of GDP increase in the primary surplus would cause a reduction in the level of the GDP path by 0.4 percent, but thereafter the debt dynamics would stabilize the debt ratio.

The new government of Japan has sought to revive the economy through a large program of quantitative easing, with the intent to boost Japan's inflation rate to 2 percent.[20] For debt sustainability, the question would then be whether achieving 2 percent inflation would improve debt sustainability by boosting the nominal (and real?) growth rate or erode debt sustainability by boosting the interest rate as the public reaches higher inflationary expectations.

It seems to be a widely accepted impression that Japan has experienced "lost decades" of growth, and an aggressive policy change designed to pull the economy out of stagnation might seem appropriate if such a view were correct. It turns out, however, that Japan's decade of the 1990s was not exactly lost, and in the 2000s its growth has actually been comparable to that of the United States when judged on the right basis. There is an optical illusion caused by Japan's aging population and stagnant population total when compared to economic performance in the United States with its younger and rising population. From 1991 to 2012, the US labor force rose by 22.7 percent, whereas the labor force of Japan rose by only 0.6 percent (IMF 2013b). One should thus have expected Japan's economy to expand by less than that of the United States.[21]

Figure 9.12 shows the time path of real GDP per number of workers in the labor force (employed and unemployed) for Germany, Japan, and the United States from 1991 to 2012.[22] Japan's economic growth performance in the past two decades looks relatively comparable to that of its peers when measured in terms of output per number of workers in the labor force. The US growth rate for output per worker is indeed higher, as indicated by the steeper US line. However, the rate for Japan is actually slightly higher than that for Germany.

---

addition to robust nominal GDP growth, correcting two decades of budget deficits requires a large and sustained fiscal consolidation...."

20. Surprisingly, in the April 2013 WEO the IMF slightly reduced rather than increased its growth outlook for Japan from its October 2012 WEO, despite the aggressive new program of quantitative easing. Average real growth in 2013–17 was placed at 1.3 percent annually in the earlier WEO but at 1.1 percent in the most recent issue (IMF 2012, 2013a).

21. Nor was stagnation in Japan's labor force caused by a falling labor force participation rate. The ratio of the labor force to the 20–64-year-old population rose modestly (from 85.5 percent in 1990 to 90.3 percent in 2010), whereas that for the United States fell modestly (from 86.2 to 82 percent) (IMF 2013b, World Bank 2013b).

22. Data are from IMF (2013b). For Germany, data for 1991–95 are from BLS (2005) and are spliced to the 1996 IMF number to correct for a break in the IMF series.

Figure 9.12   Real GDP per labor force, Germany, Japan, and United States, 1991–2012

index (1995–2000 = 100)

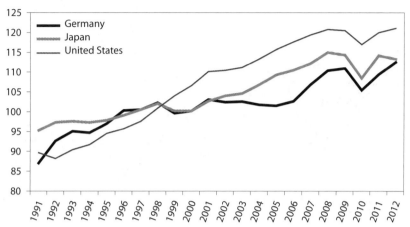

Sources: IMF (2013b); BLS (2005).

The full-period average annual growth rates of real output per worker are 1.66 percent for the United States, 0.91 percent for Japan, and 0.87 percent for Germany.[23] So there is some basis for questioning just how radically Japan needs to boost its growth, and correspondingly how realistic it is to expect far higher growth performance in Japan from different policy approaches. The stylized fact of Japan's two lost decades implicitly judges the country's growth performance against its own past, which was of course characterized by much higher growth prior to the 1990s.[24] However, as Japan has completed its phase of catchup growth, the more relevant comparison has become against growth in other rich industrial countries, rather than against Japan's own history.[25]

As for the question of possible feedback from inflation to the cost of public debt, figure 9.13 shows the time paths for annual consumer price inflation, the annual percent increase in the GDP deflator, and the average implicit

---

23. These growth rates are the coefficient in simple log-linear regressions on time.

24. Whereas growth averaged 4.5 percent annually from 1970 to 1990, the average was only 2 percent from 1990 to 2007. Kyoji Fukao (2013) estimates that total factor productivity growth contributed an average of 1.6 percent annually over 1970–90 but only 0.6 percent annually over 1990–2007.

25. Thus, whereas Japan's per capita GDP at market exchange rates was an average of only 62 percent of the US level from 1970 to 1980, it reached an average of 114 percent of the US level by 1990–2000 (calculated from IMF 2013b). In terms of purchasing power parity, per capita GDP in Japan rose from 65 percent of the US level in 1970 to 83 percent in 1990 (Maddison 2009, IMF 2013a).

Figure 9.13 Inflation in consumer prices, GDP deflator, and interest rate on government debt in Japan, 1981–2010

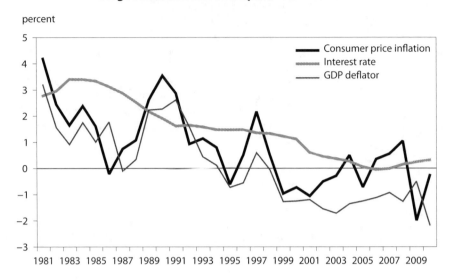

percent

Source: IMF (2013a).

net interest rate on public debt for Japan from 1981 through 2012.[26] For the three decades as a whole, average consumer price inflation was 0.81 percent, average GDP deflator inflation was 0.11 percent, and the average implicit net interest rate on government debt was 1.5 percent. If the spreads between these rates were restored to their long-term averages, then achieving 2 percent annual consumer price inflation would boost the (net implicit) interest rate on public debt to 2.69 percent, while raising the GDP deflator inflation rate only to 1.39 percent. In contrast, there is a negative rather than positive interest rate spread above the GDP deflator in the 2013–18 baseline projections of the IMF, with the deflator rising at 1 percent but the net implied interest rate at only 0.5 percent.

Although it may seem contradictory to suggest that further monetary expansion through quantitative easing could raise rather than reduce real interest rates, the shock of a paradigm shift implied by the new program might do just that, by forcing a market reassessment of interest rates and in the process focusing attention on the historically aberrant negative spread between the interest rate and the inflation rate. Indeed, after the Bank of Japan's "shock and awe" announcement on April 4, 2013 that it would double the monetary base by the end of 2014, the 10-year government bond rate declined only briefly

---

26. As before, the implicit average interest rate is based on the ratio of interest in the year in question to gross public debt at the end of the prior year. Interest is in turn calculated as the difference between the total fiscal deficit and the primary fiscal deficit, as reported in IMF (2013a).

(from 0.56 percent at end-March to 0.44 percent on April 4) and then proceeded to rise to 0.85 percent by mid-May.[27] Success at achieving 2 percent consumer price inflation might thus come at the cost of reverting the interest-rate-deflator rate spread to a more normal positive rather than negative amount. The total swing in this differential would amount to 1.8 percentage points (from –0.5 percent to +1.3 percent [= 2.69 – 1.39]). Growth would have to accelerate by 1.8 percent above the baseline, or from an average of 1.3 percent to an implausibly high 3.1 percent, to keep the debt ratio from rising above its baseline path as a consequence.[28] So it would appear that there is considerable likelihood that the new strategy could raise the debt-to-GDP ratio above the already high level as a consequence of a rise in the interest rate that more than offsets the likely rise in the nominal growth rate. In an earlier period, a further rise in Japan's debt ratio might have been dismissed as business as usual. However, with the paradigm shift from Europe indicating that even rich countries can default, it would seem highly advisable for Japan to begin the process of reducing the debt ratio rather than increase it further.

The case of Japan also raises another dimension of debt sustainability. It is sometimes argued that Japan can sustain an abnormally high level of public debt because the debt is largely held domestically rather than by foreign investors. Foreigners hold only 9 percent of the country's public debt.[29] Takeo Hoshi and Takatoshi Ito (2013, 7) specifically attribute Japan's low interest rate on government bonds to the fact that "Japanese residents...are risk-averse and home-biased," although deflation has also meant that the real interest rate exceeds the nominal rate. The two researchers posit that a debt crisis could occur in Japan once the total domestic private asset market is fully absorbed by government bonds, which in their baseline could happen by 2023. The reason is that at that point the government would need to seek funding from abroad, and there could be a quick escalation in interest rates and deterioration in debt sustainability. They find that this critical debt ceiling can be avoided only under a combination of relatively high growth and steady escalation of the consumption tax, from 5 percent at present to 25 percent. The overall thrust of their analysis would thus seem to be that Japan does indeed have a long-term

27. Leika Kihara and Stanley White, "BOJ to Pump $1.4 trillion into Economy in Unprecedented Stimulus," Reuters, April 4, 2013, www.reuters.com/article/2013/04/04/us-japan-economy-boj-idUSBRE93216U20130404 (accessed on July 1, 2013). There was a comparable but slightly later increase in long-term US interest rates, which rose from 1.67 percent for the 10-year government bond at the end of April to 2.21 percent by June 10, reflecting new uncertainty about how long the existing pace of quantitative easing would be sustained (Datastream). Note further that a surge in the Japanese stock market and decline in the yen in the first few weeks following the announcement were both fully reversed by mid-June.

28. Note, however, that for its part the IMF in its April 2013 WEO projects that the debt ratio will plateau at 243 percent of GDP by 2018, after rising from 237.9 percent in 2012 to 245 percent in 2013 (IMF 2013a).

29. Jonathan Soble, "Foreign Holdings of JGBs Hit Record," *Financial Times*, December 21, 2012.

government debt problem, even after taking account of the heavy dominance of holdings by passive domestic investors.

More generally, there is presumably some favorable influence from domestic holding in other countries as well. Investors internationally are known to have a home bias, and presumably this bias could help assure debt rollover under increasingly stressful conditions. There is some evidence that a high share of holding of government debt by nonresidents has played a role in differential severity of the euro area debt crisis. Thus, in 2010 nonresidents held 70 to 85 percent of government debt in the three economies that were eventually forced to enter into internationally assisted adjustment programs (Greece, Ireland, and Portugal) but only 40 to 50 percent in Italy and Spain, which have so far avoided doing so.[30] However, a major contradictory example exists: the case of the United States. Almost half of US federal debt held by the public is held by foreigners.[31] Yet despite the combination of rapidly rising debt (from 36.3 percent of GDP in 2007 to 72.5 percent in 2012 for debt held by the public; CBO 2013) and a relatively high foreign holding share, the US government remains the benchmark for risk-free sovereign debt.

Debt and Growth

This chapter has focused on debt crises. However, an important related debate has emerged that concerns whether high levels of public debt can depress growth even if no crisis occurs. The most prominent exponents of an adverse effect have been Carmen Reinhart and Kenneth Rogoff (2010, 575), who estimated that for advanced countries in the postwar period, median growth has been about 1 percent lower and average growth about 4 percent lower once public debt exceeds 90 percent of GDP. Subsequent discovery of a spreadsheet error revealed that the result for the average was seriously overstated, though not the result for the median.[32] Several other empirical studies have also tended to find some reduction in growth at higher debt ratios.[33] This literature remains in flux, importantly because it is unclear that the negative

---

30. Based on calculations using a dataset compiled in Merler and Pisani-Ferry (2012) and subsequently maintained by them.

31. Foreigners held 48.4 percent of US federal debt held by the public at the end of March 2013. The PRC alone held 10.5 percent (largely in the form of official foreign exchange reserves), and Japan held 9.3 percent (US Treasury 2013).

32. In the heated controversy that ensued, the two authors replied that "We have never used anything but the conservative median estimate [1 percentage point growth loss] in our public discussions...." Carmen M. Reinhart and Kenneth S. Rogoff, "Reinhart and Rogoff: Responding to Our Critics," New York Times, April 25, 2013.

33. Stephen G. Cecchetti, M. S. Mohanty, and Fabrizio Zampolli (2011) find that when public debt exceeds 85 percent of GDP, a 10 percentage point rise in the ratio of debt to GDP is associated with a reduction in annual growth by 10 to 15 basis points, considerably smaller than the 100 basis points median in the Reinhart-Rogoff results.

relationship holds up once endogeneity from a weak economy to a large fiscal deficit and rising debt is taken into account.[34]

For industrial countries there is nonetheless a long tradition that higher government debt exerts some negative influence on growth by crowding out domestic investment. This influence was called "Rubinomics" (after then-Secretary of Treasury Robert Rubin) during the Clinton administration, when rising fiscal surpluses facilitated falling interest rates and rising private investment. The US Congressional Budget Office (CBO) typically includes negative growth effects of higher public debt in its long-term budget scenarios, albeit with a wide range of uncertainty.[35]

For emerging-market economies in Asia, however, it would seem that the principal consideration linking growth to debt remains the traditional concern about a discontinuous debt crisis, which is immensely costly to output and growth. I have suggested an approach that incorporates the rising probability of default as the debt ratio exceeds high thresholds, and have used this approach to suggest that whereas the multiplier could usually be positive and high under conditions of high unemployment (and hence warrant fiscal expansion), a total-welfare-equivalent multiplier could turn negative if the economy already has a high ratio of debt to GDP and further increases would substantially increase the probability of sovereign default (Cline 2013). Again, a crucial element in the default probability is the interest rate. Debt sustainability is inherently a multiple equilibrium phenomenon, and to the extent that a sharply rising debt ratio triggers a large increase in the interest rate, the stage will be set for rising debt to shift debt from being sustainable to being unsustainable.

Conclusion

The emerging-market economies of Asia already appear to have learned the principal lessons from international experience with sovereign debt crises. They have avoided high ratios of external debt to exports of goods and services that

---

34. Ugo Panizza and Andrea Presbitero (2013) find that it does not.

35. In the CBO's June 2012 projections, the "extended baseline" of current law (which then included full expiration of the Bush administration tax cuts) placed the ratio of debt held by the public at 53 percent of GDP by 2037, down about 20 percentage points from the present level. The "extended alternative scenario," assuming full extension of the Bush tax cuts (which were in fact extended except for top brackets) and rollback of the "sequester" mandatory spending cuts (which instead were retained), placed the debt ratio at a remarkable 199 percent of GDP in 2037. The corresponding level of GDP was 6.6 percent lower (+0.3 percent to –13 percent) in the extended alternative scenario; GNP (which takes account of interest payments to foreigners) was 13.4 percent lower (–3.5 to –21 percent) (CBO 2012, 38). The difference amounts to about 0.9 percent of GNP for each 10 percentage points of GDP higher debt (= 13.4/{0.1 × 146}). The lengthy 25-year period translates these level differences into small growth differences: 0.04 percent lower annual growth (for example, 2.46 percent instead of 2.5 percent) for each 10 percentage points of GDP debt increase. Using a 50 percentage point increase from the extended baseline to arrive at a Reinhart-Rogoff 90 percent threshold, the CBO parameters imply a growth-rate loss of 20 basis points (5 × 0.04 = 0.2) rather than 100 basis points as suggested by Reinhart and Rogoff.

marked the Latin American debt crisis of the 1980s. They have sharply reduced the high ratios of short-term external debt to reserves that made them vulnerable to the East Asian debt crisis in the late 1990s. In that crisis, they avoided debt restructuring with major haircuts. The Republic of Korea in particular achieved a successful three-year stretchout of bank loans at an interest rate comparable to original terms, making it possible to weather a classic liquidity problem without recourse to insolvency-resolving haircuts.

In the second dimension of debt—the internal transfer problem associated with fiscal (as opposed to external) sustainability—the Asian emerging-market economies also have pursued sound management. Their public debt ratios are moderate (or, where high, much of the debt is concessional and hence does not represent as high a burden as market-interest debt). India faces the challenge of reducing high fiscal deficits and high inflation, but ironically the rapid increase in its nominal GDP thanks to the combined influence of high real growth and high inflation means that its public debt ratio is not yet at a dangerous level. All eight of the region's emerging-market economies examined (the PRC, India, Indonesia, the Republic of Korea, Malaysia, the Philippines, Thailand, and Viet Nam) pass the fiscal sustainability test, whereby the primary surplus must at least equal the debt-to-GDP ratio multiplied by the excess of the interest rate over the growth rate (both nominal) in order to avoid escalation of the debt ratio.

Increasing ability to rely on debt denominated in domestic currency instead of foreign currency is another strong sign of fiscal sustainability in the region, and one that reduces risk of mismatch between a government's revenue base and obligations. The Republic of Korea and Malaysia have gone the furthest in this direction, with 97 to 99 percent of government debt in the form of domestic rather than foreign debt. Thailand and the Philippines have also gone a long way, at 63 and 72 percent, respectively. Reliance on the domestic market does come at a price, but the limited data available nevertheless suggest that this premium is small for the Republic of Korea (only about 25 basis points) and is difficult to identify at all in Thailand, whereas the premium is on the order of 150 basis points in Mexico and South Africa (figure 9.11).

It is difficult to escape the conclusion that the principal sovereign debt challenge in the region going forward is more likely to be located in its richest major economy rather than in its emerging-market ones. The Organisation for Economic Co-operation and Development warns that Japan's high debt ratios place it in "uncharted territory" (OECD 2013, 107). A fiscal sustainability test suggests that Japan needs to raise its primary surplus by at least 0.8 percent of GDP just to keep the gross debt ratio, already at 238 percent of GDP, from rising. Perhaps the most sobering lesson from international debt experience in this regard is the newest lesson of all: that industrial countries can go bankrupt, as shown by the case of Greece. Although Japan does not have the special impediment faced by Greece—lack of control over the currency of its debt—the new experience of default by a rich country would seem grounds for increased attention to Japan's high debt.

Japan's major macroeconomic policy at present is the major shift toward aggressive quantitative easing with the objective of raising the inflation rate to 2 percent, a level it has not witnessed since 1989. The discussion above suggests that the conceptual framework to this reflationary push may be fragile because it seems to be premised on the stylized fact that Japan has needlessly lost two decades of growth and that deflation has been an important reason. It turns out, instead, that a stagnant labor force associated with demographics is the main reason Japan's growth numbers have not been as large as those of its industrial-country peers. Output per labor force has risen at rates fully comparable to those in Germany and, in the most recent decade, the United States. Monetary expansion might thus not bring as much growth acceleration as many might think based on the stylized international comparisons. Yet there is significant risk that the reflation will succeed in boosting the interest rate back to a more normal relationship with GDP-deflator inflation, which would mean further pressure toward a rising ratio of debt to GDP, as the increase in the real growth rate needed to offset the higher interest burden could be implausibly high.

References

Bank of Korea. 2013. Economic Statistics System, 8.7.1 External Debt. Seoul. Available at http://ecos.bok.or.kr/flex/EasySearch_e.jsp.

BLS (Bureau of Labor Statistics). 2005. *Comparative Civilian Labor Force Statistics, 10 Countries, 1960–2004.* Washington, DC.

Cavallo, Domingo. 2002. *An Institutional Coup* (April 19). Available at www.cavallo.com.ar/wp-content/uploads/an_insitutional.pdf (accessed on July 1, 2013).

CBO (Congressional Budget Office). 2012. *The 2012 Long-Term Budget Outlook.* Washington, DC.

CBO (Congressional Budget Office). 2013. *The Budget and Economic Outlook, Fiscal Years 2013 to 2023.* Washington, DC.

Cecchetti, Stephen G., M. S. Mohanty, and Fabrizio Zampolli. 2011. *The Real Effects of Debt.* BIS Working Paper 352 (September). Basel: Bank for International Settlements.

Cline, William R. 1984. *International Debt: Systemic Risk and Policy Response.* Washington, DC: Institute for International Economics.

Cline, William R. 1995. *International Debt Reexamined.* Washington, DC: Institute for International Economics.

Cline, William R. 1998. *IMF-Supported Adjustment Programs in the East Asian Financial Crisis.* IIF Research Paper 98-1. Washington, DC: Institute of International Finance.

Cline, William R. 2003. *Restoring Economic Growth in Argentina.* Policy Research Working Paper 3158. Washington, DC: World Bank.

Cline, William R. 2013. The Multiplier, Sovereign Default Risk, and the US Budget: An Overview. In *Public Debt, Global Governance and Economic Dynamism,* ed. Luigi Paganetto. New York: Springer.

Deutsche Bank. 2013. *Foreign Investment in the Major EM Domestic Government Debt Markets.* Global Economic Perspectives (April 3). New York.

ECB (European Central Bank). 2012. *Technical Features of Outright Monetary Transactions* (September 6). Frankfurt.

Fukao, Kyoji. 2013. Explaining Japan's Unproductive Two Decades. Tokyo: Hitotsubashi University, March. Photocopy.

Hoshi, Takeo, and Takatoshi Ito. 2013. *Is the Sky the Limit? Can JGBs Continue to Defy Gravity?* Tokyo: University of Tokyo.

IMF (International Monetary Fund). 2012. *World Economic Outlook* (October). Washington, DC.

IMF (International Monetary Fund). 2013a. *World Economic Outlook* (April). Washington, DC.

IMF (International Monetary Fund). 2013b. *International Financial Statistics*. Washington, DC.

IMF (International Monetary Fund). 2013c. *Fiscal Monitor* (April). Washington, DC.

IMF (International Monetary Fund). 2013d. *Regional Economic Outlook: Asia and Pacific* (April). Washington, DC.

Maddison, Angus. 2009. *Historical Statistics of the World Economy, 1-2008 AD*. University of Groningen. Available at www.ggdc.net/maddison/Historical_Statistics/vertical-file_02-2010.xls (accessed on July 1, 2013).

Mehrotra, Aaron, Ken Miyajima, and Agustin Villar. 2012. Developments of Domestic Government Bond Markets in EMEs and Their Implications. In *Fiscal Policy, Public Debt and Monetary Policy in Emerging Market Economies*. BIS Paper 67 (October). Basel: Bank for International Settlements.

Merler, Silvia, and Jean Pisani-Ferry. 2012. *Who's Afraid of Sovereign Bonds?* Bruegel Policy Contribution 2012/02. Brussels: Bruegel.

Noland, Marcus. 2000. The Philippines in the Asian Financial Crisis: How the Sick Man Avoided Pneumonia. *Asian Survey* 40, no. 3 (May-June): 401–12.

OECD (Organisation for Economic Co-operation and Development). 2012. *Economic Outlook* 2, no. 92 (December). Paris.

OECD (Organisation for Economic Co-operation and Development). 2013. *OECD Economic Surveys: Japan*. Paris.

OMB (Office of Management and Budget). 2013. *Budget of the United States Government, Fiscal Year 2014*. Washington, DC.

Panizza, Ugo, and Andrea F. Presbitero. 2013. *Public Debt and Economic Growth in Advanced Economies: A Survey*. Working Paper 78 (January). Money and Finance Research Group. Geneva: Graduate Institute.

Reinhart, Carmen, and Kenneth Rogoff. 2010. Growth in a Time of Debt. *American Economic Review* 100, no. 2 (May): 573–78.

Steneri, Carlos. 2011. *Al Borde del Abismo: Uruguay y la Gran Crisis del 2002-03*. Montevideo: Banda Oriental.

US Treasury. 2013. Major Foreign Holders of Treasury Securities (August 15). Data and Charts Center. Washington, DC. Available at www.treasury.gov/resource-center/data-chart-center/tic/Documents/mfh.txt (accessed on August 26, 2013).

World Bank. 2013a. *International Debt Statistics*. Washington, DC. Available at http://data.worldbank.org/data-catalog/international-debt-statistics (accessed on July 1, 2013).

World Bank. 2013b. *Health, Nutrition and Population Statistics*. Washington, DC. Available at http://data.worldbank.org/data-catalog/health-nutrition-and-population-statistics (accessed on July 1, 2013).

About the Contributors

William R. Cline has been a senior fellow at the Peterson Institute for International Economics since 1981. During 1996–2001 while on leave from the Institute, he was deputy managing director and chief economist of the Institute of International Finance (IIF) in Washington, DC. From 2002 through 2011 he held a joint appointment with the Peterson Institute and the Center for Global Development, where he is now senior fellow emeritus. Before joining the Peterson Institute, he was senior fellow, the Brookings Institution (1973–81); deputy director of development and trade research, office of the assistant secretary for international affairs, US Treasury Department (1971–73); Ford Foundation visiting professor in Brazil (1970–71); and lecturer and assistant professor of economics at Princeton University (1967–70). He is the author of numerous books, including *Financial Globalization, Economic Growth, and the Crisis of 2007–09* (2010) and *The United States as a Debtor Nation* (2005), and coeditor of *Resolving the European Debt Crisis* (2012).

Joseph E. Gagnon, senior fellow at the Peterson Institute for International Economics since September 2009, was visiting associate director, Division of Monetary Affairs (2008–09) at the US Federal Reserve Board. Previously he served at the US Federal Reserve Board as associate director, Division of International Finance (1999–2008), and senior economist (1987–90 and 1991–97). He has also served at the US Treasury Department (1994–95 and 1997–99) and taught at the Haas School of Business, University of California, Berkeley (1990–91). He is author of *Flexible Exchange Rates for a Stable World Economy* (2011) and *The Global Outlook for Government Debt over the Next 25 Years: Implications for the Economy and Public Policy* (2011).

Stephan Haggard, visiting fellow at the Peterson Institute for International Economics, is the Lawrence and Sallye Krause Distinguished Professor at the

University of California, San Diego, Graduate School of International Relations and Pacific Studies. He has written widely on the political economy of financial crises, stabilization, and structural adjustment and is the author of *The Political Economy of the Asian Financial Crisis* (2000). He is also coauthor with Marcus Noland of *Witness to Transformation: Refugee Insights into North Korea* (2011) and *Famine in North Korea: Markets, Aid, and Reform* (2007).

Marc Hinterschweiger has been a research analyst at the Peterson Institute for International Economics since 2008. He is also a PhD candidate in economics at Ludwig-Maximilians University (LMU) in Munich, Germany. His research focuses on the transmission mechanism of monetary policy, asset prices, and financial crises. He previously worked at the Rhenish-Westfalian Institute for Economic Research (RWI) in Essen, Germany. He assisted Joseph E. Gagnon with *Flexible Exchange Rates for a Stable World Economy* (2011) and *The Global Outlook for Government Debt over the Next 25 Years: Implications for the Economy and Public Policy* (2011).

Simon Johnson, senior fellow at the Peterson Institute for International Economics since September 2008, has been the Ronald A. Kurtz Professor of Entrepreneurship at MIT's Sloan School of Management since 2004. He was the International Monetary Fund's economic counsellor and director of the Research Department (2007–08), assistant director in the department (2004–06), and visiting fellow at the Institute (2006–07). He is also a member of the Federal Deposit Insurance Corporation's Systemic Resolution Advisory Committee, the Congressional Budget Office's Panel of Economic Advisers, the private sector Systemic Risk Council founded and chaired by Sheila Bair, and cofounder of the blog BaselineScenario.com. He is coauthor, with James Kwak, of *White House Burning: The Founding Fathers, Our National Debt and Why It Matters to You* (2012) and *13 Bankers: The Wall Street Takeover and the Next Financial Meltdown* (2010).

Masahiro Kawai is the dean and CEO of the Asian Development Bank Institute (ADBI). He was previously special advisor to the ADB President in charge of regional economic cooperation and integration. Before that he was in academia, first as an associate professor of economics at the Johns Hopkins University and later as a professor of economics at the University of Tokyo. He also served as chief economist for the World Bank's East Asia and the Pacific Region (1998–2001) and as deputy vice minister of finance for international affairs of Japan's Ministry of Finance (2001–03). His recent publications focus on Asia's economic regionalism. He holds a BA in economics from the University of Tokyo and a PhD in economics from Stanford University.

James Kwak is associate professor at the University of Connecticut School of Law. He is coauthor, with Simon Johnson, of *White House Burning: The Founding Fathers, Our National Debt and Why It Matters to You* (2012) and *13 Bankers: The Wall Street Takeover and the Next Financial Meltdown* (2010). He is also the coauthor of BaselineScenario.com, a leading blog covering economics and public policy, and an online columnist for *The Atlantic*. His articles have appeared in many publications, including *Democracy, The American Prospect, Finance and Development, New York Times, Washington Post*, and *Los Angeles Times*, and on the websites of the *Wall Street Journal, Huffington Post, NPR, Foreign Policy*, and *Financial Times*. In 2011–12, he was a fellow at the Harvard Law School Program on Corporate Governance. He has an AB in social studies from Harvard, a PhD in history from the University of California, Berkeley, and a JD from the Yale Law School. Before going to law school, he worked as a management consultant at McKinsey and Company and cofounded Guidewire Software.

Peter Morgan has been senior consultant for research at the Asian Development Bank Institute since 2008. He has 23 years of experience in the financial sector in Asia, most recently serving in Hong Kong as chief Asia economist for HSBC, responsible for macroeconomic analysis and forecasting for Asia. Before that, he served in Tokyo as chief Japan economist for HSBC and earlier held similar positions at Merrill Lynch, Barclays de Zoete Wedd, and Jardine Fleming. Prior to entering the financial industry, he worked as a consultant for Meta Systems Inc. in Cambridge, MA, specializing in energy and environmental areas, including energy policy issues in Asian countries, and at International Business Information KK in Tokyo, specializing in financial sector consulting. His research interests are in macroeconomic policy and financial sector regulation, reform, and development. He earned his MA and PhD degrees in economics from Yale University.

Donghyun Park is principal economist at the Economics and Research Department of the Asian Development Bank (ADB), which he joined in April 2007. Prior to joining ADB, he was a tenured associate professor of economics at Nanyang Technological University in Singapore. His main research fields are international finance, international trade, and development economics. His research, which has been published extensively in journals and books, revolves around policy-oriented topics relevant for Asia's long-term development, including the middle-income trap, Asia's services sector development, and Asia's aging population. He plays a leading role in the production of the *Asian Development Outlook*, ADB's flagship annual publication. He holds a PhD in economics from the University of California, Los Angeles.

Adam S. Posen is the president of the Peterson Institute for International Economics. From 2009 to 2012, he served as an external member of the Bank of England's rate-setting Monetary Policy Committee (MPC). Previously, he worked in finance in Germany following reunification; wrote the definitive book on Japan's economic crisis of the 1990s, *Restoring Japan's Economic Growth* (1998), and counseled the Koizumi government that subsequently turned Japan around; coauthored with Ben Bernanke a reform program for Federal Reserve policy and currently advises the US Congressional Budget Office; and consulted for the UK Cabinet Office on the successful London G-20 summit of 2009, prior to being appointed to the MPC. Among the most cited economists in the press, he is a columnist for the *Financial Times* and appears frequently on Bloomberg, NPR, and other programs. In April 2012, an article in the *Atlantic* magazine named him to its international team of "superstar central bankers," and in December 2012 he was profiled in the *New York Times Magazine* article "God Save the British Economy." He received his PhD and BA from Harvard University and is a member of the Council on Foreign Relations, the Trilateral Commission, and the faculty of the World Economic Forum.

Arief Ramayandi is an economist in the Economics and Research Department of the Asian Development Bank (ADB). Prior to joining ADB, he was the director for the Center of Economics and Development Studies at Padjadjaran University in Bandung, Indonesia. He has published in the field of macroeconomics and development and served as a consultant for the ASEAN Secretariat, Australian Agency for International Development (AusAID), Commonwealth Scientific and Industrial Research Organization (CSIRO), United States Agency for International Development (USAID), World Bank, and other institutions. He holds a PhD in economics from the Australian National University.

Changyong Rhee Changyong Rhee is the chief economist of the Asian Development Bank (ADB). He is the chief spokesperson for ADB on economic and development trends and oversees the Economics and Research Department, which publishes ADB's flagship knowledge products. He has over 20 years of professional experience as an economist, financial adviser, and academic. He was the secretary general and sherpa of the Presidential Committee for the 2010 G-20 Seoul Summit, as well as vice chairman of the Financial Services Commission (FSC) and chairman of the Securities and Futures Commission in the Republic of Korea. Prior to his appointment at the FSC, he was a professor of economics at Seoul National University and assistant professor at the University of Rochester. He was also a frequent and active policy adviser to the Government of the Republic of Korea, including in the Office of the President, the Ministry of Finance and Economy, the Bank of Korea, the Korea Securities Depository, and the Korea Development Institute. His key research interests include macroeconomics, financial economics, and the Korean economy. He has published many papers in these fields. He obtained his PhD in economics from Harvard University and his BA in economics from Seoul National University.

Kwanho Shin is professor of economics at Korea University. He was assistant professor at the University of Kansas for four years and occasionally taught at the University of California, Los Angeles (UCLA), Claremont Graduate University, and Claremont McKenna College as a visiting professor. He was named one of the Fifty Future Leaders in Korea by the *Seoul Economic Daily* in 2010 and a MaeKyung Economist by the *Maeil Business Newspaper* in 2011. He also served as a council member for the National Economic Advisory Council from 2010 to 2011. He has published widely on the subjects of business cycles, monetary economics, international finance, and labor economics in a number of academic journals including *American Economic Review, Journal of Monetary Economics, Journal of Econometrics, Journal of International Economics, Journal of International Money and Finance,* and *Journal of Labor Economics.* He received his BA and MA in economics from Seoul National University and PhD in economics from UCLA.

Lea Sumulong is senior economics officer in the Economics and Research Department (ERD) of the Asian Development Bank. In her current capacity, she provides support to ERD's research projects and contributes to ERD's flagship publications and knowledge products. She has over 20 years of experience in economic research and has lectured at the University of the Philippines.

Edwin M. Truman, senior fellow at the Peterson Institute for International Economics since 2001, served as assistant secretary of the US Treasury for International Affairs from December 1998 to January 2001 and returned as counselor to the secretary March–May 2009. He directed the Division of International Finance of the Board of Governors of the Federal Reserve System from 1977 to 1998. He has been a member of numerous international groups working on economic and financial issues. He is the author, coauthor, or editor of *International Economic Policy Coordination Revisited* (forthcoming), *Sovereign Wealth Funds: Threat or Salvation?* (2010), *Reforming the IMF for the 21st Century* (2006), *A Strategy for IMF Reform* (2006), *Chasing Dirty Money: The Fight Against Money Laundering* (2004), and *Inflation Targeting in the World Economy* (2003).

Shahin Vallée was appointed to the Cabinet of European Council President Herman Van Rompuy as economic advisor in July 2012. He was visiting fellow at Bruegel from October 2010 to June 2012. His research interest is essentially focused on international macroeconomics, but he is also interested in research areas at the intersection of financial markets and public policy. In particular, at Bruegel he worked on the international monetary system, European economic governance, and monetary and macroprudential policy. Previously he worked at BNP Paribas, where he occupied different roles within the research department. Between January and June 2012 he served as an advisor on European and economic issues to the Green Party's presidential campaign in France. He holds a master's degree from Columbia University in New York, a public affairs degree from Sciences Po in Paris, and an undergraduate economics degree from La Sorbonne.

Index

central bank actions, 57, 59, 62
crony capitalism, 149–56
CSF (Countercyclical Support Facility), 237
currency crises, 181
current account balance
  during Asian crisis, 111, 112f, 113, 114f
  crisis likelihood and, 124, 137
  depth of crisis and, 127–29, 128t, 137
  recovery from crisis and, 129–32, 130t–137t,
    137–38
Cyprus
  bank restructuring, 203
  denial of crisis, 191
  IMF role in, 180, 231, 232, 234
  macroeconomic performance of, 181–83,
    182t
  origins of crisis, 181–86
  as solvency crisis, 195
Czech Republic, 143

Dae-Jung, Kim, 143, 156
debt
  Asian (See Asian debt)
  domestic-sovereign links, 283–84
  dynamics of, 284–85, 291–92, 294,
    295t–296t
  emerging-market crises and, 144–48
  European, 64–66, 74, 201, 256, 281–84
  growth and, 308–309
  Japan, 8–9, 20, 20f, 303–11
  Latin America, 277–79
  sustainability of, 8–9, 261, 284–98, 309–11
  US, 142
debt crises, 181
debt-exports ratio, 286–90, 288f
debt-imports ratio, 286–90, 287f
debt overhang concept, 278
debt-reserves ratio, 286–90, 287f
de Larosière, Jacques, 200
delay phase, 187–91
deleveraging, 21–22
demand, after Asian crisis, 105–106
denial phase, 187–91
deposit guarantees, 63
depth of crisis
  Asian versus European crisis, 184–85, 186t,
    209–10
  determinants of, 127–29, 128t, 137
  measurement of, 118, 119f
Deutsche Bank, 300
diagnosis phase, 191–93
Dimon, Jamie, 160n
discount window, 62, 63, 86
Dodd, Chris, 158, 173n

Dodd-Frank Financial Reform Act of 2010,
  161n, 171–74
domestic credit. See credit
doom loop, 155–56, 200n
Draghi, Mario, 72, 185, 282

East Asian miracle, 104, 144n
EBRD (European Bank for Reconstruction
  and Development), 220, 237
ECB. See European Central Bank
Ecofin (Council of Finance Ministers of the
  European Union), 255, 264
Economic and Monetary Union (EMU), 185,
  209. See also European Monetary Union
economic environment. See also
  macroeconomic effects
  Asian versus European crisis, 194–95,
    204–208
Economic Review and Policy Dialogue
  (ERPD), 267–68
Ecuador, 270, 271
educational attainment, 39–43, 41t
EESA (Emergency Economic Stabilization
  Act), 158, 161, 162
EFSF (European Financial Stability Facility),
  191, 224, 226t, 227, 247t, 257–59
EFSM (European Financial Stabilization
  Mechanism), 191, 226t, 247t, 257–59
EIB (European Investment Bank), 220
Emergency Economic Stabilization Act
  (EESA), 158, 161, 162
emergency loans, 63, 65, 72–74
  effectiveness of, 83–87, 93
emerging-market crises. See also specific country
  or crisis
  classic, 6, 142
  features of, 144–48
  lessons learned, 141–43
  political economy of, 149–56
  US and, 156–58
employment ratio, 26
EMU (Economic and Monetary Union), 185,
  209
end users coalition, 172
ERM (Exchange Rate Mechanism), 216, 246t,
  255n
ERPD (Economic Review and Policy
  Dialogue), 267–68
ESF (Exchange Stabilization Fund), 269
ESM. See European Stability Mechanism
Eurasian Development Bank, 227
Eurasian Economic Community (EURASEC)
  Anti-Crisis Fund (ACF), 216, 224, 225t,
    227

during Asian crisis, 105, 108*f*
depth of crisis and, 127–29, 128*t*, 137
recovery from crisis and, 129–32, 130*t*–137*t*, 137–38
government power
crony capitalism, 149–56
US bailouts, 160–71
Great Depression, 89
Great Recession, 283
Greece
diagnosis of crisis, 193
IMF role in, 180, 189–90, 195*n*, 201, 203, 231–32
lessons learned, 282–83, 308
origins of crisis, 181–86
precrisis indicators, 181–83, 182*t*
regional response to, 64–65, 203, 206, 237, 252–53, 257–59, 273
as solvency crisis, 195, 291
Greenspan, Alan, 143–44
gross domestic product. *See* GDP
Group of Seven (G-7), 221
Group of Twenty (G-20), 198, 223, 227–28, 238
growth. *See* GDP

HAMP (Home Affordable Mortgage Program), 170–71
Home Affordable Mortgage Program (HAMP), 170–71
home bias, 308
housing prices
during Asian crisis, 116, 117*f*
in Japan, 4, 12–14, 15*f*, 22, 45
Hungary
Balance of Payments Assistance Facility, 205, 220*n*, 255–56
denial of crisis, 188
exchange rate regime, 204, 219
IMF role in, 180, 189, 205, 219
macroeconomic performance of, 181–83, 182*t*
origins of crisis, 181–86

Iceland
denial of crisis, 188
foreign investment in, 202
IMF role in, 180, 202
macroeconomic performance of, 181–83, 182*t*
origins of crisis, 181–86
as solvency crisis, 195
IDB (Inter-American Development Bank), 268
identification problem, 86–87

IKB, 59
import-debt ratio, 286–90, 287*f*
Independent Evaluation Office (IMF), 187, 196, 232
India, debt sustainability, 286–89, 288*f*, 290*f*, 292, 297, 298
Indonesia
crony capitalism in, 149–50, 153
debt sustainability, 286, 287*f*, 290*f*, 298*n*
diagnosis of crisis, 191
exchange rate regime, 203
IMF role in, 179, 194, 280
inflation in, 110*n*
macroeconomic performance of, 105–18, 181–83, 182*t*
origins of crisis, 181–86, 279
regional arrangements, 217–19
structural reform, 199
inflation
during Asian crisis, 6, 110*f*, 110–11
banking crises and, 29–45
crisis likelihood and, 124, 137
depth of crisis and, 127, 128*t*, 137
during global crisis, 64–65, 67*f*, 88
in Japan, 305–307, 306*f*, 311
institutional environment, 194–95, 204–208
insurance mechanisms
alternative, 7, 213
regional versus global, 7–8, 213
self-insurance, 3, 213, 218, 238–39, 279
Inter-American Development Bank (IDB), 268
interest parity condition, 113–15, 115*t*
interest rates
during Asian crisis, 107–108, 109*f*, 117, 199
central bank actions (*See* policy rates)
debt sustainability and, 309
depth of crisis and, 127–29, 128*t*, 137
domestic bond markets, 300–301, 310
in Japan, 18–20, 19*f*, 305–307, 306*f*
recovery from crisis and, 129–32, 130*t*–137*t*, 137–38
regional arrangements, 224
term structure of, 75–76, 81–83
ultra-low, 5, 58, 90–92
International Monetary Fund (IMF)
central bank response study, 92
conditional lending, 3, 194, 206, 218, 232
debt ceiling target, 298
Flexible Credit Line (FCL), 222
Global Financial Stability Report, 200
Independent Evaluation Office, 187, 196, 232
as lender-of-last-resort, 249–51
lending framework, 222–23, 234–35, 239

regional arrangements in, 8, 230, 249, 268–73 (*See also specific mechanism*)
Latin American Monetary Fund, 271
Latin American Reserve Fund (Fondo Latino Americano de Reservas; FLAR), 270
  characteristics of, 224, 225*t*, 227, 271
  history of, 214, 216
  IMF coordination, 230, 271
  success of, 249, 252, 270–73
Latvia
  Balance of Payments Assistance Facility, 205, 220, 255–56
  denial of crisis, 188
  IMF role in, 180, 189, 205, 230
  macroeconomic performance of, 181–83, 182*t*
  origins of crisis, 181–86
Lawson doctrine, 279
legal structure of regional arrangements, 227–29
Lehman Brothers collapse
  as classic crisis, 6, 142
  failure to prevent, 58, 73, 93, 160
  Japanization and, 13, 15, 17
  as peak of crisis, 57, 62, 158, 180, 283
lender-of-last-resort
  central banks as, 85, 250, 253, 264
  regional arrangements, 8, 249–51, 253, 259–60, 263–64, 269, 272–73
lending operations
  central bank, 63, 65, 72–74
    effectiveness of, 83–87, 93
  IMF
    conditionality, 3, 194, 206, 218, 232
    framework, 222–23, 234–35, 239
    regional arrangements, 227–30, 234–35, 264, 266, 271
lessons learned. *See also* policy implications
  Asian crisis, 1–3, 6, 138, 141–58, 175, 279–80
    versus European crisis, 208–10, 284
  coordination of IMF and regional arrangements, 232
  as crisis phase, 187
  debt sustainability, 284–85, 309–11
  European crisis, 283–84
Libor-OIS spreads, 59, 59*n*, 60*f*, 84, 86–87
liquidity crises
  bailouts and, 159
  versus solvency crises, 194–96, 279–80, 291
  structural reform and, 201–203
liquidity facilities
  central bank, 57, 59–74
    effectiveness of, 83–87, 93

swap lines, 62–67, 84, 213–14, 221–23, 229, 236
  as self-insurance, 3, 218, 239
  Summers Call, 221
Lisbon Treaty, 253
London inter-bank offered rate (Libor), 59, 59*n*, 60*f*, 84, 86–87, 224
longer-term refinancing operations (LTROs), 65–66, 85–86
long-term asset purchases, by central banks, 64–66, 68*f*–71*f*, 72–74
  effectiveness of, 77–83
Long-Term Capital Management (LTCM), 143–44, 157
lost decades
  in Japan, 3–4, 11, 304–305 (*See also* Japanization)
  in Latin America, 36
LTCM (Long-Term Capital Management), 143–44, 157
LTROs (longer-term refinancing operations), 65–66, 85–86

Maastricht Treaty, 220, 229, 251, 253–56, 292
macroeconomic effects
  of Asian crisis
    versus European crisis, 181–83, 182*t*
    versus global crisis, 105–18, 138
  of central bank responses, 87–89
  policy implications, 2
Macroeconomic Imbalance Procedure (MIP), 262
Mahathir, Mohamad, 179*n*–180*n*
Malaysia
  debt sustainability, 286, 287*f*, 288*f*, 290*f*, 298, 310
  exchange rate regime, 203
  IMF role in, 179
  Japanese assistance to, 191*n*
  macroeconomic performance of, 105–18, 181–83, 182*t*
  origins of crisis, 181–86, 279
  regional arrangements, 217–19
  structural reform, 199
management phase, 187
Manila Framework Group, 218*n*, 264–65
market perceptions, 193, 199–200, 228–30, 300
Maturity Extension Program (MEP), 67, 72
Mayekawa Report, 24*b*
MBS (mortgage-backed securities), 67, 72, 79, 80*n*, 82–83, 158
Medium Term Financial Assistance (MTFA), 214, 245*t*, 255, 258

MEP (Maturity Extension Program), 67, 72
Mercosur, 269
Merrill Lynch, 158, 164
Mexico
  borrowing costs, 302, 303*f*
  lending operations to, 278
  lessons learned, 143
  oligarchy and, 154
  origins of crisis, 279
  regional safety net and, 216, 229
  US leadership and, 269
MIP (Macroeconomic Imbalance Procedure), 262
Miyazawa Initiative, 218*n*
monetary policy
  during Asian crisis, 107–109, 117
    versus European crisis, 194, 198–99, 204
  depth of crisis and, 127–29, 128*t*, 137
  during global crisis, 58–72
  comparison of, 73–74
  in Japan, 21, 306–307
  recovery from crisis and, 129–32, 130*t*–137*t*, 137–38
  shocks caused by, 82
  structural reform and, 91–92
monetary unions
  European crisis and, 184–85, 204–206, 209, 282–83
  history of, 214–16, 219–21
money growth
  depth of crisis and, 127–29, 128*t*, 137
  recovery from crisis and, 129–32, 130*t*–137*t*, 137–38
money laundering, 168
mopping-up phase, 187
moral hazard
  bailouts, 175
  central bank actions, 5, 58, 90, 93
  ex ante commitments, 250
  IMF lending, 223
  "too big to fail" concept, 6, 143
mortgage-backed securities (MBS), 67, 72, 79, 80*n*, 82–83, 158
MTFA (Medium-Term Financial Assistance), 214, 245*t*, 255, 258

NAFA (North American Framework Agreement), 216–17, 269
New Miyazawa Initiative, 191*n*, 217–18
no bailout rules, 250–51, 253–54, 264
nominally comprehensive programs, 193–94
North American Framework Agreement (NAFA), 216–17, 269
North American Free Trade Agreement, 216*n*, 279

Northern Rock, 62

Obama, Barack
  political economy and, 143, 160
  rescue program design, 166–70
  structural reform, 171–74
OCC (Office of the Comptroller of the Currency), 166
OECD. *See* Organisation for Economic Co-operation and Development countries
Office of Financial Responsibility (OFR), 173
Office of the Comptroller of the Currency (OCC), 166
Office of Thrift Supervision (OTS), 166
OFR (Office of Financial Responsibility), 173
oil shocks (1973-74), 214, 277
OIS (overnight index swap) rates, 59, 60*f*, 64, 84, 86–87
oligarchy, 149–56
OMT (Outright Monetary Transactions) program, 72, 248*t*, 253, 264, 282–83
Organisation for Economic Co-operation and Development (OECD) countries, banking crises in, 30–33, 31*t*–32*t*, 48*f*–49*f*
Organization of American States, 268
original sin problem, 280
origins of financial crises, 181–82
  Asian crisis, 105, 146, 179
  European crisis, 181
  global crisis, 103
OTS (Office of Thrift Supervision), 166
outbreak phase, 187
output gaps
  during Asian crisis, 109, 110*f*
  during global crisis, 64, 65*f*, 87–88, 89*n*
Outright Monetary Transactions (OMT) program, 72, 248*t*, 253, 264, 282–83
overnight index swap (OIS) rates, 59, 60*f*, 64, 84, 86–87

Paulson, Henry, 158–59, 160, 162, 164, 167
PCL (Precautionary Credit Line), 223, 229
Peru, 230, 270
Philippines
  debt sustainability, 286, 287*f*, 288*f*, 290*f*, 310
  exchange rate regime, 203
  IMF role in, 179
  macroeconomic performance of, 105–18, 181–83, 182*t*
  origins of crisis, 181–86, 279
  regional arrangements, 217–19
PIMCO, 168
Pinochet, Augusto, 270

Romania
Balance of Payments Facility, 205, 255–56
denial of crisis, 188
exchange rate regime, 204
IMF role in, 180, 189, 205
macroeconomic performance of, 181–83, 182*t*
origins of crisis, 181–86
Rome Treaty, 254
Roubini, Nouriel, 181–82, 188, 201
Rubin, Robert, 143–44, 309
Rubinomics, 309
Russian Federation
crisis in, 143, 208, 279, 281
crony capitalism in, 150–52, 154

SAFE Banking Amendment, 172
SDR allocation, 236
Securities and Exchange Commission (SEC), 173*n*
Securities Market Programme (EU), 248*t*, 259
self-insurance, 3, 213, 218, 238–39, 279
SGP (Stability and Growth Pact), 250, 253, 256, 261, 264
Short-Term Monetary Support (STMS), 245*t*
signals of crisis, 119–21, 120*t*–121*t*
SIGTARP (special inspector general for TARP), 163, 166, 168–72
Singapore, 217–19, 229
six-pack reforms (EU), 261–64
SNB (Swiss National Bank), 62, 222
soft law, 250
solvency crises
bailouts and, 159
versus liquidity crises, 194–96, 279–80, 291
structural reform and, 201–203
South Africa, 302, 303*f*
sovereign debt. *See* debt
Sovereign Debt Restructuring Mechanism, 281
Spain
debt sustainability, 308
denial of crisis, 191
ESM loan to, 180*n*
IMF role in, 180, 231, 234
macroeconomic performance of, 181–83, 182*t*
origins of crisis, 181–86
speculative exchange rate crises, 181
spillover effects. *See* contagion
Stability and Growth Pact (SGP), 250, 253, 256, 261, 264
stabilization policy, 2
stagnation, Japanese-style. *See* Japanization
stigma effect, 229–30

STMS (Short-Term Monetary Support), 245*t*
stock prices
during Asian crisis, 115–16, 116*f*
in Japan, 4, 12–14, 15*f*
volatility of, 59, 61*f*
stress tests, 167–68
Structural Impediments Initiative, 24*b*–25*b*
structural reform
during Asian crisis, 108–109, 118
versus European crisis, 194, 199–204, 206
crony capitalism and, 155–56
in Japan, 21–26, 24*b*–25*b*, 45
monetary policy and, 91–92
in US, 172–74
stylized facts
Asian debt sustainability, 285–92
EA-5 macroeconomic effects, 105–109, 106*f*–109*f*
subprime mortgage loans, 59, 158
SUCRE (Sistema Unitario de Compensación Regional), 270
sudden-stop crises, 181, 279–80, 301, 302
Suharto, 149–50, 153–54
Summers, Lawrence
on Anglo-American model, 143–44
on market confidence, 193, 199–200
on origins of crisis, 182*n*
on policy response, 141–42, 175, 193*n*, 197*n*
Summers Call, 221
Supplemental Reserve Facility, 221
surprise phase, 187–91
surveillance
need for, 2, 187–88, 210
regional systems, 223–27, 229, 232–34, 251–52, 259–68, 272
sustainability of debt, 8–9, 261, 284–98, 309–11
swap lines
ASEAN, 214, 217–19, 242*t*, 252, 265–66
central bank, 62–67, 84, 213–14, 221–23, 229, 236
coordination of, 227–29
Latin American, 269
as self-insurance, 3, 218, 239
Swiss National Bank (SNB), 62, 222
systemic banking crises, 181

TAF (Term Auction Facility), 83–84, 86
TALF (Term Asset-Backed Securities Loan Facility), 64, 85, 169
TARP. *See* Troubled Assets Relief Program
Term Asset-Backed Securities Loan Facility (TALF), 64, 85, 169
Term Auction Facility (TAF), 83–84, 86

term securities lending facilities, 62
Term Securities Lending Facility (TSLF), 84
term structure model, 81
TFP (Trade Finance Program), 237
Thailand
  borrowing costs, 302, 303f
  crony capitalism in, 153–54
  debt sustainability, 286, 287f, 288f, 290f,
    298, 310
  denial of crisis, 188
  diagnosis of crisis, 191
  exchange rate regime, 203
  fiscal policy, 197
  foreign investment in, 201–202
  IMF role in, 179, 187
  macroeconomic performance of, 105–18,
    181–83, 182t
  origins of crisis, 146, 179, 181–86, 279
  regional arrangements, 217–19
  structural reform, 199
"too big to fail" concept, 6, 93, 143
Trade Finance Program (TFP), 237
trade imbalances, 142
Trans-Pacific Partnership, 23
Treasury (US)
  bank bailouts, 160–66, 173–74
  bond yields, 77–81, 78f–79f
  housing plan, 170–71
  Lehman Brothers collapse and, 58, 73
  nonbank institutions and, 172–73
  opposition to oversight, 174
  rescue program design, 166–70
  Wall Street consultations, 168–69, 174
Treaty of Rome, 253
Treaty on Stability, Coordination and
  Governance in the Economic and
  Monetary Union (Fiscal Compact),
  253, 261–64
Trichet, Jean-Claude, 189n, 202, 221n
Troubled Assets Relief Program (TARP), 158,
  161–66
  Congressional Oversight Panel, 162–64,
    171–72
  special inspector general, 163, 166, 168–72
TSLF (Term Securities Lending Facility), 84
Turkey, 208
two-pack reform (EU), 262–63

Ukraine, 143
unemployment rates, 64, 66f, 87–88
Union of South American Nations, 269
United Kingdom
  central bank (See Bank of England)
  fiscal policy, 198
  investment-GDP ratio, 17n
  risk of stagnation in, 46

United States
  central bank (See Federal Reserve)
  Congressional Budget Office, 309
  contagion spreading to, 65–66
  debt ceiling debacle (2011), 67
  debt sustainability, 142, 294, 297n, 308–309
  emerging-market crises and, 156–58
  financial crisis in, 158–75
    bailouts during, 6, 63–65, 143, 159–66,
    174
    housing plan, 170–71
    overall assessment, 174
    oversight concerns, 171–72
    quantitative easing during, 5, 64–66,
    72, 79–82, 88–89
    rescue program design, 166–70
    structural reform, 172–74
    subprime mortgage loans, 59, 158
  financial system as model, 143–44, 148,
    148n
  investment-GDP ratio, 17n
  Latin American region and, 268–73
  political role of, 252, 264
  real GDP per labor force, 304–305, 305f
  reliance on backroom deals, 144
  risk of stagnation in, 46
  role of nonbank financial institutions in,
    73, 172–73
  "too big to fail" concept, 143
  Treasury (See Treasury)
Uruguay, 270

Venezuela, 269, 270, 297
Very Short-Term Financing Facility, 254n,
  255n
Vienna Initiative, 220, 237–38, 247t
Viet Nam, 289n, 290f
Volcker, Paul, 173
Volcker Plan, 268, 277
vulnerability, sources of, 181–83, 188, 209,
  282, 289

Wachovia, 160
Wall Street, Treasury consultation with,
  168–69, 174
Warren, Elizabeth, 171
Washington Mutual, 160
Werner Plan, 214
World Bank, 220

Yellen, Janet, 88, 91
Yeltsin, Boris, 150

Zedillo, Ernesto, 142, 193
"zombie" companies, 4, 21–22

Other Publications from the
Peterson Institute for International Economics

WORKING PAPERS

94-1 APEC and Regional Trading
Arrangements in the Pacific   Jeffrey A.
Frankel with Shang-Jin Wei and Ernesto
Stein

94-2 Towards an Asia Pacific Investment
Code   Edward M. Graham

94-3 Merchandise Trade in the APEC
Region: Is There Scope for
Liberalization on an MFN Basis?
Paul Wonnacott

94-4 The Automotive Industry in Southeast
Asia: Can Protection Be Made Less
Costly?   Paul Wonnacott

94-5 Implications of Asian Economic
Growth   Marcus Noland

95-1 APEC: The Bogor Declaration and the
Path Ahead   C. Fred Bergsten

95-2 From Bogor to Miami...and Beyond:
Regionalism in the Asia Pacific and the
Western Hemisphere   Jeffrey J. Schott

95-3 Has Asian Export Performance Been
Unique?   Marcus Noland

95-4 Association of Southeast Asian
Nations and ASEAN Free Trade Area:
Chronology and Statistics
Gautam Jaggi

95-5 The North Korean Economy
Marcus Noland

95-6 China and the International Economic
System   Marcus Noland

96-1 APEC after Osaka: Toward Free Trade
by 2010/2020   C. Fred Bergsten

96-2 Public Policy, Private Preferences, and
the Japanese Trade Pattern
Marcus Noland

96-3 German Lessons for Korea: The
Economics of Unification
Marcus Noland

96-4 Research and Development Activities
and Trade Specialization in Japan
Marcus Noland

96-5 China's Economic Reforms:
Chronology and Statistics
Gautam Jaggi, Mary Rundle, Daniel H.
Rosen, and Yuichi Takahashi

96-6 US-China Economic Relations
Marcus Noland

96-7 The Market Structure Benefits of Trade
and Investment Liberalization
Raymond Atje and Gary Clyde
Hufbauer

96-8 The Future of US-Korea Economic
Relations   Marcus Noland

96-9 Competition Policies in the Dynamic
Industrializing Economies: The Case of
China, Korea, and Chinese Taipei
Edward M. Graham

96-10 Modeling Economic Reform in North
Korea   Marcus Noland, Sherman
Robinson, and Monica Scatasta

96-11 Trade, Investment, and Economic
Conflict Between the United States and
Asia   Marcus Noland

96-12 APEC in 1996 and Beyond: The Subic
Summit   C. Fred Bergsten

96-13 Some Unpleasant Arithmetic
Concerning Unification
Marcus Noland

96-14 Restructuring Korea's Financial Sector
for Greater Competitiveness
Marcus Noland

96-15 Competitive Liberalization and Global
Free Trade: A Vision for the 21st
Century   C. Fred Bergsten

97-1 Chasing Phantoms: The Political
Economy of USTR   Marcus Noland

97-2 US-Japan Civil Aviation: Prospects for
Progress   Jacqueline McFadyen

97-3 Open Regionalism   C. Fred Bergsten

97-4 Lessons from the Bundesbank on the
Occasion of Its 40th (and Second to
Last?) Birthday   Adam S. Posen

97-5 The Economics of Korean Unification
Marcus Noland, Sherman Robinson, and
Li-Gang Liu

98-1 The Costs and Benefits of Korean
Unification   Marcus Noland, Sherman
Robinson, and Li-Gang Liu

98-2 Asian Competitive Devaluations
Li-Gang Liu, Marcus Noland, Sherman
Robinson, and Zhi Wang

98-3 Fifty Years of the GATT/WTO: Lessons
from the Past for Strategies or the
Future   C. Fred Bergsten

98-4 NAFTA Supplemental Agreements:
Four Year Review Jacqueline McFadyen

98-5 Local Government Spending: Solving
the Mystery of Japanese Fiscal
Packages   Hiroko Ishii and Erika Wada

98-6 The Global Economic Effects of the
Japanese Crisis   Marcus Noland,
Sherman Robinson, and Zhi Wang

98-7 The Relationship Between Trade and
Foreign Investment: Empirical Results
for Taiwan and South Korea
Li-Gang Liu, The World Bank, and
Edward M. Graham

99-1 Rigorous Speculation: The Collapse
and Revival of the North Korean
Economy   Marcus Noland, Sherman
Robinson, and Tao Wang

99-2 Famine in North Korea: Causes and
Cures   Marcus Noland, Sherman
Robinson, and Tao Wang

99-3 Competition Policy and FDI: A
Solution in Search of a Problem?
Marcus Noland

99-4 The Continuing Asian Financial Crisis:
Global Adjustment and Trade
Marcus Noland, Sherman Robinson, and
Zhi Wang

Imagine There's No Country: Poverty, Inequality, and Growth in the Era of Globalization   Surjit S. Bhalla
September 2002   ISBN 0-88132-348-9
Reforming Korea's Industrial Conglomerates
Edward M. Graham
January 2003   ISBN 0-88132-337-3
Industrial Policy in an Era of Globalization: Lessons from Asia   Marcus Noland and Howard Pack
March 2003   ISBN 0-88132-350-0
Reintegrating India with the World Economy
T. N. Srinivasan and Suresh D. Tendulkar
March 2003   ISBN 0-88132-280-6
After the Washington Consensus: Restarting Growth and Reform in Latin America   Pedro-Pablo Kuczynski and John Williamson, eds.
March 2003   ISBN 0-88132-347-0
The Decline of US Labor Unions and the Role of Trade   Robert E. Baldwin
June 2003   ISBN 0-88132-341-1
Can Labor Standards Improve under Globalization?   Kimberly Ann Elliott and Richard B. Freeman
June 2003   ISBN 0-88132-332-2
Crimes and Punishments? Retaliation under the WTO   Robert Z. Lawrence
October 2003   ISBN 0-88132-359-4
Inflation Targeting in the World Economy
Edwin M. Truman
October 2003   ISBN 0-88132-345-4
Foreign Direct Investment and Tax Competition
John H. Mutti
November 2003   ISBN 0-88132-352-7
Has Globalization Gone Far Enough? The Costs of Fragmented Markets   Scott C. Bradford and Robert Z. Lawrence
February 2004   ISBN 0-88132-349-7
Food Regulation and Trade: Toward a Safe and Open Global System   Tim Josling, Donna Roberts, and David Orden
March 2004   ISBN 0-88132-346-2
Controlling Currency Mismatches in Emerging Markets   Morris Goldstein and Philip Turner
April 2004   ISBN 0-88132-360-8
Free Trade Agreements: US Strategies and Priorities   Jeffrey J. Schott, ed.
April 2004   ISBN 0-88132-361-6
Trade Policy and Global Poverty
William R. Cline
June 2004   ISBN 0-88132-365-9
Bailouts or Bail-ins? Responding to Financial Crises in Emerging Economies   Nouriel Roubini and Brad Setser
August 2004   ISBN 0-88132-371-3
Transforming the European Economy   Martin Neil Baily and Jacob Funk Kirkegaard
September 2004   ISBN 0-88132-343-8
Chasing Dirty Money: The Fight Against Money Laundering   Peter Reuter and Edwin M. Truman
November 2004   ISBN 0-88132-370-5

The United States and the World Economy: Foreign Economic Policy for the Next Decade
C. Fred Bergsten
January 2005   ISBN 0-88132-380-2
Does Foreign Direct Investment Promote Development?   Theodore H. Moran, Edward M. Graham, and Magnus Blomström, eds.
April 2005   ISBN 0-88132-381-0
American Trade Politics, 4th ed.   I. M. Destler
June 2005   ISBN 0-88132-382-9
Why Does Immigration Divide America? Public Finance and Political Opposition to Open Borders   Gordon H. Hanson
August 2005   ISBN 0-88132-400-0
Reforming the US Corporate Tax   Gary Clyde Hufbauer and Paul L. E. Grieco
September 2005   ISBN 0-88132-384-5
The United States as a Debtor Nation
William R. Cline
September 2005   ISBN 0-88132-399-3
NAFTA Revisited: Achievements and Challenges   Gary Clyde Hufbauer and Jeffrey J. Schott, assisted by Paul L. E. Grieco and Yee Wong
October 2005   ISBN 0-88132-334-9
US National Security and Foreign Direct Investment   Edward M. Graham and David M. Marchick
May 2006   ISBN 978-0-88132-391-7
Accelerating the Globalization of America: The Role for Information Technology   Catherine L. Mann, assisted by Jacob Funk Kirkegaard
June 2006   ISBN 978-0-88132-390-0
Delivering on Doha: Farm Trade and the Poor
Kimberly Ann Elliott
July 2006   ISBN 978-0-88132-392-4
Case Studies in US Trade Negotiation, Vol. 1: Making the Rules   Charan Devereaux, Robert Z. Lawrence, and Michael Watkins
September 2006   ISBN 978-0-88132-362-7
Case Studies in US Trade Negotiation, Vol. 2: Resolving Disputes   Charan Devereaux, Robert Z. Lawrence, and Michael Watkins
September 2006   ISBN 978-0-88132-363-2
C. Fred Bergsten and the World Economy
Michael Mussa, ed.
December 2006   ISBN 978-0-88132-397-9
Working Papers, Volume I   Peterson Institute
December 2006   ISBN 978-0-88132-388-7
The Arab Economies in a Changing World
Marcus Noland and Howard Pack
April 2007   ISBN 978-0-88132-393-1
Working Papers, Volume II   Peterson Institute
April 2007   ISBN 978-0-88132-404-4
Global Warming and Agriculture: Impact Estimates by Country   William R. Cline
July 2007   ISBN 978-0-88132-403-7
US Taxation of Foreign Income   Gary Clyde Hufbauer and Ariel Assa
October 2007   ISBN 978-0-88132-405-1
Russia's Capitalist Revolution: Why Market Reform Succeeded and Democracy Failed
Anders Åslund
October 2007   ISBN 978-0-88132-409-9

Economic Sanctions Reconsidered, 3d ed.
Gary Clyde Hufbauer, Jeffrey J. Schott, Kimberly
Ann Elliott, and Barbara Oegg
November 2007
    ISBN hardcover 978-0-88132-407-5
    ISBN hardcover/CD-ROM 978-0-88132-408-2
Debating China's Exchange Rate Policy
Morris Goldstein and Nicholas R. Lardy, eds.
April 2008   ISBN 978-0-88132-415-0
**Leveling the Carbon Playing Field: International
Competition and US Climate Policy Design**
Trevor Houser, Rob Bradley, Britt Childs, Jacob
Werksman, and Robert Heilmayr
May 2008   ISBN 978-0-88132-420-4
**Accountability and Oversight of US Exchange
Rate Policy**   C. Randall Henning
June 2008   ISBN 978-0-88132-419-8
**Challenges of Globalization: Imbalances and
Growth**   Anders Åslund and
Marek Dabrowski, eds.
July 2008   ISBN 978-0-88132-418-1
China's Rise: Challenges and Opportunities
C. Fred Bergsten, Charles Freeman, Nicholas R.
Lardy, and Derek J. Mitchell
September 2008   ISBN 978-0-88132-417-4
**Banking on Basel: The Future of International
Financial Regulation**   Daniel K. Tarullo
September 2008   ISBN 978-0-88132-423-5
**US Pension Reform: Lessons from Other
Countries**   Martin Neil Baily and
Jacob Funk Kirkegaard
February 2009   ISBN 978-0-88132-425-9
**How Ukraine Became a Market Economy and
Democracy**   Anders Åslund
March 2009   ISBN 978-0-88132-427-3
Global Warming and the World Trading System
Gary Clyde Hufbauer, Steve Charnovitz, and
Jisun Kim
March 2009   ISBN 978-0-88132-428-0
The Russia Balance Sheet   Anders Åslund and
Andrew Kuchins
March 2009   ISBN 978-0-88132-424-2
The Euro at Ten: The Next Global Currency?
Jean Pisani-Ferry and Adam S. Posen, eds.
July 2009   ISBN 978-0-88132-430-3
**Financial Globalization, Economic Growth, and
the Crisis of 2007–09**   William R. Cline
May 2010   ISBN 978-0-88132-4990-0
Russia after the Global Economic Crisis
Anders Åslund, Sergei Guriev, and Andrew
Kuchins, eds.
June 2010   ISBN 978-0-88132-497-6
Sovereign Wealth Funds: Threat or Salvation?
Edwin M. Truman
September 2010   ISBN 978-0-88132-498-3
**The Last Shall Be the First: The East European
Financial Crisis, 2008–10**   Anders Åslund
October 2010   ISBN 978-0-88132-521-8
**Witness to Transformation: Refugee Insights
into North Korea**   Stephan Haggard and
Marcus Noland
January 2011   ISBN 978-0-88132-438-9

**Foreign Direct Investment and Development:
Launching a Second Generation of Policy
Research, Avoiding the Mistakes of the First,
Reevaluating Policies for Developed and
Developing Countries**   Theodore H. Moran
April 2011   ISBN 978-0-88132-600-0
How Latvia Came through the Financial Crisis
Anders Åslund and Valdis Dombrovskis
May 2011   ISBN 978-0-88132-602-4
**Global Trade in Services: Fear, Facts, and
Offshoring**   J. Bradford Jensen
August 2011   ISBN 978-0-88132-601-7
NAFTA and Climate Change Meera Fickling and
Jeffrey J. Schott
September 2011   ISBN 978-0-88132-436-5
**Eclipse: Living in the Shadow of China's
Economic Dominance**   Arvind Subramanian
September 2011   ISBN 978-0-88132-606-2
**Flexible Exchange Rates for a Stable World
Economy**   Joseph E. Gagnon with
Marc Hinterschweiger
September 2011   ISBN 978-0-88132-627-7
**The Arab Economies in a Changing World,
2d ed.**   Marcus Noland and Howard Pack
November 2011   ISBN 978-0-88132-628-4
**Sustaining China's Economic Growth After the
Global Financial Crisis**   Nicholas R. Lardy
January 2012   ISBN 978-0-88132-626-0
Who Needs to Open the Capital Account?
Olivier Jeanne, Arvind Subramanian, and John
Williamson
April 2012   ISBN 978-0-88132-511-9
**Devaluing to Prosperity: Misaligned Currencies
and Their Growth Consequences** Surjit S. Bhalla
August 2012   ISBN 978-0-88132-623-9
**Private Rights and Public Problems: The Global
Economics of Intellectual Property in the 21st
Century**   Keith E. Maskus
September 2012   ISBN 978-0-88132-507-2
**Global Economics in Extraordinary Times:
Essays in Honor of John Williamson**
C. Fred Bergsten and C. Randall Henning, eds.
November 2012   ISBN 978-0-88132-662-8
**Rising Tide: Is Growth in Emerging Economies
Good for the United States?** Lawrence Edwards
and Robert Z. Lawrence
February 2013   ISBN 978-0-88132-500-3
**Responding to Financial Crisis: Lessons from
Asia Then, the United States and Europe Now**
Changyong Rhee and Adam S. Posen, eds
October 2013   ISBN 978-0-88132-674-1

SPECIAL REPORTS

1   **Promoting World Recovery: A Statement on
Global Economic Strategy***
by 26 Economists from Fourteen Countries
December 1982   ISBN 0-88132-013-7
2   **Prospects for Adjustment in Argentina,
Brazil, and Mexico: Responding to the Debt
Crisis***   John Williamson, ed.
June 1983   ISBN 0-88132-016-1
3   **Inflation and Indexation: Argentina, Brazil,
and Israel***   John Williamson, ed.
March 1985   ISBN 0-88132-037-4

WORKS IN PROGRESS

Launching a Comprehensive US Export Strategy
Howard F. Rosen and C. Fred Bergsten, editors
**Banking System Fragility in Emerging
Economies**   Morris Goldstein and Philip Turner
The Future of the World Trade Organization
Gary Clyde Hufbauer and Jeffrey J. Schott
**China's Rise as Global Direct Investor:
Policy Implications**   Daniel H. Rosen and
Thilo Hanemann
**Fueling Up: The Economic Implications of
America's Oil and Gas Boom**   Trevor Houser

DISTRIBUTORS OUTSIDE THE UNITED STATES

**Australia, New Zealand,
and Papua New Guinea**
D. A. Information Services
648 Whitehorse Road
Mitcham, Victoria 3132, Australia
Tel: 61-3-9210-7777
Fax: 61-3-9210-7788
Email: service@dadirect.com.au
www.dadirect.com.au

India, Bangladesh, Nepal, and Sri Lanka
Viva Books Private Limited
Mr. Vinod Vasishtha
4737/23 Ansari Road
Daryaganj, New Delhi 110002
India
Tel: 91-11-4224-2200
Fax: 91-11-4224-2240
Email: viva@vivagroupindia.net
www.vivagroupindia.com

**Mexico, Central America, South America,
and Puerto Rico**
US PubRep, Inc.
311 Dean Drive
Rockville, MD 20851
Tel: 301-838-9276
Fax: 301-838-9278
Email: c.falk@ieee.org

Asia (*Brunei, Burma, Cambodia, China,
Hong Kong, Indonesia, Korea, Laos, Malaysia,
Philippines, Singapore, Taiwan, Thailand,
and Vietnam*)
East-West Export Books (EWEB)
University of Hawaii Press
2840 Kolowalu Street
Honolulu, Hawaii 96822-1888
Tel: 808-956-8830
Fax: 808-988-6052
Email: eweb@hawaii.edu

Canada
Renouf Bookstore
5369 Canotek Road, Unit 1
Ottawa, Ontario KlJ 9J3, Canada
Tel: 613-745-2665
Fax: 613-745-7660
www.renoufbooks.com

Japan
United Publishers Services Ltd.
1-32-5, Higashi-shinagawa
Shinagawa-ku, Tokyo 140-0002
Japan
Tel: 81-3-5479-7251
Fax: 81-3-5479-7307
Email: purchasing@ups.co.jp
*For trade accounts only. Individuals will find
Institute books in leading Tokyo bookstores.*

Middle East
MERIC
2 Bahgat Ali Street, El Masry Towers
Tower D, Apt. 24
Zamalek, Cairo
Egypt
Tel. 20-2-7633824
Fax: 20-2-7369355
Email: mahmoud_fouda@mericonline.com
www.mericonline.com

United Kingdom, Europe
(*including Russia and Turkey*), **Africa,
and Israel**
The Eurospan Group
c/o Turpin Distribution
Pegasus Drive
Stratton Business Park
Biggleswade, Bedfordshire
SG18 8TQ
United Kingdom
Tel: 44 (0) 1767-604972
Fax: 44 (0) 1767-601640
Email: eurospan@turpin-distribution.com
www.eurospangroup.com/bookstore

**Visit our website at:
www.piie.com
E-mail orders to:
petersonmail@presswarehouse.com**